Acadia Parish, Louisiana

A History to 1920
Volume II

by

Mary Alice Fontenot

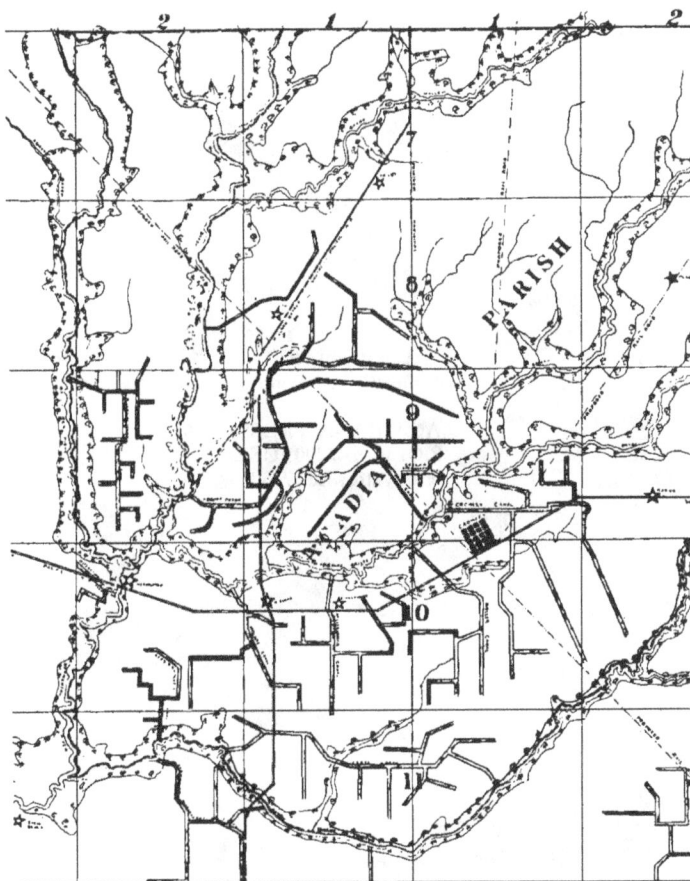

The network of irrigation canals.

ACADIANA PRESS
Lafayette, Louisiana

ACADIANA PRESS
P.O. Box 42290, USL
Lafayette, La. 70504

Printed by Moran Industries, Inc.
Baton Rouge, Louisiana

CONTENTS

Foreword

In this second volume of Acadia Parish history the author attempts to trace the development of the parish from 1900 to 1920. Material contained in the first volume, which covers pre-history to 1900, is not repeated here except in brief summations necessary for continuity.

The main sources of information used in this work, as in the first volume, were newspapers (1899-1920), other published material, legal documents, church records and oral history. Original files of the first Crowley newspaper, 1899 to 1904, were made available for research by the management of the *Crowley Post-Signal*; the remainder, 1904 to 1920, was secured from the Acadia Parish Library. Some of the files (both the private collection belonging to the *Post-Signal*, and those in the library) are of the weekly paper, the *Crowley Signal*, while others are of the *Daily Signal*. This explains the seemingly arbitrary use of both publications as source material for certain time periods. It may be helpful to students and researchers, especially those using the microfilmed files of the Crowley paper of this period, to know that all editorial matter of any importance appearing in the Saturday weekly had been already printed in preceding issues of the daily paper, Monday through Friday.

The general objective of this book is to bring together information about the events and personalities that dominated the news during the period under study. Incidents involving folkways and/or human interest material have been included to add color to the narrative.

The cut-off date of 1920 has been consistently followed, except in accounts of the rice mills and several post–1920 facts concerning the career of Sol Wright, the "Wizard of Rice."

The author realizes that many subjects treated could bear expansion; for instance, parochial and municipal politics, Crowley's churches and medical history, to name several. Also, that the main body of oral history remains virtually untouched. It is hoped that these topics will be more fully developed within the near future, and that one of Acadia's most valuable historical resources—the recollection of its senior citizens—will be more widely recognized and utilized.

—MARY ALICE FONTENOT

Introduction

A history of a Louisiana parish should accentuate all the distinctive characteristics of the particular culture as it reviews the historical events behind that culture's development. Mary Alice Fontenot, in her desire to relate the full story of Acadia Parish, has given us a detailed and intimate picture of life in what is perhaps Louisiana's most quintessential "prairie parish."

Her first volume in a two-volume series, *Acadia Parish Louisiana: a History to 1900*, won the Louisiana Literary Award for 1976 as the most valuable contribution to the state's literature. In this effort she was encouraged and assisted by the Reverend Paul B. Freeland, D.D. Dr. Freeland's untimely death in 1976 shortly after publication left Ms. Fontenot without her trusted editor and research navigator. Nevertheless, with the help of family and friends, the author persisted in her writing of the second volume. During the ensuing two years she examined volumnious civil and church records, spent many hours going through newspaper files, and compiled numerous oral histories taken from the nooks and crannies of Acadia Parish.

From the banks of the Mermentau River to the southern environs of Eunice, from Bayou Nezpique to the upper regions of Bayou Wykoff and the cotton lands around Church Point, the author has combed the countryside and townscapes of Acadia Parish in an attempt to frame an historical identity and to measure Acadia's contribution to Louisiana's culture. She is successful in her efforts to provide a new focus for the interested reader. Attakapas Indians, Spanish-owned *vacheries*, French-speaking Acadians, early Anglo-Saxons from the South and the Northeast, and Middlewestern latecomers at different intervals occupy the center stage of Louisiana's prairie heartland. In this remote southwestern corner of imperial St. Landry various ethnic islands of pioneer settlers succeeded in building a culture and an economy noted for its diversity and high level of material prosperity.

Acadia Parish can be described as both a Louisiana and a Southern anomaly. Its agricultural staple was rice, not cotton; slavery was a relatively unimportant institution and economic design; isolation was an important theme of life as late as 1880; the languages of French and German were often more pervasive than English in one community after another. Midwestern farmers with accents characteristic of rural Kansas and Illinois were later scattered over a landscape bereft of sharecroppers, tar paper shanties and Southern drawls.

Even the traditional architecture of the parish reflects a Midwestern house-type motif which conjures up the imagery of a Grant Wood painting. Slim-lined farm houses with Gothic gables and spare porches rear up from a somber prairie. The starkness, the solemnity of it all, can be replicated a thousand-fold in America's Cornbelt region far to the north.

Acadia is a composite of much that is Midwestern, Acadian, old Anglo-Saxon and Germanic, with a *soupçon* of Jews, Lebanese and Italians. The typical elements of Southern civilization, such as the plantation experience, a large black population, and the extremes of a white aristocracy and a poverty-prone tenant class have always been held in abeyance. Few places in rural Louisiana have modified the pattern of Southern life as much as this youthful parish.

Acadia retains its uniqueness. Verily, it does not even qualify as a classic American melting pot as previously suggested. It is perhaps more like a peculiar Louisiana *salad bowl*. The ingredients are discernible, each retains its special flavor, but a universal blending has never been deemed necessary.

—DR. TIMOTHY F. REILLY
Assistant Professor of Historical
and Regional Geography
University of Southwestern
Louisiana

The Parish

Acadia became Louisiana's 59th parish on October 11, 1886, by official proclamation of S. D. McEnery, governor of Louisiana. The decision to carve the new parish out of St. Landry had been made by the qualified voters of the mother parish in a referendum held October 6, 1886.[1]

Some five months later, on March 1, 1887, voters of the new parish went to the polls to select a location for the parish seat of government. The three contenders for the honor were Rayne, incorporated as a town in 1883; Crowley, a new town, not yet two months old; and a tract of land centrally located in Prairie Hayes. The result of the voting was Crowley, 689; Rayne, 560; Prairie Hayes, 519.[2]

The parish governing body was set up in November, 1886, when the governor appointed members of the police jury to represent the five wards of Acadia. Appointees were Dr. B. E. Clark, Homer Barousse, B. H. Harmon, Paul E. Fremaux and Melon Doucet.[3]

Other parish officers were elected at the March 1, 1887, election. They were Elridge W. Lyons, sheriff; R. T. Clark, clerk of court; John Crawford Lyons, state representative; Dr. R. C. Webb, coroner.[4]

The parish set up a sixth ward in 1896, and a seventh was established in 1908.[5]

Other police jurors (1888-1920) include C. T. Duhon, Dennis Miller, Cesaire Breaux, J. E. Daigle, Adam Reed, Emanuel Maignaud, W. W. Duson, Theo Flash, Joseph Flash, John Green, J. K. Toler, Homer David, F. J. Klein, F. J. Bernard, W. M. Hoyt, Ben Stagg, Ursin Daigle, Telesmar Guidry, W. A. McClelland, J. B. Richard, William Sarver, J. M. Crabtree, Dr. G. E. Brooks, Alexandre Richard, Martin Guidry, Gaudens Pousson, S. D. Wilder, W. F. Brooks, W. J. Zaunbrecher, Edward Daigle, Alcee Langley, J. H. Stakes, Pierre Bellard, John Marsh, Theophas Simon, A. Edwin Ortego, Edgar Guidry, Leopold Cart, R. C. Webb, C. H. Richard, Albert Breaux, Emile Petitjean, Wallace Dupont, G. P. Haines, J. B. Stakes, M. W. Scanlan.[6]

C. C. Duson was Acadia's first elected state senator, serving a four-year term beginning in 1888. Others (1892-1932) were D. B. Hayes, James Webb and Homer Barousse. State representatives and their terms of office were Joseph D. Bernard, 1888-1892; J. W. House, 1892-1896; J. W. Young, 1896-1900; P. S. Pugh, 1900-1904; W. H. Carver, W. M. Egan, 1904-1908; E. O. Bruner, W. A. McClelland, 1908-1912; W. A. McClel-

[1] Fontenot and Freeland, *Acadia Parish*, etc. 253, 254
[2] *Ibid*, 276
[3] *Ibid*, 258, 259
[4] *Ibid*, 277
[5] *Crowley Signal*, July 25, 1908
[6] Minutes, Acadia Parish Police Jury, *Crowley Signal*, 1888-1916

1

land, Edward Daigle, 1912-1916; L. B. DeBellevue, W. J. Zaunbrecher, 1916-1920.[7]

Assessors for the same period were David B. Lyons, 1887-1890; W. C. Chevis, 1890-1892; W. F. Brooks, 1892-1900; A. C. Lormand, 1900-1908; Martin Guidry Jr., 1908-1916; W. T. McBride, 1916-1932.

Coroners: Dr. R. C. Webb, 1887-1888; 1892-1900; Dr. George E. Brooks, 1888-1892; Dr. F. R. Martin, 1900-1904; Dr. G. C. Mouton, 1904-1908; Dr. H. C. Webb, 1908-1916; Dr. Z. J. Francez, 1916-1958.

Sheriffs: Elridge Lyons, 1887-1900; Joseph W. Murrell, 1900-1908; Louis Fontenot, 1908-1928.

Clerks of court: Raymond T. Clark, 1887-1904; Gus E. Fontenot, 1904-1926. Deputy clerks were Dallas B. Hayes and F. M. Fontenot.

Philip Sidney Pugh was Acadia's first judicial officer, elected district judge in 1904. Pugh served one term. John J. Robira was the first parish resident to be elected district attorney, winning that office in 1908. Others (to 1920) were C. B. DeBellevue and Percy T. Ogden.

While the majority of Acadia's voters belonged to the Democratic party, which returned to power in Louisiana in 1877, at one time the Republicans claimed some prominent leaders. The roster of active Republicans in 1900 included F. C. Labit, J. C. Wynne, J. E. Powers, M. W. McNeil, Fremaux Istre, J. P. Hoyt, Dr. J. F. Naftel, Dr. L. C. Pulliam, P. S. Lovell, S. B. McElhinney, M. S. Little, H. C. Wilkins, C. C. Duson, Dr. J. F. Morris, L. C. Greene, W. H. Lewis, M. L. Andrew, Dr. N. B. Morris, B. M. Lambert, J. E. Daigle, A. B. Allison, Dr. R. C. Webb, J. A. McAyeal, J. Judd, L. L. Adams and P. J. Chappuis.[8]

The party was strong enough at that time to run two candidates for parish offices: B. M. Lambert for state representative and Dr. N. B. Morris for coroner. Both were defeated, as might have been expected, but made respectable showings at the polls, considering the temper of the times. In the 1904 general election Republicans got about 10 per cent of the vote.[9]

The Socialist party was active during Acadia's early years. A mass meeting, to nominate a ticket for the party, took place in the Crowley city hall in 1904, and a Socialist rally was held there in 1909. The only names given in the meeting notices were those of E. M. Mann and R. B. Grace.[10]

Until 1906 the high man in a political race was the winner. A new election law went into effect in 1906 which required that the winning

<hr>

[7] *Crowley Signal, Daily Signal,* 1888-1916. Additional listings of Acadia Parish officials will be from this same source, unless otherwise noted

[8] *Crowley Signal,* Feb. 10, Mar. 24, Sept. 22, 1900

[9] *Crowley Signal,* Apr. 21, 1900; *Daily Signal,* Apr. 20, 1904

[10] *Ibid,* Jan. 16, 1904; *Ibid,* Mar. 5, 1909

This handsome building was Acadia's second courthouse, first used in 1904. W. L. Stevens was the architect for the $68,414 building.

candidate have a majority over all other candidates, or face the second high man in a second primary.[11]

For the first time in its 16-year history Acadia Parish was out of debt in 1902. Sheriff Murrell's annual report to the police jury showed a substantial surplus: the tidy sum of $21,000.[12]

C. C. Duson has been called "the father of Acadia."[13] It is certainly a fact that the separation from the mother parish could not have been effected without the cooperation of Duson, at the time St. Landry's most powerful politician. Once the parish was established, Duson had a great deal to do with the development of the area. He and his younger brother,

[11] *Daily Signal*, Sept. 7, 1906
[12] *Crowley Signal*, Mar. 15, 1902
[13] *Daily Signal* editorial, May 14, 1904

3

W. W. Duson, owned large tracts of land within the confines of the proposed new parish, and had set up a real estate agency to handle sales of these lands. Through the vigorous promotion programs staged by the real estate firm of W. W. Duson and Bro., thousands of new families were brought into the parish which the Dusons had helped to create.[14]

The decision to replace the first courthouse, completed in 1888, was made in 1901 by the Acadia Parish Police Jury at its November meeting. Tom Lovell of Waco, Texas was awarded the contract on a bid of $68,414. W. L. Stevens was the architect. The handsome new building was first used in the early part of 1904.[15]

Controversial Issues

One of the controversial issues that arose during Acadia's early years was the licensing of saloons. The prohibitionists, as the anti-liquor organization was called, claimed as adherents some of the parish's most prominent residents. The anti-liquor campaign won out in 1908; in an April referendum the parish was voted dry. The measure was both unpopular and ineffective; after 16 months another election was called and the licensing of saloons was returned to its former legal status.[16]

Another matter that caused controversy was the dipping law, enacted to control an infectious disease in cattle transmitted by the cattle tick. The better informed agricultural leaders of the parish adopted the practice of dipping cattle in 1915, in an effort to eradicate the disease. At that time community dipping vats had been constructed at different points in the parish by Joseph and Harry Roller, S. D. Wilder, C. E. Kemmerly, E. T. Lovell, O. Abshire and F. M. Milliken of Crowley; M. McMillan, Iota; C. W. Prather, Mowata; J. W. McCain, Ellis; Martin and Dermas Petitjean, J. B. Richard, Rayne; W. M. Hoyt, Estherwood, and Henry Bossley, Egan. S. W. Rhodes, Acadia's first agricultural demonstration agent,* began pushing the preventative measure soon after his appointment in 1914. Trouble arose in 1919 when dipping cattle became compulsory and E. P. Shreve, agricultural inspector, announced that the dipping law would be strictly enforced. Several of the dipping vats were set on fire and burned; the Leon Matthews vat at Iota was blown up by dynamite.[17]

The first graveling of parish roads, a necessity for the increasing use of the automobile, started in 1915 with the graveling of a half mile stretch of road on the west side of Bayou Plaquemine Brulee. A new bayou

---

[14] Fontenot & Freeland, *Acadia etc.* 226-229; *Crowley Signal*, Mar. 9, 1907

[15] *Crowley Signal*, Nov. 16, 1901; Sept. 19, 1903; Jan. 9, 1904; *Daily Signal*, Apr. 16, 1902

[16] *Crowley Signal*, Feb. 15, 1908; Nov. 12, 1910

* Acadia's first home demonstration agent was Erin Dore Canan, appointed to the post in 1917.

[17] *Daily Signal*, June 8, 1915; Aug. 31, 1914; Apr. 14, June 19, 1919

bridge, called Long Bridge, was nearing completion at the time. A substantial barrier had been erected the length of the steep grade, where several fatal accidents had happened during high water.[18]

The following year plans were drafted to gravel the Old Spanish Trail paralleling the Southern Pacific track from Mermentau to the Lafayette Parish line.[19]

The Acadia Parish Bar

Members of the legal profession who practiced law in Acadia Parish (to 1920) include J. E. Barry, Philip J. Chappuis, James L. Dorman, Thomas R. Smith, J. G. Medlenka, Robert Montgomery, W. R. Percy, Jules Gil, Shelby Taylor, Percy Holt, Percy Ogden, John J. Robira, A. R. Breeland, W. J. Carmouche, Felix J. Samson, Leon I. McCain, P. S. Pugh, Hampden Story, Adolphus Stamps, James A. Gremillion, Harry Gueno, L. B. DeBellevue, Abner Chappuis, Howard E. Bruner, C. B. DeBellevue, Denis T. Canan, Lawrence Pugh, M. J. Varnado and A. C. Chappuis.[20]

Schools

The establishment of schools was one of the high priority projects undertaken by leaders during the formative years of Acadia Parish.

The first school board was set up in 1887. The board was composed of William Sarver, president; D. W. Hoyt, secretary; Jean Castille, J. Wesley Young and D. C. Calkins. Members were appointed to the school board until 1908 when the office became elective.[21]

The office of secretary carried the same duties as that of superintendent and later came to be known by that title. James Edward Barry succeeded D. W. Hoyt in the position, serving from 1889 to 1906. John Hiram Lewis, superintendent from 1906 to 1913, was replaced by Jerry W. Oxford, 1913-1920.[22]

Other school board members (to 1920) were J. A. Williams, Samuel Cart, H. C. Wilkins, W. F. Brooks, L. V. Fremaux, Jean Castex, W. N. Green, W. B. Milligan, J. E. Daigle, L. F. Schamber, I. G. Jarvis, Dr. C. L. Powers, R. E. Cunningham, E. L. Harmon, S. W. Steen, F. M. Bergeron, Etienne Stagg, Yves Sensat, Alcee Henry, John A. Hunter, H. J. Fisher, R. M. Wainwright, Ursin Daigle, Albert Hains, A. B. Delahoussaye, B. F. Toler, Fernest Reed, Joseph Francois, A. P. Holt, J. T.

[18] *Ibid*, Feb. 25, 1915
[19] *Ibid*, Aug. 1, Oct. 3, 1916
[20] *Crowley Signal, Daily Signal*, to 1920
[21] *Acadia Sentinel*, July 16, 1887; *Crowley Signal*, Oct. 3, 1908
[22] Unpublished material researched by Paul B. Freeland and Dorothy B. McNeely

The first motorized school bus in Acadia Parish. The wood and metal body was built about 1918 by John Finley.

6

Nixon, Joseph Leonard, Oliver Broussard, Dr. W. T. Patterson, W. A. Morgan, Samuel D. Wilder, H. L. Redlich, Henry Bossley, Dr. Z. J. Francez, J. D. Murrell, Churchie Singletary, Charles Duhon, F. J. Klein, Ellis Hoffpauir, Charles Schamber, W. A. McClelland, Sam McManus, J. P. Nibert.[23]

Consolidation of some 50 small rural schools with the larger schools in established communities began about 1906, under the administration of Superintendent J. H. Lewis. Pupils who lived at a distance were transported in horse-drawn conveyances called wagonettes.[24]

An 1899 survey showed 5,206 children, age 6 to 18, in Acadia Parish. Of this number 4,250 were white and 936 were black. Within a 10-year period this number had almost doubled; the school census of 1910 showed 8,719 of school age in the parish: 7,130 white and 1,589 black. Crowley alone accounted for 1,200 of the school age children.[25]

Some 53 buildings were in use in 1909 for teaching purposes. Of these, three of the school houses were of brick construction and the rest were frame buildings. Two churches were among the buildings used for classes, and five of the buildings were provided the school board without charge. Libraries were established in 39 of the schools. Total enrollment for the 1908-1909 session was 5,016: 4,284 white and 732 colored.[26]

Many long-forgotten place names of Acadia Parish were created by the locations of the numerous small schools in operation before consolidation was effected. Schools were often named for the individual giving the land, or the builder of the school house. Some of the school names, like Richard, have endured; most faded from memory as soon as the little prairie school houses were dismantled and the lumber hauled away.

For the 1899-1900 school session there were 46 schools in operation in Acadia Parish. Of this number only 14 were in established communities such as Crowley, Rayne, Morse, etc. Names of these schools and the teachers assigned, other than those considered elsewhere are listed as follows in the *Crowley Signal* of September 16, 1899:

Ward 1: Phillips School, Maggie Conway; Arceneaux School, Nellie Cunningham; Leyden School, Patrick Leyden.

Ward 2: Milligan School, Annie Steen; Thibodeaux School, Ella Hazelwood; Dejean School, Daisy White; Prairie Hayes School, Gertie Abbott; Plaquemine Brulee School, no teacher.

Ward 3: Savoy School, Sidney Savoy; Ben Johnson School, Henry B. Redlich; Harmon School, Mattie Latta; Bergeron School, M. E. Normand.

Ward 4: Andrepont School, Barrie Brooks; Neville Reed School,

[23] Acadia Parish School Board minutes, published in *Crowley Signal*, to 1920
[24] *Crowley Signal*, Jan. 12, 1907
[25] *Ibid*, Mar. 31, 1900; Oct. 8, 1910
[26] *Daily Signal*, Mar. 5, 1909

Viola McMillan; McCain School, J. A. Patton; H. J. Daigle School, Miss L. Hardy; Freeland School, Margaret Borell.

Ward 5: Linebarger School, Grace Waddington; William Woods School, Cornelius Scully.

New schools put into operation between 1900 and 1905 were the Anding, Gum Point, Dugas, Petitjean, Larcade, Riverside, Green Point, Oil Field, Hundley and Camile LeBlanc schools.

The locations of many of these early schools can be determined by the names, especially those which were named for individuals. For example, the Petitjean and Larcade schools could be in but one locality—around Rayne, where the prominent families of Petitjean and Larcade settled. The Oil Field school had to be where oil was discovered in 1901. The Bergeron school near Church Point was named for one of the directors, F. M. Bergeron; the Hundley school for a pioneer family at the north end of the parish, the Ben Johnson school for a well known resident of Ward 3. The Camile LeBlanc school was in Ward 5 where Camile Le-Blanc had property.

Newspaper accounts and minutes of the school board meetings are also sources of information on locations of early schools. Many of the country schools were used as voter registration points and polling places which helped to keep the place names alive longer.

The Railroads

The importance of railroads to an agricultural area in the days prior to motorized vehicles was never more clearly demonstrated than in Acadia Parish. Without the trains the development of the rice industry would have been stalemated.

In the case of Acadia accessibility to a railroad was a major factor in the creation of the parish and the selection of the parish seat. The Louisiana Western railroad, later to become the Southern Pacific, was completed through the area in 1880. A branch line of the Southern Pacific, from Midland northeast to Eunice, extended shipping and travel facilities for Acadia.

Another link with the marketplace was the Opelousas, Gulf and Northeastern, constructed in 1906 and 1907. The 64-mile line, from Melville to Crowley, came through Church Point, Branch and Rayne. The first train arrived in Crowley September 30, 1907 and was greeted with fanfare and celebration. Thomas H. Lewis of Opelousas, called "father of the line," was presented a gold-headed cane.[27]

The third railroad, the Colorado Southern, New Orleans and Pacific,

---

[27] *Ibid*, Aug. 2, 1906; *Crowley Signal*, Oct. 5, 1907. The railway, known as "the OG," was taken over by the Texas and Pacific in 1906

commonly known as the Frisco, reached Crowley in June, 1907. The completion of the track to Crowley was marked by a ceremony at which one gold and one silver railroad spike were driven by Crowley Mayor Shelby Taylor and W. W. Duson respectively. The first train carrying about 300 passengers came in to Crowley December 15, 1907.[28]

Executions

Two executions by hanging, one legal and one illegal, have taken place in Acadia Parish. An unknown negro was lynched in Crowley in 1901, and a convicted murderer was hanged in 1910.

The following account of the lynching, headlined "Negro Stretches Hemp," is from the *Crowley Signal* of July 27, 1901:

An unknown negro man was lynched at the entrance of the court house yard by a mob of from 300 to 500 persons Friday afternoon, July 19, at 5:45 o'clock.

An hour before he opened fire with a 44-Colts revolver on Officer Turner, who attempted to arrest him. After emptying his gun at the officer he started to run, reloading his weapon, and began shooting promiscuously at the pursuing crowd and at citizens whom he chanced to meet in his flight. The negro fired probably thirty to forty shots before he was captured and disarmed. One hour and twenty minutes after the first shot was fired, the body of the negro was dangling at the end of a rope at the hands of an infuriated mob and the first lynching in the history of Acadia parish had taken place. So rapid was the work that the negro was jerked into eternity without any knowledge having been gained as to his name or where he came from.

The negro alighted from the 4:24 fast mail and his suspicious look attracted the attention of Officer James Turner, who attempted to place him under arrest. But the negro resisted, ran a few steps and began shooting at him. The officer pulled his own gun and fired at the retreating negro, who stationed himself behind a platform on the west side of the depot. Both emptied their revolvers, but none of the shots took effect.

While the officer was reloading his gun the negro started on a run down West Front street in the direction of Coontown. He saw that a crowd was following him and began shooting promiscuously at everyone in his reach. He passed the delivery wagon of Lawrence Bros.' wholesale house and shot at the negro driver, the bullet striking the seat within a few inches of the driver's feet. As the crowd pressed him he turned and fired upon it, and as he passed the American mill he began shooting at C. J. Freeland, who was standing on the platform in front of the mill, but again missed. He kept fully two blocks ahead of the pursuing mob, which was rapidly growing. When he reached the crossing leading to the Union rice mill, he changed his course and went south, making a straight cut for the woods. Shots were being fired at him by his pursuers every step, but he reached the timber without being hit.

Very few of those who were pursuing the negro were armed and only a few ventured into the deep thicket in pursuit until after guns and

---

[28] *Crowley Signal*, June 29, Aug. 3, Dec. 21, 1907

ammunition were sent out from town. The timber was soon surrounded on all sides and blood hounds set on the negro's trail.

By this time the pursuing party numbered two hundred or more and the fact that the report became current that the escaping desperado was Prince Edwards, wanted in Shreveport for the murder of John Gray Foster, only added to the excitement. The crowd, armed with Winchesters, shotguns, pistols and clubs, entered the woods behind the hounds, who soon struck the trail and followed it in a southeasterly direction.

It was not many moments before the dogs were close upon the trail of the negro, who, to escape them, ran out of the timber into a corn field near the residence of P. S. Lovell, a half mile south of town.

The dogs were at the negro's heels and a crowd not far behind him. He was almost exhausted, but his first impulse was to shoot, as he stopped and turned around to face the crowd, and again drew his gun. But a dozen Winchesters and shotguns were leveled at him and he was warned to throw up his hands. He then dropped his gun and cried out. "I surrender, I surrender, don't shoot." Some say several shots were fired at him while others deny it. However, he was not hit.

The negro was placed in a buggy and brought to town by Hugh Frere. John Raezor and several other citizens, and taken to the jail yard. He was given over to Deputy Sheriff Holland Lyons and Officer A. V. Johnson.

Jailor Paul Hebert was in a crowd searching for the negro in another part of the woods and had the keys of the prison in his pocket. The mob began surging around the officers and the prisoner and it was only by fighting their way through that he was finally locked in the jail corridor down stairs. But the mob was determined in its purpose and regardless of the protests of the officers they finally pried through the corridor door and by force pulled the quivering brute into the jail yard. Ready hands seized the brute and wild yells filled the air as he again came in view. The negro was given no time to talk. The rope was placed around his neck and he was almost dragged to the south entrance of the court house square where the rope was thrown over a limb of a tree and the body was soon dangling in the air. Before he was pulled up the negro cried piteously for mercy, but the crowd surrounding him was deaf to his pleadings.

When he was first pulled off the ground he grasped the rope with his hands, which served to relieve the strain upon his neck. Cries were raised on all sides to lower him and tie his hands behind him. This was done, whereupon, kicking and strangling, the soul of the negro was jerked into eternity.

Two or three citizens made a rush toward him as if to protect him but they were promptly and roughly forced back by the mob.

At the time the lynching was taking place Sheriff Murrel, in company with Chief of Police Lyons, Deputy Sheriff John B. Marshall and Constable George Fremaux, was watching the bridge over the Roller canal south of town, where it was expected the negro would come out of the woods, and knew nothing of the lynching until he came back to town and saw the negro's body dangling from the limb.

The sheriff, as soon as he arrived upon the scene, cut down the form and called for a physician, who examined the body and pronounced it lifeless. As the words came from the doctor's lips a hundred yells went up from the crowd surrounding the body. Then a rush was made for souvenirs. The rope was cut into hundreds of pieces and the buttons were cut from his clothes.

The grand jury, convened to investigate the lynching, examined 15 witnesses but failed to indict anyone.[29]

In 1910 Armas Woods, a convicted murderer, was hanged in the parish jail. Woods, a black man, was charged with the beating death of Mansur Nacer, a young Lebanese, at the John Pietro store on September 9, 1908.[30]

Epidemics

Acadia Parish weathered three yellow fever scares, several serious outbreaks of smallpox and the flu epidemic of 1918 during its first 35 years of existence.

The yellow fever epidemic of 1888 resulted in a brief quarantine imposed by the town of Rayne. Nine years later, in 1897, the entire parish quarantined for six weeks. Persons without a health certificate were not allowed to enter, freight went undelivered, and guards stood duty at railroad stations and on all roads leading into the parish.[31] If any Acadia residents died of the disease in 1888 and 1897 the deaths were not reported in the newspapers.

A parish-wide quarantine went into effect again in 1905 during the epidemic that claimed thousands of victims in the state, especially in New Orleans. The Acadia quarantine lasted three months, August through October. During that time all travel and commerce with the outside world came to a halt. By this time the causes of the disease were better understood, and the disease carrier, the mosquito, had been identified.

Emergency measures went into effect throughout the pairsh. The police jury set up a detention camp in the old Mike Coleman house west of the city; Dr. E. M. Ellis, Crowley health officer, ordered all open water receptacles to be covered with oil, the Crowley Oil and Mineral Company supplied hundreds of barrels of crude oil to pour into ditches, ponds, barrels and cisterns to eradicate mosquito larvae. Crowley Mayor P. J. Chappuis declared a half holiday so that residents could cut weeds, clean up rubbish, cover cisterns with screen wire. The death of one parish resident, Joshua C. Sills of Rayne, was attributed to the disease.[32]

Outbreaks of smallpox plagued all areas of the parish until World War I. Cases were isolated by having the victims brought to a pest house, where nursing care and food were provided. Immune persons were employed to work in the pest house and to fumigate the houses of victims. During the smallpox epidemic of 1899-1900 the police jury, on motion of W. W. Duson, appropriated $1,000 for the care of smallpox victims.[33]

---

29 *Ibid*, July 27, 1901
30 *Daily Signal*, Sept. 9, Nov. 2, 1908; *Crowley Signal*, Feb. 19, 1910
31 Fontenot-Freeland, *Acadia*, 211
32 *Daily Signal*, Aug. 17, 1905
33 *Crowley Signal*, May 13, 1899; Jan. 13, 20, 27, 1900

In the spring of 1901 Dr. F. R. Martin reported that he, Dr. Homer Chachere and Dr. D. D. Mims had vaccinated 500 Crowley residents in a house-to-house campaign against smallpox. Thirty four cases, found within the corporate limits of the town, were reported confined in 17 houses which had been marked with yellow flags warning of the infection within.[34]

Except for a few cases reported in 1905, there were no further smallpox scares until 1914 when 250 cases were reported. In 1916 several cases were reported in the north and northwest portions of the parish.[35]

Typhoid posed another threat to the well being of Acadia residents, but if there were epidemics during the period under study such were not reported in the newspapers.

The flu epidemic of 1918 took a heavy toll. One report claimed there were as many as 2,000 cases in the parish. Schools were closed, church services in Crowley and Rayne suspended. A number of deaths were attributed to the flu.[36]

Infant Mortality

Many infants and young children of Acadia Parish died of diseases which have since been virtually wiped out. The most common causes of death in young children during the first two decades of the century were membranous croup, a contagious disease resembling diphtheria; diphtheria, and cholera infantum, an illness said caused by excessive heat, improper feeding and bad sanitation.

Leprosy

Several cases of leprosy were discovered in the parish between 1904 and 1914. One victim was an old man who lived near the oil field, another was a resident of the Estherwood area who died of the disease in 1910. In 1914 Dr. Z. J. Francez, parish coroner, discovered 12 cases of leprosy in the vicinity of Morse and Mermentau Cove. The victims were persuaded to go the the state leper colony for treatment.[37]

Animal Diseases

Diseases affecting livestock caused great losses to Acadia's farm people in the days before mechanized farm machinery. Lack of knowl-

---

[34] *Ibid*, Mar. 10, 1901
[35] *Daily Signal*, Apr. 13, 14; May 11, 18, 1914; Mar. 14, 1916
[36] *Crowley Signal*, Oct. 12, 1918
[37] *Daily Signal*, June 1, 1904; July 21, 1914; *Crowley Signal*, July 9, 1910

edge of how to treat and control such diseases was blamed for their spread. In 1901 the body of a mule, dead of charbon (anthrax), was left out in the woods to decay; as a result hundreds of animals became infected and died. This brought a mandate by the police jury that carcasses of all dead animals had to be burned or buried in lime at least two feet deep in the ground.[38]

During the charbon epidemic of 1903 a number of humans contracted the disease by skinning the dead animals in order to use, or sell, the hides. The infected individuals became ill, but none died.[39]

A sickness known as "blind staggers" which affected horses and mules was another disease that crippled farming efforts when it reached epidemic proportions.[40]

---

[38] *Crowley Signal*, July 6, 1901; Aug. 1, 1903
[39] *Ibid*, Apr. 11, 1903
[40] *Ibid*, Aug. 3, 1907

The Rice Industry

The history of rice cultivation in Acadia Parish goes back to the days of the first prairie settlers, who planted the grain for their own use. The rice, called providence rice, was planted in the shallow ponds which once dotted the flat prairies; the success of the crop was entirely dependent upon natural rainfall.

German farmers of the Fabacher and Robert's Cove colonies are credited with being the first to cultivate rice on high land, also the first to grow rice for commercial purposes. The Germans found that they could aid providence by storing rainwater for irrigation in reservoirs made by throwing up levees around the ponds and marshy places.

Further improvements in irrigation, new methods of harvesting and the establishment of local rice mills resulted in tremendous growth of the rice industry between 1890 and 1900.

The expansion and development carried over into the new century and reached a peak about 1905.

The story of one man's dogged determination to perfect a domestic variety of rice—an undertaking that had all the earmarks of an "impossible dream"—and another man's vision of opening up additional thousands of acres of rice production are two major highlights of the history of the rice industry during the 20-year period covered by this work.

The first man dreamed his great dream and made it come true entirely by his own efforts. The second man's plan for a giant irrigation system could have worked—but ended in dismal failure. The life work of both men was inspired by the golden grain which had become the precocious agricultural giant of the southwest Louisiana prairies.

The two men were Salmon Lusk Wright, rice farmer-scientist, and Welman Bradford, engineer-surveyor and canal builder. Wright achieved lasting fame as the developer of domestic seed rices which revolutionized the industry; historically speaking, Bradford all but lost his canal-building identity when J. Franklin Schell took over the building of the immense irrigation system.

Profile of a Genius

S. L. Wright's contribution to rice farming interests of the United States dominates the entire history of the industry, overshadowing whatever had already happened and whatever was to happen. His awesome genius in breeding new rice varieties, which reversed the direction of a major food industry, has few parallels in the history of agriculture.

Born in Rockville, Indiana, April 26, 1852, "Sol" Wright spent 10 years farming wheat at Albany, Oregon, before coming to Acadia Parish in 1890. He was successful as a rice farmer from his first year. His 320-

S. L. Wright, 1852-1929

acre farm five miles southwest of Crowley, for which he had paid $1,500, brought him $1,900 that first harvest—$400 more than the cost of the farm.[1]

Less than a decade after he came to Louisiana Wright was recognized as one of the leading farmers of the rice belt and as an authority on seed rice. He had scientifically sound ideas on every phase of rice cultivation—his farming techniques were away ahead of his time—and he shared this knowledge, gained from his own experience, with all and sundry.

At that time (1901) new settlers from the northern states continued to come into the area in large numbers. There were virtually no sources of information on rice culture, and the newcomers knew virtually nothing about rice farming. Sol Wright could appreciate their position; he knew how to help them, and he proceeded to do so in a most thorough fashion, through the columns of the Crowley newspaper and a local farm publication.[2]

"I have been in the rice business more than ten years and therefore feel competent to give advice to newcomers," he wrote by way of introduction. Then he went into detailed directions on how to prepare the land for planting, how to select the best seed and what amounts to use per acre.[3]

Wright even had his own methods of controlling red rice, a wild rice with red grains that spreads with amazing rapidity and devaluates the quality of the crop. On lands where red rice had taken over Wright advised the farmer to "plow about five inches deep and turn the red rice under deep so that it will not grow." Also he thought the red rice could almost be choked out if the farmer could succeed in getting a good thick stand of the white rice. It was important, Wright warned, that when red rice was found heading out in a field that it be cut out at once. He had small patience with those farmers who held to the belief that white rice spilled in the field turned to red rice during the winter lay-over. "The man who thinks white turns red by laying in the mud all winter is to be classed with those who think the world is flat and the moon made of green cheese," was his captious summation.[4]

The ex-wheat farmer had acquired some expertise on the proper way to irrigate rice. Rice, he said, should be flooded two to four inches deep. If the rice fell down, it was because it was too thinly planted, or had been flooded too deep.[5]

Something of Wright's exact and painstaking procedures can be learned from an abstract from the above-cited article:

---

[1] *Country Gentleman*, magazine, July 24, 1920
[2] *The Rice Journal and Gulf Coast Farmer*, a monthly publication by Signal Printing Co.
[3] *Crowley Signal*, Feb. 23, 1901
[4] *Ibid*
[5] *Ibid*

"I have good seed rice at $5 a barrel. My best seed rice, that is, better than imported, is $7 a barrel. How did I get it better than imported? I bought the best imported seed I could get, at $9 a barrel, gave it a thorough fanning, and when I drilled it I stopped up one of the middle holes in my drill so I had a vacant space of 16 inches every eight feet for my men to walk in so they would not get lost and make skips while going through to hand pick the rice. I put my men through each piece from two to three times. It is generally thought that rice that has been raised here for one year will beat the imported yielding, and I am inclined to think it is true."

Wright's first crop of rice was the so-called "providence" rice, the success of the crop dependent entirely on rainfall for irrigation. After that first season Wright bought water from a canal company until 1902, when he put down his own well. The well, adequate for the acreage to be flooded, was 10 inches in diameter, drilled to a depth of 293 feet. The pit for the pump was 20 feet deep, later deepened to 50 feet to accommodate a steel pit.[6]

(A freak accident happened at this well. According to the *Crowley Signal* of June 27, 1903, Willis A. Hill was caught in the machinery of the irrigation well, pulled down 20 feet into the pit then brought back up again. Hill's only injury was a broken leg. The bizarre part of the incident was that when Hill was returned to the surface the only clothes left on his body were his shoes.)

More rice "how to" by Wright appeared in print in 1903, in the September issue of the *Rice Journal* and *Gulf Coast Farmer*. Asked to contribute an article on field work, Wright wrote that the subject was so broad that he couldn't cover it in one article, "so shall mention a few things I regard as of great importance."

It took something like 1,500 words and about 25 column inches of 7-point type to cover the "few things." The article brought the farmer up to date on rice field irrigation, with complete and explicit directions on how to construct levees, how best to drain a field after the rice matured and some specific guidelines on this phase of cultivation.[7]

Wright's articles also give some insight into some of the early techniques used by the pioneer rice farmers of the area, and how changes came about. For instance: "When I came to southwest Louisiana about 13 years ago, we all thought that levees should be run for six- to eight-inch falls between cuts. About six years ago we began to think of three-inch falls; and some of us began to use them. . . . My observation has shown that the change was a wise one. I am firmly convinced, however, that the change did not go far enough. I made my levees closer together for the present crop than for any other, but feel they are not yet close enough. I

---

[6] *Country Gentleman*, July 24, 1920
[7] *Crowley Signal*, Sept. 5, 1903

aim to levee my land this winter for a two-inch fall, being certain that it will pay me."[8]

Without benefit of government bulletins, without anything except his own trial-and-error experiments, Wright came up with a simple method of accurately locating the levees in so small a fall. He set gauges that were marked every two inches, as two-inch marks are indicated on a ruler. When the gauges were set in the water one mark was at the surface, the other two inches deeper. Then, by drawing off the water until the second mark was even with the surface, a level was had that was two inches lower than the first. To run the levee for any level it was only necessary to draw a furrow along the thin edge of the water. "This will locate the levee more accurately than any other method," Wright wrote. "It is a cheap method. The farmer can do the work, without hiring a high-priced man for several days. Running a levee by the edge of the water one is better able to tell just when it is safe to straighten a levee so as to avoid some of the sharp angles that would appear in the line run by a civil engineer."[9]

Wright had found that the more shallow flooding would control weeds better; he advised however, that should the grasses get ahead of the rice, deeper flooding was indicated. He had also observed that after the rice had finished stooling it needed deeper water, four to six inches. "I have observed that deeper water produces deeper mud," he wrote. "Just what the reason is, I cannot say. Possibly hydrostatic pressure has something to do with it. . . . Rice does better when the ground is soft to the greater depth."[10]

The article included advice for the interim period between cutting and threshing the rice. "After rice is matured, there are three important things to use care with. (1) Do not drain the field until the crop is made, till the grains begin to harden. Then draw the water off quickly. To do this, it will be necessary to have good drainage facilities. See that they work. They are likely to fool you. (2) Do not cut the grain till it is ripe. The low grade of much rice is due to the grain being cut too early. It is robbed of some of the elements necessary to its curing well. (3) Do not thresh till rice is dry. This is to avoid rotten, musty, and stackburnt rice. By observing these three points, it may happen that the farmer will market his rice a little later, but on the whole he can afford it. On the average he will make a better profit, and his profit is surer."[11]

The articles written by Wright are uncluttered with scientific data and terminology and therefore could be easily understood by any literate farmer of his day. His highly readable writing style, coupled with an ability to convey information in a clear and logical manner, add interest and value to his published material, which constitutes yet another of his contributions to the agricultural interests of the time.

---

[8] *Ibid*

[9] *Ibid*

[10] *Ibid*

[11] *Ibid*

Wright was the first person to challenge the status quo of seed rice. From the start of the giant industry all interested persons—from planters to millers to canal men and everyone in between—accepted the fact that there were only two kinds of rices available for planting. These were the Japan and Honduras varieties, both imported. Seed from the importations did well the first and second year, but disintegrated the third year, so that every third year new seed must be brought in from the country where it originated. An estimated 250 tons of Japan seed was imported by Crowley mills alone in 1903; this averaged out, for the rice belt, about 25 tons per mill.[12] That was the way it was and everyone accepted it. Except Sol Wright.

In 1903 when his 13th rice crop was about to mature Wright announced that he would raise only seed rice in the future. Wright seed was already well known in Acadia Parish; he had advertised fancy Japan seed rice for sale as early as 1901. In connection with his plan to specialize in seed rice Wright said his aim was to rid his farm entirely of red rice, and he confidently predicted that this would by accomplished by the spring of 1904. He evidently succeeded; in the spring of 1905 he advertised for sale 1,500 barrels of domestic Japan seed rice "free from red and all foul seeds."[13]

During those years of testing out best methods of running levees, controlling red rice and such, Wright was on another experimental quest: to develop a pure bred American rice. He had strong feelings about the need for a domestic variety. Later, after his work was recognized, he was to be widely quoted on this point.[14]

The need for a better stock, American or foreign, was becoming increasingly urgent. The available seed rices were mostly hybrids; after two generations the grains would break up in the milling process. Yields were decreasing at an alarming rate each year.[15] Intrusion of salt water into the irrigating streams for two successive seasons followed by bad market years had already seriously crippled the rice business. The young industry had all the symptoms of a terminal illness.

Hard times in the Louisiana rice belt were attributed to several factors: worn-out land, late planting, not enough or too much rain at the wrong times, any other condition over which the farmer had no control. Sol Wright was the one person who recognized the symptoms for what they were. Because he had begun his long range experiments during a time of plenty he was able to come up with a cure at the time it was most needed—during the lean years.

The human interest and drama in the Sol Wright story were recognized by professional writers during his lifetime and after. Some 30 years

---

[12] *Daily Signal*, Feb. 6, 1903
[13] *Crowley Signal*, Aug. 8, 1903; Feb. 2, 1901; *Daily Signal*, March 7, 1905
[14] *Daily Signal*, Nov. 9, 1911; Mar. 26, 1918
[15] *Ibid*, Dec. 6, 1912

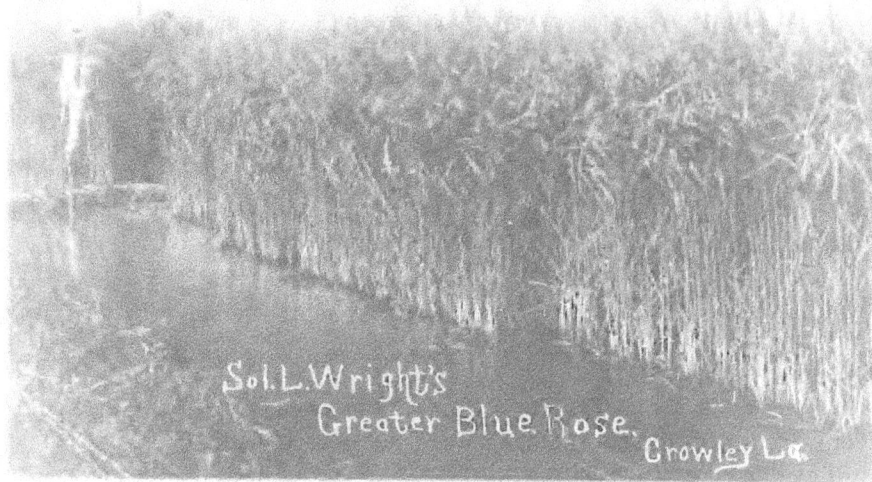

A magnificent stand of Blue Rose rice on the Wright farm southwest of Crowley. At one time there were some 500 varieties of rice growing on the 50 acres reserved for experimental purposes.

after his death Frances Parkinson Keyes, one of America's best known novelists, adapted his life story for one of her works of fiction.[16] In 1914, when Wright was well on his way to fame as a rice breeder, a *Times-Picayune* reporter, Herman J. Seiferth, wrote a sensitive article on Wright which was re-printed in the *Daily Signal* of November 18, 1914. The in-depth article, the most complete resume of Wright's work published during that period, deserves to be reproduced here in its entirety:

> The rice farmer says that Sol Wright saved his industry.
>
> The rice miller affirms that Sol Wright preserved rice as a profitable crop.
>
> The Federal government, while pointing to its own work and willingness, admits that Sol Wright has accomplished more for rice than anybody else, and accounts for the fact on the ground that Sol Wright is a genius, who arises once in a century, and that his achievements are no disparagement of the orderly, systematic progress of scientific experiment.
>
> Who is Sol Wright?
>
> His unabridged name is Salmon L. Wright, sixty-two years of age,

---

[16] Keyes, Frances Parkinson, *Blue Camellia*, author's note, pp vii-x, Julian Messner, 1957

and he is a rice farmer, near Crowley. You can see him almost daily on the streets of the bustling town, medium in height, spare of build, wearing an overcoat before the weather makes it imperative, with thin graying mustache and his mild blue eyes curtaining dreams. And always he carries a little bouquet of rice in his hand. That rice is the symbol of the vision that absorbs him. He has always been eager to share his vision with the world, and he will expand upon it and expatiate upon it to whoever will listen. At first he was regarded as a crank, then as a savior, and it will not be many years before the fuller realization will make him wealthy, although he is still a comparatively poor man, for, so far, his discoveries have enriched others, rather than himself.

Sol Wright was born on an Indiana farm. When he approached manhood he joined in the rush to the West. He had never enjoyed much schooling, he did not possess much means, but he was one of the most ardent students and lovers of nature, and when he started a wheat farm in Oregon he at once became devoted to the study of wheat. When the experts came around to form estimates of the crops they lingered to talk to Wright, for the gentle farmer always had some wonders to relate and show. When their reports were issued they were unconsciously tinged with Wright. He might have achieved for wheat what he has done for rice, but the cold climate was too much for him and his health broke down. The doctors told him he would have to move, and he sold his last crop before it was grown. That came near being the only stroke of modern business of which the farmer sage ever was guilty. A terrible freeze came along and killed the crop, for which he had been paid. The purchaser was willing to accept his loss in good part, and it is doubtful Mr. Wright could have refunded the money had he so desired. But he remained on the spot, showed the buyer how to take advantage of the plowing and other work that had been done, and assisted in the quick cultivation of a spring harvest, which reimbursed him for the disaster.

Then Mr. Wright came South and bought his rice farm, giving notes for part of the price. The first crop was so bountiful that he was able to pay off all his debt. That was twenty-four years ago, and he has never thought of leaving the land that was so generous to him in the crisis of his life. He also won back his health under the sunny skies of Louisiana, and, although never robust, the gifts which the section bestowed upon him inspired him to pay back the blessings a hundred fold.

For years Mr. Wright was very little different from the farmers around him. His genius was unsuspected, and he laid no claim to any superior knowledge. His faculty was not of the meteoric kind that blazes a pathway with a brilliancy that makes men pause to marvel and pay tribute. He was the dreamer afield who solves the secret of nature, and, with reverent touch and infinite patience, follows almost invisible threads until the glory of the miracle is plain and the golden result is within the faithful lover's keeping. It was the tireless wooing of years that was rewarded by the development of the Blue Rose rice.

Before the perfection of that variety the rice grower was in despair. The land that had almost paid for itself every year yielded constantly diminishing harvests. Some said that was due to the failure to replenish the fertility of the soil, but the crude and even scientific rebuilder failed to restore former conditions. Dr. Knapp,* the first great champion of the

---

* Dr. Seaman A. Knapp, founder of agricultural extension work, played a conspicuous part in the early development of the Louisiana rice industry.

21

industry, obtained the aid of the United States in a quest for better seed, and did succeed in introducing several kinds that increased the harvest. But the seed deteriorated, various pests attacked the new breeds, and soon the planters were faced with the same hopeless fight. The government established its station, began experiments which will eventually improve the seed and land both, but in the meantime there was dire need for betterment.

About the only heartening prospect was the result being achieved with Japan rice, and it was this constant talk of Japan that supplied the spur Mr. Wright required in order to crystallize and concentrate his endeavor. Crystallize is the keynote of the quest that was pursued to victory. The crystal is the foundation of profit in rice growing. The crystal was the mirror of the Wright deal.

When the cover of the grain of rice is removed and the grain exposed it is often found to be part chalky substance. This chalky portion leads to breakage and loss in milling. The crystal portion of the cereal, which is firm and resists the severest test in milling without breakage makes the head rice, which regulates the main return from the crop. A barrel of rough Japan rice was calculated to yield eighty pounds of head rice, while Honduras most of the time only gave fifty pounds. It was a matter of seed selection and breeding that was beyond the ken of the ordinary planter. The old types had never been bred properly, and it was the bad breeding that caused the starchy, chalky grains that broke up badly in the milling process. The heads produced contained two types of rice, the chalky and the crystal. The chalky grain took after its ancestors that were mixed with the type. The problem was to eliminate the chalk.

Mr. Wright was no scientist. All he knew was nature. Breeding rice meant the same principle as propagating animals so as to perpetuate the finest qualifications and cover the thoroughbred lines. He had the clear understanding of his goal, and his intimacy with nature's methods was his only equipment for reaching it. He had his thoroughbred Italian bees before him, and because of his faith in the thoroughbred he could go among them unharmed and observe every stage on the purest scientific process they practiced. He noticed the most minute methods of nature's exercise in achieving the perfect growth. And then there was infinite patience, the indisputable symbol of genius. Night after night, though weary from the long day's toil, he sat beside his lamp with his sheaves before him. He laid open thousands of grains with his cramped fingers and carefully examined each grain. The grains that came nearest the standard he had in mind he laid aside and replanted next day. As soon as these produced new grains the latter were subjected to the same rigid scrutiny.

It required only a few lines to detail the plodding pursuit and its purpose, and volumes could not describe the ecstasy of the one magnificent minute when the grain for which he had striven many months lay glistening in his palm, a tiny speck, full formed and clear crystal, destined to become the progenitor of a species without the defects and the drawbacks of those that had prevailed.

Even a story such as this has place for a mother-in-law. Mr. Wright is as proud of his family as of his greatest attainments. He attributes thoroughbred characteristics to his wife and to his children, and he has conferred their names upon the rices of the superior breeds that he has evolved. His mother-in-law was on a visit to his farm when he was at the height of his momentous search, and each night, as he bent over his

The "Wizard of Rice" and a sheaf of headed rice of which Sol Wright was particularly proud. The picture was taken in 1917.

magic grains, she was wont to rail him good naturedly about his absorbing task. On the fateful evening she told him a story of a priest in the section who applied himself assiduously to the culture of roses. The cleric had produced many rare and fragrant beauties, and one of his parishioners, in a spirit intended to be sarcastic, asked him why he did not raise a blue rose.

"Ah, my dear friend," he responded, "if I could to that I would not have to remain your priest."

It was while half listening to the anecdote that the perfect grain revealed itself in his hand. Mr. Wright, trembling with the joy of triumph, extended his prize between his feverish fingers and exultantly exclaimed:

"Here is the rice I have been looking for and you have named it for me!"

So was the Blue Rose born. The unattainable had been reached.

But that was only the beginning. From that one grain, sown in the spring of 1909,** there were 125,000 acres of Blue Rose harvested this season. One man and his own effort established the American mastery over Japan.

But the single grain was only the start of a time of trial that would have discouraged and defeated the average man. The progeny of the grain had to be nurtured and watched. From the stalks of subsequent fruition two of the perfect grains had to be gathered. One was planted and the other retained for comparison with the yield. Victory was not complete until resultant rice exactly matched the mother seed, and until every grain upon the stalk was uniform and true to type. And after the variety was thoroughly developed and permanency assured there were new difficulties. Mr. Wright's fate was not different from the experiences of Columbus and the long line of human benefactors. Many to whom he offered the seed regarded him as a crank whom it was not worth while even to humor. For he was poor and stood alone. Others were convinced by his confidence and claims, but they feared to hazard the cultivation. Rice had to be sold to the mills, and the mills had their grades for Japan and for Honduras rice. There was no grade for Blue Rose, and the mills might refuse to handle it at any price, so that the daring grower might pay high for his courage.

So the Blue Rose went begging, and at first Mr. Wright almost impoverished himself pushing his find.

Recognition came the next season, but almost too late for the pioneer. The Blue Rose not only made the highest yield per acre, but it stood the highest test in the mills. There was less waste and more clean product. A barrel of rough netted a hundred pounds of head rice, and commanded the highest price. Then there was a rush for Blue Rose, but the seed was mostly in other hands. Men who hesitated and scoffed paid $9 a barrel for the new breed, and were glad to get it. It was hailed as the salvation of the Louisiana industry. Japan was eliminated from Acadia, and wherever he rode, Mr. Wright's eyes were greeted with fields of bright, beautiful yellow, instead of the dark, weather-beaten hue which distinguished the former crops. The yield was 25 to 50 per cent greater. The stalk fuller and stiffer, and that not only made it easier to harvest but provided a succulent feed that will give impetus to cattle raising, al-

---

** This is an error, probably typographical. Information from other sources gives 1907 as the year the parent seed was sown. This is substantiated by the Wright family.

Edith Wright and a "bouquet" of the rice her father named for her. A later variety, Lady Wright, was named for the wife and mother, Laura Cook Wright.

though the agricultural experts say that it will not do for silage owing to the air in the cane, inducing fermentation too rapidly.

When Blue Rose came into its own planters enthusiastically laid the matter before the United States government. They thought that the national department should back the American rice developer to the extent of paying his expenses around various rice sections so that he could educate and supply the growers to their own advantage. The department ruled that such a move would be impossible, as it would be devoting the government's money to exploiting the sale of privately owned seed.

Frank A. Godchaux, president of the Louisiana Rice Milling Company, early became a convert. The large yield per acre, the large yield in the mill, he declared, would enable the State to combat the importation of foreign rice, always commanding a relatively higher price than the Japanese cereal, and he offered to place all his buyers and graders at the disposal of the father of Blue Rose, or even to buy his seed outright and dispose of it through the company's forces. The Southern Rice Growers Association said that it had proved its supremacy planted beside every other variety, and upon every type of soil, and was the strongest weapon designed to keep foreign rice out of the country. The association offered to distribute all the seed of Mr. Wright's own raising. But as largely told, most of the seed was in other hands, because Mr. Wright could not win the needed support at the crucial period. Worse than that, others who raised his rice without his skill in selection and his conscientiousness in conformity to breed, disposed of seed in which quality had become mixed and the result was bound to be deterioration.

But both the rice farmers and Mr. Wright had learned their lessons, and the outlook is that the developer will eventually break the old rule and find fortune while he is still alive. The Blue Rose was not the limit of his vision. He has improved upon it. He has taken the Honduras rice in hand, and has bred it up into the Edith rice, with a little longer and thicker and more cylindrical shaped berry, clear and white, which will mill fifteen pounds more head to the barrel. He has perfected an early prolific, the very title of which proclaims its purpose.

And his effort along the avenue of crystal enhancement has brought about what he deemed his crowning achievement, the Louisiana Pearl. From a food standpoint, he says, this will be the greatest rice in the world, with very heavy yield in field and mill, and the prospect for 115 pounds and more of head rice to the barrel, a figure deemed impossible before.

Some of these seeds will not be on the market for a year or so, for Mr. Wright is beginning to think of his own financial welfare, though the gratification of improvement is his main pleasure, as well as making the State independent of foreign invasion and benefiting the people among whom he made his home. They now have more faith in him, and his confidence in himself and them has risen in proportion. He now farms partnerships with the farmers who trust in him, furnishes them with the new seeds, and guides the cultivation, and when the crops come in there will be ample grain for both. Of course, as there are many planters in the new compacts there will be larger reward for Mr. Wright.

In that way it will come about that the prophet will attain both honor and wealth in his own country. But nobody will begrudge him the success that all are sure will come, for he will have helped the country more than he has ever demanded for himself.

The "prophet" did indeed attain honor in his own country, but never the predicted wealth. He was "written up" in the home town newspaper when his new seed first began to make news: "S. L. Wright . . . has been for 20 years experimenting for the purpose of developing a new type of rice that will unite the best qualities of Honduras and Japan . . . has at last succeeded. Mr. Wright calls his new type of rice Blue Rose American."[17] Shortly thereafter another newspaper article reported that Blue Rose seed was being sold for $9 a barrel. This, at a time when milling rice was bringing $1 to $3.50 per barrel, was the big news. The years of patient and exhaustive work in developing the rice were summed up in less than a dozen lines of type: "Six years ago he selected the original seed from a head of Shinriki rice. Selecting the most perfect seeds he planted them and in the following years carefully selected the most perfect seeds. Eventually, by the process of selection, the new type was developed."[18] Even so, it may be said that the Crowley newspaper did more to promote Wright's great work than any other medium.

Other Wright varieties were in various stages of development at the time that Blue Rose became available for distribution. A report on Wright's Early Prolific appeared as early as 1911: an Estherwood area farmer, Drozin Broussard, got 23 sacks to the acre on his Early Prolific seed, and the rice graded No. 1 straight through. A third variety, known at that time as Wright's improved Honduras, was credited with "remarkable milling qualities, due to a total absence of chalk in the grains."[19]

Reports such as these drew agronomists and agricultural specialists to the Wright farm. They observed and studied Wright's methods, ended up with the same conclusions: that he had "developed some very valuable types of rice, possessing most of the good qualities of the old types, besides additional good qualities of their own, and lacking the bad qualities of the old varieties." All agreed that in his development of the varieties Wright had pursued the most approved scientific methods of selection and breeding.[20]

By the end of 1911 Wright was being hailed as "the Burbank of rice." The title most frequently given him was "the wizard of rice;" he was also called "the gentle genius," perhaps the most apropos title of all.[21]

However, this "gentle genius" could show his tough side, like when the reputation of his precious rices was threatened. In 1914, well after Blue Rose had become a household word in the industry, the New Orleans Board of Trade was taken to task by Wright for having listed his Blue Rose as Java, an Oriental variety. Interviewed by the press concern-

[17] *Daily Signal*, Aug. 8, 1911
[18] *Ibid*, Aug. 24, 1911
[19] *Ibid*, Oct. 10, 26, 1911
[20] *Ibid*
[21] *Ibid*, Dec. 2, 1911; Aug. 20, 1919; Oct. 22, 1915

Graphic proof of Sol Wright's break-through in rice breeding is provided by the photos on these pages. The four hulled grains of rice all came from the same pannicle of rough rice, shown at right. The one perfect grain, a mutation (or, as Sol Wright called it, a "mongrel"), became the parent of Blue Rose.

ing the matter, Wright, with justifiable pride, made the following statement:

> I originated the Blue Rose rice. It is strictly an American rice and I gave it an American name. I have given no one authority to change the name. I have sold it as Blue Rose for three years. Its reputation is so great it has acquired the name of 'Famous Blue Rose.' It is the most popular rice in America. This rice was not discovered by accident, but was built by scientific process and I am still improving upon it. It is the only purebred rice grown in America.
>
> Why the New Orleans Board of Trade should undertake to change the name to an inferior foreign hybrid rice is something I cannot understand. It cannot be that they are trying to increase the popularity of Blue Rose for it has built up its own reputation and is in greater demand than any other rice. It looks more like they want to change the name to Java, so that the inferior Java can be imported and sold on the good reputation built up by Blue Rose.
>
> When I went to work to improve rices a number of years ago, I

found that practically all the rices were hybrids. My work has been to classify and weed out the undesirable mixtures and produce pure bred rices that will grow grains all of the same texture, and other uniform and desirable qualities. I have originated a number of these new types that are superior to any rices that can be found elsewhere. The Blue Rose is the first of these types to be put on the market.

I am producing these new types for the benefit of the American rice grower, and not to enable some man to import an inferior foreign rice and sell it on the good reputation built up by one of my new purebred rices. The New Orleans Board of Trade has made a mistake in attempting to change the name of Blue Rose to Java, and should in all fairness, at once correct this mistake.[22]

The error was corrected, and an apology was made by the president of the Board of Trade.[23] It was not altogether a matter of smoothing Wright's ruffled feathers; serious financial complications and loss could have resulted. At the time Blue Rose was commanding a half cent more than Java; if Blue Rose had been denied the classification, the farmers would have suffered in consequence.[24]

Later, the Rice Miller's Association made the same mistake. Wright angrily charged that the association was seeking to discount his work and to destroy the identity of Blue Rose because of its popularity.[25] Whether or not Wright's charges were justified is not known. The actions of the two agencies might have been due to carelessness. Be that as it may, the resulting statewide publicity in each case helped to further establish Blue Rose for what its propagator said it was: an American rice with an American name, developed especially for American farmers.

Wright's caustic remarks, quoted in the press at the time of the controversy, may have made him appear a boastful, arrogant type of person. Such was not the case. The gifted rice breeder was in reality an humble man, but one to whom "it was given to know that he had done well." When he said: "I have originated a number of new and improved types of rice that are superior to any rices that can be found else-where. . . . I am introducing two new types this fall and winter that are extremely valuable rices . . . these rices will just about change the entire seed rice picture of the United States within the next two years. . . ."[26] he was speaking only truth. He knew exactly what he was talking about—such remarks were merely statements of fact, and no one knew this better than Sol Wright.

Nor was he the brooding recluse that his concentration and absorption with his experiments might seem to indicate. He was a genial, out-going person who liked to be with people, especially those who would listen to him expound on his favorite subject—his rices. A clear picture of

[22] *Ibid*, Nov. 9, 1914
[23] *Ibid*, Nov. 19, 1914
[24] *Times-Picayune*, Nov. 17, 1914
[25] *Daily Signal*, Oct. 22, 1915
[26] *Ibid*

Sol Wright, the man, emerges from newspaper and magazine articles published during his lifetime. A New Orleans reporter described him as "lean, lank, slow-speaking. He talks Darwin's 'Origin of the Species' but has never read it."[27]

The fact that Wright was not a geneticist always impressed writers. His work was termed "a narrative of American achievement, a tale of endless, patient toil and observation by an obscure rice grower, who without special training for his work clung tenaciously to his idea."[28]

It is obvious that Wright was a special favorite with newspaper people, which is generally an excellent guideline for judging a person's popularity with his contemporaries. "Uncle Sol," as he came to be known in the press, was "good copy." He could be depended upon to provide something worth printing even if it was only a quip. For example, when he was ready to introduce one of his improved Blue Rose varieties he was quoted: "The only objection to this rice is that it can overwork the farmer at harvest time, when he must haul the immense yield to market."[29]

Since it took a farmer an entire season to test out Wright's claims for his rice, it is surprising that the word got around as quickly as it did. Wright's early supporters—Drozin Broussard, Frank Godchaux and officials of the Southern Rice Growers Association, were not the only ones who believed. The home parish planters who were pioneers in Blue Rose cultivation included A. Kaplan, Dan J. Feitel, W. M. Hoyt, J. P. Hoyt and J. A. Leighton.[30] As early as 1912 the *Signal* editorialized: ". . . those few farmers who have tried Wright's Blue Rose are enthusiastic over the results, the yield being several times that of ordinary rices."[31]

And "those few farmers" were more than repaid for their confidence in Wright's new seed. Blue Rose brought Acadia Parish an estimated $6 million in 1913.[32]

Another early user of Wright rice seed was T. T. Atteberry, manager of the huge Jones Brothers rice farms at Mowata. Wright supplied the seed, Atteberry planted and cultivated under Wright's supervision, and the two shared the profits. Atteberry was one of the first farmers to plant Early Prolific.[33]

Frank Milliken, Crowley manager of the Southern Rice Growers Association (later the American Rice Growers Association), was undoubtedly Sol Wright's chief disciple. Milliken boosted Wright's work by exhibiting samples of his rices at association meetings in Louisiana and Texas.[34] At Christmas, 1912, Wright was presented a $150 gold watch,

[27] *New Orleans Item*, Apr. 21, 1918
[28] *Southwest Trail*, July 1915
[29] *Daily Signal*, Oct. 24, 1919
[30] *Ibid*, Nov. 30, 1912; Nov. 15, 30, Dec. 4, 1913
[31] *Ibid*, Dec. 6, 1912
[32] *New Orleans Item*, Apr. 21, 1918
[33] Daily Signal, Dec. 4, 1913; July 20, 1914; Mar. 11, Aug. 26, Sept. 3, 1915
[34] *Ibid*, July 25, 1916

inscribed, a gift from the farmers and businessmen of Acadia Parish, in gratitude for having originated Blue Rose. The presentation was made by Frank Milliken,[35] who, in all probability, had instigated the movement and taken up the subscription. Wright was cited by directors of the association as "one of our number who has succeeded in developing the best purely American rice grown, and outranking any foreign grown variety of similar character introduced into the rice belt."[36] Milliken was probably behind this recognition, and could also have instigated the previously mentioned request for government aid.

By the end of 1913 the good reports on Blue Rose were literally pouring in, and orders for the seed came from Texas, Oklahoma, Tennessee, Mississippi, Arkansas and Missouri. J. P. Hoyt had calls for orders of Blue Rose seed up to $10,000; W. M. Hoyt reported Blue Rose seed more in demand than any other variety, owing to better yield and germination, plus endurance qualities in standing up when ripe in the fields. The tough, vigorous straw of Blue Rose was a quality with strong appeal for farmers. Blue Rose straw held the head well up and could withstand long periods of bad weather. This, like the crystal berry, had not come about by accident or chance. The toughness of the straw was also the result of careful selection by Wright over a period of years.[37]

Blue Rose was first mentioned in rice sales in the spring of 1914. The sale was reported by the Southern Rice Growers Association and the lot included 860 sacks of Blue Rose, at $4.27 a barrel; 690 sacks of No. 7 (another Wright variety) at $3.88, and 200 sacks of Japan, at $2.48.[38] Prior to this the only rices named in sales were Japan and Honduras.

Rice acreage in 1914 was not as large as 1913, but it was predicted that the quality—due to the planting of the new variety, Blue Rose—would offset the shortage from a financial standpoint. The prediction was borne out. The first Blue Rose of the 1914 season brought $4.25 per barrel. Throughout that season quotations in the rough rice market report showed Blue Rose bringing from 25 to 50 cents more than Honduras.[39]

Of the 1914 acreage, 17 per cent was Blue Rose, with an anticipated yield of 25 per cent of the total crop. The rice was found to have a larger yield than other varieties, and was of a superior milling quality, bringing larger profits to both producer and miller. The prediction was that there would be no danger of overproduction, as Blue Rose would compete in the European market with Java, the highest grade rice known to general trade in Europe.[40]

Farmers from each rice producing state—Arkansas, California and

---

[35] *Houston Daily Post*, Dec. 26, 1913

[36] *Daily Signal*, June 30, 1913

[37] *Ibid*, Nov. 15, 1913; Feb. 14, 1914; Mar. 27, 1916

[38] *Ibid*, Apr. 13, 1914

[39] *Ibid*, May 19, Aug. 22, Oct. 6, 1914

[40] *Ibid*, editorial, Dec. 5, 1914

Texas—ordered Wright seed by the carload. Sales continued to mount as record yields and top prices were reported.[41] By the time the United States got involved in World War I rices developed by Wright accounted for 90 per cent of the crop. The four most popular varieties—Blue Rose, Louisiana Pearl, Early Prolific and Edith—were Wright propagations. In addition he had improved Blue Rose and developed several other varieties. Before the war ended the government took over all available supplies of Blue Rose.[42]

Wright spent time traveling to the rice producing states to advise planters on how to secure best results from good seed and other recommended practices. When the federal government turned down the association's request for aid to subsidize Wright's work so that he could travel for this purpose he went anyway—at his own expense. He spent a week in Arkansas in 1915, advising rice farmers of that state concerning varieties and best cultural methods.[43] He also visited Texas and California, making the trips without compensation.[44] He was interested in one thing only—the success of the American rice farmer who planted his American rice seed.

Wright maintained and reaffirmed his early stand that he had created "American seed for American farmers." Once a party of South Americans came to Crowley and toured his experimental garden. They asked to buy seed. Wright refused, on the grounds that he reserved his seed rices for his own countrymen. Later, through friendly correspondence, it was learned that one of the foreigners had sneaked some Wright seed into his pocket. The man planted the few grains on his South American farm and got the nucleus of a future crop. Just when he began to dream of a fine harvest of his own "imported" seed, his plan was circumvented through accident and a bit of poetic justice—a horse got in and ate up the whole planting.[45]

Had Sol Wright been able to patent his rice varieties he would have become an instant millionaire.[46] As it was he was never wealthy, but the success of his rices did provide a comfortable living for his family.

Wright's agricultural interests were not completely confined to rice. He was one of the first Acadia Parish farmers to take steps to improve his beef herd.[47] He was also an enthusiastic apiarist, and at one time experimented with breeding a species of stingless bees.[48]

It has been said of Wright that he gave his bees credit for cross-pollinating his rices. He did know, however, that rice is self-pollinating.

[41] *Ibid*, Feb. 15, Mar. 6, Apr. 7, Nov. 25, 1916; Sept. 26, Oct. 3, 1917
[42] *Ibid*, May 2, 1918; Aug. 24, 1915; Sept. 11, 1918
[43] *Ibid*, Nov. 13, 1915
[44] Interview, S. L. Wright Jr., Sept. 20, 1977
[45] *Ibid*
[46] Interview, Lindsey Baur, Oct. 26, 1977
[47] *Crowley Signal*, Oct. 15, 1910
[48] *New Orleans Item*, Apr. 21, 1918

Questioned about rice pollinization by a reporter, Wright answered: "Rice fertilizes itself." He explained that the pollen is not on the outside of the hull, as is generally believed, but on the inside with the grain, and pointed out that the pollen can be transferred from one grain to another. He also knew that the miniscule rice blooms open only once a day, and noted that "bees do not cross-pollinize much because the blooms remain open so short a time. But it helps."[49]

The unanswered question appears to be: how much did the bees contribute to the development of the new varieties? This may be a question that the rice breeder himself could not have answered. Obviously he believed in his bees; he kept 200 hives of fine Italian bees in close proximity to the one-acre plot where only carefully selected, superior grains of rice were planted. Wright himself observed the bees going from one tiny rice bloom to another. With thousands of the willing cross-breeders so readily available during the hour or so each day that the blooms opened, it is possible that the bees helped more than is generally believed.[50]

"Uncle Sol" was a familiar figure on Crowley streets. He came to town almost every day, driving the five miles by horse and buggy during the early years. Daily trips to the post office and freight depot were necessary—there was no rural mail delivery at the time, and he was carrying on a large seed rice mail order business. A gregarious person by nature, after he completed his business rounds for the day he could be seen on the streets talking with whomever would listen, fingering the inevitable grains of rice he carried in his pocket, and holding forth on the merits of whatever variety of rice he was experimenting with at the time. He enjoyed playing checkers and often would spend time at the Southern Rice Growers Association office playing the game with friends.[51]

Wright was a skilled clog dancer, a talent he learned while farming wheat in Oregon. At the time construction was underway on the Pacific railroad from Portland to San Francisco. The place where Wright lived was a favorite stopping place for traveling actor troupes, and it was from these performers that he picked up the dance steps. He enjoyed the dancing; it was his favorite recreation. He built a wooden platform about halfway between his Acadia Parish farm house and the barn, and here he would practice dancing, not only for entertainment but as a form of physical activity that he considered beneficial to body and mind. He entertained with his dancing at rice conventions in Texas and on other occasions, notably his 66th birthday party.[52]

His evenings, except for special occasions, were all spent the same way: examining grains of hulled rice under a magnifying glass, by the light of a kerosene lamp. In night clothes and robe he would sit for hours at a

[49] Ibid
[50] Interview, S. L. Wright Jr., Oct. 25, 1977
[51] Daily Signal, Feb. 2, 1915; Nov. 18, 1914; Mar. 13, 1915
[52] Ibid, Apr. 27, 1918; interview, S. L. Wright Jr., 1977

time carefully hulling the grains by hand, scrutinizing each grain from every angle, measuring and taking notes.[53]

Wright devised his own methods of measuring rice grains, in addition to using a standard ruler. One such method was to place a pin across two grains of Honduras, then try to push a grain of one of his varieties under the pin. Invariably, because the Wright-bred grain was the more plump, the pin would be pushed off the Honduras grains.[54]

The process of selection—discarding the imperfect grains, reserving the better specimens—went on night after night, year after year. Even though the search was crowned with such phenomenal success, he continued, for the rest of his life, to look for better rices.[55]

Family life played a meaningful role in Wright's life. His wife was strongly supportive of everything he did and took an active part in it in addition to giving him moral reenforcement. She helped him with keeping records and when the post office mailbox began to overflow with mail from all over the world, it was she who took over the correspondence, answering each letter in her own handwriting. Her husband honored her by naming one of his most valuable varieties Lady Wright. Sol Wright and Laura Cook were married September 30, 1901. Their four children, Lillian, S. L. Jr., Edith and Rose Mary spent their childhood immersed in the father's rice experiments.[56]

Recognition first came to Wright in 1907 when he was awarded a gold medal for exhibiting a sheaf of Japan rice at the Jamestown Tercentennial. After 1911, when Blue Rose was first introduced, he won awards for his rices at a number of agricultural fairs in Louisiana and Texas.[57]

He was appreciated by the people of Acadia Parish, as has been shown. On his 66th birthday in 1918 friends gathered at the Wright home to show "appreciation of his 27 years citizenship in this community, during which time he has become a world figure in the rice industry." P. J. Chappuis made the presentation of a silver water service with these words: "The rice growers of the world will appreciate your work long after you have gone . . . we desire to express our appreciation now."[58]

The "gentle genius" died at home February 9, 1929, at age 77. He would have applauded the tribute to his work which appeared in the Crowley newspaper the day after his funeral:

"To attempt to set a value upon Sol Wright's contribution to the rice industry and southwest Louisiana would be like putting a price on the soil, the sunshine or the elements that go into a crop. For the rices he

---

[53] *Beaumont Enterprise*, Nov. 20, 1914

[54] *Southwest Trail*, July, 1915. A rounder berry was considered more desirable for milling purposes.

[55] Interview, S. L. Wright Jr., 1977

[56] *Crowley Daily Signal*, Jan. 17, 1942; interview, S. L. Wright Jr., 1977

[57] Interview, S. L. Wright Jr., 1977

[58] *Daily Signal*, Apr. 27, 1918

developed were brought out at a time when old varieties seemed to have worn out and when the very condition of the business called for remedy.

"Every rice market report, every warehouse receipt book and every article on rice carries words that in themselves are testimonials to the importance of the man who died here Saturday. His perseverance and his determination demonstrated the effectiveness of his method of approaching his labors and undertaking his quest for something better. His monument is renewed each year when the fields turn green, then bend to the harvest."[59]

Addendum

Sol Wright and his daughter Edith reigned as king and queen of the first Crowley Rice Festival, held in September of 1927.[60] A brief resume of Wright's work is included in the *Yearbook of Agriculture*, official publication of the United States Department of Agriculture, 1936 edition, and is also in the *National Cyclopedia of American Biography*, James T. White & Co., New York, 1943.

A historical marker citing Wright's work was placed at the Wright farm in 1968 by the Louisiana Tourist Commission under the sponsorship of the Louisiana Farm Bureau. The resolution adopted by the sponsoring state agency read: "The varieties he developed and distributed produced 70 to 80 per cent of all rice grown in the United States for many years, and is still providing breeding stock for many of the varieties in use today, and have been worth hundreds of millions to American rice growers. The site of his work should be appropriately marked in recognition of one of the nation's greatest agricultural enterprises and one of its greatest plant breeders." The presentation, by James Graugnard, president of the state organization, was made at Rice Festival time to a grandson, S. L. Wright III.[61]

Other than this his memory is honored through contributions made by his children and their spouses: Wright Park in Crowley, established for a playground by the donation of a city block by Rose Mary Wright Hoffpauir and her husband, Paul C. Hoffpauir,[62] and Blue Rose Museum, founded by S. L. Wright Jr. and his wife Frances Wynn Wright, at the site of the experimental farm.

The Great Canal

Welman Bradford, born in Ascension Parish in 1869, was by profession a civil engineer and surveyor. He began experimenting with rice culture in the Rayne-Branch area of Acadia Parish about 1888. He was a leader in parish affairs; he served as treasurer for the town of Rayne, also as official surveyor for Acadia Parish.[63]

[59] *Ibid*, Feb. 11, 1929, editorial, "An Annual Monument," by W. W. Duson Jr.

[60] *The Acadian*, Sept. 14, 1927

[61] *Crowley Daily Signal*, Oct. 1, 1968

[62] *Ibid*, July 18, 1951

[63] Perrin, William H., *Southwest Louisiana, Biographical and Historical*, Part II, 254; Fontenot and Freeland, *Acadia Parish, etc.* 143

Bradford's first experiments with rice irrigation were on the John E. Pelton farm (the old William Wikoff Spanish grant) in the late 1890s, when he persuaded Pelton to let him prove his theory of gravity irrigation by "contouring" his rice field. Bradford claimed to have originated the idea that rice could be grown in only a few inches of water, provided there be shallow levees so constructed as to hold an even depth all over the field. The contouring on the Pelton farm, Bradford said, was the actual birth of "gravity irrigation," and further claimed that the system he originated had subsequently been introduced over the entire rice growing region of Louisiana, Arkansas and California.[64]

Bradford conceived his colossal irrigation scheme prior to 1899, as some of the recorded rights-of-way contracts he secured are dated that year. At that time securing sufficient water for growing rice was an ongoing problem, despite the great advances made in irrigation procedures. By the end of 1901 there were 16 irrigation canals in Acadia Parish, watering a total of 78,300 acres of rice lands. Of the 16 seven were large pumping plant and canal systems, watering from 2,000 to 20,000 acres, and the remainder privately owned canals irrigating from 200 to 1,200 acres. These canals drew from the major waterways of the parish. In addition there were some 300 deep wells furnishing water for Acadia-grown rice.[65]

These irrigating systems were mostly in the southern half of the parish, the location dependent upon the water source. This left thousands of acres in the northern portion of the parish—including the "providence" rice lands of the Mamou and Faquetaique prairies—totally dependent on rainfall. There was, of course, the option of putting down deep wells, but at the time Bradford initiated his plan deep wells were just beginning to come into general use in the rice belt, and only the more affluent rice planters could afford the installations.[66]

Bradford's proposition, simply stated, was to construct a super canal, 250 feet wide and some 60 miles long, to convey water from Bayou Courtableau, a branch of the Atchafalaya River, through St. Landry into Acadia Parish, thence to the rice lands of Calcasieu, watering rice fields on both sides all along the canal route. The water would be furnished individual farmers for a share of the crop, probably one fifth, which was the water rate established by the existing canal companies.

In the spring of 1902 Bradford was confronted with a major problem: competition. A surveying party was in the Washington area to select a line for an irrigation canal from Washington to the Mermentau River. The newspaper report stated that a similar project (Bradford's) had "fallen through" only months previously on a proposal to build a canal from Bayou Cocodrie near Washington to "some point in Acadia, extending

[64] *Daily Signal*, June 29, 1917
[65] *Crowley Signal*, spec. ed., Dec. 21, 1901
[66] *Ibid*, Feb. 16, 1901

through Prairie Mamou." Both canals were to start in the Washington area—one above the town and the other below; both enterprises were said to be backed by capital in the neighborhood of $5 million.[67]

The report that Bradford's project had fallen through was premature. Some weeks later the Opelousas newspaper stated that Bradford had "a large force in the field, with plows, scrapes and spades," and crews of workmen were "pushing the work." At the same time J. Franklin Schell was identified as the builder of the second canal. Both construction companies, the paper stated, were backed by "ample capital."[68]

It would appear unlikely that two such large ventures would have been going on at the same time in the same vicinity and with the same goal: to provide water for the Louisiana rice belt in Acadia and Calcasieu Parishes. But local tradition confirms that there were two separate canal projects, one by Bradford and the other by Schell, going on at the same time at Washington.[69]

The magnitude of the Bradford plan—and some of the wishful thinking it engendered—are detailed in an article published in the Crowley *Daily Signal* of July 4, 1902:

> The New Orleans correspondent of the Manufacturer's Record writes the following concerning the proposed Bradford irrigation canal:
>
> An English syndicate represented by George Thompson Jr. of New York city is about to begin the construction of a great irrigation canal seventy-five miles long and 250 feet wide, to run from Washington through St. Landry and Acadia parishes to the Bayou Nez Pique, and into Calcasieu parish.
>
> The water supply, which is ample, will be obtained at Washington, situated on a branch of the Atchafalaya. The canal will be called Bradford, after the Crowley civil engineer who surveyed the route and obtained the rights of way for the proposition. Capitalists of England were interested and sent their representative to report on the project, and the reports compiled were in every sense most highly favorable. The result was the speedy conclusion that the canal should be built.
>
> Modern irrigation appliances will be provided and the capacity of the canal made sufficient to irrigate from 500,000 to 700,000 acres of land. The route of the ditch will be through one of the peculiar tracts which in this state are called prairies, and which at the present time produce nothing, yet when irrigated will be capable of producing from twenty-five to thirty-five sacks of rice per acre. Members of the State board of engineers have recently declared that this was one of the very richest portions of the state, and this declaration, too, was made before the canal project was as much as thought of.
>
> Messrs. Thompson & Bradford, who are now on the ground engaged in the preliminaries of grading and digging, expect to return north in a few days, after all contracts for excavation are closed. They expect soon to place contracts for machinery, pumping plants and rice mills, as it is a

---

[67] *Opelousas Courier*, quoted in *Daily Signal*, May 19, 1902
[68] *Opelousas Courier*, June 28, 1902
[69] Interviews, S. A. Pierrel, Loved Montgomery, Jr., Alphonse Wartelle, L. A. Zernott, 1977

part of the plan of the syndicate to place mills along the canal to mill the rice which will be raised, and not only this, but to construct a railroad from Washington to the Southwest as a still better outlet for the product of the farmers they will induce to locate there from all parts of the Northern and Western states, and perhaps from England. Banks will be established at Washington and at other necessary points in order to facilitate the farmers in their pecuniary needs and as a business proposition as well. It will require from $1,500,000 to $2,000,000 to construct the canal. The canal, when completed, will add materially to the area of the rice belt. The scheme is one that will build up whole towns, increase assessments and revenues and add to the rapidly increasing wealth.

Some three months later even more ambitious plans were made known. The canal would be deep enough to permit barge and steamer navigation, and an electric railway system was to built along the right-of-way. The canal would draw its water from the Atchafalaya, and through that river and Bayou Courtableau entrance would be had into the Mississippi, thus giving an all-water route to New Orleans, Memphis, St. Louis and other river ports. Financial backing was put up by six New York capitalists, including George Thompson. Bradford was quoted as saying the canal project "would revolutionize the rice industry in Louisiana."[70]

Bradford was at his camp at Washington in fall of 1902 supervising work on the canal. He also spoke to civic groups in Jennings and Crowley, soliciting support for a plan to build a railroad to Jennings from the point where his proposed canal would cross Bayou Nezpique. Bradford's company was the Columbia Irrigation and Navigation Co., and he was the secretary for the company.[71]

Meanwhile Schell and a large party of capitalists made an overland tour of the proposed canal territory and were entertained in Eunice.[72] At this point Bradford seems to have faded from the picture; there was no further mention of his canal in the Crowley newspaper. The *Signal*, however, continued to carry progress reports on the Schell canal.

Three Acadia Parish residents were directors in Schell's canal company. They were Dr. R. C. Webb and George E. Sears, officials of the Rayne Rice Milling Company, and O. H. Terwilliger of Crowley. Other directors included three St. Landry Parish leaders: Dr. J. A. Haas and J. H. Lawler of Opelousas, and Leon Wolff, head of the bank at Washington. Some of the other company officials held important positions: one was a member of Congress from Pennsylvania, another the vice president of a New York brokerage concern, a third, the president of a New Orleans bank.[73]

The corporation, chartered as the Union Rice and Irrigating Co., was

---

[70] *Daily Signal*, Oct. 23, 1902
[71] *Ibid*, Nov. 6, 8; Dec. 16, 1902
[72] *Ibid*, Nov. 29, 1902
[73] *Ibid*, Feb. 27, 1903

capitalized at $6 million. Dr. Webb, the treasurer, spent a month in New York on company business. On his return he told reporters in New Orleans that the project was the largest of its kind ever organized; that the plan was to irrigate lands in the Prairie Hayes and Prairie Mamou areas of Acadia Parish by utilizing the natural fall of the land in St. Landry, which was about a foot to the mile. The water would be brought through the main canal and its laterals by gravity flow, therefore no relift would be necessary. Projected time for full scale operation was the fall of 1904.[74]

Meanwhile three carloads of equipment arrived at the construction site near Washington and brought crowds of the curious, plus newspaper comment. The shipment included two excavating machines, one of which weighed five tons. Nothing of the like had been seen before in southwest Louisiana.[75]

A more in-depth account of the irrigation plan appeared in newspapers a few months later. In summary, the engineer's survey showed that water would flow a distance of 35 miles, from Bayou Courtableau to Bayou Nezpique, by force of gravity without relift. The country was found to slope uniformly in a southwesterly direction, and the survey showed that the canal should run due west from the top of the bluff above Bayou Courtableau, a mile north of Washington, to Bayou Nezpique. By dropping laterals from the main canal in a southwesterly direction between the bayous a natural fall could be secured to irrigate lands in Robert's Cove, Prairie Hayes, Faquetaique and Mamou prairies. To the north the surveys showed that water could be thrown into the rice regions of the Ville Platte prairie without relift. By cutting a tailrace about 4,000 feet long from Courtableau to the bluff above Bayou Carron just south of Washington an "inexhaustible source of water could be emptied into a canal at that point" by lifting the water 75 feet.[76]

The project was hailed with unbridled enthusiasm by state newspapers. Predictions were that the irrigation plan would create great wealth for the entire state, more than $50 million; that it would build cities, factories, mills, schools, churches, libraries—moreover, the canal would induce large numbers of northern farmers to move to the area, as well as provide employment for thousands.[77]

In the fall of 1903 Schell started his promotional tours—the first of an even dozen—for the Pennsylvania capitalists whom he hoped would provide the financial backing for the canal. They came to Louisiana by special car and spent two days inspecting the route of the canal and learning about the rice industry. Some months afterwards Schell said that the Pennsylvanians who had visited Crowley earlier had all invested in company bonds. Schell stated that all was well with the project; however,

---

[74] *Ibid*
[75] *Ibid*, Feb. 16, 1903
[76] *Crowley Signal*, June 20, 1903
[77] *Ibid*

The Union Irrigation Company's plant and a portion of the main canal near Washington. The planning and actual construction of the immense irrigation system, designed to bring water from the Atchafalaya River to the rice fields of southwest Louisiana, went on for more than a dozen years. (Reproduced from the *Rice Journal and Southern Farmer*, March 1, 1913)

41

"financial stagnation had interfered to some extent with the company's plans for raising money."[78]

In June of 1906 members of another party of visiting Pennsylvania stockholders were cued-in on the canal deal. The location of the pumping plant, they were informed, was 65 feet above sea level; four engines, of 1,000 horsepower each, were to be installed together with four 36-inch centrifugal pumps. Water would be drawn from a coulee connected with Courtableau and conveyed through a pipe 250 feet in length to the main canal. Water from Courtableau would be lifted 60 feet from the bayou to the top of the ridge at Washington, along which a canal 350 feet wide would be constructed. Gravity would do the rest. The plan was to build five miles of main canal to start, then extend it 30 more miles.[79]

Whether or not Bradford was still working on his project at this time is not known, but he was still coming and going between Crowley and Washington during 1905 and 1906.[80] In the fall of 1906 he resigned his position as Acadia Parish surveyor and went to Brazil at the invitation of the government of that country to take charge of rice growing experiments undertaken by the Brazilian government.[81]

Meanwhile the irrigation project had bogged down completely. Franklin Schell spent a year in Pennsylvania "advancing the interests of the canal." He announced a change of plans: the pumping plant would consist of two pumps instead of four.[82]

Mid-January of 1908 found construction, five years behind schedule, actually beginning. The arrival of two large grading machines, drawn by mammoth traction engines, further excited the citizenry. Elaborate plans were made to celebrate the start of construction on January 16, with speeches by Gov. N. C. Blanchard and Dr. S. A. Knapp of the United States Department of Agriculture.[83]

By June of 1908 two miles of the main canal were reported completed, but again the work must have been halted. It wasn't until February of 1909 that a contract for constructing the canal was let to L. B. Constant of Bunkie, who agreed to have 100 teams of mules at work by March 10, and to complete the main canal and two laterals by June 1.[84]

Work on the pumping plant was indeed underway by March. The pit for the machinery was excavated to a depth of 45 feet; the huge pit measured 85 by 65 feet. More than 4,000 feet of railroad iron was used to reinforce the concrete foundations and retaining walls for the pumping plant. (One man lost his life during this phase of the construction. Robert Zernott of Washington, hauling in heavy equipment for the pumping plant

---

[78] *Ibid*, Feb. 6, 1904
[79] *Daily Signal*, June 7, 1906
[80] *Ibid*, May 17, 1905; Mar. 3, May 31, 1906
[81] *Ibid*, Sept. 4, 1906; *Crowley Signal*, Apr. 13, 1907
[82] *Crowley Signal*, Apr. 13, 1907
[83] *Ibid*, Jan. 11, 18, 1908
[84] *Daily Signal*, Feb. 22, June 13, 1908

by mule team, was crushed to death when the massive load accidentally shifted.)[85]

Construction evidently came to another standstill in the fall of 1909. For the third time that year Franklin Schell brought in a party of 57 Pennsylvanians to check out the project and the rice industry in general. At the time excavating on the intake canal, from Bayou Courtableau to the intake of the pump (a distance of about four and three quarter miles) was still going on.[86]

After that progress on the huge project continued on a fairly regular basis. Fifty mule teams were at work excavating for a drain under the main canal in late January, 1910; the 72-inch centrifugal pump was on the site, including the 110-foot impeller, which weighed 42,000 pounds, and the lower half of the pump was on its foundations in the bottom of the pit. One of the 1,000 horsepower engines had been delivered, the other engine and the boilers had been shipped, the smoke stacks and discharge pipes were on hand ready for installation.[87] In late May people in the rice industry got ready to entertain Franklin Schell and more Pennsylvania backers—the 12th such tour of inspection.[88]

Five miles of the main canal and six miles of laterals were completed early in 1911. The pumping plant installation was ready. There was only one unfinished sector—the intake canal leading from Courtableau to the pumping plant, and 175 men were at work on that.[89]

The long awaited opening of the Schell Canal took place on April 8, 1911. The event was celebrated with fanfare and speeches, including an address by Gov. J. Y. Sanders. Some 4,000 persons watched as Schell's daughter, Irma, pushed the button that "started an enterprise which is greater than anything Louisiana or the south has ever known."[90] There was high praise for Franklin Schell; he was termed a genius, and given full credit for conceiving the idea and carrying it through "despite apparently unsurmountable obstacles." It was his brain "that conceived the tremendous idea of diverting the silt-laden waters of the Mississippi feeders to the prairies of southwest Louisiana, and it has been his brains and his nerve and unbeatable courage that has brought the enterprise up to the present point."[91]

But the company's construction headaches were not yet fully allayed. Three weeks after the grand opening the dredge boat was again at work on Bayou Carron, the waterway which furnished an inlet to the pumping plant for the water from Courtableau. After the big plant began working it was found that the improvised canal was not deep enough;

[85] Interview, L. A. Zernott, May 27, 1977
[86] *Daily Signal*, Oct. 9, 1909
[87] *Crowley Signal*, Jan. 29, 1910
[88] *Ibid*, May 28, 1910
[89] *Daily Signal*, Jan. 2, 1911
[90] *Ibid*, Apr. 10, 1911
[91] *Ibid*, editorial, Apr. 8, 1911

also, the dirt that was removed from the canal was not placed far enough from the edge. Consequently heavy rains had washed quantities of the dirt back into the inlet, making it necessary to dredge again.[92] Later on that fall there was a hassle with the Corps of Engineers over a company proposal to build a lock at the mouth of Bayou Courtableau in order to maintain water communication between Courtableau and the Atchafalaya.[93]

The canal was in successful operation during the summer of 1912. It pumped water on 3,000 acres of rice, some of which was heading out by mid-July. Public faith in the enterprise was still evident: the starting of the big pumps was said to be an event which "marked an epoch in the history of the rice industry" and one that would greatly increase rice acreage.[94]

The final curtain on the ill-fated project did not fall until 1918. By 1913 the company was bankrupt;[95] in 1915 it was reported sold at a sheriff's sale to Mrs. Lena Mann for the nominal sum of $5,000.[96] This sale was evidently for only a part of the property, as W. A. Billingsley and associates bought the system at a receiver's sale in 1917 for $99,275 cash. There was an attempt to put it back into operation: Major W. A. White, a New Orleans engineer, was employed to examine and report on the feasibility of such a plan.[97] Billingsley tried for several months to get planters interested in water rent contracts. Farming interests did not take too well to his proposals—he asked for a guarantee for five years planting of a given acreage and one fourth of the crop as water rent.[98]

The last stage in the disintegration of the great system took place in October of 1918. The plant site, consisting of 188 acres, plus rights-of-way of about 900 acres, were sold by Billingsley to Richard Hollier of Opelousas, who planned to re-sell the land.[99]

Causes of the failure of the venture are not altogether clear. A. S. Pierrel of Washington, born in 1885, was a young man during the building of the canal and clearly remembered many of the details when interviewed in 1977. He recalled that 1911 was a bad year for the rice crop. After the rice was cut and shocked that fall, incessant rains caused the grain to sprout and rot in the fields before it could be threshed. Pierrel also said that the relatively small amount of rice (3,000 acres) irrigated by the system that year could not, even in a good crop year, have produced enough rice to pay the operational expenses of the canal, and in addition he pointed out some engineering mistakes in the construction.

[92] *St. Landry Commoner*, quoted in *Daily Signal*, July 3, 1911
[93] *Daily Signal*, Oct. 27, 1911
[94] *Ibid*, July 20, 1912
[95] Fontenot, M. A., article, "*The Schell Canal*," Opelousas *Daily World*, Jan. 19, 1969
[96] *Daily Signal*, Feb. 22, 1915
[97] *Ibid*, Apr. 10, 1917
[98] *Ibid*, May 29, July 18, Aug. 11, 1917
[99] *Opelousas Clarion*, quoted in *Crowley Signal*, Oct. 26, 1917

Other reasons advanced for the failure of the plan includes withdrawal of funds, insufficient water in Bayou Courtableau, inadequate drainage facilities to get the water off the ripened rice in the shock.[100]

In a requiem for the great project the *Opelousas Clarion* paid tribute to Schell's 18 years of effort:

> The great dream of J. Franklin Schell has, at least for the time being, passed, though no man with the genius, indomitable energy and will of Mr. Schell can ever be said to have been defeated in any undertaking. It may seem a simple deferring of his plans and aspirations, for the feasibility of his scheme is acknowledged by all. Mr. Schell has been a great builder for this section, notwithstanding his canal project has temporarily failed, for through his perseverance new blood, new money and new prices for land were brought to the section contiguous to his canal.[101]

Welman Bradford was given no credit for originating gravity irrigation for low level rice field flooding, an idea later confirmed by S. L. Wright's experiments.[102] Nor were his pioneering efforts with the irrigation plan ever recognized. During the six or more years that he tried to work out his dream he too had problems; several lawsuits, seeking to revoke rights-of-way contracts he had secured in St. Landry and Acadia, were filed against him. One such suit, instituted by Ferdinand M. Wartelle, also sought an injunction to stop the canal construction, even though Bradford had paid Wartelle $1,200 for the right-of-way. Wartelle charged that Bradford had been at work on the canal through his (Wartelle's) property "in a haphazard sort of way, in his own name, and on his own initiative and responsibility;" and that Bradford was "impecunious and totally irresponsible financially."

District Judge E. T. Lewis ruled in favor of Bradford. Wartelle's attorneys took his case to the Louisiana Supreme Court, which in 1904 upheld the lower court's decision.[103]

After the successful termination of his work in Brazil Bradford returned to Louisiana with a new dream for large-scale rice irrigation.[104] His new canal idea was even more extensive and ambitious than the first—he planned to draw water from the Red River north of Natchitoches and bring it down by gravity fall to the southwest Louisiana rice fields. The system would have taken four years and $15 million to complete.[105]

Bradford succeeded in getting some impressive support for his plan and continued to promote it for four years,[106] but with the country involved in a world war he had small chance of carrying it through.

---

[100] Interviews, Sept. 14, 1977, Gus Anderson, L. A. Zernott, Paul Mayne
[101] *Crowley Signal*, Oct. 26, 1918
[102] *Ibid*, Sept. 5, 1903
[103] Miscellaneous suits No. 13, St. Landry Parish court records
[104] *Daily Signal*, Oct. 12, 1914; June 29, 1917
[105] *Ibid*, Jan. 19, 1918
[106] *Ibid*

Harvest scene on the Hains brothers farm about 1920. Shocked rice in the field was loaded into mule-drawn wagons and hauled to the thresher. The men standing in the wagons near the thresher are feeding the bundles of rice into the machine with pitchforks. (Reproduced from Barnett glass negative, Freeland Collection, USL)

The Rice Mills

The new century started off very well for Acadia's rice people. The year 1899 was a good year for rice, so was 1900,[107] and when it was a good year for rice everything else in the rice belt was good.

Indications were that the region was entering into an era of prosperity that could only get better as time went on. New businesses sprang up in every town and settlement, old businesses continued to do well. Rice fever was epidemic in Acadia Parish—except around Church Point, where cotton would continue to be king long past the scope of this chronicle. Everybody else wanted to get on the rice bandwagon, be it in the line of cultivation, milling or marketing.

The first few years of the century constituted the great era of mill building in Acadia Parish. From 1900 to 1903 13 new rice mills were constructed, giving the parish a total of 18 operating mills. The mills already in operation, given in the order of building, were the Acadia of Rayne; the Crowley, Eagle, People's Independent and American mills of Crowley. A sixth Crowley mill, the Southwest Louisiana mill, was destroyed by fire in 1899.

The large number of mills was attributed to toll milling, a practice which for many years had been considered a necessary evil by rice planters. In toll milling the mill charged the farmer a fixed price for milling and selling his rice. In addition, the mill retained the by-products of the milling process, such as bran, which could be sold as feed for farm animals, and hulls, used as fuel by many of the mills.[108]

Toll milling was profitable to the miller as the farmer bore all the losses and the miller was certain of his profit, no matter what the price of the finished product might be. The enormous profits led to the establishment of more mills than was necessary. Toll milling, always unpopular with the farmer, began to give way in the early 1900s. By 1905 the practice had been abolished and the mills were buying rough rice outright from the farmer.[109]

Available information on the rice mills of the parish includes names of original milling company officers and principal stockholders, and in many instances the names of the people employed by each mill. These listings identify the pioneer rice men who were active in the milling industry prior to 1910.

The good times of the turn of the century disappeared during 1901 and 1902 when severe drouths wrought havoc not only with providence rice, but with canal-irrigated rice as well. The canal pumps drained the water in the Mermentau and its tributaries so low that salt water from the

---

[107] *Crowley Signal*, Oct. 27, 1900
[108] *Ibid*, Mar. 31, 1900; *Rice Journal and Southern Farmer*, Mar. 1, 1913
[109] *Ibid*, Oct. 6, 1900; *Ibid*

Gulf of Mexico entered the streams and was pumped onto the rice. Damage to the rice crops was estimated to have been in the millions.[110]

The intrusion of salt water brought about one of the most controversial issues in the history of the rice industry—the construction (and destruction) of the Mermentau dam.

Bad weather that fall caused a serious set-back in harvest operations. Incessant rains made the rice sprout on the ground and in the shocks; discouraging reports came in from all sides. By late October many hundreds of acres were still uncut, and a great deal of cut rice was rotting in the fields. It was indeed an unfortunate year for rice farmers—no water during the growing season when it was needed, too much at the harvest when it wasn't needed.[111]

The years 1903 and 1904 were times of plenty, crop-wise, but the bountiful crops brought low prices. The 1903 crop was the largest in history to date, but the price was the lowest in history—due to over-production and allegedly poor judgment in marketing. Rice was sold at prices below the cost of production, hitting a new low in the American rice industry. The picture brightened in 1905—the crop was short, and better prices prevailed. The good prices were also attributed to other factors, one of which was the elimination of the toll milling system. While it had been recognized that toll milling was the only way to free rice planters from the commission merchants, yet leaders in the industry felt that the time had come when toll milling had served its purpose. Less than 30 percent of the 1905 crop was handled on toll. The crop was mostly handled on a cash basis, which enabled the planters to receive cash returns as soon as the rice was harvested and threshed instead of waiting several months until it could take its turn to be milled and sold.[112]

Another practice on its way out was that of cash advances, at eight per cent interest, made to farmers by the mills. By the fall of 1905 a new system of selling rice had begun. This was the sealed bid system, when buyers made bids on lots of rice. The amount of the bid was based on estimates of random samplings of the rice offered for sale.[113]

Rice fever began going down in 1905. Remembering the depressed market caused by the overproduction of the previous two years, agricultural leaders continued to stress crop diversification,[114] and some of the farmers began to take heed. The great era of construction of mills and canal systems had come to an end. No further great gains were made by the industry until 1912, when Blue Rose, the first domestic variety of rice, was introduced to the trade.

---

[110] McNeely, Dorothy B., "Mermentau Dam Secret for 70 Years—Revealed," *Crowley Post-Signal*, Apr. 17, 1977; *Daily Signal*, June 29, Aug. 21, 1902

[111] *Daily Signal*, Oct. 8, 21, 1902

[112] *Ibid*, Aug. 13, 1904; Dec. 16, 1905

[113] *Ibid*, Apr. 30, 1904; *Crowley Signal*, Oct. 7, 1905

[114] *Daily Signal*, Mar. 10, 1905

The Ida rice mill of Rayne, as it appeared in 1905 after it was taken over by J. D. Marks. The Ida, destroyed by fire in 1908, was formerly the historic Acadia, the first mill built in Acadia Parish.

Acadia-Daboval-Ida

The first rice mill in Louisiana outside of New Orleans was the Acadia mill of Rayne. The mill was built in 1887 and began operations in the fall of 1888. A. S. Chappuis was president of the company, M. Arenas was treasurer and August L. Chappuis secretary. In 1890 Emile Daboval bought an interest in the mill and the name was changed from the Rayne Rice Mill and Manufacturing Company to the Acadia Rice Milling Company. The mill was oftentimes referred to as the Daboval mill because Emile Daboval was identified for so long with the business.[115]

One of the old style pestle-and-pounder types, the mill's capacity was about 100 barrels of clean rice per day. The mill was remodeled in 1898 and new machinery installed. In 1903 J. D. Marks bought the mill and re-christened it the Ida Rice Mill.[116]

Marks, one of the early merchants of Crowley, got into the rice business prior to 1900. He was president of the company which built the Marks mill in Crowley in 1898. After he bought the mill in Rayne Marks employed J. C. Corbett, a Crowley contractor, to enlarge the facility to include large two-story warehouses for rough and clean rice, and other major improvements. Offices were handsomely finished in hard oil and red ingrained paper with gilt borders. The clean rice sample room was

---

[115] Fontenot and Freeland, *Acadia Parish*, etc. 137, 327
[116] *Crowley Signal*, Aug. 29, 1903

papered in blue—the blue color enhanced the appearance of the clean rice samples. The mill office was equipped with a Postal Telegraph system.[117]

The Ida was a moderately sized mill, the capacity being 400 barrels in 12 hours. At the start of the milling season in 1905 the employees were Miss Kate Mudd, stenographer; J. Breaux, clean rice department; Frank Gilbert, grader; Ernest Petitjean, assistant warehouseman; Theodore Dickerson, miller; W. S. Casey, engineer.[118]

The Ida was in operation until December 1908 when it was destroyed by fire. The loss was estimated at $80,000—$40,000 for the mill and the remainder for the rough and clean rice stored in the warehouses.[119] A tragic footnote is that four years earlier a fire at the Marks residence in Crowley had caused the death of Marks' beautiful young daughter, Ida, for whom the mill was named.[120]

Pickett-Crowley

Crowley's first rice mill, the Pickett, was chartered March 1, 1893. A small two-story building was erected by Squire A. Pickett and equipped with the necessary machinery, some of which had been invented and patented by Pickett himself. The engine for this mill served a double purpose: the 50-horsepower unit was used at a pumping station during the irrigation season, then moved to the mill in time for milling.[121]

The Pickett mill was reorganized in 1895 as the Crowley Rice Milling Company.[122] The enlarged capacity of the mill in 1900 was 1,400 sacks. John Green was mill manager and P. B. Lang headed the clean rice department. Other pioneer employees were A. M. Finley, stenographer; Jerry Hogan, mill supervisor; George Gill, engineer; Gilbert Baillio and J. B. Fontenot, warehousemen; F. A. Voorhies, rice grader; Otto Mayer, clean rice warehouse; R. H. Kleiser, millwright; A. P. Bookover, shipping clerk; Eddie Hogan, office boy.[123]

The first rice packaging plant in the United States was domiciled in the Crowley mill. In 1902 John Green, Crowley mill manager, installed rice packaging machinery. The equipment was geared to package 40 one-pound cartons a minute; the rice was automatically weighed and packed into boxes on which rice recipes were printed. The operation required two girls to hold the boxes to be filled, two more to paste up the box tops, and a man to pack the filled boxes into wooden crates and nail up the tops.[124] Crowley Rice Food Co. was chartered in 1903 with the following principal

---

[117] *Daily Signal*, Mar. 12, 1904; Dec. 14, 1907
[118] *Crowley Signal*, Sept. 30, 1905
[119] *Ibid*, Dec. 26, 1908
[120] *Daily Signal*, Nov. 29, 1904
[121] Fontenot and Freeland, *Acadia, etc.* 327
[122] *Ibid*, 344
[123] *Crowley Signal*, Oct. 13, 1900; Oct. 12, 1901
[124] *Ibid*, Mar. 1, 1902

stockholders: J. B. Foley, John Green, A. B. Allison, Charles J. Bier, Dan Blum, A. Kaplan, C. J. Freeland, W. H. Hunter, Jr.[125] The eight men named were all leaders in the rice industry at the time.

The packing plant began operations in October of 1903 under the firm name of Columbia Rice Packing Co. Capacity was 48,000 cartons a day. F. B. Purdy of Battle Creek, Mich., was plant supervisor; six girls and three men were employed.[126] In March of 1904 the *Daily Signal* reported that the Columbia Rice Packing Company had shipped 2,000 cases of rice in packages, and was then negotiating for the sale of 1,500 more cases. "Demand for these goods is increasing daily, and the promoters of the enterprise feel that they are on the right track," the article stated.[127] Despite this optimistic prediction, very little else appeared in the press concerning the project. Mention was made in August of 1904 that J. O. Fremaux was the bookkeeper and stenographer for the packing company, so it can be assumed that the firm was in operation at that time.[128]

A Beaumont firm bought the packaging machinery in 1909. The report of the sale stated that the Crowley company had been organized in 1903 to package rice in one, two and three pound cartons, but that "the product had not been put on the market."[129] Since this is inconsistent with the information published in 1904, it would have been more accurately stated to say that the firm had been unable to establish a trade.

The Crowley mill was one of the mills absorbed by Louisiana State Rice Milling Co. in 1911.[130] The mill was dismantled in 1913. At the time of the dismantling one of the workmen, Caezar Francez, was killed and his brother Louis badly injured when a 12 by 12 beam fell on them.[131]

Eagle-United States

Crowley's second mill, the Eagle, was built in 1893, a few months after the Crowley mill, and was operated by Star Rice Milling Co. The principal stockholders were George B. Green, John P. Hoyt and J. A. Crooker. The following year the mill was sold at a sheriff's sale to P. S. Lovell for something over $700. Later J. E. Platt acquired the mill and rebuilt it.[132]

The mill was destroyed by fire early in 1899. Platt rebuilt and operated the mill until 1902, when it was taken over by a stock company. Officers and main stockholders in the company were Dan Blum, W. C.

---

[125] *Ibid*, June 6, 1903
[126] *Ibid*, Oct. 31, 1903
[127] *Daily Signal*, Mar. 17, 1904
[128] *Ibid*, Aug. 15, 1904
[129] *Ibid*, June 29, 1909
[130] *Ibid*, Mar. 20, 1911
[131] *Crowley Signal*, Apr. 13, 1913
[132] *Daily Signal*, Apr. 7, 1906

The United States, one of the mills which became a part of the Louisiana State chain, was used to mill rice flour during World War I. Formerly the Eagle, the mill was built in 1893, destroyed by fire and rebuilt in 1899. (Freeland Archives photo, Acadia Parish Library)

Cullumber, W. P. Campbell, John P. Burgin, S. A. Irving, S. M. Hundley and J. E. Platt.[133]

After three seasons of operations the mill was ordered seized as the result of a $300 suit brought by Philip Rahm. Other persons, unidentified, were reported holding judgments against the business. At the sheriff's sale J. Frankel bought the mill for $30,000. The company was reorganized under the firm name of the United States Rice Milling Co. Directors were W. E. Lawson, W. E. Hunter, E. E. Paramore of St. Louis, Jacques and Joseph Trautman of New Orleans.[134]

The mill was among those absorbed by the Louisiana State Rice Milling Co. in 1911. During World War I the mill was used to make rice flour. The property and building were eventually bought by Clem Samson and the mill building was converted into a warehouse. The property is presently (1977) owned by the Supreme Rice Milling Co.[135]

People's Independent

The People's Independent mill, one of A. Kaplan's multi-enterprises, was built in Crowley about 1896. Located on south Parkerson Avenue just south of the railroad tracks, the mill became a landmark; it was operated

---

[133] *Crowley Signal*, Feb. 18, May 13, 1899; Sept. 29, 1900; *Daily Signal*, Apr. 15, 1902
[134] *Daily Signal*, Feb. 28, Apr. 7, May 18, 21, 1906
[135] *Ibid*, Apr. 28, 1911; interview, Lindsey Baur, Nov. 4, 1977

The People's Independent mill, built about 1897, was in operation in Crowley for 60 years. The mill was one of those absorbed by Louisiana State in 1911. (Freeland Archives photo, Acadia Parish Library)

for 60 consecutive years. Mill employees in 1900 included C. J. Bier, manager and clean rice man; J. F. Coleman, clean rice assistant; A. S. Kennedy, head bookkeeper; M. J. Barnett, assistant bookkeeper; Charles January, cashier; Joseph Wright, stenographer; Frank Walker, mechanical engineer; W. A. Porter, miller; John Mallett, warehouseman; J. W. McGraw, shipping clerk; William Malter, sampler. A. Kaplan was president of the company and Miron Abbott vice president.[136]

Southwest Louisiana-Flash

During the summer of 1897 construction was begun on a fifth mill in Acadia Parish. This was the Southwest Louisiana mill, sometimes called the Flash mill, built by Joseph Flash and Dr. S. T. Pulliam. Construction was slowed down due to the yellow fever quarantine, and the mill did not begin operations until January 1, 1899. Shortly thereafter the mill was destroyed by fire. The mill was small; its capacity was about 200 barrels a day.[137]

Marks

The Marks mill, built in Crowley in the fall of 1898, was destined to

[136] Interview, Oswald Lyons, Nov. 9, 1977; *Crowley Signal*, Sept. 22, 1900

[137] *Crowley Signal*, Prosperity Number, May 1898; Fontenot-Freeland, *Acadia, etc.* 327; interview, Lindsey Baur, Nov. 4, 1977

have a long and varied career, and several identities. President of the mill company was Jefferson Davis Marks, who was later to have large interests in rice mills at Morse and Rayne. Louis Sternberger was vice president of the company, and J. D. Belton was mill superintendent.[138]

American

The American mill was chartered in 1899 with a capital stock of $20,000. Main stockholders, each with 50 shares of stock, were J. J. Thomas, J. W. Roller, C. J. Freeland and T. B. Freeland. In 1900 the mill personnel included C. J. Freeland, manager; W. J. Harrison, clean rice; Ransom Nockton, bookkeeper; Eva Hill, stenographer; Frank Keith, warehouseman; Archie Elder, assistant warehouseman; Charles Calamari, miller; Joe Sarver, solicitor; J. W. Wynn, shipping clerk; Ed Kennedy, engineer.[139]

Before its second season the American mill was expanded. The company bought a large warehouse at Gueydan to store the rice from that section, overhauled the mill at Crowley and built a two-story addition to the mill warehouse. The following year another large rough rice warehouse was added, and the existing warehouse enlarged. Warehouses were whitewashed on the inside as a fire retardant and as protection against insects. New and improved machinery was installed.[140]

In less than 10 years after it was built the Freeland brothers had complete ownership of the mill. Officers in 1907 were T. B. Freeland, president; J. W. Roller, vice president; C. J. Freeland, secretary-treasurer. Mill personnel included Ed Harrington, miller; R. A. Nockton, bookkeeper; Allen Moffet, assistant salesman; Frank H. McKnight, warehouseman. In the fall of 1908 the Freelands bought out Roller's interest. A few days later the mill was destroyed by fire. The loss, partially covered by insurance, was estimated at about $80,000.[141]

Within two weeks of the disastrous fire the Freelands announced the purchase of Star B, formerly the Marks mill. The Marks-Star B, which had been idle for several years, was sold to the Freelands by the Louisiana Irrigation and Milling Co. for $35,000, and became the American mill.[142]

The American mill company was re-chartered in 1919, with a capital stock of $800,000. Owners were the Freeland brothers and R. A. Nockton. The mill was operated by the Freeland family until 1960 when it was closed down.[143]

[138] *Crowley Signal*, Mar. 23, 1901
[139] *Ibid*, Aug. 12, 1899; July 21, Oct. 5, 1901
[140] *Ibid*, July 21, 1900; Aug. 10, 1901
[141] *Ibid*, Dec. 14, 1907; Sept. 28, Oct. 3, 1908
[142] *Ibid*, Oct. 17, 1908; Nov. 16, 1909
[143] *Daily Signal*, Nov. 24, 1919; interview, Sidney Baker, Nov. 9, 1977

Star

The Star mill went up early in 1900. W. W. Duson and A. R. McMurtry headed the stock company which built the mill. Others in the company, with a paid up capital stock of $50,000, were Peter F. Dorr, Dr. J. F. Naftel, E. T. Slocum of Detroit, J. C. Morris of New Orleans, George Ferre of Dalton, Ill., A. B. Allison, J. W. Roller, B. R. Garland and Miron Abbott.[144]

The Star, located just west of the American, was on land bought from T. J. Toler. Its capacity was 600 sacks in 12 hours. The facility included two large two-story warehouses. Storage capacity for rough rice was 75,000 bags.[145]

In the spring of 1901 the Star company bought the Marks mill and renamed it the Star B, the original Star mill being designated as Star A. Both mills were under the management of A. B. Allison. The company also owned the Louisiana mill at Jennings.[146]

Personnel of Star A for the 1901-1902 milling season included Paul F. Pritchard, clean rice department, assisted by F. H. McKnight; S. P. Johnson, bookkeeper and cashier; L. H. Lawrence, stenographer; F. M. Milliken, rough rice; B. J. Thompson, shipping clerk; Phillip Rettig, weigher; William Hoelzel, milling superintendent for both Star A and Star B; W. D. Parker, engineer.[147]

The three Star company mills—Star A, Star B and the Louisiana mill at Jennings—were among the six mills purchased by the Louisiana Irrigation and Milling Co. in 1904. The background of this corporation will be presented in a separate section.

The Star company was reorganized in 1907 with a capital stock of $75,000. Officers and directors were A. B. Allison, president and manager; J. R. Roller, vice president; E. E. Edmundson, secretary-treasurer. Directors included P. S. Lovell, P. H. Dorr, B. M. Lambert, F. M. Milliken and L. A. Williams. The new company consisted of former stockholders of the Louisiana Irrigation and Milling Co.[148]

The company's Star A was sold at public auction on November 16, 1911. Liquidating commissioners were J. R. Roller, L. A. Williams and F. M. Milliken. Frank Godchaux was the only bidder, at $30,000. The mill was operated for a while by Louisiana State then shut down.[149]

Pelican-Conover-Louisiana

Two rice mills located in Jefferson Davis Parish should be considered

---

[144] *Crowley Signal*, Jan. 27, Mar. 23, Sept. 28, 1901
[145] *Ibid*, Feb. 3, 1900
[146] *Ibid*, Mar. 23, June 15, Sept. 28, 1901
[147] *Ibid*, Sept. 28, 1901
[148] *Ibid*, Aug. 3, 1907
[149] *Daily Signal*, Nov. 6, 1911; interview, Lindsey Baur, Nov. 4, 1977

along with the Acadia Parish mills, as both were built by Acadia residents. The Pelican mill was built on the west bank of the Mermentau River at Mermentau by Jean Castex Sr. in 1897. The mill was sold at a sheriff's sale in 1903 to W. B. Conover for $7,500 and was thereafter operated as the Conover mill.[150]

The other out-of-parish mill was the Louisiana mill, organized in 1900 mainly by Acadia Parish businessmen. C. D. Bonin was president; other officers were Desire Richard and Theopha Simon, vice president and secretary-treasurer-manager respectively. Later in 1900 Dr. J. F. Morris, another Acadia resident who invested heavily in the rice industry, was named president.[151]

The mill was bought in 1901 by the Star company of Crowley. Stockholders included W. W. Duson, Dr. J. F. Morris of Pomona, Calif.; Dr. J. F. Naftel, Crowley; A. R. McMurtry, A. B. Allison, P. L. Lawrence. The output of the mill was sold through the Crowley office.[152] The mill was one of the six bought by the Louisiana Irrigation and Milling Co. in 1904.

Eureka

The Miller-Morris Canal Co., named for William Miller and Dr. J. F. Morris, let the contract to build a rice mill at Estherwood in the summer of 1899. In 1900 the canal and mill were bought by the Kaplan interests, at a price of some $90,000.[153]

The mill, named the Eureka, had a capacity of 1,000 barrels in a 24-hour run. The warehouse could hold 30,000 sacks of rice, and in 1907 25 men were employed by the mill. Officers of the company were A. Kaplan, I. M. Lichtenstein, S. B. Daniels. Mill personnel in 1907 included M. J. Barnett, manager; E. G. Baumgarten, miller; Frank Giozza, assistant miller; C. E. Hebert, shipping clerk; J. O. Fremaux, cashier-bookkeeper; H. C. Fremaux, engineer; H. S. Hebert, operator of the Postal Telegraph located in the building.[154]

Some of the earlier employees of the Eureka mill were Jake Garvey, Alex Brown, J. Fleet Coleman, Henry Meadus, Percy Levy and P. O. Fowler.[155]

The Eureka was one of the mills absorbed by Louisiana State. After it was finally shut down the foundation building was used as a warehouse for the canal company. In later years Johnny Unverzagt rebuilt the mill. It is presently (1977) being operated by Robert D'Aquin.[156]

[150] *Crowley Signal*, June 20, 1903; Dec. 14, 1907
[151] *Ibid*, Mar. 31, 1900; *Daily Signal*, Oct. 13, 1900
[152] *Crowley Signal*, May 18, June 29, 1901
[153] *Ibid*, July 1, 1899; June 16, 1900
[154] *Ibid*, Dec. 14, 1907
[155] *Ibid*, Mar. 10, 1900; *Daily Signal*, June 24, 25, Aug. 15, 1904
[156] Interviews, 1977, Lindsey Baur, B. C. Delahoussaye

The National Pembroke mill, built in Crowley by a New Orleans concern in 1900. The mill was taken over by Louisiana State and was moved to Kaplan in 1917. (Freeland Archives photo, Acadia Parish Library)

National-Pembroke

The Pembroke mill was built at Crowley in 1900 by the National Rice Milling Co. of New Orleans. The foundation construction of the mill was said to have been "entirely new to the people of this section." The bottom of the foundation pits were first filled to a depth of eight inches "with a concrete of crushed brick and cement, and upon this solid foundation are laid the strong and massive brick pillars, cement mortar being used instead of lime."[157]

Other features of the mill construction included an automatic fire extinguishing system, and a 20,000 gallon water tank which topped the top story of the mill.[158]

This water tank made news in 1904. The wooden tank burst, flooding the engine room and strewing the yard with broken staves. M. Berlinger, the miller, and Henry Wilson, the engineer, were standing near the engine room door and barely had time to get to shelter before the mass of twisted hoops, broken staves and thousands of gallons of water "came down like a hammer blow and shook the building to its foundations."[159]

---

[157] *Crowley Signal*, June 16, 1900
[158] *Ibid*, Sept. 7, 1901
[159] *Daily Signal*, Mar. 18, 1904

57

Among pioneer rice men associated with the Pembroke mill were Louis Gueno, Henry G. Holbrook, E. G. Garic and the Carver brothers, Hiram and Will.[160]

The Pembroke, one of the Crowley mills absorbed by Louisiana State, was moved to Kaplan in 1917. The machinery and buildings of the Pembroke, together with those of the Morse and Gueydan mills, were used to construct the Agnes mill, named for Frank Godchaux's wife, Agnes Putnam.[161]

White Swan

The first of two mills built at Morse was the White Swan, constructed in 1900. Principal stockholders in the company were J. M. Crabtree, Dr. F. R. Martin, C. F. Matthews, N. J. Zaunbrecher, Joseph Leonards, C. H. Hurd, Dr. C. H. Wright, W. E. Lawson, J. S. Mauboules, W. F. Brooks, H. J. Landers.[162]

The location of the mill was considered ideal; it was situated in the heart of a large rice producing area between four irrigating canals. The capacity was 1,400 barrels in 24 hours. Among the early employees were Edgar B. Roy, clean rice; A. P. Inglis, bookkeeper; Harry Lawrence, stenographer; O. Richard, Walter Smith, H. Richard, graders; L. C. Green, shipping; Alfred A. Lanaux, miller; Ted Reilly, assistant miller; Arthur Crawford, engineer.[163]

A year after the White Swan began operations it was purchased by a company composed of local and northern capitalists, and placed under the management of the Star milling company of Crowley. Officers of the company were T. J. Toler, Dr. F. R. Martin, A. B. Allison; directors included W. W. Duson, M. Abbott, George Ferre, E. C. McMurtry, P. L. Lawrence, G. H. Brooks, A. R. McMurtry, T. Catlin, W. J. and C. T. Naftel, Dollinge & Brown, J. C. Morris, Alex Smock.[164]

The White Swan was taken over by the Louisiana Irrigation and Milling Company in 1904, later was absorbed by Louisiana State. J. Frankel, A. B. Allison and Alex Brown were the main officers in 1907, when the mill force included Richard F. Smith, J. M. Chiasson, J. J. Cassidy, E. W. Fremaux, A. Crawford. The mill employed 30 men during the operating season.[165] The White Swan was one of the Acadia Parish mills absorbed by Louisiana State.

Union

Another of Crowley's early mills was the Union, built in 1900. Direc-

[160] *Ibid*, Mar. 18, Aug. 16, 20, 1904
[161] *Ibid*, Jan. 25, 1917; interview, Lindsey Baur, Nov. 4, 1977
[162] *Crowley Signal*, May 5, 12, 1900; *Daily Signal*, Oct. 19, 1900
[163] *Daily Signal*, Oct. 19, 1900
[164] *Crowley Signal*, Oct. 19, 1901
[165] *Ibid*, Dec. 14, 1907

tors of the mill company were James R. Webster, J. F. Foley, J. B. Foley, C. C. Keigley, B. F. Carper, Z. Frank Schultz, W. J. Naftel and M. Z. Mayes, all of Crowley. Some 40 to 50 rice producers composed the company. The mill, with a capacity of 1,600 barrels in 24 hours, was located west of the brickyard, on 13 acres known as the Col. Pickett property.[166]

Employed at the Union for the first season of operation were Ben Reynolds, clean rice department; John Schexneyder and Joe Mayes, rough rice; E. M. Gibson, shipping; J. F. Christman, bookkeeper; Joe Harrel, office clerk; Cal Wells, millwright; Ed Harrington, assistant. The newest equipment was installed, including a lighting plant, steam heat and a reception room for farmers.[167]

The mill plant and machinery were sold at a sheriff's sale November 23, 1907, to satisfy a debt of $3,369 owed O. P. Shreve.[168]

The Union was renamed the Rice City Mill in 1911 when it was taken over by a new company, the Brown Rice Milling Co., with a capital stock of $40,000. Alex Brown, manager of the White Swan at Morse, was president and general manager. Among the incorporators were W. E. Ellis, H. M. Bone, W. H. Hunter Jr. and George W. Little.[169]

The mill was subsequently absorbed by Louisiana State. Located at the west end of "Mill Row," in 1916 it was sold by Louisiana State to T. Simon and W. H. Carver.[170]

Two years later a new corporation, headed by J. A. Sabatier of the Iota mill, bought the Simon mill. Other officers were W. E. Lawson and R. F. Smith. The mill was renamed the Federal; some years later it became the Mutual mill. The mill, owned by an Arkansas firm, is in operation at present (1977).[171]

Iota Mill

The Iota Rice Milling Co. was organized in March of 1901 with C. C. Duson as its first president. Other officers and directors were Dr. L. A. Clark, J. A. Sabatier, H. J. Daigle, W. S. Robertson, Gustave Bordelais, W. E. Lawson.[172]

Sabatier, the secretary-treasurer and general manager, had formerly operated a general merchandise store in Crowley, and owned a store and implement business in Iota. Other early employees of the Iota mill were

[166] *Ibid,* Mar. 10, 1900
[167] *Ibid,* Oct. 13, 1900
[168] *Ibid,* Oct. 17, 1907 legal advertisement
[169] *Daily Signal,* July 13, 1911
[170] *Ibid,* Jan. 31, 1916
[171] *Ibid,* Mar. 8, 1918; interview, Lindsey Baur, Nov. 4, 1977; J. J. Cassidy, Nov. 29, 1977
[172] *Crowley Signal,* Mar. 23, 1901

The Iota mill was built in 1901. The mill was often identified with J. A. Sabatier, long-time manager. (Photo courtesy Gerald Wright)

Louis Prados, clean rice; John D. Belton, miller; Louis Andrus, J. H. Sabatier, rough rice.[173]

The mill was among those absorbed by Louisiana State and was continued in operation until 1915 when it was closed down.[174] The following summer the mill was sold to an independent milling concern headed by J. A Sabatier. Associated with him were G. A. and A. J. Sabatier. The plant, which had been dismantled, was re-equipped, and was reported to have had a successful first season of operation under the new management.[175]

The mill was destroyed by fire in the late 1930s.[176]

Rayne Mill

Five rice mills were constructed in Acadia Parish during the year 1902. The first of these was the Rayne mill, organized in February of that year with a capital stock of $50,000. Dr. R. C. Webb was president of the corporation and Mervine Kahn was vice president. J. C. Corbett was the contractor who built the mill and large warehouse.[177]

Among early employees were Frank Richwood, J. W. Buchanan, Travis Webb, Jules Perrodin, Charles Bruner, Bennett Irion. The mill employed 25 men during its operating season. In 1907 the officers and

[173] *Ibid*, Oct. 12, 1901
[174] *Daily Signal*, Nov. 15, 1915
[175] *Ibid*, Dec. 27, 1916
[176] Interview, B. C. Delahoussaye, Nov. 11, 1977
[177] *Crowley Signal*, Feb. 8, 1902; *Daily Signal*, Apr. 7, 1902

directors were Dr. R. C. Webb, O. Broussard, R. C. Holt Jr., W. H. Hunter Jr., C. C. Keigley, J. W. Buchanan, Joseph Birg, A. W. Berdon and Joseph Leonard.[178]

The Rayne mill became a part of the Louisiana State organization in 1911.

Hunter

The Hunter brothers, W. H. of Vermilion Parish and Sam of Shreveport, formed a private corporation and built a rice mill in Crowley in 1902. James A. Petty was the contractor for the mill, located on the Southern Pacific railroad east of Star B (the American). The mill had a capacity of 1,200 barrels in 12 hours and the equipment included attrition mills to grind chaff into stock feed and oil burners for fuel.[179]

---

[178] *Signal* Ch. Ed., Dec. 14, 1907
[179] *Crowley Signal*, Feb. 15, 1902

The Standard mill, about 1920. The mill was originally built to handle the enormous rice crops produced at the Jones Brothers' farm at Mowata. (Freeland Collection photo, USL)

The mill was destroyed by fire in 1907. The loss of the mill and large warehouse was estimated at $100,000. The owners carried $67,000 in insurance.[180]

Jones-Standard

The Jones mill was operated as a private concern for 10 years. The mill, built by the Jones brothers in 1902, was operated for one purpose: to mill the rice produced on the Jones' farm in the vicinity of Mowata. J. A. Petty was the contractor for the mill, located east of the Hunter mill. The mill capacity was 2,500 barrels in 24 hours, and its adjuncts included a large rough rice warehouse. Pete Wikoff was one of the early mill managers.[181]

In 1912 the mill was sold to a Houston concern and the name changed to Standard mill. W. K. Morrow and P. E. Paine were main stockholders in the company. That fall the mill was equipped with a sprinkler system for fire protection; the 50,000 gallon water tank was pressurized for this purpose. After World War II the mill became the Roberts mill, with Millard and "Pinky" Roberts as owners and operators.[182]

Morse Mill

The community of Morse in the southwest corner of the parish acquired its second mill in the summer of 1902. Main stockholders were H. A. Mauboules, H. Richard, C. F. Matthews, J. B. Cade, J. S. Mauboules, Robert Morris, C. H. Wright, Alcee Henry, L. C. Greene, C. A. Butcher, J. H. McCampbell and C. C. West.[183]

After the first year's operation the stock owned by Matthews and Greene, plus all treasury stock, was bought by J. D. Marks. Remaining stockholders included Robert Morris, Jules and Jack Mauboules, Alcee Henry, Dr. C. H. Wright, Jake Kollitz, Honore Richard, C. C. West, J. H. McCampbell of Jennings, A. Crawford, Eugene Trahan and others.[184]

Shelton G. Meng was secretary-manager in 1907. Other employees included Andrew Kober, miller; Felix J. Arceneaux, rough rice; S. W. Elberson, engineer. The mill employed 15 men when running.[185]

J. D. Marks bought the mill in 1909 for $40,000, later moved the mill to Memphis, Tenn.[186]

---

[180] *Ibid*, Apr. 13, 1907
[181] *Daily Signal*, Apr. 17, 18, 1902; July 26, 1904; interview, Lindsey Baur, 1977
[182] *Ibid*, May 16, Nov. 25, 1912; interview, Lindsey Baur, Winston Atteberry, 1977
[183] *Daily Signal*, May 21, June 2, 1902
[184] *Crowley Signal*, July 18, 1903
[185] *Signal*, Ch. Ed., Dec. 14, 1907
[186] *Daily Signal*, Aug. 23, 1909; Apr. 20, 1911

Midland Mill

Rice planters and land owners in the Midland area got together in 1902 to build the Midland mill. The company, organized May 31, 1902, included William Hoyt, C. H. Cowen, O. R. Hopson, P. L. Lawrence, C. H. Griffin, W. W. Duson, J. O. Fremaux and C. H. Hurd. $30,000 of the $50,000 capital stock was subscribed at the organizational meeting. Charter members of the company also included J. F. Istre, J. M. Crabtree and W. F. Spurgeon.[187]

James A. Petty was awarded the contract to build the mill. Among the early employees were W. G. Garvey, L. T. Bliss and John Marsh.[188]

The mill was reorganized in 1903. Officers were C. H. Cowen, W. W. Duson, A. B. Allison, O. R. Hopson and C. T. Bliss. Interested farmers included William Spurgeon, C. H. Cowen, Fremaux Istre, Jesse Miers, Charles Hurd, C. Vogue, J. M. Crabtree, the Hoyt brothers, S. L. Wright and others.[189]

The Midland mill was bought by the United States Rice Milling Co., which in turn was bought by the Louisiana Irrigation and Milling Co. In 1911 it was absorbed by Louisiana State and subsequently moved to Eunice.[190]

Egan Mill

A rice mill was built at Egan in 1903, the prime movers being W. M. Egan, Miron Abbott, P. B. Lang, W. W. Duson, J. W. Smith, Frank C. Labit and Frank Scanlan. A number of farmers in the area took stock in the mill. The building work was done by J. C. Corbett, Crowley contractor. P. B. Lang was general manager of the mill.[191]

The mill went into receivership in 1907, with Miron Abbott named receiver. In 1910 the mill was moved to Vidalia by Isadore Marks, to be operated by the Vidalia Rice Milling Co. Andrew Kober, at the time with the Planter's mill of Abbeville, went to Vidalia to rebuild the mill at its new location.[192]

Estherwood Mill

A milling company, with a paid up stock of $50,000, was organized in 1902. Main stockholders were W. M. Hoyt, George Wolverton, S. G. Watkins and E. T. Hoyt. More than 50 farmers in the area bought stock, and 75,000 sacks of rice were pledged. The company planned to build an

[187] *Ibid*, June 2, 25, 1902
[188] *Ibid*, June 16, 1902; Mar. 3, 18, 1904
[189] *Crowley Signal*, June 27, 1903
[190] *Ibid*, Feb. 2, 1907; interview, Lindsey Baur, 1977
[191] *Crowley Signal*, June 20, July 4, 1903; *Daily Signal*, July 10, 1904
[192] *Crowley Signal*, Dec. 7, 1907; Apr. 9, May 7, 1910

800-barrel capacity mill at Estherwood,[193] but the plans were never carried out.[194]

Liberty Mill

In 1918 Liberty Rice Mills, Inc., put up a mill at Morse. Officers were Alex Brown, W. L. Trimble and J. O. Fremaux. The mill was later sold to Mrs. S. E. Gueno and sons, A. D. and Albert Gueno. About a year later the mill was destroyed by fire and was not rebuilt.[195]

Simon-Supreme

Veteran miller T. Simon, former owner of the Union-Federal mill, built a new mill in Crowley in 1919. The mill cost was estimated at $50,000, with the machinery about $150,000. H. J. Andrus was the contractor for the mill, located on the site of the old American mill, on the south side of the SP track. The mill continues in operation (1977) under the management of Gordon Dore and is owned by the Dore family.[196]

Edna-Mermentau

Victorin Maignaud, one of Mermentau's pioneer businessmen, converted his sawmill into a rice mill in 1890. The mill was named the Edna.[197]

Fifteen years later the following classified advertisement appeared in the *Crowley Signal* of October 21, 1905:

> FOR SALE—Rice mill, two warehouses, six acres of land. Apply Gus E. Fontenot, Crowley, or V. Maignaud, Mermentau.

The rice mill offered for sale is believed to have been the Edna.

The next published information about a rice mill on the Acadia Parish side of the Mermentau River was in 1914, when the Mermentau Rice Farmers' Mill Co. was organized. Prime movers in the company were officials of the Callahan Lumber Co. of Midland, who bought the Maignaud rice mill and land extending to the river from the V. Maignaud heirs for $3,000. The company announced its intention to rebuild the mill, and a number of farmers were said to have been interested in the mill.[198] Plans to reactivate the mill were not carried out.

Some two years afterwards J. J. Cassidy bought the mill and announced his plans to remodel and repair the badly deteriorated old mill in time for the 1917-1918 season. The property included the side tracks and

[193] *Daily Signal*, May 26, 1902
[194] Interview, Lindsey Baur, 1977
[195] *Daily Signal*, June 21, 1918; interview, J. J. Cassidy, Nov. 29, 1977
[196] *Daily Signal*, Mar. 22, 1919
[197] Fontenot and Freeland, *Acadia*, 173, 174
[198] *Daily Signal*, May 1, 9, 1914

water privileges, and also what was considered a distinct asset for the times: ". . . the proposed Old Spanish Trail passes within nine feet of the mill doors." Cassidy, the mill owner, had been head miller at the American and had 15 years experience.[199]

After World War I the mill was taken over by a stock company. Main stockholders were Joseph J. Cassidy, T. B. Freeland, J. E. Cassidy and C. J. Freeland. The mill was subsequently owned and operated by L. J. Bartell and P. M. Lyons, then by B. C. Delahoussaye. Delahoussaye re-sold to Cassidy, Edmond D'Aquin and Eddie Davis. It is presently (1977) owned and operated by Evans Cormier.[200]

Louisiana State

A firm which was to dominate rice milling interests for the next half century was organized in 1911 by Frank A. Godchaux. This was Louisiana State Rice Milling Co., which in six months time gained ownership and control of 28 Louisiana rice mills.

The mammoth company was first organized as Louisiana State Rice Co., a sales organization. Eighteen country mills got together early in March, 1911 to buy and sell clean rice; within a few days $95,000 of the capital stock of $500,000 had been subscribed. Frank A. Godchaux was president and manager. Directors included A. Kaplan, C. S. Morse of Jennings, W. B. Conover, Lake Arthur; J. A. Foster, Lake Charles; J. W. Myers, Rayne; John Green and J. Frankel of Crowley, and George Hathaway of Jennings.[201]

The milling company was organized at New Orleans in September, 1911, with capital stock of $9½ million and more than $2 million of that amount subscribed. The list of incorporators included several new names: Alex Brown, John P. Burgin, J. A. Sabatier and W. H. Hunter Jr.[202]

Twelve Acadia Parish rice mills were among the 28 absorbed by Louisiana State. These were the United States, Crowley, People's Independent, Union, Star A and Pembroke of Crowley; the Midland, White Swan of Morse, Eureka of Estherwood, Rayne, Egan and Iota mills. This left the parish with but one independent operating mill—the American of Crowley. The Jones mill was in operation at the time, but cannot be classified as an independent mill since its only output was rice grown on the Jones' farm.[203]

The company was reorganized in 1916. President Godchaux, queried concerning the reorganization, said that it had been done because of

---

[199] *Ibid*, Oct. 23, 1916
[200] *Ibid*, June 26, 1919; interviews, J. J. Cassidy, Lindsey Baur, B. C. Delahoussaye
[201] *Ibid*, Mar. 20, 1911; interview, Lindsey Baur, 1977
[202] *Ibid*, Sept. 11, 1911
[203] Interview, Lindsey Baur, 1977

growth of the business; that the firm needed extra capital, and the reorganization represented an addition of $560,000 to the working capital through the issuance of that amount of preferred stock in the company.[204]

Labor Conditions

During the early years rice mill hands worked a 12-hour day—from 7 a.m. until 7 p.m., with no break at noon, for $1.50 per day. These conditions led to a strike in the fall of 1901. Mill workers organized the Crowley Mill Men's Labor Union and went on strike for a 11-hour day at the same pay. A petition to this effect, signed by 59 mill workers, was presented to A. B. Allison of Star A mill; similar petitions were delivered to management persons of the other Crowley mills.

A labor leader named C. E. Haralson was the apparent instigator of the walk-out and organizer of the union. The only other names mentioned were Ed P. Guidry and J. L. Coleman, listed as officers of the union. One newspaper story stated that a number of Negro workers had quit work "for fear of violence from white strikers" indicating that only white workers had gone on strike. White labor leaders had threatened the black workers, it was rumored.

The petitions and the walk-outs were ignored; the mills continued operations with the help of non-strikers and outside labor. All strikers were black-listed.[205]

Mill men were quoted in the newspaper on their views of the situation. John Green, connected with three of the mills, said he saw no reason for the strike. Boys of 15 to 17, he pointed out, who had been getting as much as $1.50 per day, had now lost their jobs by walking out. J. E. Platt, owner of the Eagle mill, and C. J. Freeland of the American, said they would never re-hire anyone who walked out. W. W. Duson, interested in four of the mills, wrote a letter to the editor of the *Signal* supporting management in the strike. He pointed out that many of the mills gave employment to their men during the off-seasons by putting them to work on the canals and at other industry-related jobs. Mills, he said, were paying good wages; "we pay 12 hours wages for 12 hours labor."

The millers' actions brought criticism from area newspapers. The *Lake Charles American* was of the opinion that there was "no way . . . to settle a labor complaint except by either granting the demands or by telling the complainants fairly and squarely why it cannot be done." The *Beaumont Journal* expressed shock and surprise: "Outside of the highly protected sweat shops of the north and east, the *Journal* was ignorant that employees were required to work as long as 12 hours a day."[206]

Labor shortages often hampered the harvest and fall warehouse

---

[204] *Daily Signal*, Aug. 25, 1916
[205] *Crowley Signal*, Oct. 26, Nov. 2, 1901
[206] *Ibid*, Nov. 2, 1901

work. In the fall of 1903 farmers were said to be paying "as much as $1.75 per day" for farm hands, and the mills were paying $1.50 a day for warehouse labor. The reason given for this particular labor scarcity: a great exodus of country Negroes to the northern states.[207]

A project to employ Orientals on farms in the rice belt did not work very well. Some Japanese farmers were brought into the Gueydan area in 1906. They were said to have become despondent over weather conditions; they abandoned the rice farms and returned to their homeland.[208]

During the first World War the Kaplan interests brought in some Mexican labor to help with the harvesting. Twelve of the 70 men and their families were sent ot Iota, where the men were put to work in the rice mill. The labor force was secured through the US Government Employment Service Bureau of Laredo.[209]

Louisiana Irrigation and Milling Co.

A company combining both irrigation and milling was organized in 1904. This was Louisiana Irrigation and Milling Co., which continues in operation today (1977).

The main stockholders at the time the firm was chartered were C. C. Duson, W. W. Duson, Miron Abbott, J. Frankel, A. B. Allison, E. C. McMurtry, J. R. Roller, P. H. Dorr, P. L. Lawrence, L. T. Bliss and Martin D. Abbott, each with five shares of stock at $100 a share.[210]

The LIM company, as it came to be known, represented a consolidation of six mills and six canals.

Five of the six canals were in Acadia Parish: the Abbott-Duson, Ferre, Crowley, Roller and Midland canals; the sixth was the Grand canal of Calcasieu Parish. The main canals and laterals totaled 254.48 miles. Four of the six mills were in Acadia Parish: Star A and Star B of Crowley, the Midland mill and White Swan of Morse. The other two were the Lousiana mill of Jennings and the Roanoke mill, Calcasieu Parish. The six mills had a combined capacity of 3,900 barrels in 12 hours.[211]

The company also owned 10 independent warehouses with a combined storage of 500,000 bags, and controlled 100,000 acres of irrigable land. The holdings included eight main pumping plants, 11 relift stations with a combined pumping capacity of 54 million gallons of water an hour. Main source of water was the Mermentau River and its tributaries. In 1904 the LIM canals irrigated 60,000 acres of rice; the rent received was 104,500 bags of 185 pounds each, or 470,250 bushels.[212]

---

[207] *Ibid*, Oct. 17, 1903
[208] *Daily Signal*, Sept. 27, 1906
[209] *Ibid*, Sept. 23, 1918
[210] *Crowley Signal*, Mar. 12, 1904
[211] *Daily Signal*, May 27, 1905
[212] *Ibid*

Some 400 men were employed by the 12 independent companies amalgamated into LIM. With their families, these represented about 2,000 people, exclusive of stockholders, who were interested in the fortunes of the 12 companies. The directors, in 1905, were E. C. McMurtry, J. R. Roller, P. H. Dorr, P. L. Lawrence, L. T. Bliss, M. D. Abbott.[213]

The LIM disposed of its mills in 1907. The six mills were taken over by the Consolidated Mill Co. The six mills were sub-divided into smaller milling companies. Two of the Acadia Parish mills in the combine, Star A and White Swan of Morse, were taken over by a company headed by A. B. Allison, while Star B went to the Duson-Abbott interests.[214]

The company went into receivership in 1916. James W. Billingsly was appointed receiver and in turn named W. H. Hunter Jr. general manager for LIM interests. That year the company had 38,500 acres under irrigation of which 31,500 acres were in Acadia Parish, the rest in Jefferson Davis. The company operated entirely on a share crop basis, instead of as formerly on a share and cash basis combined, and the new arrangement worked out in a satisfactory manner.[215]

A year later the company was completely reorganized and P. L. Lawrence was named president. Plans were made to take the concern out of the hands of the receivers as soon as the necessary legal steps could be taken. The reorganization was on the same basis as the company had before the receivership, the capitalization remaining $1,500,000. Other officers were C. J. Freeland, vice president; George Hathaway, second vice president; T. B. Freeland, secretary-treasurer; S. P. Johnson, assistant secretary-treasurer. The 14-member board of directors included W. M. Hoyt, W. W. Duson, J. R. Roller and P. H. Dorr. The majority of the stock was owned by Lawrence and the Freeland brothers.[216]

The Canals and Irrigation

Acadia Parish was truly "the cradle of southwest Louisiana's irrigation industry." It was here that a unique and practical system of agricultural irrigation, contrived to suit the topography of the Acadian prairies, was initiated and developed. This was the canal system of rice irrigation which was responsible for making Louisiana America's chief rice producing state. The system had other far-reaching results, such as an increased demand for harvesters, threshers, harrows, plows and other farm implements; steam engines and pumping plants; as well as machinery and construction material for rice mills. It opened up the market for some 75,000 head of northern mules and horses, plus millions of bushels of corn and

[213] *Ibid*
[214] *Crowley Signal*, June 15, July 20, 1907
[215] *Daily Signal*, Feb. 14, July 28, 1916
[216] *Ibid*, Jan. 10, 1917

Primitive—but practical—methods of artificial irrigation are shown in these two photos of the system on the Hoyt brothers farm in the western part of Acadia. Top photo shows the pump installation in the coulee; bottom photo is of the camp set-up at the pumping plant during flooding season. (Photos courtesy Lucille Hoyt Hoffpauir)

The wilderness that once characterized the wooded areas along Acadia's waterways gradually gave way to the ingenuity and inventiveness of pioneers in the rice industry. In top photo is an old-time steam engine being "refueled" with water from the tank wagon, while the lower scene shows the relift flume on the Hoyt canal framed by the pastoral beauty of moss-festooned trees. (Photos courtesy Lucille Hoyt Hoffpauir)

oats to feed these work animals. Land values soared as more and more land was reclaimed for rice farming.[217]

Rice had been grown on the southwest Louisiana prairies for half a century before artificial irrigation was conceived. This was the so-called providence rice—the crop depended on sufficient rainfall. A landowner would plant from 25 to 40 acres of rice on the lowest portion of his quarter or half section of land, using vacant lands adjoining as water sheds. Flats and low places, which needed but little irrigation, became the rice fields. Profits from this simple method stimulated farmers to enlarge their operations, and led to improvements. Farmers began damming up the gulleys and holding water in reservoirs during the winter for use during the rice growing season in summer. This method, first used by German rice farmers in the Robert's Cove area, supplied the demand for 50 to 60 acres of rice on each quarter section. If more rice was planted, the water supply was insufficient. The years 1891 and 1892 were exceptionally rainy years; farmers were successful in raising rice on higher land, which proved that rice could be raised anywhere in the parish, provided sufficient water was available.[218]

The first use of water from the streams to irrigate rice was the primitive buckets-on-a-continuous-chain method initiated in 1888 by the Abbott brothers. The first irrigation canal, constructed by C. C. Duson in 1890, was a small project on Bayou Plaquemine Brulee; this proved unsatisfactory, but did not discourage further experimentation. By the end of 1901 a network of 17 canals was in operation, watering more than 80,000 acres in Acadia Parish alone.[219] The uncertainty in cultivating large quantities of rice had been eliminated.

One of the first requisites for canal building was the selection of a suitable site for the pumping plant. The banks of a tidewater stream, where prairie lands came as near the stream as possible, was the ideal location. This would cut down on the building of long flumes, which was an expensive process, especially when such had to be built through timber and across swampland.[220]

Pumping plant machinery was heavy and required solid foundations. Such were secured by excavating the clay to a depth of six to 10 feet and constructing foundations of brick and cement on which the engines and boilers rested. Foundations for the pumps were usually made by driving cypress piling down a depth of 12 to 20 feet. After the machinery installa-

[217] Crippen, Charles L., "Surface Canals," *Crowley Signal*, Feb. 16, 1901; Babineaux, Lawson P., "History of Rice Industry in SW La.," University of Southwestern Louisiana thesis, 1967, 39

[218] *Crowley Signal*, Feb. 16, 1901; Fontenot-Freeland, *Acadia, etc.*, 182

[219] Fontenot-Freeland, *Acadia*, 325; *Crowley Signal*, Oct. 6, 1900; Dec. 21, 1901

[220] Crippen, Charles L., "Surface Canals," *Crowley Signal*, Feb. 16, 1901. All further descriptive material concerning canal building will be from this same source unless otherwise noted.

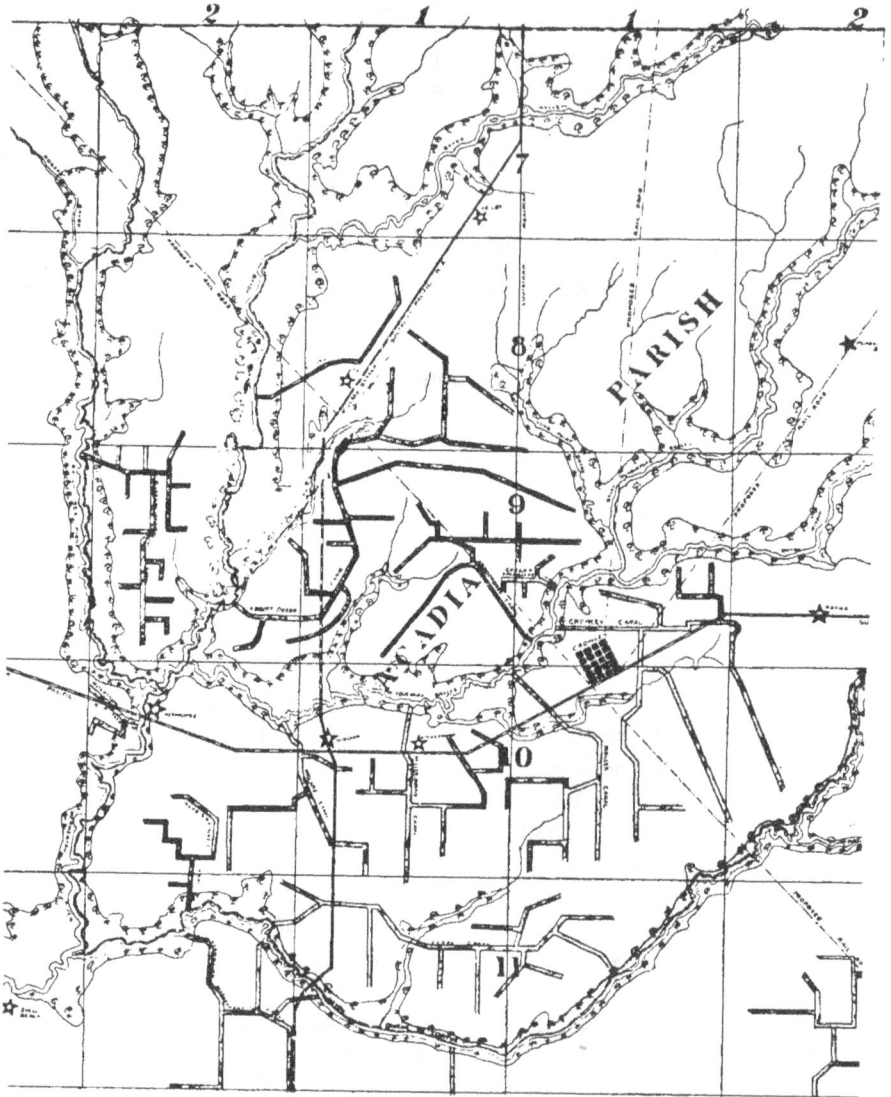

The network of irrigation canals is shown in this 1901 map of Acadia Parish. Even at that early date canals were furnishing water for some 80,000 acres of rice.

tion was completed a cypress flume was built, connecting the pump with the canal proper.

Because the water in the streams was from 15 to 20 feet below the level of the land, the canals had to be of the surface type. The canals were constructed by throwing up two levees from 50 to 200 feet apart, the dirt being taken from the outside of the levees.

The levees were from four to 10 feet high, according to the topography of the country through which they passed. The levee bases were from 12 to 20 feet wide, with five-foot crowns. Usually the highest ridge was selected for canal-building, and since no dirt was taken from the inside, the water was thus kept above the fields which were to be irrigated.

The first step in canal levee building was to plow up the bed of the levee and pulverize the soil to eliminate clods or lumps that might cause the levees to leak. From experience the levee builders learned that to obtain best results the levees should be put up with drag scrapers and mules, as the constant tramping and stamping done by the teams made the levees more compact and solid than if done by the regular grading machinery in use at the time.

When deep gullies or small streams were encountered the water was carried over by flumes. Canals were kept as full as possible. Whenever water was needed for the fields on either side of the canals, openings were made from four to six feet wide and wooden boxes and gates were inserted through which the water was drawn off into laterals or branch canals, leading away in every direction. The number of miles of laterals that were connected with a canal was usually double the mileage of the main canal; thus a canal 12 miles long would have in addition 25 miles of laterals. Much care was necessary in the placing of the wooden gates and boxes because of the workings of minks, crawfish and muskrats, and the general tendency to wash out.

In Acadia the land becomes higher as one goes away from the streams, so that often in a distance of four or five miles the level of the country would be four or five feet higher than where the canal started. At such points it was necessary to establish a relift; a new canal would be started, levees would be built up five or six feet high, pumps and engines put in, and the work of re-lifting the bayou water into the higher level canal would begin. Some of the irrigating systems had as many as four relift stations and could water lands 43 feet above the level of the streams from which came the water supply.

Wherever a natural drain was encountered, cypress boxing was put in to allow the water to pass under the canal. Each canal company employed a superintendent, who had charge of the plant and also managed the levee workers and gave instructions concerning the distribution of water. Operated from a rental system, the farmer usually paid one fifth of his crop for water.

The water from Acadia Parish streams was found to be soft and free from obnoxious seeds, and of the right temperature to give best results to the crop. The streams ran through timber, a half to three miles wide; therefore fallen leaves and the decayed vegetation of centuries were taken by the great pumps and spread over the fields as fertilizer.

Surface canal construction went on with such rapidity that by the early part of 1901 there were in southwest Louisiana 40 canals, aggregating a length of nearly 500 miles, with about 1,000 miles of laterals, irrigating some 200,000 acres. The systems, which required an expenditure of energy equal to 20,000 horsepower working day and night, cost more than $2½ million, an impressive amount for the times.

Abbott-Duson

The largest of the early canal systems in Acadia was the Abbott-Duson, which irrigated some 20,000 acres. Officers of the company in 1900 were W. W. Duson, C. C. Duson, B. M. Lambert, Miron, M. D. and C. Abbott, all of Crowley. Two pumping plants were on the canal; the first on Bayou des Cannes 12 miles northwest of Crowley, and the secondary or relift pump, where the water had to be pumped up 10 feet, was three miles east of the main plant.

The first station lifted the water from the bayou to an elevation of 24 feet and had a capacity of 90,000 gallons a minute. The plant was equipped with six large boilers, two Corliss engines with 24-inch cylinders and 48-inch stroke, each of 420-horse power, and six 18-inch double suction Iven's pumps. The relift station was equipped with three boilers, one Corliss engine and two 36-inch pumps.[221]

Ferre

The Ferre canal, constructed about 1897, extended east from Bayou Queue de Tortue. Stockholders and directors in 1900 were A. R. McMurtry, Marshall, Ind.; W. W. Duson, John W. Roller, Alex B. Allison and George Ferre of Dalton City, Ill., for whom the canal was named. Irrigating capacity at the end of 1901 was 15,000 acres.[222]

Miller-Morris

The Miller-Morris was Acadia's third largest irrigation canal in 1901, capacity-wise, with 12,000 acres under irrigation. William Miller and Dr. J. F. Morris were the originators. In 1900 the canal was sold to a stock company, of which A. Kaplan, W. W. Duson and C. J. Bier were the main officers. Directors included Isidore Hechinger, I. M. Lichtenstein and H. Lichtenstein.

The pumping station, located one mile north of Estherwood on Bayou Plaquemine Brulee, in 1900 pumped water through 23 miles of main canal and laterals.[223]

The canal company was reorganized in 1905 with a capital stock of $75,000, with 750 shares at $100 each. Incorporators, each with five shares of stock, were P. J. Chappuis, P. J. Pavy, George H. Tinker, James L. Wright, George H. Einsiedel, Dan J. Feitel.[224]

[221] *Crowley Signal*, Oct. 6, 1900; Dec. 21, 1901
[222] *Ibid*
[223] *Ibid*
[224] *Daily Signal*, Mar. 23, 1905

In 1908 new machinery was added to the old plant on the bayou north of Estherwood. During the pumping season the plant would pump 80,000 gallons a minute through the 30 miles of main canal to irrigate some 12,000 acres. Engineers were R. E. Gill and J. W. Embry, Sr.[225]

An interesting sidelight on the Morris canal's operations is that the company bought muskrat pelts in 1909, offering 12½ cents per pelt, because of the great damage done to the canal levees by the animals. A large quantity of pelts was reported brought in.[226]

In 1916 the canal company, known as the United Irrigation and Rice Milling Company, was supplying water for some 8,000 acres. A. Kaplan was president and general manager, and J. W. Embry Sr. was engineer. The pumping plant was said to be "one of the model plants in the area," with the engines, pumps and other equipment kept spotless and shining at all times, with no dirt or grease in evidence.[227]

Crowley

Built in 1896, the Crowley canal was enlarged several times and by 1901 was watering rice acreage totaling 10,000 acres. W. W. Duson, also interested in a number of other canal companies, was president of the corporation. Miron Abbott was vice president and C. L. Crippen secretary. Located one and a half miles northwest of Crowley on Plaquemine Brulee, the plant supplied water for about 3,000 acres belonging to Duson, and for some 30 to 40 farmers who bought water from the company.

The Crowley canal was the town's first swimming pool. Young people from Crowley and the surrounding area made up swimming parties in the summer to bathe in the canal flume when the pumps were running.[228]

Roller

The Roller canal, with a flooding capacity of 8,000 acres, extended south from Bayou Plaquemine Brulee for 18 miles. The water was lifted from the bayou a height of 24 feet. Stockholders and directors in 1900 were W. W. Duson, P. H. Dorr, Anthony B. Longenbaugh, Joseph R. Roller, John Roller and George Ferre.[229]

Midland

The Midland canal was completed in the spring of 1899. Thirty farmers made use of its facilities in 1900; irrigation provided that year totaled 5,000 acres, 200 acres of which were cultivated by the canal company.

[225] *Crowley Signal*, May 16, 1908
[226] *Daily Signal*, Feb. 27, 1909
[227] *Ibid*, June 29, 1916
[228] *Crowley Signal*, Oct. 6, 1900; Dec. 12, 1901
[229] *Ibid*, Oct. 6, 1900

Palmer P. Laughlin was president of the company, C. C. Duson was vice president and Dr. John F. Naftel secretary-treasurer. Principal stockholders included Dr. John N. Randall, B. F. Cloud, William J. Naftel, W. W. Duson, O. B. Gorin, A. H. Hill. The water source was Bayou Plaquemine Brulee and the lift had an elevation of 20 feet. John Marsh was manager of the plant in 1903.[230]

Acadia

The Acadia canal, built by C. C. Duson, was under construction in 1900. The main pumping plant was built at Pointe-aux-Loups Springs on Bayou des Cannes, about 18 miles northwest of Crowley. The water was lifted 29 feet from the bayou and carried through a cypress flume built on trestles 28 feet high, for a distance of a half mile. The flume was 15 feet wide and four feet deep and ran nearly full when the four pumps were in operation.

A half mile from the pumping station the water emptied into the canal proper, which was 100 feet wide and about five miles long, not counting the laterals. The canal crossed the Midland-Eunice branch railroad at a point one and a half miles above the town of Iota; the water was relifted here seven feet and carried onto a higher level. Company officers in 1900 were C. C. Duson, George Croker of New York City, and R. R. Duson. The system's capacity at the end of 1901 was 2,000 acres.[231]

These seven were the major irrigating systems of the parish up to 1902, supplying water for the rice grown by the canal owners and the farmers along the route of the main canals and laterals. Five of the seven—the Abbott-Duson, Ferre, Crowley, Roller and Midland canals —were taken over by the Louisiana Irrigation and Milling Company in 1904.

Another canal system to be considered was Riverside, which watered lands in the western part of Acadia but was owned by a Jennings corporation. The main canal began from the east bank of Bayou Nezpique about 10 miles north of the village of Mermentau. The primary pumping plant lifted the water 25 feet; a mile and a quarter farther on another station lifted it an additional seven feet. In 1900 the company furnished water to 40 farmers having a total acreage of 2,500 acres, also 500 acres of its own cultivation.[232]

Also there were nine private canals in operation by 1901, watering some 7,500 acres of privately owned rice lands. Of these, the Hurd-Wright canal, capacity 1,200 acres, was the largest. Water source was Bayou Queue de Tortue. Charles Hurd and Dr. C. H. Wright owned the canal. Other private canals, watering from 200 to 1,000 acres were the

---

[230] *Crowley Signal*, Apr. 22, 1899; *Daily Signal*, Feb. 6, 1903
[231] *Crowley Signal*, Oct. 6, 1900; Dec. 21, 1901
[232] *Ibid*, Oct. 6, 1900

Green-Shoemaker, Jean Castex, Paul Fremaux, Philibert Simon, Wilder, Philip Lapleau, Fremaux Istre and Maignaud canals.[233]

A number of Acadia Parish residents had large interests in canal systems outside the parish limits. One of these plants was the Watertown Farm and Irrigation Company. The canal was on the west side of the Mermentau in Calcasieu (later to be Jefferson Davis) Parish. At the pumping station the water was 65 feet deep and a lift of 14 feet was all that was necessary. In 1900 the canal was only about three miles long and watered less than a thousand acres. Company officers were J. F. Shoemaker, J. Frankel and John Green. In 1902 the Grand canal, owned by the Jennings Irrigating Company was bought out by a stock company which included W. W. Duson, Miron Abbott, A. B. Allison, E. C. McMurtry, George Hathaway, U. S. Phillips and George Ferre. A. Kaplan of Crowley also invested heavily in irrigation canals of Vermilion Parish.[234]

Other early canal systems were the Millerville, Mamou and Hoyt canals. The Mamou Canal Company was chartered in 1902 with a capital stock of $40,000. Major stockholders were A. Kaplan, J. A. Sabatier and George Sabatier. The plant was about 20 miles north of Crowley in Mamou prairie and watered some 5,000 acres in 1908.[235]

Deep Wells

During the early years of rice irrigation in southwest Louisiana deep wells were used more extensively in Calcasieu Parish than in Acadia. Only about 12,500 of the 50,000 acres flooded by deep wells in 1901 were in Acadia; the rest were in Calcasieu, which at that time took in what is now Jefferson Davis Parish.[236]

However, the largest deep well plant in the rice belt was located in Acadia. This was the installation at the Jones Brothers' farm. Winston and Henry Jones and their sister, Patty Jones Williams of Mobile, Ala. owned 12,500 acres of the best farmland in the state, about half of which was located in Acadia Parish; seven sections were in the northern part of the parish, at what was later to be known as Mowata. The immense farm was managed by T. T. Atteberry, who moved his family from Eutaw, Ala., to the area in 1902. The three years prior to 1907 were extremely dry years; in order to properly irrigate their rice fields it was necessary for the Jones to put down 14 new water wells, giving the farm the largest deep well system in the rice country.[237]

Acadia can also claim the first deep well for irrigating rice lands. Jean

[233] *Ibid*, Dec. 21, 1901; interview, Lindsey Baur, 1977
[234] *Ibid*, Oct. 6, 1900; Feb. 15, 1902
[235] *Daily Signal*, Nov. 18, 1902; Aug. 25, 1909
[236] *Crowley Signal*, Feb. 16, 1901
[237] *Crowley Signal*, Apr. 13, 1907; interview, Winston Atteberry, Mar. 20, 1977

Castex of Mermentau at an unspecified time used a water well with a two-inch bore to flood his rice. The well was driven by a windmill.[238]

The number of deep well installations was to multiply many times in the ensuing years, but the natural streams were to remain the chief source of water for rice irrigation purposes in Acadia Parish.[239]

Providence Rice

Some providence rice was raised in south Louisiana as late as 1914. That year Henry Holbrook, a buyer for Louisiana State, bought the first rice of the season at Chataignier, a settlement about eight miles northeast of Eunice. The rice, Honduras variety, was said to have been raised without artifical irrigation.[240]

Published crop and weather reports indicate that providence rice was grown more extensively in the extreme northwest portion of the parish in the vicinity of Basile, and in the Prairie Hayes area.[241]

The year 1900 was known as "the providence rice year," because of excessive rainfall. Farmers in the Fabacher-Basile area harvested a bumper crop; both the yield and the quality of the rice was very good, and the farmers were "jubilant over the success of their providence crop."[242]

The Mermentau Dam

After the invasion of salt water for two consecutive years and the resulting damage to the rice crop, the growers, millers and canal men decided to make an effort to alleviate the situation. In November of 1902 a meeting was held in Jennings and a committee named to investigate the feasibility of building a dam on the Mermentau to hold back the brackish water. Crowley was represented on the committee by A. Kaplan, Miron Abbott and George H. Tinker.[243]

Engineers inspected the river from the railroad bridge at Mermentau to the Gulf. They found that the highest banks were at the point where the river pierced the Grand Cheniere ridge.

John Wharton Maxcy, civil engineer of Houston, was engaged to inspect the proposed site and draw up specifications for a dam 400 feet wide with a lock 40 feet wide by 125 feet long made of creosoted lumber

---

[238] Ginn, Mildred Kelly. "History of Rice Production in Louisiana." *Louisiana Historical Quarterly*, Vol. 23, 570

[239] Booklet, "Acadia Parish Resources and Facilities," 1946 survey by La. Dept. Public Works and Acadia Parish Planning Board, 33

[240] *Daily Signal*, Aug. 7, 1914

[241] *Crowley Signal*, Mar. 31, Apr. 14, 1900; Aug. 3, 1901; July 18, 1903; July 13, 1907; July 16, 1910; *Daily Signal*, Sept. 8, 1906

[242] *Crowley Signal*, Aug. 11, Sept. 9, Oct. 13, 1900

[243] McNeely, Dorothy B., "Mermentau Dam Secret for 70 Years—Revealed," *Crowley Post-Signal*, Apr. 17, 1977. Further information on the dam, unless otherwise noted, will be from this same source.

and pilings, surmounted by a movable superstructure consisting of 44 shutters, or gates. More than 50 sets of specifications were let out for bids. Maxcy's estimate was under $50,000 and his bid was accepted.

Meanwhile the Rice Irrigation and Improvement Association was organized and chartered. Capital stock was fixed at $250,000 and divided into 10,000 shares at $25 per share. Officers were Miron Abbott, Charles A. Lowry, George H. Tinker and S. J. Johnson.

In January of 1903 Congress authorized the association to construct a lock and dam on the river, provided the work be done under the supervision of the United States Corps of Engineers and that the cost and maintenance be paid for by the association.

The sale of stock in the corporation produced little more than half of the total cost of the construction, which ended up at $130,000. The association asked Congress for assistance in paying for the work. When this effort failed the rice men turned to the Louisiana Legislature for aid. This resulted in the creation of the Mermentau Levee District which became law on July 4, 1904.

The Levee District act began a storm of controversy. Landowners in the Mermentau Basin reacted in alarm; they feared they would be taxed for the necessary costs of construction and maintenance of the dam. Members of the association traveled the area in an attempt to reassure residents that the tax would affect only the corporations and individuals who actually pumped water from the river. Full texts of the speeches made were printed in rice belt newspapers.

The fight against the levee board was led by Henry L. Gueydan of Vermilion Parish. George H. Tinker, secretary of the association, was the leader for the proponents. This led some newspapers to refer to the project as "Tinker's Dam."

The storm of oratory, pro and con, raged for several months. A suit filed by eight residents of Vermilion, Acadia and Calcasieu resulted in a restraining order against the newly appointed board of commissioners of the Mermentau Levee District. The suit charged that the levee board was a "cover behind which to hide and disguise the true intent and purpose, which is to buy a system of dams and locks now already constructed by a private corporation near Grand Cheniere in the Mermentau River."

After a year of hearings and court procedures Judge J. E. Barry dissolved the injunction, thus sustaining the "dam people" and stating that the "plaintiffs had no right to complain until they were hurt."

The reaction of the "plaintiffs" was to dynamite the dam. An estimated one third of the 44 sections was systematically destroyed by "unknown parties." The repairs took five months, but by planting time the dam was again operable. That fall watchmen at the dam were seized, bound and gagged while 17 sections were destroyed. In each dynamiting obvious care was taken not to damage the lock. Two more dynamitings took place in 1909.

The War Department was requested to make the decision as to whether the dam should be maintained or destroyed. The decision rested with them for seven years—from 1909 to 1916—before the final order was issued to remove the remains of the dam at the expense of the company.

The dam was first dynamited on Oct. 2, 1905. On receiving the news of the dynamiting a party from Crowley left to inspect the damage. Miron Abbott, C. C. Duson, R. R. Duson, J. F. Shoemaker, George H. Tinker, Frank Randolph and M. G. Wilkins drove to Mermentau then took a boat to Grand Cheniere. The investigating group spent two days at the dam. The estimate of the damage was given as $10,000; later estimates placed the damage at from $20,000 to $30,000.[244]

Residents of Grand Cheniere believed that the dam was responsible for the river water backing up, causing flooded conditions which had resulted in great losses. Not so, said the proponents. Tinker claimed that the dam construction had facilitated the passage of water, and that his statement could be backed up by a Tulane engineer. He further maintained that heavy rainfall was responsible for the damaging floods in the area; the flow of water at the dam had been checked by government engineers, he said. Nonetheless the Grand Cheniere people believed that their homes were menaced by the dam.[245]

These matters were threshed out at a meeting held in Jennings in November of 1905. C. C. Duson was one of the dam proponents who addressed the meeting; later, he was head of a committee to meet with the Cheniere people to effect a compromise. The dam proponents hoped that by making certain adjustments in the dam construction that the residents of Grand Cheniere would be satisfied. But Cheniere residents were said to be "deaf to all dam propositions;" they wanted the dam moved up river several miles, to a place called Brown's Island. But this location, the dam people said, would do no good for rice.[246]

In the spring of 1906 the citizens of Grand Cheniere filed a protest with the federal government claiming flood losses from the dam, also that the construction was an obstruction to navigation. Some months later the U.S. Corps of Engineers published the report of their investigation which stated that the dam was not an obstruction to navigation.[247]

The second dynamiting of the dam took place July 26, 1907. A small crowd of men surprised the three guards at the dam, bound them and set charges of dynamite. The men held the guards up with Winchester rifles and stood over them while others placed the dynamite. The men worked quickly and carefully. The dynamite charges were exploded by electricity.[248]

[244] *Daily Signal*, Apr. 20, 1906; *Crowley Signal*, Oct. 7, 1905; Apr. 20, 1906
[245] *Crowley Signal*, Nov. 18, 1905
[246] *Ibid*, Nov. 18, Dec. 9, 1905
[247] *Daily Signal*, May 3, Aug. 6, 1906
[248] *Crowley Signal*, July 27, 1907

Opponents of the dam were successful in getting the Mermentau Levee Board Act repealed. Three of the politicians who were opposed to the Act and who helped to get it repealed were Alcee Henry, Joseph Flash and E. O. Bruner. The Act was said to be one "that made every farmer, merchant, clerk, laboring man, in fact, everybody who lived within said district pay a tax of 10 mills to hold fresh water for canal people who were selling the same water back to farmers at enormous prices."[249]

The third crisis didn't come until 1909, when two attempts were made to destroy the structure with dynamite. The first was a failure, the second partially successful as part of the superstructure was destroyed. Rice farmers, threatened by salt water, asked the War Department to settle the question.[250]

The final disposition of the case occurred in 1916 when the War Department decided that the dam constituted a menace to navigation and ordered that the wreckage be dynamited and carried off.[251]

A federal investigation was made and indictments brought against six residents of Cameron Parish charged with blowing up the dam. The case was never brought to trial and eventually the indictments against the accused were nolle prossed in federal court.[252]

A related incident, but of relatively minor importance, happened in Acadia Parish in 1908. John P. Burgin, a farmer in the south part of the parish, built a dam in Bayou Queue de Tortue about 900 feet long. The purpose of the dam was to store water for rice irrigation. The dam was provided with floodgates which were kept open except during and just before pumping season. Burgin owned about 1,000 acres in Ward 5 of Acadia Parish, also had land across the bayou in Vermilion Parish.

When the floodgates were installed Burgin was notified by the district attorney of Vermilion Parish to appear and answer complaints about the dam. Burgin went to Abbeville, along with six other property owners said to be affected. All testified that no damage had been done by the dam. Nevertheless that night six men cut holes in the dam with axes and saws; one of Burgin's employees tried to prevent the vandalism, but was run off by one of the men who was armed with a pistol. The identity of the men was said to have been known; strangely enough, they were not landowners in the area affected.[253]

Irrigation Problems

The discovery of oil in Acadia Parish in 1901 created a new problem for rice farmers in the oil field area. In the summer of 1906 a delegation of

[249] *Ibid*, Nov. 2, 1905
[250] *Daily Signal*, Apr. 3, May 15, 1909
[251] *Ibid*, Aug. 5, 1916
[252] *Ibid*, Oct. 8, 1909: Aug. 5, 1916
[253] *Crowley Signal*, Apr. 4, 1908

farmers from around Egan appeared before the police jury with a complaint that Bayou des Cannes—the source of water for their rice fields—had become contaminated from salt water gushers in the oil field. The delegation was composed of John Wilson, Henry Bossley, Louis Leger, Paul Trump and Frank Scanlan.

The farmers affected tried throwing up a levee to dam the flood of brackish water in the bayou. Evidently this measure was not satisfactory, as shortly thereafter three members of the farmers' committee—Bossley, Leger and P. B. Lang—came to town and hired an attorney to represent their interests.[254]

The following spring, prior to rice flooding time, it was announced that no more salt water would be emptied into the bayou. All of the salt water would henceforth be pumped into the great earthern storage tanks at the oil field and held there until pumping season was over. There was available storage for eight million barrels of the salt water.[255]

The threat of salt water was renewed at the beginning of the pumping season in 1909 when the current in the Mermentau began flowing upstream. The north wind drove the fresh water out and the water level in the river went down six inches.[256]

Excessive rainfall plagued farmers in 1911. Heavy rains during September seriously damaged shocked rice in the fields. Early Honduras was reported overripe and beginning to shell or sprouted in the shock. Rice in the fields on poorly drained land suffered the most damage. Where rice in shocks had to stand in water the result was soft, musty, imperfect grains, which downgraded the price.[257]

A prolonged drouth and fear of salt water damage in 1917 drove rice people to seek relief from a unique source. Those farmers who were willing to put up cash in the amount of $5,000 to employ a rainmaker were asked to contact W. A. Morgan or F. M. Milliken. The rainmaker, a professional by the name of Peter Fellman, said his plan was to operate from a tall building; asbestos balloons, filled with certain chemicals, would be released from the top of the building. The balloons would explode at a certain height, the chemicals would be released, thereby causing rainfall.[258] Since there was no follow-up report on the scheme the conjecture is that either the proponents were unable to raise the necessary $5,000, or a good rain wiped out the rainmaker's project.

Rice Miscellany

Some of the less important aspects of the rice industry and several

[254] *Daily Signal*, July 10, 18; Aug. 27, 1906
[255] *Crowley Signal*, Apr. 13, 1907
[256] *Daily Signal*, May 12, 1909
[257] *Ibid*, Sept. 4, 5, 28, 1911
[258] *Ibid*, June 23, 1917

industry-related incidents reported during the early years are of interest and shed more light on the way things were during the pioneer years of the business. For example, a Crowley resident and prominent farmer (unidentified) paid what was for those days a stiff fine—$15 and costs—in city court for permitting a thresher engine belonging to him to be taken over one of the crossing bridges in town without having planked the bridge under the wheels. The engine, a 15-horsepower machine, was over the maximum weight (5,000 pounds) permitted by municipal ordinance to cross bridges without planking.[259]

Another harvest time difficulty: getting the rice to the mills. Farmers hauled rice to the mills day and night in mule-drawn wagons. At these times dry weather and moonlit nights brought thankful smiles to every rice farmer's face.[260]

A source of curiosity to rice men of 1903 was "a quaint specimen of rice mill machinery," on exhibit at the Crowley mill. The "machinery" was an old rice pounder, used in the olden days to beat the hulls off the grain. The pounder was the property of S. D. Broussard who lived on the Mermentau River. The pounder had been made more than 60 years before by Broussard's father, Napoleon Broussard.[261]

In the early days of country milling the clean rice was packed in barrels for shipping by rail. By 1904 bags had supplanted the barrels. However, the railroad company complained when inferior quality bags were used, as oftentimes these ripped and tore in transit. The railroad threatened a rate increase unless better grade bags were used.[262]

The rice industry gave rise to several inventions. One of these was a compound to control red rice, weeds, water grasses and water lilies. The compound, patented by Joseph Flash of Acadia Parish and a New Orleans man named Bedford, was sold in barrels of 250 to 300 pounds, at a price of $2.75 per hundred pounds at the factory in New Orleans. Flash was in charge of sales in the Acadia area.[263] The success or failure of the product was not established; however, rice farmers continued the practice of burning over their fields to get rid of red rice.[264] Another invention was an automatic rice grader, patented by Percy Lyons in 1907.[265]

The rapid developmemt of the rice industry made Crowley a trading center for mules and horses, especially for mules, as their endurance and sure-footedness made them particularly valuable as draft animals in the rice fields. Twenty one carloads of mules were reported sold in Crowley within a six-weeks period in 1906. The five sales stables at that time were operated by Lackey and Duvall, L. S. Cornett, West brothers, A. Rake-

[259] *Crowley Signal*, Nov. 7, 1903
[260] *Ibid*, Oct. 10, 1903
[261] *Ibid*, Dec. 5, 1903
[262] *Ibid*, Sept. 26, 1903
[263] *Ibid*, Dec. 8, 1900
[264] *Ibid*, Nov. 9, 1901
[265] *Ibid*, Feb. 16, 1907

straw and A. Nichols, the last named having leased the sales stables of J. C. Welch.[266]

Brokerage

Crowley's first clean rice brokerage firm was the Rice Millers and Growers Association, organized in 1898. Officers and directors were L. E. Robinson, C. A. McCoy, A. B. Allison, C. A. Lowry, John Green, J. P. Haber, C. S. Morse, Miron Abbott, C. J. Freeland, H. C. Lake and J. Frankel. The firm had office rooms over the Signal and Toler buildings. John Green was general manager.[267]

The world's largest rice brokerage firm, organized in Acadia Parish in 1904, went out of business after two and a half years of operation. This was the American Brokerage Co., which during its brief life had expanded to include offices in six of the country's largest cities: San Francisco, Charleston, New Orleans, Chicago, New York and St. Louis.

The original incorporators included Miron Abbott, John Green, J. D. Marks, J. F. Christman, W. E. Ellis, J. B. Foley, J. Frankel, J. A. Sabatier, A. B. Allison, W. E. Larson, Jules Mauboules, C. J. Freeland, P. S. Lovell, Dan Blum, W. H. Hunter Jr., W. W. Duson and P. B. Lang.

The company occupied a suite of eight rooms in the Toler building over the First National Bank. James C. Harvey was the first office manager; others were A. B. Allison, James L. Wright and Fleet Coleman. W. E. Trotter was in charge of the San Francisco office.[268]

The Louisiana Commission Co., dealt only in rough rice. Officers of the firm, organized in 1902, were John Green, J. Frankel, P. B. Lang and D. S. Loeb.[269]

Both clean and rough rice were bought and sold by the Crowley Rice Exchange, which went into business in 1904. Officers and directors were Charles J. Bier, Miron Abbott, Wade D. Marshall, J. F. Christman, John Green, W. H. Hunter, A. B. Allison and T. B. Freeland. The business was operated for less than two months. A rough rice exchange by the same name was operated in 1908 by L. A. Williams and Wade Marshall.[270]

Promotion

Forerunner to today's Rice Council of America was the Rice Association of America, the aims and objectives of which were to promote rice as a food. The association sponsored a Rice Kitchen at the St. Louis Fair

[266] *Daily Signal*, Jan. 24, 1906
[267] *Crowley Signal*, Jan. 5, 1901
[268] *Daily Signal*, July 16, 22, 1904; June 2, Dec. 16, 1905; Dec. 18, 1906
[269] *Ibid*, Mar. 15, 1902
[270] *Ibid*, Apr. 30, June 10, 1904; *Crowley Signal*, June 6, 1908

in 1904. Locke Breaux, well-known rice buyer of New Orleans, was chairman of the Rice Kitchen committee, which selected Charles D. McAyeal, Crowley hardware dealer, to manage the promotional facility in St. Louis during the great exposition.[271]

Another project to promote rice as food was a book of rice recipes published in 1910. The cookbook, titled "The Creole Mammy Cook Book," had a picture of a colored "mammy" on the cover. The model for the "mammy" was the nurse employed to help care for the children in the family of Dr. M. L. Hoffpauir. The cookbook was said to be in great demand. A Crowley photographer, E. W. Ewing, made picture postcards of the "mammy" (unidentified by name) which were used to promote sales of the cookbook.[272]

All branches of the rice industry in Acadia Parish shared in supporting these promotion schemes. In 1916, when the first talk came up of putting a nationwide advertising campaign, the Freeland brothers and A. Kaplan were the first to put up money.[273]

Mechanization

Motorized farm implements, other than thresher machinery, began to come into use in Acadia Parish about 1910. One such implement was a three-horsepower binder engine tested that year on the Jay Freeland farm. The engine was attached to the binder for the purpose of propelling the machinery only, not hauling the machine. Farmer Freeland bought the engine; he said he had been using six and seven mules to work the binder; with the engine he could get by with three. Large gas traction engines to do plowing and general farm work were introduced the following year. The machine could do the work in one fourth the time; 20 acres could be plowed in a day, at half the expense of mule power. Within a few years 20-horsepower tractors that could pull two six-foot binders were in use, also rotary tillers that could do the work of three old-style tillers.[274]

By-Products

A recurring dream of manufacturing paper from rice straw began in Acadia Parish in 1900, when the Duson brothers attempted to get a paper manufacturing plant for Crowley. The Dusons claimed that they had commissioned experiments that demonstrated that rice straw could be used to make a good grade of paper. The brothers were successful in getting some northern capitalists interested in the plan,[275] but the plant

[271] *Daily Signal*, Mar. 5, Apr. 23, 1904
[272] *Crowley Signal*, Mar. 12, 1910
[273] *Daily Signal*, Nov. 3, 1916
[274] *Crowley Signal*, Aug. 20, 1910; *Daily Signal*, Mar. 2, 1911; Sept. 26, 1913; Apr. 14, 1916
[275] *Crowley Signal*, Apr. 21, Oct. 27, 1900

did not materialize. Similar proposals came up from time to time over a period of some 40 years, but nothing was ever accomplished. The people of Crowley were reluctant to risk the pollution and the unpleasant odor that ordinarily goes along with such a plant.[276]

One plant using a rice by-product operated successfully in Crowley. This was the Nutriline plant, constructed on First Street in 1904 at a cost of $80,000. Product of the plant was stock feed, the main ingredient of which was rice bran from which the oil had been extracted. The operation was the result of experiments involving the use of rice by-products which had been made by F. M. Pratt of Decatur, Ill., and experts from the Louisiana Experiment Station of Baton Rouge. The oil, which was extracted from the bran by a new process, could be used for commercial purposes such as making soap. Removal of the oil from the bran prevented the feed from becoming rancid; therefore the process helped to increase the commercial value of the bran. Officers of the company, chartered as the Lawrence Feed Co., were P. L. Lawrence, F. M. Pratt, R. M. Lawrence, M. Abbott, W. W. Duson, Clem Erisman and A. B. Allison.[277]

Rice hulls, or chaff, caused industry headaches from the beginning. As early as 1890 the Rayne Town Council ordered all rice chaff removed from the corporate limits of the town because it was considered a health hazard. Some of the mills used the hulls as fuel, but this only created another problem. The Crowley Council in 1903 adopted an ordinance ordering the mills that burned chaff as fuel to "find effectual means of arresting and suppressing the soot." The whys and wherefores of the ordinance pointed out that great quantities of the rice chaff soot settled over residences, stores and premises, and created "an intolerable nuisance." Some 15 years later residents were continuing to complain about chaff cinders blowing in and messing up sleeping porches, galleries and clean clothes hung on the line.[278]

At one time during the early 1900s the price of rice was so low that farmers fed the rough grain to their livestock. This resulted in at least one animal casualty: E. T. Hoyt lost a valuable horse when it choked to death on rice.[279]

Rice flour was milled in Crowley during the critical food shortages during and after World War I. In the summer of 1919, 25 cars of rice flour were shipped from the old Eagle mill, at that time operated by Louisiana State, for export trade.[280]

---

[276] Hair, Velma Lee, "The History of Crowley, Louisiana," *Louisiana Historical Quarterly*, Vol. 23, 52
[277] *Daily Signal*, July 29, 1904
[278] Fontenot & Freeland, *Acadia, etc.* 137; *Crowley Signal*, Dec. 19, 1903; *Daily Signal*, Oct. 28, 1919
[279] *Daily Signal*, June 1; 1905
[280] *Ibid*, June 7, 1919

"The Young Octopus"

What appears to have been an attempt by one company to gain control of the entire rice industry was made in 1900. Farmers were asked to contract to sell all of their rice for four years to the American Rice Growers Distributing Co., chartered in Acadia Parish on Nov. 5, 1900. The proposal was that if 75 per cent of the rice growers would sign such contracts the company could begin operations and would be enabled to stabilize the fluctuating prices of the grain.[281]

The company was composed mainly of New York capitalists, one of whom was the world-famed financier, William K. Vandebilt. Other directors were Alex W. Hellenborg, James P. McGovern, Anderson T. Herd, William H. Dowe and Charles N. Gray, all of New York; W. W. Duson and Miron Abbott of Crowley. Some weeks before the charter was filed Herd came down from New York to lay the groundwork for the organization; C. C. Duson went with him to Beaumont to present the proposal to Texas farmers. The firm opened rough rice offices in the Toler building in Crowley with J. Frankel as chief grader. L. T. Bliss of New York City was installed as chief custodian of all warehouses in the combine. Other names mentioned in connection with activity in Crowley were Herd, W. W. Duson, Abbott and John Green.[282]

The announcement of the formation of the company aroused some strong feelings. The Gueydan newspaper referred to the company as "the young octopus" and "the rice combine" and charged the firm with "seeking to monopolize the rice trade and regulate prices to the consumer." It is not known how long the company operated, or even if it operated at all, although the Crowley newspaper reported "the big company has commenced business." A large sum of money, the amount not known, was reported to have been received by the company from New York.[283]

A proposition of a similar nature also fell through a few years later. In 1904 a man by the name of John W. Gates tried to interest rice people in another marketing plan. A meeting was held in Beaumont to organize a company which would control the output and establish uniform prices and grades for rice. Gates planned to form a stock company with a capital stock of $1.5 million; the millers, irrigators and growers were to put up half that amount, and Gates the other half. Milling companies would subscribe not less than $10,000 and canal companies $5,000. Warehouses were to be located at distributing points throughout the country. The parent company would receive a fixed commission for marketing the rice, which would be sold at a price fixed by a 15-member board of directors. Whatever rice was not sold by the end of the rice year would be bought by

---

[281] *Crowley Signal*, Oct. 6, Nov. 10, 1900
[282] *Ibid*, Oct. 6, Nov. 10, 17; Dec. 15, 1900
[283] *Ibid*

the company. The plan, it was explained, was not expected to raise the price of rice, but to make it uniform on the basis of grades, and to reduce the cost of marketing.[284]

Southern Rice Growers

Of all the efforts made to assist farmers in marketing their rice the most successful was the formation of the Southern Rice Growers Association. Since the start of the industry marketing had been controlled by brokers and middlemen who manipulated the market. The result was the producer received widely fluctuating prices for his rice, ranging from below production costs to outrageously high prices. This was said to have served only one purpose—to enrich the speculator.

The first step towards organization came in October of 1910 when some 800 farmers, millers, irrigators and businessmen met at the Opera House in Crowley to discuss ways and means to achieve better and more stable prices. Southern Rice Growers served as a sales agency; farmers signed two-year-contracts and paid 10 cents a bag commission. The organization developed into a powerful marketing concern and accomplished its goal of stabilizing the price of rice.[285]

The two men most prominently associated with Southern Rice Growers in Acadia Parish were Frank Milliken, manager of the Crowley office, and Joe Wynn, in charge of the Rayne office. In 1915 the Crowley office was moved into a historic building—the old frame structure on Second Street which had originally housed the Duson brothers real estate office. The place also served as a hangout where farmers could exchange quips and complaints about the market and the weather, and play checkers during the slack season.[286]

Rice Experiment Station

The first experimental work done by the United States Department of Agriculture in the Louisiana rice belt was in 1901 when the USDA sent Frank Bond to Acadia Parish to study artificial irrigation. A 40-acre tract on the Abbott brothers farm three miles northwest of Crowley was selected for his studies. Bond's work included studying the flow of water in the canals, the cost of construction and machinery, placement and construction of flumes, average rainfall and the rate of water evaporation.[287]

Five years later a rice experiment station was set up on the J. F.

[284] *Daily Signal*, Mar. 21, 22, 24; Apr. 1, 5, 1904
[285] Babineaux, Lawson P., "A History of the Rice Industry of Southwest Louisiana," USL thesis, 1967; *Rice Journal and Southern Farmer*, Immigration Spec., Mar. 1, 1913; *Crowley Signal*, Oct. 15, Nov. 26, 1916
[286] *Daily Signal*, June 15, 1915; interview, Lindsey Baur, 1977
[287] *Crowley Signal*, Mar. 2, Aug. 3, 1901

Shoemaker farm, just south of the corporation limits of Crowley. About eight acres were set aside for experimental plantings. A small building housed the laboratory and tools. H. E. Ney, an agriculture student from Louisiana State University, was in charge of the work. That first year he planted several hundred varieties of rice gathered by the USDA from various foreign countries in an attempt to learn which varieties were best suited for Louisiana. Ney also experimented with fertilizers for rice cultivation.[288] J. B. Dodson was the man in charge of the station in 1907, and C. E. Sellers was the official observer of rainfall and evaporation in 1908.[289]

Agricultural leaders felt the need for expanded facilities to help solve some of the problems facing the rice planter. Rice land was decreasing in productivity; there were no adequate controls of insects, rice weeds and plant diseases. Irrigation and drainage methods needed scientific study; information was needed on factors that influenced milling quality, farmers needed some answers to questions about what crops to combine with rice for successful rotation.

These needs were brought out at a meeting held in the Acadia Parish courthouse in the spring of 1908. Dr. W. R. Dodson, director of the state experiment station, was the main speaker at the meeting. Action taken included naming a committee of P. S. Lovell, Sol Wright, Dr. J. F. Naftel, Thomas Show and J. F. Shoemaker.[290]

That summer the Louisiana Legislature passed a bill, introduced by Rep. E. O. Bruner of Acadia, to establish an experiment station,[291] but it was not until the following year that any further action was taken. The Crowley Board of Trade took up the cause, another committee was named, J. G. Medlenka offered a lease on 60 acres of land on Bayou Queue de Tortue as a site for the station. The new committee named consisted of J. F. Shoemaker, C. A. Chalifour, Sol Wright, Jay Freeland, A. B. Longenbaugh and Medlenka.[292]

Acadia didn't get the station without a fight. The rice people of Calcasieu Parish decided they could use such a facility; the police jury of that parish put up $5,000. Acadia Parish upped the bid: the police jury appropriated $3,000 and Crowley citizens raised an additional $4,000. The total included the value of land given for the site. The location selected, one of three Crowley sites offered, was a 60-acre tract west of Crowley owned by L. S. Cornett and A. B. Longenbaugh. The site was said to have been chosen because of accessibility; the location was near the railroad and spur tracks, also two public roads, and the soil was typical of the rice belt.[293]

---

[288] *Daily Signal*, Mar. 24, Apr. 27, 1906
[289] *Crowley Signal*, Mar. 2, 1907; Dec. 27, 1908
[290] *Ibid*, Mar. 14, 1908
[291] *Ibid*, July 4, 1908
[292] *Daily Signal*, Feb. 18, 1909
[293] *Ibid*, Mar. 3, 29, 31, 1909

The Rice Experiment Station, about 1913. The experimental farm, set up in 1909, was located on a 60-acre tract west of Crowley. (Freeland Collection, USL)

F. C. Quereau was the first resident manager of the station, assigned there in May of 1909. A few months later he was joined by J. Mitchell Jenkins, special agent for the USDA. When Quereau, a captain with the Crowley National Guard unit, was called to active service in 1916, Jenkins was put in charge of the station, assisted by C. B. Anders.[294]

One of the many early projects undertaken by the experiment station was to find a control for a rice blight known as "straight head." This was a disease that caused rice heads to fail to fill out, so that the head did not bend over at maturity but remained straight up, thus the descriptive name.[295]

[294] *Ibid*, May 3, July 15, 1909; July 15, 1916
[295] *Ibid*, May 17, 1911

The Oil Field

Oil speculation in Acadia Parish, set off by the quick riches found at Beaumont's Spindletop in January of 1901, was begun in the spring of that year. Drilling companies were formed almost overnight and appeared to breed other drilling companies; six such companies were chartered in Acadia Parish in less than a month's time.

Within a short while men from all areas of the parish—farmers, business and professional men—became involved in oil speculation. The list of names appearing in the oil company charters reads like an early "Who's Who" of Acadia Parish.

In the months after the Spindletop discovery there was a number of reports of oil indications in the parish. Gas was discovered on the surface of the ground in lower Mamou Prairie, there were reports of similar findings at Ebenezer. A primitive gas test was devised; a stick or a pipe was driven into the earth, then removed. If gas from the hole ignited when a match was struck, the presence of oil was indicated.[1]

A different type test for gas took place at the E. Wellman farm, about two and a half miles north of Crowley across Long Bridge. A 75-pound water cooler was inverted in 10 inches of water (in a low place or in a pond), which left a vacuum in the top of the cooler about eight by eight inches. The faucet of the cooler was then opened and a lighted match applied. The trapped gas inside the cooler caused an explosion and "two bricks, one chunk of wood and part of a man's weight went up quick as a flash, much to the astonishment of the spectators."[2] The bricks, wood and "part of a man's weight" were evidently used to hold the cooler down in the water.

The center of oil prospecting interest was identified in a letter written by H. C. Wilkins of Evangeline to the *Crowley Signal.* "The find at Majuba Hill is nothing new," Wilkins wrote. He said that for 15 years he had known of escaping gas three quarters of a mile northeast of Evangeline, but until the Beaumont discovery nothing was thought of it. "Now," he wrote, "prospectors, visitors and land seekers throng the place daily." Wilkins noted that land prices in the area had advanced to $200 an acre. "We will make a summer resort of Majuba Hill, which overlooks the entire lower Mamou Prairie," Wilkins predicted.[3]

Welman Bradford, the parish surveyor, was the first to find indications of oil in Mamou Prairie. The subsequent organization of the Crowley Oil and Mineral Company, Acadia's first drilling company, was a direct

---

[1] *Crowley Signal*, Apr. 13, 1901
[2] *Ibid*, Apr. 27, 1901
[3] *Ibid*

91

Derricks sprang up on Prairie Mamou like toadstools after a summer rain when oil was discovered in Acadia Parish in 1901. The photo above shows the field at the height of production about 1905. (Freeland Archives photo)

result of Bradford's discovery. Bradford had secured an option on the land which the company later leased.[4]

W. W. Duson, president of the Crowley Oil and Mineral Company, initiated the Acadia oil rush in April of 1901. Duson went to Lafayette and successfully negotiated with Judge J. G. Parkerson, attorney for a land company, to buy 639.45 acres in Section 48, T9SR2 West, the John McDaniel Spanish land grant.[5]

Stockholders in the Crowley Oil and Mineral included Hampden Story, C. L. Crippen, Dr. F. R. Martin, Miron Abbott, Gus Fontenot,

---

[4] *Crowley Daily News*, Oct. 5, 1901
[5] *Crowley Signal*, Apr. 20, 1901

92

Thomas R. Smith, C. C. Duson, P. S. Pugh, W. F. Brooks, Welman Bradford, H. R. Silvernail, Dr. H. Chachere, Dr. D. D. Mims, W. L. Trimble, A. Jumonville and P. L. Lawrence.[6]

The contract to drill the first well was awarded to W. E. Patterson. The derrick was completed and the pipe was on hand by early June. Crowds gathered to watch when the drilling began about June 21.[7]

Another drilling company, composed of Jennings business men, acquired holdings adjacent to the Crowley tract. The Jennings people secured the services of the Heywood brothers* of Spindletop fame to do the drilling from them. The two wells went down simultaneously. Both companies began drilling the same day, with the Crowley group getting an hour's headstart.[8]

Drilling pipe broke in the Jennings well and a new well site was selected. The same thing happened to the Crowley well; after the drill pipe broke a new well was started.[9]

Work on the two wells continued for several weeks. Then, on September 21, 1901 the Jennings well gushed at 1,700 feet, establishing the first oil field in Louisiana.

The news of the oil strike was brought to Crowley by P. J. Chappuis, attorney for the Jennings company.[10]

The gusher spewed sand and oil for seven hours, until a nearby rice field resembled a black lake. Sand 12 inches deep surrounded the derrick for 100 feet. Finally the well choked itself off with sand almost up to the well casing.[11]

The report set the entire region wild with excitement. Great crowds gathered at the well site when gushing began again some weeks later. Those getting too near were showered with oil.[12]

Within two weeks after the first well came in a controversy developed between the Crowley newspapers and newspapers in Jennings and Lake Charles. The out-of-parish papers persisted in calling the oil field "the Jennings Field." The Crowley papers identified it as "the Mamou Field."**

While no one could gainsay the fact that the field lay well within the boundaries of Acadia Parish, the first well had been brought in by a Jennings-based company.

The feuding had its ridiculous aspects. The *Lake Charles American* editorialized: ". . . the attempt of the Duson tribe of Indians to rob Jen-

---

* The Heywoods later bought out the Jennings people
** The oil field was not known as the Evangeline Oil Field during the early years

[6] *Ibid*, Apr. 13, 20, 1901
[7] *Ibid*, June 8, 22, 1901
[8] *Crowley Daily News*, Oct. 5, 1901; *Crowley Post-Signal*, May 12, 1976
[9] *Crowley Daily News*, Oct. 5, 1901
[10] *Crowley Signal*, Sept. 21, 1901
[11] *Crowley Post-Herald*, May 24, 1970
[12] *Crowley Signal*, Oct. 19, 1901

nings of her oil fields has evoked a roar of indignant remonstrance from Mermentau to Laccasine. Public meetings have been held in Jennings, new companies organized and preparations made to hold the field at all hazards."[13]

Months later the Jennings newspaper tried fanning the coals. The editor of the *Jennings Times* wondered "if the *Crowley News* man is another Rip Van Winkle. He continues to call the Jennings field the Acadia field, when everybody knows that Jennings won it by right of conquest over a year ago."[14]

Crowley Oil and Mineral finally got its gusher, almost a year after the Jennings well came in. The well, less than 100 feet from the Jennings well, came in at 1:43 p.m. September 11, 1902, spouting oil 110 feet into the air. Within the year the company brought in a second well and started on a third. By the end of 1904 Crowley Oil and Mineral owned 14 producers and had started paying out handsome dividends.[15]

Other companies brought in producers. Almost every well came in gushing 2,500 to 10,000 barrels a day. One well produced 2½ million barrels in less than two years under its own pressure. The field produced more per acre than any other field in the nation and by 1905 was labeled "the greatest in the history of the oil business."[16]

The oil flowed free, unhampered by restrictions and conservation laws governing production. Each driller rushed to keep others from draining the black gold from under the land he was drilling on.

After a peak of more than nine million barrels in 1906 production began to decline. By 1909 production had gone down to less than two million barrels.[17]

The first oil field fire resulted when lightning struck a large storage tank on July 15, 1902. The fire raged for six days, attracting large numbers of the curious to the scene. On the third day one of the gushers caught fire; the rumbling and roaring column of flame and smoke shook the ground and lit up the night skies for miles. The *Signal* put out an extra, headlined "Vast Fortunes Going Up in Smoke."

Crowley livery stables ran out of carriages, buggies and horses, such was the demand for vehicles to convey visitors to the scene. Driving was hazardous; the roads were in bad condition and 10 carriages and buggies were smashed the first two days of the fire.

The blaze was finally put out by steam.[18]

A spark caused by friction from a new derrick pulley was believed to have been the cause of the second fire which erupted on August 25, 1904.

[13] *Ibid*, Oct. 5, 12, 1901
[14] *Daily Signal*, June 21, 1902
[15] *Daily Signal*, Sept. 11, Dec. 20, 1902; *Crowley Signal*, Dec. 24, 1904
[16] *Crowley Post-Herald*, May 24, 1970; *Daily Signal*, Feb. 3, 1905
[17] *Daily Signal*, July 23, 1906; Oct. 29, 1912
[18] *Ibid*, July 15, 16, 17, 18, 21, 1902

It took live steam from eight large boilers to extinguish the flames when five oil gushers took fire in 1904. The damage was estimated at $100,000. (Freeland Archives photo).

Steam from eight large boilers extinguished the fire after two days. Loss was estimated at $100,000 by Charles A. Morse and C. C. Duson.[19]

More than 100 derricks were blown down, 40 buildings wrecked and pipelines broken in a windstorm in April, 1909. Less than a month later fire caused $10,000 damage in the business section that had developed near the field.

Buildings destroyed were Dr. Trezevant's drug store, Theo Kahn's clothing and gent's furnishing; Guidry's cold drink stand; Fontenot's gambling house, J. J. Price's saloon building and contents of pool tables, cold drinks and bar; George White's barber shop and pool room; A. Taylor's cold drink and fruit stand; Pat Cosgrove's gambling house and a third pool room, the owner unidentified.[20]

Although pipelines were constructed, there were storage problems

---

[19] *Ibid*, Aug. 25, 26, 27, 1904
[20] *Ibid*, Apr. 13, May 7, 1909

that defied solution during the first years of high production. Large earthen tanks or reservoirs were constructed as well as steel tanks. Negro and Mexican labor was imported to dig the earthen tanks. At one time 300 teams were at work on the reservoirs. Even when storage capacity reached three million barrels and with the oil flowing through pipelines to Egan, Mermentau and Jennings and being taken out in railroad tank cars, storage remained a major problem.[21]

What to do about waste oil and salt water posed other serious problems for the new industry. As early as 1905 there were complaints that waste oil from the Mamou field was polluting the waters of the Mermentau. In 1906 William L. McFarlain filed suit, alleging that oil had killed trees and damaged crops on his property. The oil had seeped from earthen storage tanks into a dammed-up gully which overflowed McFarlain's land after a rain. The court awarded the plaintiff $1,000 damages.[22]

The disposal of salt water brought other headaches. The Haywoods had facilities for storing eight million barrels of salt water, but the other companies got rid of it by dumping into the Mermentau, Bayou des Cannes and tributaries at the rate of 125,000 barrels a day.[23]

The salt water damaged rice and other crops. Irate farmers held protest meetings, finally took legal action to prevent further pollution of the streams. The court ordered the oil companies to refrain from emptying salt water into streams used for irrigation during the rice growing season, from March 1 to September 1.[24]

Many lawsuits were filed by landowners seeking to retrieve some of the riches they had so blithely signed away before the field was established. Litigation in many cases continued for years.

---

[21] *Ibid*, Aug. 29, Sept. 24, Dec. 10, 1904
[22] *Ibid*, May 8, 1905; May 1, June 23, 1906
[23] *Crowley Signal*, Apr. 11, 1908
[24] *Daily Signal*, Aug. 8, Sept. 3, 1911

Crowley

Crowley: the only town in Acadia Parish that did not develop naturally; the planned, man-made town, the two-months-old upstart of a municipality that had the presumption to bid for, and win, the parish seat.

Crowley was founded by the Duson brothers, C. C. and W. W., with the support and financial backing of a group of Opelousas business and professional men.[1]

Cornelius C. Duson, called "Curley" by his friends, was the older of the brothers. A man of dynamic personality, he was one of the most influential political figures in the history of St. Landry Parish. He had high level connections all the way from the Opelousas courthouse to Washington, D.C. He was sheriff of St. Landry Parish for 14 years, from 1874 to 1888; he served a term as state senator and was appointed a United States marshal by President Theodore Roosevelt, a position he held at the time of his death in 1910.[2]

William W. Duson, less flamboyant than the popular sheriff, was a businessman of foresight and imagination. His numerous enterprises included real estate, newspaper publishing, rice farming, milling and irrigation; banking and oil speculation. At one time his holdings totaled more than $1.5 million; financial reverses caused him to end up in relatively modest circumstances.[3] During the years of parish development he donated land for literally dozens of institutions—churches, cemeteries, schools and parks—in all sections of Acadia.

Crowley was named for Pat Crowley, the contractor who graded the roadbed for the Southern Pacific through Acadia Parish. The railroad company had placed a switch, or spur tract, on property owned by Michael Coleman, and as a courtesy to the contractor had named it the Crowley Switch.[4]

The location of the Crowley Switch just west of land owned by the Dusons made the property desirable as a town site. The Dusons tried to make a deal with Coleman, but he refused to sell or trade. The town builders then persuaded the railroad company to relocate the Crowley Switch on their property on the main line east of the Coleman tract.[5]

The switch played an important role in the development of the new town, which was situated in the middle of a prairie. All of the material that went into the construction of the first buildings was brought in by railroad cars which were switched onto the spur track for unloading.

At the beginning of 1900 Crowley was about to celebrate its 14th

---

[1] Fontenot and Freeland, *Acadia Parish*, 244
[2] Summary, *Acadia Parish*, Chapter XIII
[3] *Crowley Signal*, May 14, 1910
[4] *Daily Signal*, Dec. 15, 1906
[5] *Ibid*

Parkerson Ave. View. Crowley, La.

Crowley's principal business street, Parkerson Avenue, from a photo-postcard made about 1912 or before. The wide thoroughfare was hardsurfaced in 1912, a neutral ground constructed and ornamental electric lamp posts installed. (*Crowley Post-Signal* photo)

birthday. Construction on the first building in the town site had begun January 4, 1887, barely three months after Acadia was established as a separate parish. This date has traditionally been celebrated as the birthday of the town.[6]

While Crowley's early development could hardly be described as booming, nonetheless progress of a steady and substantial nature can be noted. The greatest growth during the early years was the 1890-1900 decade, when the town gained almost four thousand residents, increasing from 420 in 1890 to 4,414 in 1900.[7]

The original area of the town, as laid out by Leon Fremaux, was exactly one square mile lying north from the Southern Pacific tracks to Northern Avenue and between Eastern and Western Avenues. South Crowley, the section south of the railroad tracks, was laid out in 1897.[8]

In 1902 the corporation limits were extended south to Bayou Blanc, and an additional fourth of a mile on the west was taken in.[9]

The first large scale extension of the city began in 1919 when P. L. Lawrence undertook the development of 94 lots. The residential area, situated north and west of the city, became known as the Lawrence Addition.[10]

Crowley's main business district built up from the Southern Pacific depot north to the courthouse along Parkerson Avenue, the extra wide street that bisects the town.

The period of greatest business construction was from 1899 to the beginning of 1903, when new and better buildings replaced many of the old structures. As new buildings went up on the avenue, the old buildings were moved into the middle of the wide expanse of Parkerson Avenue so that business could go on as usual. In February of 1903, for the first time in three years, the view down the avenue from the depot to the courthouse was unobstructed. The last building to be removed from the street was that of Chris Memtsas, the fruit dealer, whose store had temporarily occupied the intersection of Parkerson and Third Street.[11]

City Officials, 1888-1920

Dr. D. P. January was Crowley's first mayor, elected by acclamation at a public meeting held January 6, 1888, the day the town was officially incorporated. Members of the first council were Jac Frankel, Hiram W. Carver, J. T. Stewart, D. B. Lyons.[12]

---

[6] Fontenot-Freeland, *Acadia Parish*, 266

[7] *Daily Signal*, Dec. 27, 1911

[8] *Crowley Signal*, Dec. 21, 1901

[9] *Daily Signal*, Aug. 6, 1902

[10] *Ibid*, July 1, 1919

[11] *Daily Signal*, Feb. 23, 1903

[12] Unpublished research by Paul B. Freeland and Dorothy B. McNeely. All further references to Crowley officials will be from this same source unless otherwise noted.

Dr. January served 10 months and was replaced by James T. Stewart. After four months in office Stewart moved to Opelousas.

A. R. Burkdoll, the controversial editor of the *Crowley Signal*, was appointed mayor March 1, 1899. Burkdoll had carried on an editorial feud with Will Chevis, editor of the Rayne newspaper. Challenged to a duel by Chevis, Burkdoll resigned as mayor and editor and moved away.

Other mayors (to 1920) were Gus E. Fontenot, D. R. January, P. J. Chappuis, J. E. Barry, W. P. Campbell, Shelby Taylor, Dallas B. Hayes, W. M. Egan.

Mayors who served more than one term were Chappuis, mayor for four terms, 1894 to 1898, and 1902-1906; Shelby Taylor, elected to a second term in 1908 then resigned to serve as Louisiana railroad commissioner and W. M. Egan, elected for five consecutive terms of two years each.

Serving on the board of aldermen, 1889 to 1920, were: D. R. January, Mador Kahn, John Oertling, C. L. Crippen, R. N. Lyons, W. N. Milton, E. V. Rudrow, M. J. Andrus, B. M. Lambert, John Egan, T. J. Toler, J. G. Sloane, A. G. Quinn, Ben E. Black;

Dr. H. C. Webb, John Green, Hampden Story, P. L. Lawrence, W. E. Patterson, Miron Abbott, C. D. Andrus, Dr. Homer Chachere, H. E. Lewis, P. S. Pugh, Sam Irving, Aaron Loeb, A. B. Allison, L. A. Kloor, Robert McMicheal, Ben R. White, J. H. Lewis, L. H. Clark;

Louis Fontenot, W. G. Adams, W. H. Hunter, J. D. Marks, Dr. F. R. Martin, Theophas Simon, J. F. Bernard, N. John, L. V. Johnson, H. W. Lackey, E. J. Saal, L. A. Stagg, W. E. Scott, Floyd Williams;

M. Berlinger, J. W. Cheney, Dr. E. M. Ellis, T. B. Freeland, A. D. Gueno, G. R. Harmon, J. G. Medlenka, S. P. Johnson, A. Melancon, J. W. Miles, E. L. Vinet, A. F. Dacosta, Jens Nelson, D. G. Richard, J. R. Thompson, A. S. Wright, John Bethany, E. L. Savoie, Henry Newman, L. P. Gaudin, R. A. Nockton.

Aldermen serving more than one term on the council were Carver, Lyons, Rudrow, C. D. and M. J. Andrus, Toler, Loeb, Black, Clark, Egan, Lambert, Webb, Chachere, Kloor, John, Marks, Berlinger, Johnson, Medlenka, Vinet, Miles and Bethany.

A. V. Johnson, appointed in 1889, was Crowley's first marshal. J. M. Lyons, appointed marshal in 1900, was named chief of police in 1904.

Business and Commerce

By 1900 Crowley could list among its assets an electric light and water works plant, telephone service, an ice plant, an efficient fire company, three schools and a round dozen churches.

In addition there were hotels and boarding houses, three banks, a home loan company, and a number of business firms and individuals representing almost every type of merchandise and service offered at that time to the buying public.

The following, compiled from advertising and random references in the *Daily Signal*, *Crowley Signal*, *Rice City News* and *Crowley Mirror*, lists the names of Crowley trade persons, 1900 to 1905, and the occupations and services they represented. Some of the businesses date back to the town's founding and were in continuous operation throughout the five-year period, and beyond. Others stayed open for a short time only, while some changed ownership and were continued under new firm names.

Bakers: Bertrand Bazerque, W. B. Kelley, J. A. Parker, M. Plitt, A. Pefferkorn, Frank Nassans, W. D. Marshall, J. B. McAfee.

Barbers: Louis Kloor, Felix and William Lina, E. Louviere, Cliff Guidry, Rodney Roddy, Ed Lyons, A. E. Hall, L. Smith.

Blacksmiths: Henry Loewer, J. Judd, M. Kluwe, Reynaud & McBride, Quinn & Villien, F. A. Waschka, Reiber & W. C. Fleshman, Christianson & Hoag, Troy F. Ewing, F. P. Shuler.

Bottling plant: Phil Schenkel.

Building contractors: J. A. Toups, C. L. Hormell, B. F. Castain, D. T. Russell, William Davidson, Joseph Corbett, James A. Petty, McElhinney & Lewis, F. W. Steinman, Joe D. White, Henry J. Yentzen, H. J. Andrus.

Building supply dealers: Wirt Collins, T. J. Toler, Eckhardt Manufacturing, F. S. Butler, E. H. Ellis, J. A. Toups, Stewart and Lewis.

Confectioners: Mrs. E. Guidry, Charles Fields, W. C. Thompson, C. K. Memtsas, J. A. Thornton, E. V. Rudrow, Hugh Frere.

Coal dealers: Phil Schenkel, H. L. Bourgeois.

Dairymen: Wall Brothers.

Draymen: T. H. Hoffpauir, J. H. Smith.

Druggists: T. B. Hutts, Mrs. Jennie Hamilton, Paul Eckels, D. H. Emery, Chachere & Mims, N. B. Morris, W. T. Ellison.

Electricians: H. W. Thomas, G. E. Miles.

Feed and grain dealers: Naftel Brothers, Lawrence Brothers, Simon, King & Wilder; Brooks Brothers and Wolverton.

Fish and oyster dealers: Philip Candiloro, J. B. Grimaldi.

Fruit, vegetable and game dealers: Frank Memtsas, J. D. Koch.

Furniture dealers: Clarence E. Berdon, Alcee Jumonville, F. W. Heath.

Furniture repair: Joe Koko, W. A. Chachere, Pearce and J. I. Godso.

General merchandise, drygoods, clothing, shoes, notions dealers: Jac Frankel, J. A. Sabatier, Simon & Bonin, Marcus and Reisfeld, Kaplan and Blum, W. L. Doss, J. Kollitz & M. L. Feitel, A. N. Keller, Ed Martin, R. E. Hines, H. Roos, B. A. Antakly, Miller & Kaplan, M. A. Wolfson, Landau Bros., Johnson & Grehan, M. J. Daniels, J. L. Godchaux, S. R. Gerson, A. D. de Generis, W. L. Trimble,

Albert, L. A. and Ben Stagg, Sam Aldrick, H. Miller, J. Cohn, M. Sarkes, Nahmi John, G. B. Vetro, S. Joseph.

Grocers: John Hetzel, J. J. Price, S. O. McBride, S. M. Rucher, J. W. Whipple, Haydell and Sealy, L. B. Hayes, H. H. Hawkins, V. P. Hickman, M. J. Daniels, W. P. Campbell, J. Z. Vinsy, Freeman Bros., Mike Ellis, W. W. Higginbotham, T. Simon, Skolfield & Bradley, E. H. Tanner, Mrs. Alfred Martin, Phineas Foreman, H. H. Hankins, J. E. Babin, Salem Deher, Nahmi John, K. Khalid, A. Amuny, Jean-Marie Lina.

Hardware and implement dealers: J. A. McAyeal, R. A. Lagarde, T. J. Toler, Henry Loewer, B. F. Tanner, William E. Hockaday, H. W. Lanz, F. B. Coffall, W. E. Patterson, G. B. Thompson, C. C. Lyons, Stagg Brothers, Black Brothers, F. M. Joplin.

Harness and saddle dealers: D. R. Kelsey, Linus H. Walker.

Insurance men: W. M. Egan, L. R. Deputy, Guy S. Norton, Neal Davidson, J. C. Stafford, W. W. Duson, Thomas H. Lewis, Jr., J. L. Barrett, Will Egan, W. L. Burke, John F. Egan.

Jewelers: L. T. Little, J. F. Jackson, Dave C. Ferguson, Frank Vagliente, Hollins Brothers, C. F. Monaco.

Laundries: Jake Hoffman, George Key.

Livery stables: C. J. Welsh, D. E. Lyons, Luther Johnson, John R. Carter, T. L. Gardiner, Lackey & Duvall, L. S. Cornett, West Bros. & Redman, R. M. Carter, Carver Bros. & Tate, Norwood Milton.

Machine shops: Champion Iron Works, Acadia Iron Works, James Christian Foundry and Repair Shop, American Foundry and Machine Works.

Meat markets: Walton A. Lyons, C. Trahan, Harmon & Lumpkin, Hoffpauir & Spell, James Tally, George Dorr, Sam Roe, L. B. Chachere, Sigur and Ousse, Johnson & Lupper, A. O. Sigur, Paul C. Hanagriff.

Milliners: Grace Botsford, Vogan Sisters, Virgie Hutchinson, Julia Wise, Mrs. G. M. Hauks, Mrs. Louis Kernan, Mrs. Maud Farmer, Eula Luckett.

Mule dealers: Newton Nichols.[13]

Musical instrument dealers: W. C. Murrel, J. P. McGee.

Newsstands: T. J. Hinchliffe, J. T. Barrett, W. D. Marshall, Joseph Rowe.

Nurserymen: L. P. Morton.

Oil dealers (illuminating and lubricating): M. Ellsworth.

Painters, wallpaper hangers: F. S. Button, Willie and Henry Fontenot, Henry Newman.

Photographers: F. A. Vonder Heiden. E. Barnett, B. A. Barnett, A. Henno (tintypes), Pipes & White (transients).

Plumbers: F. G. Marx, F. G. Marx Jr., Adolph Paul Marx, Miles Bros., O. K. Plumbing & Electric.

---

[13] Mules were also sold at livery stables.

Real estate: W. W. Duson and Brother, A. C. Lormand, D. R. January.

Pool halls: Denis Canan Sr., George Parker.

Restaurant men: A. D. LeBlanc, M. Pizzini, C. Boquoi, A. G. and J. S. McElhenney, N. A. Dugas, Walton A. Lyons, Coles & Burns, A. Floyrn, D. T. Canan Sr., Jim Wing, C. A. Ranson, J. A. M. Clount, George Bouchez, Heinz & Burr, Simon & Bonin, John Zeller.

Saloon keepers, bartenders: Robert Mull, G. N. Gilly, John Zeller, S. Tusa, J. D. Bonin, Tom Carver, Rufus Lyons, John Schenkel, John Kristner, Jerry Cahill, J. W. White, L. A. McKinnon, Joe Lormand, V. H. Williams, S. H. Stovall, D. T. Canan Sr., J. H. Spann, N. John, C. A. Foulcart, Mike Coleman, Cornett & Boudreaux, Jake Schuler, Tom John.

Sewing machine salesmen: W. Price.

Sign painters: Frank Barry.

Tailors: F. A. Rudrow, U. S. Scarbrough, W. G. S. Harmon, Earl S. Hercherath, Tony Coro, Joseph Hayes, Harmon & Lyons, Lucian Marx, Paul Marx, J. F. Keller, Paul Barraco, Lester Lyons, D. Feldman.

Tin shops: A. M. Fontenot, Louis Fontenot, Harvey Sanders, Robert Kleiser.

Tombstone dealers: R. W. Knickerbocker.

Well drillers: L. H. Thompson, Cornett & Carter.

Wholesale firms: Green-Shoemaker, Lawrence Bros., Brooks Bros.

Wood yards: Phil Schenkel, White & Higginbotham, J. J. Bradley.

Undertakers: J. K. Toler, Stephen M. Toler, James Raney.[14]

Crowley's first bank was the Crowley State Bank, organized in 1892. The 1901 directors were P. S. Lovell, W. E. Ellis, J. M. Pintard, John Green, Miron Abbott, R. T. Clark and J. Frankel.[15]

The Acadia Bank opened for business January 23, 1899. A. M. Finley was cashier in 1902. The list of officers and directors in 1904 included J. Frankel, J. A. Sabatier, Eugene Lewis, W. E. Lawson, J. F. Morris, Jac Mayer, P. S. Lovell, J. G. Medlenka.[16]

First announcement of the opening of a third bank in Crowley was in May of 1900, and the name given was the People's Bank. The list of principal stockholders included B. M. Lambert, T. J. Toler, W. W. Duson, C. C. Duson, P. L. Lawrence, A. B. Allison, Gus Fontenot, H. Chachere, Hollins Bros., and Pat Crowley of Lake Charles, for whom Crowley was named.[17]

The name of the institution was changed to First National Bank of

---

[14] The hearse, drawn by two black horses, was provided by the C. J. Welsh livery stable.

[15] *Crowley Signal*, Dec. 21, 1901

[16] *Crowley Signal*, Jan. 19, 1901; *Daily Signal*, Nov. 11, 1902; Apr. 27, 1904

[17] *Crowley Signal*, May 19, July 28, 1900

Acadia, and opened for business on September 2, 1900.[18] In 1906 the bank bought the lot on the southeast corner of Parkerson and Second Street for $6,500, exclusive of improvements, from W. W. Duson. The property had been known as "the old Chinese restaurant corner."[19]

The bank went into liquidation February 10, 1915 and was immediately reorganized as First National Bank of Crowley. Officers and directors were W. L. Trimble, P. J. Chappuis, L. A. Williams, D. W. Thibodeaux, G. B. Thompson, C. J. Freeland, J. S. Mauboules, J. B. Foley, T. T. Atteberry.[20]

First National became a Federal Reserve institution in 1918. The capital stock was increased to $100,000 and some new stockholders, including Mervin Kahn, Alex Brown, W. A. Morgan and G. A. Kennedy, were taken in. Announcement was made in October of 1919 that the bank would erect a seven-story building and had increased its capital and surplus to a total of $300,000.[21]

Crowley's second financial institution was the Crowley Building and Loan, organized in 1893. Officers and directors in 1901 were J. G. Medlenka, J. Frankel, W. E. Ellis, W. E. Lawson, L. A. Kloor, A. Kaplan and C. D. Andrus.[22]

Crowley's first hotel was the Crowley House, the second building to be constructed in the new town in 1887. (The first building in Crowley was the Duson real estate office.) Two other hotels were erected in 1888: the Magnolia House, also called the Hinchliffe Hotel, run by Thomas Hinchliffe, and the Davis House, where J. C. Davis was the innkeeper.[23]

Other Crowley hotels in operation during the early years of the century were the Commercial, Pizzini, Vinsy, and the Manhattan Hotel. Also mentioned were the Riley House, O'Quinn House, and the Austin House, but it is not known if these were hotels catering to the traveling public or boarding houses. James Lormand opened the Rice City Hotel in 1909, and the Egan Hotel, built in 1913, was opened January 1, 1914 with George Dorr, manager.[24]

New tradespersons mentioned in print for the first time in 1905 included two new barbers, A. L. Ringuet and Sevenne Hebert; O. Dore, V. Vallien Jr. and L. B. Hayes, grocers; the Tony Kasich cafe; Beulah Myers and Blanche Hayes, milliners, Ed Smith, hardware, Abram Frank, tailor.[25]

Business notes in 1906 included the establishment of the Dave Mitchell mercantile firm; two new barbers, Phil Rettig and Felix Orgeron, and

[18] *Ibid*, Oct. 6, 1900; Dec. 21, 1901
[19] *Daily Signal*, July 16, 1906
[20] *Ibid*, Feb. 12, 1906
[21] *Ibid*, Mar. 18, 1918; Oct. 27, 28, 1919
[22] *Crowley Signal*, May 25, July 6, 1901
[23] *Ibid*, Aug. 25, 1888
[24] *Signal* files, 1900-1920; Oct. 15, 1909; Dec. 9, 1913
[25] *Daily Signal*, Jan. 9, Feb. 8, Mar. 2, 6, 23; Oct. 7, 21, 1905

the steam laundry under new ownership, R. A. Nockton and J. W. Wynn.[26]

In January of 1907 the old Pizzini restaurant on the corner of Third and Parkerson was remodeled for Paul Eckel's drug store. On April 1 Dan Blum opened a grocery store and Jac Mayer succeeded H. Roos Company in the dry goods business. At this time M. S. Favinger advertised a marble works business and Jens Nelson operated a planing mill. The five dairies supplying the town with milk were operated by dairymen named Wall, Durio, Bouillon, Dupree and Babin.[27]

The long time chief engineer at Crystal Ice Plant, A. F. Horn, took over the managership of the plant in 1910.[28]

Crowley's first cotton gin was put into operation in 1908. O. Dore was the manager and O. T. McBride the ginner.[29]

In 1912 George Key was operating a Chinese laundry in Crowley. Some of the neighborhood groceries and fruit stands were run by Joseph Khaled, Joe Cagnina, S. Saloom, William Amuny, V. Pizzalatto, A. M. Zwan, J. Raslan, Mrs. Mathilda George, Paul Karre.[30]

Three new businesses which opened in Crowley in 1912 were Central Lumber Company, Ellis G. Keller, W. E. Lawson and J. Nelson; W. T. Culpepper, jewelry, and Kennedy's. Culpepper had been conducting a jewelry business in Rayne for 10 years. Kennedy's was a branch of the G. A. Kennedy store in Rayne.[31]

Thompson and Lyons, first chartered in 1902, became Thompson-Reiber in 1913. American Land Company, organized by A. Kaplan, Jack Piloff and Dan J. Feitel, was chartered in 1913.[32]

The year 1913 witnessed the construction of three buildings which were to become Crowley landmarks: the three-story Egan Hotel, the new Methodist Church and the post office-federal building.[33]

D. P. Egan bought the long-established McAyeal Hardware in 1915, then a year and a half later sold the hardware department of his store to John F. Egan and D. M. Hills.[34]

Dominic Serio offered free delivery of fresh shell oysters from his Parkerson Avenue stand in 1915.[35]

Crowley's pioneer business devoted to the maintenance and repair of motorized vehicles was Acadia Garage, chartered in 1916 by J. T. Hinchliffe, George B. Nye and E. T. Lovell. The business was identified by a mammoth electric sign requiring 140 light bulbs to spell out the word

---

[26] *Ibid*, June 30, July 14, Nov. 12, 1906
[27] *Crowley Signal*, Jan. 26, Apr. 6, Dec. 14, 1907
[28] *Ibid*, Mar. 12, 1910
[29] *Daily Signal*, Feb. 12, 1912
[30] *Ibid*, Aug. 20, 1912
[31] *Ibid*, June 23, 1919; Oct. 22, Dec. 16, 1912
[32] *Ibid*, Mar. 31, Apr. 13, 1913
[33] *Ibid*, Aug. 20, 1913
[34] *Ibid*, Mar. 8, 1915; Sept. 15, 1916
[35] *Ibid*, Aug. 27, 1915 classified ad

"garage" in two-foot high letters. Leonard Hooker took over the managership of the battery station at the garage in 1919, the same year that E. L. Savoie bought out the business.[36]

The establishment of new businesses, stalled during World War I, was resumed in 1919. Ford Motor Company was chartered by J. A. Boggs, W. E. Lawson and John A. Finley. The firm built a two-story brick building on the corner of Fifth and Parkerson, formerly occupied by the B. Meyer and Son grocery. A new pharmacy, the People's Drug Store, opened August 1 in the Egan Hotel building. Owners were Drs. R. B. Raney, J. W. Faulk and E. J. Petitjean of Church Point. E. L. Gaudet was the pharmacist. A New Orleans firm, H. T. Cottam and Co. Ltd., bought out the Green-Shoemaker wholesale grocery, valued at $100,000. Henry L. Hautot was the new manager.[37]

Also in 1919 B. Bazerque's French Bakery was turning out 1,500 loaves of bread a day. The pioneer Crowley baker was assisted by his wife and three sons, Albert, Bertrand Jr. and Frank.[38]

A company to manufacture horse collars in Crowley was organized in 1919. C. C. Lyons was president of the Crowley Pneumatic Collar Company. Stockholders included P. L. Lawrence, T. T. Atteberry, A. F. Horn, R. L. Martin, W. W. Duson and W. H. Moore.[39]

Frontage on Parkerson Avenue, 60 by 120 feet, brought a price of $7,000 in 1919 when Southern Amusement Company bought the lot between Lyons' Tailor Shop and Blum's Grocery[40] as the location for the Acadia Theater.

Civic Progress

Prior to 1900 telephone service in Crowley was limited to daytime use. In February of 1900 the service was extended to include an unspecified number of hours at night. Cumberland Telephone and Telegraph Company bought the Crowley exchange late in 1900. The franchise had been originally granted to A. B. Pickett, and the system had been operated for four years by Luther V. Johnson, Albert H. and Linn T. Perkins.[41]

The exchange, as improved by Cumberland, had a new 500-drop switchboard of cherry wood with highly polished brass drops, 10 toll lines and five operators: two for local calls, two for toll lines, and one night or relief operator.[42]

[36] *Ibid*, July 26, Aug. 23, 1916; June 30, July 24, 1919
[37] *Ibid*, June 16, 27, July 28, 1919
[38] *Ibid*, July 9, 1919
[39] *Ibid*, Dec. 11, 1919
[40] *Ibid*, May 21, 1919
[41] *Crowley Signal*, Feb. 10, Nov. 17, Dec. 1, 1900
[42] *Ibid*, Jan. 12, 1901

At that time long distance telephone service was considered one of the marvels of the changing technology. A long distance call in 1902 brought awed comments: Jones Brothers rice mill of Crowley placed a call to St. Louis, a distance of more than 900 miles; the call went through in less than six minutes, it was reported by Ada Bailey, the toll operator. The calling party said they could hear each other "as well as if in the same city."[43]

Telephone service was gradually extended to the rural areas of the parish. In 1915 a new line, extending five miles south of Crowley, had two subscribers, J. A. Wilder and S. L. Wright.[44]

Crowley had two wire services, Postal Telegraph and Western Union, during the early years of the century.[45]

Civic improvements during 1900 included:

—The installation of water troughs for the convenience of farmers coming to town. The Dusons provided two such facilities, one in front of the courthouse on Parkerson, and another in the center of the avenue just south of First Street. The base of the 16-foot-high troughs was of brick with stone finish. At the top was a cluster of five incandescent lights. Each had three iron troughs for watering horses, and drinking places for the general public. W. W. Duson's name was on one of the troughs, and C. C. Duson's on the other.[46]

—Guidelines for the construction of plank walks were set forth by the town council as follows: boards four feet long and one inch thick were to be placed cross-wise on three two-by-four stringers, except on Parkerson, where the walks were 10 feet wide on four stringers. The ordinance providing for the sidewalks specified that when brick buildings were put up the sidewalks should be of concrete.[47]

—A street sprinkler, to wet down the heavy dust during dry spells, was put into operation in the spring of 1900; at the same time a new grandstand, to seat 300, was erected in the ball park.[48]

—A city dump ground was secured and a town scavenger appointed in October, as provided by town ordinance. Duties of the scavenger, in addition to picking up dead animals and disposing of the carcasses, included cleaning and disinfecting privies once every 60 days (unless the owner did his own work), the owner to pay the scavenger 50 cents (or $3 a year) for all privies and water closets so cleaned. The scavenger's salary was set at $40 per month. Also in October police officers, in conformity with a town ordinance, began wearing new regulation uniforms.[49]

The principal highlight of 1901 was the completion and acceptance by

[43] *Daily Signal*, Nov. 18, 1902

[44] *Ibid*, Jan. 8, 1915

[45] *Crowley Signal*, June 15, 1901

[46] *Ibid*, Jan. 20, 1900

[47] *Ibid*, July 28, 1900

[48] *Ibid*, Mar. 24, 1900

[49] *Ibid*, Oct. 13, 1900

the town council of the $21,000 city hall and market, the town's first municipal building. The two-story building, located at the east intersection of Parkerson and Hutchison, accommodated municipal offices on the second floor, and the fire department and public market stalls on the ground floor.[50]

The installation of street lights and a fire ordinance were among important actions taken in 1901. The fire ordinance prohibited any buildings on Parkerson, from the courthouse to the depot, being built of materials except stone or brick.[51]

Town jail repairs claimed attention during the early part of 1902. The jail, located west of the courthouse near the standpipe, was described as "only a frail plank affair at best." The repair work was precipitated by the escape of seven hoboes, who had been jailed on charges of drunkenness and vagrancy. Escape was effected after one of the prisoners whittled a board in two with his pocketknife. An eighth prisoner declined to go along with the escapes—his term was about up. The repair work included covering large cracks in the wall boards and the building put in such condition that "it would not be considered cruel to make parties stay in prison overnight."[52]

Extension of the corporation limits and setting up a park commission were also undertaken in 1902. The town limits were extended south to Bayou Blanc, and Parkerson Avenue was opened across the Southern Pacific tracks to South Crowley. At the same time the old crossing, about 150 feet east of Parkerson, was closed because of the new depot to be built by the railroad company.[53]

The mayor named 18 citizens to look after the town squares which had been set aside by the town founders to be used as parks and recreation areas. The four parks, which had been named for stockholders in the Southwestern Louisiana Land Company, and the commissioners appointed were:

Levy Park: John Green, W. E. Ellis, J. G. Medlenka, W. E. Lawson, A. P. Holt.

Meyer Park: J. H. Lewis, J. A. Carlisle, E. Cornwell, W. D. Jenkins, J. E. Barry.

Bloch Park: Louis Deputy, Ed Lee, Cornelius Hoffpauir.

Duson Park: H. C. Ross, J. A. Spann, I. C. Chapman, Marcel Thomas, Valsin Vallien Jr.

The appointees lived in the various sections of the town in the immediate vicinity of the parks they were chosen to look after.[54]

---

[50] *Crowley Signal*, Mar. 16, 1901; *Daily Signal*, Nov. 18, 1900

[51] *Crowley Signal*, Apr. 13, June 1, 1901

[52] *Ibid*, Nov. 2, 1901; Jan. 11, 1902

[53] *Daily Signal*, Aug. 6, 27, 1902

[54] *Ibid*, Aug. 7, 1902

Crowley Becomes a City

By official proclamation of Louisiana Governor W. W. Heard, Crowley became a city on December 16, 1903 by virtue of having 5,000 inhabitants. The census was taken by Newton Lyons.[55]

Improvement and extension of street lighting took place in 1905. The city bought 20 new street lights, bringing the total installation to 44. Another lighting improvement was noted that fall, when dark and gloomy weather brought requests from many citizens that electric current be made available for daytime as well as nighttime use.[56]

A $100,000 bond issue for municipal improvements carried almost

[55] *Crowley Signal*, Dec. 12, 26, 1903
[56] *Daily Signal*, Mar. 14, 1905

Parkerson Avenue in 1913, decorated with flags and bunting for a July 4th celebration. The street was hardsurfaced with creosoted wooden blocks.

unanimously in 1906. The proposal was to use $50,000 for a sewerage system to serve practically all that portion of the city east of Avenue F. Plans called for the sewerage to be emptied into Bayou Plaquemine Brulee north of the city. The remainder of the funds was earmarked for a $20,000 improvement in the water system, and $30,000 for a school in South Crowley.[57]

The decision to hardsurface the main business street came in 1912, when property owners on Parkerson Avenue petitioned the city council. At this time the city had 30 miles of concrete sidewalks; property owners had taken down fences around their residences as the sidewalks were constructed, thereby improving the appearance of the town.[58] The council at first chose vitreous brick as the street hard-surfacing agent, then changed to creosoted wooden blocks.[59] The improvement included installation of ornamental electric lamp posts on the neutral ground which created a "white way" at night that made Crowley the envy of its neighbors. Total cost of the improvement, borne by Parkerson Avenue property owners, was about $56,000.[60]

Palm trees, donated by the three Crowley banks, were planted on the grass-seeded neutral ground. The beautification program was continued by the Civic League which provided about two dozen more palms.[61]

The wood block "paving" was not satisfactory. The blocks swelled and warped after the first rain, and the street was constantly in need of repair. A movement to replace the blocks with concrete was started in the fall of 1919.[62]

An extension of electrical service took place in 1912. Residents of Promised Land, that section of Crowley lying west of Western Avenue, petitioned the council for the service, after raising about $100 to help pay for the work. The area east of Western, designated "the old colored section," did not have electrical current at the time.[63]

Public dance halls in Crowley were closed down by action of the city council in 1914. At the same time metal flues were condemned as fire hazards. A city ordinance made it mandatory that brick or stone be used instead of the metal.[64]

Progress in Crowley, as elsewhere, came to a standstill during World War I years. Post-war recovery was slow, due to the drastic drop in the price of rice in 1919.[65]

---

[57] *Ibid*, Nov. 5, 1906
[58] *Ibid*, Feb. 7, 1912; Jan. 25, 30, 1911
[59] *Ibid*, Feb. 7, Apr. 23, 1912
[60] *Ibid*, Nov. 21, 1912; editorial, Oct. 24, 1919
[61] *Ibid*, Apr. 17, 1913; Mar. 10, 1916
[62] *Ibid*, editorial, Oct. 24, 1919
[63] *Ibid*, Feb. 10, 1912
[64] *Ibid*, Nov. 26, 1914
[65] Interviews, Lindsay Baur, J. J. Cassidy, 1978

Firemen and Fires

Until 1901 when the city hall was completed, the Crowley Fire Department was quartered on Fifth Street, between Parkerson and Avenue G. When the new fire hall was dedicated in the spring of 1901 a gala celebration took place. Firemen, dressed in full uniform, paraded from the old headquarters to the new, marching to music provided by the Crowley Cornet Band.[66]

The formal organization of a fire company in 1898 had been a vital move for the protection of life and property. Risk of fire was very high, with frame buildings put up close together, rice mills and warehouses filled with highly combustible material, and the use of flammable oil for lighting and fuel.[67]

A public announcement in the spring of 1900 informed residents that "it would be no longer necessary to fire revolvers and shotguns and yell like Comanche Indians" to give the fire alarm in Crowley. Police whistles had been ordered for every member of the fire department.[68]

The following year the waterworks whistle was being used as a fire alarm, then the city bought its own fire whistle: the Union rice mill's "wildcat" whistle, which had a distinctive sound, different from anything else in the town. The whistle was installed on top of the power house.[69]

First fire alarm boxes were installed along Parkerson Avenue in 1905. The three alarm boxes were placed as follows: one in the Southern Pacific freight depot; one on a telephone pole at the Acadia Bank corner, and the third near the Vienna Bakery. Keys to the alarm boxes were carried by all policemen and were also placed at nearby business houses.[70]

Horses to draw the fire truck were provided by Crowley livery stables until 1905, when the city bought two fine draft horses especially for the use of the fire company. The horses were purchased in Missouri by E. Duvall. The first motor truck was bought by the city in 1916 at a cost of $1,700.[71]

During the early years the 30-plus members of the department were divided into four groups headed by captains. M. S. Little was listed as chief in 1904. At an election held in the fall of 1904 John Mallett was named chief, G. E. Miles assistant chief, Phil A. Goldstein second assistant and W. J. Miles captain of division 4. Wesley Miles became the new fire chief in 1911.[72]

---

[66] *Crowley Signal*, Apr. 6, 1901
[67] McNeely, Dorothy B., "New Fire Department Celebrated July 4th, 1899." *Crowley Post-Signal*, July 3, 1977
[68] *Crowley Signal*, Apr. 28, 1900
[69] *Ibid*, Apr. 6, 1901; May 16, 1903
[70] *Ibid*, Dec. 16, 1905
[71] *Crowley Signal*, Oct. 7, 1905; *Daily Signal*, Aug. 26, 1916
[72] Daily Signal, June 11, 1904; Apr. 4, 1911; *Crowley Signal*, Sept. 14, 1904

Central Fire Station, about 1913. At left is the standpipe, the metal reservior that held the city's water supply.

A new two-story fire station was built in 1912. The frame building was located at the corner of Hutchinson and Court Circle.[73]

There were no major fires in Crowley in 1900 and only one in 1901 when James Christian's machine shop was destroyed, resulting in a loss of $3,500.[74]

Three fires were reported in 1902. Freeman Brothers grocery on Parkerson and the Austin House, a boarding place run by Mrs. Lizzie Chan, burned in the spring. A loss of $7,000 was sustained when fire destroyed the West Brothers and Redman livery, corner of Third and Avenue G, and damaged Acadia Iron Works and Black Brothers buildings.[75]

A warehouse, photography studio and a large store building went up

[73] *Daily Signal*, May 16, 1912
[74] *Crowley Signal*, Aug. 31, 1901
[75] *Crowley Signal*, Mar. 1, 1902; *Daily Signal*, Mar. 18, May 20, 1902

in flames in 1903. The warehouse belonged to Brooks Brothers and the loss was estimated at $16,000. The second fire burned the Acadia Bakery, Barnett's Studio and the T. J. Toler building and damaged several other structures.[76]

Crowley firemen fought at least eight bad fires in 1904. Buildings burned included a Chinese restaurant, tailor shop, Nassan's bakery, Felix Lina's barber shop, Toler lumber yard, L. S. Cornett livery, McBride and Reynaud blacksmith shop and the Button paint store. Damage was lighter in 1905. John Hetzel's grocery store and an unoccupied residence belonging to Dr. F. R. Martin were the only two fires reported.[77]

The Hunter rice mill burned in 1907, a loss of $100,000, and a $25,000 loss resulted when the Abbott pumping plant was destroyed. That same year five buildings in west Crowley went up in flames. One was a large building formerly owned by Marcel Thomas. The other four belonged to J. G. Medlenka.[78]

Fires caused damages estimated at almost $100,000 in 1908. The greatest loss, $80,000, was in the fall when the American rice mill burned. Other buildings burned that year included an unoccupied residence owned by H. M. Bone; eight small buildings owned by M. D. Coleman and a two-story structure belonging to J. A. Spann.[79]

Fires in 1909 took a heavy toll. A late January fire destroyed the W. W. Duson mansion, built in 1904 at a cost of $16,000. In the fall fire erupted after an explosion in the power plant, destroying the plant and leaving the city without lights and water. Damage was estimated at $20,000. Later in the year three buildings, occupied by Toler lumber yard, S. M. Toler undertaking parlor and W. C. Danum's tin shop burned, causing a loss of $13,250.[80]

The only fire of any consequence reported during 1910 and 1911 was when the N. John and Brothers store, corner of Second Street and Avenue F., burned down in March of 1911.[81]

Three fires caused losses of more than $60,000 in 1912. The Brooks and Clark warehouse, two freight cars and 6,000 bags of rice burned in February. In October six frame structures, including the N. John and Brothers saloon and small store on Avenue B and Second, a second saloon and three restaurants were burned. The John saloon, rebuilt immediately on the same site, burned for the second time three weeks later.[82]

The city was free of large fires for almost two and one half years.

[76] *Crowley Signal*, May 16, 1903; Jan. 2, 1904
[77] *Daily Signal*, Aug. 1, 3, 1904; May 5, July 4, 1905; *Crowley Signal*, Nov. 26, 1904
[78] *Crowley Signal*, Feb. 23, Apr. 20, 1907
[79] *Ibid*, Jan. 4, Oct. 3, 1908
[80] *Daily Signal*, Feb. 1, Sept. 20, Dec. 6, 1909
[81] *Ibid*, Mar. 9, 1911
[82] *Ibid*, Feb. 10, Oct. 3, Nov. 21, 1912

The W. W. Duson mansion, destroyed by fire in 1909. The residence, typical of many built in Crowley during the period, was built in 1904.

Then in 1915 three businesses were burned out—Marx tailor shop, Ringuet's barber shop and Graham Meyer's variety store.[83]

Firemen fought two major fires in 1916 and one in 1917. Buildings burned in 1916 were the Jens Nelsons's sash and blind business at First and Avenue E., and the A. M. Zwan home and store on west Hutchinson. The Jay Freeland home was burned in December of 1917.[84]

Post Office

Jac Frankel, Crowley's first merchant, was also the town's first

[83] *Ibid*, May 20, 1915
[84] *Ibid*, May 9, Dec. 4, 1916; Dec. 11, 1917

postmaster. The register of postmasters shows Frankel appointed post-master of ''Crowleyville'' Feb. 26, 1887. An entry dated May 14, 1887 shows the name of the town changed to Crowley. Other postmasters (to 1920) were J. A. Williams, 1889; Dallas B. Hayes, 1893; Frank C. Labit, 1897; A. C. Lormand, 1914.[85]

A new two-story post office building was erected on Second Street in 1900. Postal business was transacted on the ground floor; the second floor was reserved by W. W. Duson for the accommodation of northern home-seekers. The first concrete sidewalk in Crowley was around this building, laid by Duson.[86]

The Crowley post office achieved second class status in 1901, when postal receipts for the year went well over the required amount of $10,000. Free delivery started June 1, 1903, with three carriers delivering mail twice a day.[87]

In 1910 the federal government bought property at the corner of Third and Avenue G as the site for a new post office and federal building, to cost $46,000.[88]

Rural mail delivery began in 1914.[89]

Vice and Prostitution

Despite the highly moralistic character of the church-going town leaders, Crowley had problems connected with public morality. Early in its history the town banned all forms of gambling, and violators were severely punished. Persons found keeping disorderly houses within the corporation limits were given stiff fines or jail sentences. This policy was continued until 1909 when the city council passed an ordinance establishing brothels in a restricted district. The move was based on the premise that the moral interests of the town could best be served if all of the so-called houses of ill repute were in one location, permitting easier supervision and control. Ordinance 349 provided that all bawdy houses be located in west Crowley between Fourth and Hutchinson and extending one block west of Western.[90]

The establishment of the district, which gave official sanction to the practice of prostitution within the corporate limits of the city, became the most controversial issue in the history of Crowley. A petition signed by 250 Crowley women was side-stepped by the council. A. P. Holt, spokesman for the women petitioners, told the council members that their

---

[85] Register of Postmasters, National Archives and Records Service
[86] *Crowley Signal*, Sept. 29, Nov. 3, 1900
[87] *Ibid*, Apr. 6, 1901; June 6, 1903
[88] *Daily Signal*, Mar. 31, 1913
[89] *Ibid*, May 1, 1914
[90] *Crowley Signal*, Sept. 2, 1899; Apr. 13, 1901; *Daily Signal*, Apr. 22, 1904; Mar. 6, 1912

action "was a license on crime and debauchery;" that the district "could only degrade the morals of the rising generation." If the mayor and council knew of brothels, Holt contended, then it was "their duty to suppress, not to license, more." J. H. Lewis, superintendent of schools, appeared before the council to offer further protests. Lewis reminded that "a new school house for colored (children) was right across the street from where the district was laid out." The signed petition and the two spokesmen were ignored. An appeal by H. C. Ross, minister, educator and leader of the black community, was also passed over.[91]

Some weeks after the issue was debated Crowley police raided six houses located on Sixth and Seventh Streets and arrested six women on charges of prostitution. The judge warned the women they must move to the restricted district "or get out of town."[92]

Holt, a Sunday School superintendent, was again the spokesman in 1912 when 247 citizens agitated against the district. An ordinance introduced in 1914 to outlaw the district was vetoed by Mayor W. M. Egan. Voting to close the district were Aldermen D. G. Richard, E. L. Vinet, J. W. Miles and A. Melancon. Voting to maintain the district were Aaron Loeb, J. Nelson and A. Dacosta. The action took place at the council meeting of October 6, 1914.[93]

Several of the regulations governing the operation of the houses within the restricted district are contained in Ordinance 422, adopted by the council in December of 1914. The ordinance provided that "all inmates of any house of ill fame located in Crowley . . . be examined at least once a month." The ruling specified that the cost of the physical examination and health certificate was not to be more than 75 cents, and ordered lattice work put up on the front porches of all houses in the district. Another ordinance, passed in 1917, prohibited the inmates of the district from being on the streets except between the hours of 10 a.m. and 2 p.m.[94]

Fires broke out often in the vice district. Seven buildings were destroyed in 1915, causing a loss of $20,000. The buildings included a grocery store, saloon, restaurant, dance hall and three houses. A 1917 fire destroyed two buildings.[95]

Names of the women who operated the houses were published in news stories, such as reports of the fires, fights, arrests and such. When men were involved in the fights and resulting arrests their names were not given. An example: in 1917 two men, described only as "prominent and well known" were involved in a fight and cutting scrape in the restricted district. One of the men was reported in serious condition and the other

[91] *Daily Signal*, May 21, July 7, 1909
[92] *Ibid*, Aug. 24, 1909
[93] *Ibid*, Mar. 6, 1912; Oct. 9, 1914
[94] *Ibid*, Dec. 15, 1914; Apr. 11, 1917
[95] *Ibid*, Jan. 25, 1915; July 23, 1917

wounded by a hatchet. The men were not identified by name; the two women involved were listed by name.[96]

The district was finally closed in 1918, after almost nine years of uninterrupted operation. E. L. Vinet, member of the council, gave notice at the March meeting that he intended to submit an ordinance to abolish the district. The following month the district was outlawed by unanimous vote of the council, and those concerned given 90 days in which to comply. A large area was affected by the ordinance, which covered both white and black elements of the district.[97]

Lebanese, Italian Colonies

Before the United States entered World War I Crowley had a Lebanese colony of some 60 persons and almost as many Italians. The foreign-born members of both colonies were for the most part naturalized Americans engaged in small businesses in the city, and were known as peaceable, law-abiding citizens and staunch members of the Roman Catholic church.[98]

Lebanese residents of Crowley included the families of Nahmi, Joseph, Tom, Pietro and L. John; J. A. Antakly, M., Charles and G. B. Vetro; John and B. Sarkes; Salem Deher, Emile Joseph, K. Helo, John Joseph, Joseph Khaled, S. Saloom, William, A. and A. A. Amuny Jr., A. M. and B. M. Zwan; Joseph Raslan, James Raslan, F. Hamsony, Mrs. Mathilda George, Paul Karre, Mrs. K. Kalid, A. J. Khaled, S. Karre and Mrs. Emile Reggie.

Nahmi John, native of the village of Cyro on Mt. Lebanon, was the first of his family to locate in Crowley. He came about 1898 and was joined shortly thereafter by his four brothers. All of the brothers became Crowley businessmen; by 1910 they owned six stores in Crowley. Nahmi John, the acknowledged head of Crowley's Lebanese colony, returned to the old country in 1909 to settle the family estate. He sold the ancestral olive grove on the slopes of Mt. Lebanon, where his family had lived for untold generations, returned to Acadia Parish and invested the entire proceeds in Crowley real estate and a large farm near Bayou Queue de Tortue. In 1908 John became the political leader of Crowley's third ward and served three terms on the Crowley City Council.[99]

James Antonious Antakly owned a store on Hutchinson Avenue in 1902. On October 22, 1909 Antakly had his name legally changed to James Antonious Azar. A son of this merchant, Dr. James A. Azar, achieved a

[96] *Ibid*, Mar. 24, 1917
[97] *Ibid*, Mar. 7, Apr. 3, 1918
[98] *Crowley Signal*, Jan. 8, 1910; *Daily Signal*, Oct. 21, 1916
[99] *Crowley Signal*, Feb. 1, 1908; Jan. 8, July 16, 1910; *Daily Signal*, Oct. 26, 1916

brilliant reputation for himself as the sanitary inspector for the Louisiana State Board of Health investigating hookworm disease in the state.[100]

Emile Joseph and Joseph Raslan both operated stores in South Crowley. Raslan came to Crowley about 1896; he was a brother of Mrs. Mary Khaled. John Sarkes had a large general store in west Crowley; A. Amuny and Salem Deher owned grocery stores.[101]

The Syrian-American Benevolent Association, with N. John as president, was organized in Crowley in 1910. Other officers were Paul Karre, A. J. Khaled and James Raslan. The association began with 16 charter members.[102]

At that time the Syrian (Lebanese) colony of Crowley numbered 59 persons. Of these 27 were adult males, 15 adult females and 17 children. They owned and operated 16 stores in Crowley and owned 34 separate pieces of real estate.[103]

At least one of the Italian merchants was in business in Crowley by 1900. This was Philip Candiloro, who operated a fish market and fruit store. Other early arrivals were Tony Coro, a tailor in 1901; Sam Anzolina, Joe Cagnina, Frank Guerico, Peter Tegnina, V. Pizzalatto, Joe Failla, F. Messina, Louis Pizzalatto, Joseph Cagnina, V. Y. Martorana, Charles Robello, Nick Scalco, Joe Fazzio and D. Serio.[104]

Crowley's Churches

Since its beginning Crowley has been a church-going community. By 1900 ten congregations were functioning in the town: Methodist Episcopal (South), Central Methodist, First Baptist, Episcopal, St. Michael's Catholic, Presbyterian, Lutheran, Morning Star Baptist, Jewish, and Christian (Disciples of Christ).

The first congregation and church was Methodist Episcopal (South), organized in 1887 by Rev. H. O. White. Services were held in a one-room schoolhouse. A church, built on property donated by W. W. Duson, was completed in the spring of 1889.[105]

Groundbreaking ceremonies for a new Methodist church took place on Thanksgiving Day, November 28, 1912. Montagne Brothers of Abbeville was awarded the contract on a bid of $28,380.[106]

For some 30 years, from 1889 to 1919, Crowley had two Methodist congregations. Central Methodist, known as "the northern persuasion,"

[100] *Crowley Signal*, Jan. 4, 1902; *Daily Signal*, Nov. 10, 1909; Aug. 11, 1911
[101] *Daily Signal*, Aug. 11, 23, 1916; *Crowley Signal*, June 6, 1903; Dec. 28, 1901
[102] *Crowley Signal*, Jan. 8, 1900
[103] *Ibid*
[104] *Crowley Signal*, Sept. 29, 1900; June 22, 1901; *Daily Signal*, Mar. 8, 1904; Aug. 12, 1912; May 22, 1918
[105] Fontenot-Freeland, *Acadia Parish*, 308
[106] *Daily Signal*, Nov. 29, 1912

was organized in 1889. A church was dedicated in 1892 and Rev. W. F. Abernathy was first pastor.[107]

A Baptist congregation was organized February 10, 1889 and the first church was dedicated April 3, 1892. Rev. J. B. Harrell was first pastor.[108] The church was moved to the corner of Avenue G and Fifth, across the street from its original location, in 1902. During the time of moving Sunday services were held in Crowley City Hall.[109]

Rev. James H. Spearing organized the Episcopal congregation in 1893. The first church was built in 1900 on a lot just north of the courthouse. The church was remodeled in 1916; new brick piers were installed, the structure strengthened by placing four ornamental trusses beneath the ceiling to reinforce the framework, and the edifice was painted, inside and out.[110]

The first Catholic church, a frame structure, was built in 1892 on Eighth Street between Avenues H and G. In 1900 the building was moved to property on Avenue F, between Hutchinson and Fifth. The church was a mission of the Iota church until 1897 when it was established as an independent church parish. Rev. F. Wenceslaus Geens was the first resident pastor.[111] Both black and white Catholics attended the same services. Black members used the pews in the rear of the church.

A three-story convent, to serve as a residence for the nuns who staffed the parochial school, was finished in 1902.[112]

A new $40,000 church was dedicated in May of 1912.[113]

Rev. P. Van Alfen, who succeeded Father Geens as pastor, died in 1907 while visiting his native Holland. Rev. J. H. Cartisser was pastor for two years and was replaced by Rev. A. F. Isenberg, editor of the New Orleans *Morning Star*.[114]

Priests who served as assistants and interim pastors (to 1916) included Revs. M. A. Jiamona, Emile Reynal, Charles Deviral, J. V. Monteillard, A. A. Ethier, J. A. Heil, J. W. Jansens, Leo Kerysch.[115]

The Catholic Knights of America was organized in 1902, with 50 members. The Knights of Columbus was formed April 12, 1908. When Archbishop Blenk of New Orleans came to Crowley in 1908 on a confirmation tour he was met at the depot by a delegation of Knights of Columbus, Catholic Knights of America, Altar Society and Children of Mary members.[116]

[107] Unpublished research by Rev. Paul B. Freeland, D. D. Freeland Archives, Acadia Parish Library
[108] *Ibid*
[109] *Daily Signal*, Oct. 25, 27, 1902
[110] Freeland research; *Daily Signal*, Feb. 9, 1916
[111] *Morning Star*, Aug. 24, 1978
[112] *Daily Signal*, Oct. 6, 1902
[113] *Ibid*, May 9, 1912
[114] *Crowley Signal*, June 1, Nov. 23, 1907; *Daily Signal*, Nov. 12, 1909
[115] *Crowley Signal*, Nov. 18, 1905; Apr. 18, 1908; *Daily Signal*, June 16, 1909; Aug. 28, 1911; June 26, 1912; May 2, Aug. 1, 1914; June 20, 1916
[116] *Crowley Signal*, Mar. 8, 1902; Apr. 18, May 23, 1908

View of west Hutchinson during the horse-and-buggy days. At left is a partial view of the first St. Michael's Catholic Church.

Dr. George Fraser was first pastor of the Presbyterian Church, organized in Crowley in 1889. The first church was built in 1894.[117]

The German Evangelical Lutheran Church, on the corner of Eighth and Avenue F, was dedicated March 31, 1895. The congregation was organized in 1894 by Rev. H. Gellert. Services were held in both the German and English languages.[118]

The Christian (Disciples of Christ) congregation was organized in 1898 by Rev. Claude L. Jones. The first pastor, Rev. W. O. Stephens, came to Crowley in 1901. The church, built in 1902 at the corner of Avenue G and Hutchinson, cost $3,100.[119]

Jewish residents attended services in Lake Charles until 1904, when Congregation Emmanuel was formed in Crowley. Services were conducted in the Masonic Temple by Dr. L. Warsaw of Lake Charles until

---

[117] Freeland research
[118] *Daily Signal*, Mar. 3, 1904
[119] Freeland research; *Crowley Signal*, Oct. 19, 1910; Nov. 11, 1902

1906, when Nathan Michnick became the first resident rabbi. By 1907 the congregation numbered 100 and Rabbi Michnick was holding regular services in the Masonic Temple.[120]

The Crowley Ministerial Union was formed in 1901 with six members: Revs. D. F. Wilkinson, Floyd Vaughn, J. M. Life, J. F. Wynn, F. D. Van Valkenburg and C. P. Smith.[121]

Cemeteries

The first cemetery, located near the center of the town, was moved about 1893 to what was then the outskirts of Crowley. The new location was on land that had been set aside by the town's founders for both Protestant and Catholic burial places.[122]

For many years Ellen Duson Foreman, familiarly known as "Aunt Diddie" was in charge of the Protestant section of the cemetery. She was assisted by her sister, Mrs. R. T. Clark and members of the Crowley Cemetery Association in the upkeep and beautification of the cemetery. Wrought iron fencing replaced the individual fences around family plots; driveways, paths and flower beds were laid out and all graves marked.[123]

Crowley Schools

The establishment and support of educational institutions was one of the top priorities in Crowley's early history. Within two years after the town was founded civic leaders got together and put up funds to establish Acadia College, where students could earn the equivalent of a high school education. Land for the school was donated by Southwestern Louisiana Land Company. The school, patronized by students from a wide area, was in operation for 10 years, from 1889 to 1899, at which time the three-story building was destroyed by fire.[124]

Acadia College was replaced by Crowley University School, also known as the Lewis University School, which offered high school and business courses. J. H. Lewis founded the school in 1900. Lewis headed the school until 1906, when he became superintendent of schools for the parish. Crowley University School was closed shortly afterward.[125]

By 1900 enrollment at the Crowley public school had reached 150,

[120] *Daily Signal*, Apr. 27, May 13, 1904; Apr. 10, Oct. 15, 1906; *Crowley Signal*, June 1, 1907

[121] *Crowley Signal*, Oct. 19, 1901

[122] *Ibid*, Jan. 27, 1900; Oct. 3, 1903

[123] *Crowley Signal*, Feb. 20, Dec. 10, 1904; *Daily Signal*, Apr. 16, 1913

[124] McNeely, Dorothy B., "Acadia College: Educating the Rural Louisianian," *Crowley Post-Signal*, May 15, 1977

[125] *Crowley Signal*, June 23, Aug. 11, Sept. 22, 1900; *Daily Signal*, Sept. 15, 1906

with four teachers instructing the eight grades: A. P. Holt, Daisy White, Celeste Barry and Mrs. Lou Williams.[126] Other early teachers were J. I. Johnson, Mae Perkins, Winnie Hayes, J. D. Dunovant, Eula Milton, Elizabeth Camp, Edward B. Stover, Sallie Spencer, Carrie Naftel, Edie Watson, Maggie Hunter and Mary Wynn.[127]

Plans for a new school building, to accommodate both the elementary and high school departments, were finalized in 1901. H. C. Voss was awarded the contract on a bid of $22,945. The first commencement was held in 1905 when a high school graduating class of seven—six girls and one boy—received diplomas. Graduates were Cecile Williams, Clara Carper, Genevieve Smith, Julia Wilder, Lottie Coleman, Sarah Landau and Oscar Grey.[128]

A second grade school was established in 1903, in South Crowley. Dora E. Gibson and Mary Nixon were the first teachers at the school. A new brick building to house the six grades was built in 1907, at a cost of $15,000.[129]

In addition to the early public schools and private high schools, Crowley also had two schools operated in connection with churches: St. Michael's Catholic School, and the Lutheran School. The Catholic school opened in September of 1900 with about 125 pupils enrolled. Sister Mary Clementine of the Sisters of Perpetual Adoration was in charge, and was assisted in teaching by three other nuns.[130]

During the early years black as well as white children were enrolled at St. Michael's. In 1902 Father Van Alfen, pastor of St. Michael's, reported that the nuns were instructing 200 in the white school "and 75 in the colored school."[131]

The first graduate of St. Michael's was Marie Lognion, the lone member of the class of 1903.[132]

Both boys and girls were accepted as pupils at the schools. Many were from out of town and boarded at the convent. In 1908 the faculty was composed of Sisters Mary Alberta, superior; Margaret Mary, Mary Gertrude, Mary Gobnait and Mary Lucilla. Sister Gertrude was in charge of the boys.[133]

Classes for the Lutheran school, taught by the pastor, were held in the church from about 1902 to 1914. Elementary subjects, religion and the German language were taught. Pastor-teachers during this period were Rev. H. Meibohm and Rev. F. W. Abel.[134]

---

[126] *Crowley Signal*, Oct. 6, 1900
[127] *Crowley Signal*, Sept. 16, 1899; Sept. 14, 1901; *Daily Signal*, Oct. 13, 1902
[128] *Crowley Signal*, Apr. 27, 1901; *Daily Signal*, May 17, 1905
[129] *Crowley Signal*, June 6, 1903; Nov. 23, 1907
[130] *Ibid*, Aug. 11, 1900
[131] *Ibid*, Jan. 11, 1902
[132] Meaux, Ena Broussard, unpublished research, Ledoux Library, LSU at Eunice
[133] *Crowley Signal*, Sept. 12, 1908
[134] *Daily Signal*, Aug. 21, 1902; Sept. 14, 1909; Sept. 1, 1911; Sept. 13, 1913

Several private schools were in operation during Crowley's early years. Mrs. J. L. Irion conducted a private school in South Crowley, in 1901 and 1902. A private school for first, second and third grades was operated in 1908 by Hazel Cornett.[135] Early kindergarten classes were taught by Mrs. John T. Nixon and Miss Iberia Gassie, later by Miss Dora Jumonville.[136]

A business school, Crowley Commercial College, was opened in 1919 by J. O. Lyons.[137]

Civic Organizations

The Progressive Union was Crowley's first civic organization, formed in 1903. Officers were P. J. Chappuis, J. A. McAyeal, Miron Abbott, J. M. Pintard and Frank Randolph. The second such organization was the Crowley Board of Trade, activated in 1907. J. A. McAyeal was president and L. A. Williams secretary.[138]

The Acadia Commercial Club was organized in 1919 with W. W. Duson president and C. W. Lyman chairman of the board of directors. Forty three Crowley businesses were pledged to membership.[139]

Fraternal and Social Organizations

Fraternal and social organizations had early starts in Crowley. These included the Masonic Lodge, Knights of Pythias, International Order of Odd Fellows, Elks Lodge, Woodmen of the World, Ancient Order of United Workmen, Imperial Order of Red Men, Catholic Knights of America, all organized before 1904.

A Masonic building was erected in 1902, on property given by W. W. Duson. Located on the corner of Hutchinson and the Court Circle, the handsome building was dedicated December 29, 1902.[140]

Crowley began a campaign in 1906 to secure the Odd Fellows Home, an institution for relatives of the organization's members. In its bid for the facility the city gave 20 acres of land and $9,000 and won out over Shreveport and Alexandria. The large brick structure, located north of the city, was dedicated March 15, 1911.[141]

The first Boy Scout troop in Louisiana outside of New Orleans was

---

[135] *Crowley Signal*, Sept. 28, 1901; Sept. 5, 1908; *Daily Signal*, Sept. 3, 1902
[136] *Daily Signal*, Sept. 13, 1909; Aug. 30, 1913; Sept. 1, 1914; *Crowley Signal*, Jan. 16, 1904
[137] *Daily Signal*, June 2, 1919
[138] *Crowley Signal*, Mar. 28, 1903; June 1, 1907
[139] *Daily Signal*, Mar. 21, 26, 29; Apr. 3, 1919
[140] *Ibid*, May 23, June 20, Dec. 30, 1902
[141] *Ibid*, Mar. 14, Aug. 26, 1906; Mar. 15, 1911

The Odd Fellow's Home, long a Crowley landmark. The institution, dedicated in 1911, was located north of the city.

organized in Crowley in 1911. P. A. Goldstein was the first troop leader.[142]

The Elks Lodge took over the Grand Opera House in 1919. The purchase price was $80,000.[143]

Several women's organizations of a social and cultural nature, and numerous church groups functioned during the period being studied. The most durable of the social organizations was the Crowley Woman's Club, formed in 1900.*

Autos

The first "horseless carriage" came to Crowley and Acadia Parish in

---

* The club is continuing its activities at present, 1979

[142] *Ibid*, Feb. 9, 1911

[143] *Ibid*, Nov. 5, 1919

1900. C. C. Duson owned the automobile, an $850 Foster Wagon that had a speed of 30 miles per hour.[144]

A Crowley physician, Dr. N. B. Morris, bought the second automobile in 1902. By 1907 the city could count five autos, and when the Acadia Auto Club was organized in 1909 there were 18 members on the club roster.[145]

Recreation and Amusements

Picnics and fish frys in the woods along the bayous, band concerts in Levy Park, train and boat excursions, baseball games, swimming in the irrigation canals provided recreation for Crowley's pioneers.

During the summer of 1901 W. W. Duson put up a pavilion and bath houses on the irrigation canal north of the city. Such large numbers of people went out to the bathing platform that during the 1904 season a hack, or transfer line, was established to transport bathers every evening on a regular schedule.[146]

Garden socials, with Japanese lanterns strung up for illumination, euchre and flinch parties, and indoor musicals were popular forms of home entertainment. Favorite songs of 1900 were ''My Kentucky Babe,'' ''Goo-Goo Eyes,'' and other ragtime tunes. Mrs. W. W. Duson headed the list for home talent; her services as a vocal entertainer were much in demand.[147]

The Opera House

The city's principal entertainment center, Dave Lyons' Opera House, was the mecca for thousands of patrons for 18 years. The two-story building at the corner of Parkerson and Fifth, was constructed in 1901 at a cost of $18,000. The stage, the largest between New Orleans and Houston, was 43 feet wide and 20 feet high. About 800 persons crowded the theater for the opening presentation, a minstrel show, in November of 1901. Road shows, with special scenery and orchestras, played one-night stands at the Opera House. The theatre was renovated in 1909 when Lyons began showing motion pictures.[148]

An entertainment highlight of 1908 was the presentation in Crowley of two popular road shows, Buffalo Bill's Wild West Show with Col.

[144] *Crowley Signal*, Dec. 8, 1900

[145] *Daily Signal*, Sept. 6, 1902; Sept. 23, 1909; *Crowley Signal*, May 4, 1907

[146] *Crowley Signal*, June 1, 1901; *Daily Signal*, July 22, 25, 1904

[147] *Crowley Signal*, June 30, Sept. 29, 1900; *Daily Signal*, May 24, 1904

[148] *Crowley Signal*, Dec. 22, 1900; Aug. 21, Nov. 23, 1901; *Daily Signal*, Jan. 5, 1906; Oct. 9, 1909

The grandstand and race track at the Fair Grounds in 1908. The Acadia Parish Fair provided a showcase for the agricultural products and creative works of parish residents.

William Cody in person, and "The Clansman," with the original New York cast of 40.[149]

Crowley had two other movie houses by 1909: L. B. Chachere's Wonderland, featuring movies and vaudeville, and J. M. Pintard's Electric Palace movie house. The Wonderland was sold to a company composed of G. E., Wesley and J. R. Miles, Dr. John C. Copes and W. E. Scott. The name was changed to the Elite Theater.[150]

The Acadia Theater opened December 14, 1919 under the management of B. Toler. Miss Ruby E. Holliman played organ music during the presentation of the silent motion pictures.[151]

With the majority of its influential citizens subscribing to the Protestant ethic, Crowley had less interest in horse racing than neighboring towns populated mainly by Acadian Catholics. The one early racing park in operation was on Mike Coleman's property a mile west of town near the Southern Pacific railroad. A grand stand was erected in 1902 and two-day racing events were scheduled on a regular basis. After the grandstand at the Fair Grounds was built in 1908 horse racing, harness racing and even auto racing were popular for a time.[152]

"The Rice City"

Crowley's title of "Rice City of America" originated in 1900 and from that time on was used with increasing frequency.[153]

Fish and Game

In the line of food, even the less affluent of Crowley's pioneer residents lived well. Fish and game were plentiful. All of the parish streams, before the intrusion of salt water, oil, waste and other pollutants, were fished for bass, perch, catfish and other edible fresh water fish. The swampy areas yielded bullfrogs, crawfish and turtles.

During the winter months the countryside abounded in waterfowl, such as wild ducks and geese. Birds such as doves, quail, snipe, grosbecs and papabottes (upland plovers) were plentiful in the rice fields. Professional hunters sold wild game to city markets as well as to individuals. On moonlight nights hunters could walk along the irrigation canals and shoot hundreds of wild ducks; this went on until 1908, when night hunting was prohibited.[154]

---

[149] *Daily Signal*, Oct. 28, 1908
[150] *Ibid*, Mar. 10, June 2, 7, 1909
[151] *Ibid*, Dec. 11, 1919
[152] *Crowley Signal*, Feb. 2, June 6, 1902; *Daily Signal*, Oct. 31, 1908
[153] *Crowley Signal*, June 30, 1900; Oct. 17, 1903; Mar. 9, 1907
[154] *Crowley Signal*, Feb. 17, 1900; Aug. 17, 1907; Dec. 27, 1908; *Daily Signal*, July 21, 1905

Crowley's Trees

Even though Crowley was laid out on a treeless prairie, early in its history the town was envied for the many beautiful shade trees lining its wide streets.

Planting trees, begun when Crowley was founded in 1887, was continued for several decades. During idle hours employees were sent to the woods for trees to beautify property belonging to the Duson real estate firm, and on city streets.[155]

The Bank of Acadia sponsored a tree-planting project in 1910. The bank distributed to the farmers of the parish 12,000 catalpa trees. The catalpa, or Indian bean, a rapid-growing shade and ornamental tree, was also desired because it harbored a variety of caterpillar used as fishing bait. The bank was also responsible for the planting of 500 oak trees along the streets of Crowley.[156]

Military Units

The Crowley Rifles, Company F, Louisiana National Guard, was mustered in November 25, 1902 by Gen. Allen Jumel of Baton Rouge at ceremonies held in city hall. The roster listed 41 names. The company was mustered out in 1909 due to lack of interest, then re-activated in 1915 as Company B.[157]

The company was sent to the Mexican border in 1916 when depredations by the outlawed bandit, Pancho Villa, caused President Woodrow Wilson to order the National Guard to reinforce United States troops at points along the Rio Grande.[158]

The unit answered a second call to the colors in 1918 when the United States entered World War I.

Crowley Newspapers, 1888-1920

A review of the history of Crowley's first newspaper, the *Crowley Signal*, shows that the publication changed hands several times between 1888 and 1920.

The weekly newspaper, formerly the *Rayne Signal*, was brought to Crowley by W. W. Duson and renamed the *Crowley Signal*. Duson bought the six-month-old Rayne newspaper, the first in Acadia Parish,

---

[155] Interview, Vernon Sonnier, 1977
[156] *Crowley Signal*, Mar. 19, 1910
[157] *Daily Signal*, Nov. 26, 1902; Jan. 16, 1909; Mar. 29, 1915
[158] McNeely, Dorothy B., "Pancho Villa's Border Raids Activated Company B.," *Crowley Post-Signal*, Mar. 27, 1977

Lt. Isaac B. Broussard was cited by General John J. Pershing for leading his battalion in the Meuse-Argonne drive of World War I, on November 10, 1918. Lt. Broussard was in the famed "Lost Battalion."

from George Addison and C. W. Felter on September 1, 1886. He moved the plant to Crowley, sold a half interest to A. R. Burkdoll and began publishing the *Crowley Signal* early in 1888.[159]

Duson bought out Burkdoll in 1889, then on May 30, 1896 sold the paper to L. S. Scott, who bought new equipment and started publication of the *Daily Signal* on September 1, 1898. The daily, with up-to-date wire service news, was delivered by carrier.[160] The weekly paper, composed mostly of re-used type from the daily editions, also contained columns of parish news, contributed by correspondents from a wide area.

In 1902 the two newspapers were sold to a stock company composed of Acadia Parish businessmen, including Scott, who retained 250 of the 1,000 shares issued. The purchase price of $30,000 was said to have been the highest price ever paid for a newspaper (in Louisiana) outside of New Orleans.[161]

Names of stockholders and the number of shares each owned were Miron Abbott, 50; W. W. Duson, 50; A. Kaplan, 50; J. Frankel, 40; Gus Fontenot, 10; P. B. Lang, 10; John Green, 10; J. F. Shoemaker, 10; W. E. Ellis, 20; P. S. Lovell, 20; J. E. Platt, 5; A. B. Allison, 10; C. J. and T. B. Freeland, 20; G. H. Brooks, 4; T. J. Toler, 20; E. H. Ellis, 10; O. R. Hopson, 4; W. M. Egan, 4; P. L. Lawrence, 10; W. T. Patterson, 10; Thomas R. Smith, 4; Hollins Brothers, 10; Frank C. Labit, 10; H. E. Lewis, 10; Story and Pugh, 4; J. A. Petty, 5; John A. McAyeal, 5; Ben E. Black, 5; George E. Sears, 10; J. L. Murrel, 5; C. L. Crippen, 10; J. B. Foley, 10; B. M. Lambert, 10; R. T. Clark, 5; August L. Chappuis, 4.[162]

The company also owned the *Rice Journal and Gulf Coast Farmer*, a monthly magazine devoted to promoting the rice industry and farming interests of the region; did job work and printed other publications, one of which was the *Epworth Star*, published by the Methodist Episcopal Church (South).[163]

Scott continued active management of the company until November of 1902 when he left Crowley and went to Indiana. He was replaced as editor by Frank Randolph, who had bought an interest in the company.[164]

Officers and directors of the company, elected in 1904, were Miron Abbott, W. E. Ellis, Frank Randolph, John A. McAyeal, W. W. Duson, A. Kaplan, J. Frankel, P. B. Lang, Charles Springer. At that time subscribers paid 15 cents a week or 50 cents a month for delivery by carrier.[165]

Randolph stayed with the *Signal* for three years, then left to work for

---

[159] *Abbeville Meridional*, Jan. 14, 1888

[160] *Signal*, 50th Anniv. Ed., "History of the *Daily Signal*," 1949, 30

[161] *Daily Signal*, June 20, 1902; Baton Rouge *Morning Advocate*, quoted in *Daily Signal*, July 14, 1902

[162] *Daily Signal*, June 20, 1902

[163] *Daily Signal*, June 30, 1902; *Crowley Signal*, Mar. 20, 1901

[164] *Daily Signal*, Feb. 28, 1903; *Crowley Signal*, Oct. 17, 1903

[165] *Daily Signal*, Mar. 1, 1904

the Lake Charles newspaper, returned to the Crowley paper two years later, in 1907. Meanwhile he had been replaced by first, H. M. Sheppard, then Paul J. Braud and Frank T. Nixon.[166]

When Randolph returned as editor John Nixon was made manager, a position he held only three years due to his untimely death in 1909.[167]

The newspaper plant was sold at a bankrupt sale April 6, 1912. The new owners were C. J. and T. B. Freeland and P. L. Lawrence. All three publications, the daily and weekly newspapers and the *Rice Journal*, were continued without interruption.[168]

Randolph left again in 1911, this time for good. He accepted a position as publicity director for the American Rice Growers Association, later became managing editor of the *Beaumont Journal* and *Enterprise*.[169]

Other editors and managers (to 1915) identified in the newspaper were Lawrence L. Luehm, Newell C. Nugent, Homer Clark, Marx B. Kahn, editors; J. W. Cheney and W. C. Kelly, managers.[170]

A statement of ownership published March 30, 1915 listed the Freeland brothers and P. L. Lawrence owners; J. F. Christman, editor; Matt Shaefer, business manager. The average circulation was 725. Names of the entire staff were published for the first time in the 1916 Christmas edition. The list included C. J. and T. B. Freeland, P. L. Lawrence and R. A. Nockton, owners; Otto C. Lightner, managing editor; Col. S. L. Frisbie, editor; Felix Thibodeaux, cashier; Lee Babin, advertising; Henry G. Lafleur, foreman; C. P. Pond, binding department; William J. Bellott, machine operator; T. E. Minton, compositor; William Mays, utility; Willie Navarre, pressman; Calice Trahan, assistant pressman; Eldridge Foreman, devil (apprentice printer).

The listing included the names of the carriers, Guy Lyons, Edwin Youse, Francis and Edward Webb, Frank Copes and Oren Irving, and the rural correspondents: Captain John M. Taylor, Iota; Lloyd Franques, Church Point; Ben Toler, Ellis; Mrs. Emilien Miller, Nezpique; J. P. Hoyt, Estherwood; Mattie Prather, Mowata; Alice Petry, Prosperity; Ruth Robinson, Cole's Gully; Manette Daboval, Rayne; Jake Fortner, Branch; Mrs. J. A. Broussard, Evangeline; John Sarver and Dr. C. J. Edwards, Abbeville and Vermilion Parish.

During World War I publication of the daily newspaper was suspended for a little over five months, from October 1, 1918 to March 10, 1919. Reasons for the suspension were that the paper had lost the majority of its regular employees to the armed service, newsprint was both scarce and high priced. The weekly, the *Crowley Signal*, was continued. When

[166] *Crowley Signal*, Nov. 25, 1905; *Daily Signal*, June 25, July 11, 1906
[167] *Daily Signal*, Feb. 9, 1909
[168] *Ibid*, Apr. 9, 29, 1912
[169] *Signal*, Anniv. Ed., 30
[170] *Daily Signal*, Mar. 9, July 8, 11, 1912; Apr. 27, June 23, 1914

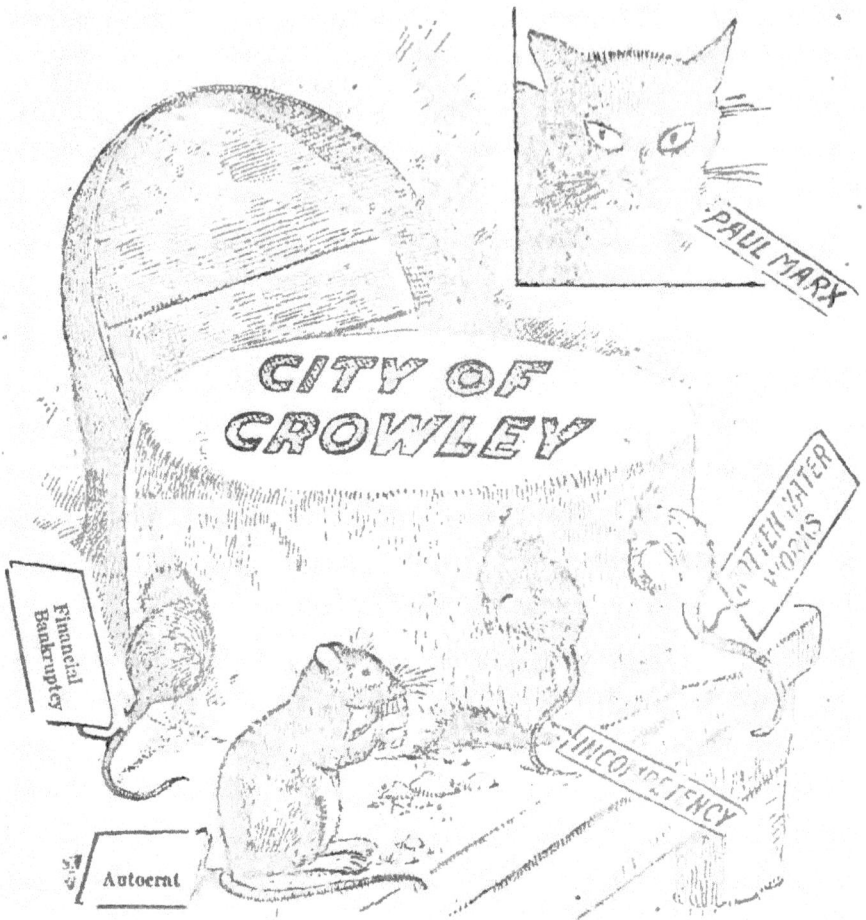

Let the Cat In!

PAUL MARX

CITY OF CROWLEY

Financial Bankruptcy

Autocrat

Political cartoon used on the front page of the *Daily Signal* of February 4, 1918 left no doubt in readers' minds as to which candidate the newspaper was backing in the mayor's race.

the daily paper was resumed the paper had a four-page format. W. B. Waddie was editor during the war months.[171]

The fourth change of ownership occurred in the fall of 1919 when the new owners, W. W. Duson Sr., W. W. Duson Jr. and H. R. Cocreham were announced. James G. Gabelle of Montreal became the new editor and J. W. Worthington the business manager.[172]

The *Signal* did not, as a rule, involve itself in partisan politics during the period under study. One notable exception was in 1918, when the

---

[171] *Ibid*, May 8, Sept. 20, 1918; Mar. 10, 1919
[172] *Ibid*, Oct. 15, Nov. 15, 1919

paper supported Paul Marx for mayor. Marx opposed the incumbent, William M. Egan.[173] Bitter enmity had developed between the newspaper management and Mayor Egan four years earlier, in 1914, when the newspaper criticized the Egan administration for failure to close the red light district, operating in a restricted area with the permission of the city council. The end result was a libel suit filed by Egan against the newspaper asking $50,000 damages.[174] The case was brought before the Louisiana Supreme Court, which ruled in favor of the defendants, reversing a lower court decision,[175] but the feuding was carried on through the 1918 municipal election.

Six other newspapers, published in Crowley between 1895 and 1915, were either consolidated with the *Signal* or phased out.

The first was the *Creole American*, brought from Lafayette to Crowley in 1895, which was taken over by the *Signal* in 1897.[176]

The *Crowley Mirror*, published twice a week, began about 1896. John T. Nixon, later to be affiliated with the *Signal*, was the editor.[177] The *Mirror* is believed to have suspended publication (or merged with another newspaper) before the summer of 1901, as Nixon was listed as editor of the *Crowley Daily News* at that time.[178] The *Crowley Daily News* stopped publication in March of 1905.[179]

The most durable of the *Signal*'s early competitors was the *Rice Belt News*, published for 10 or more years, from 1896 to an undetermined date between 1906 and the fall of 1908. Several issues of the newspaper are in the Freeland Archives in the Acadia Parish Library. The issue of April 8, 1904 was Volume 9, Number 15. The newspaper, a weekly, was published at an office located at 123 East Third Street, Crowley. Officers of the corporation were P. J. Chappuis, J. F. Shoemaker, John T. Nixon, W. E. Lawson, Thomas R. Smith and P. S. Pugh. The same company published the *Crowley Daily News*.[180]

When Nixon, the *Rice Belt News* editor, was made manager of the *Signal* in April of 1906, Louis Nussbaum succeeded him at the *Rice Belt News*.[181]

Three other newspapers made brief appearances in Crowley between 1908 and 1916. The *Crowley Acadian*, a short-lived semi-weekly, began publication in September of 1908. The proprietor was D. L. Stumps, who moved his paper to Texas after some four and a half months.[182] A weekly,

---

[173] *Ibid*, Feb. 4, 1918
[174] *Ibid*, July 3, 1915
[175] *Ibid*, Feb. 12, 1917
[176] Fontenot-Freeland, *Acadia Parish*, 317
[177] *Crowley Mirror*, June 16, 1900
[178] *Crowley Signal*, July 20, 1901
[179] *Daily Signal*, Mar. 10, 1905
[180] *Ibid*, July 11, 1902
[181] *Ibid*, July 11, 1906
[182] *Crowley Signal*, Sept. 12, 1908; *Daily Signal*, Feb. 2, 1909

the *Rice City News*, edited by Louis Nussbaum, was published for seven months in 1911-1912.[183]

The *Daily Rice City News* made its initial appearance February 22, 1915. The paper was published for an undetermined length of time by Southern Publishing Company. Dupre (first name not given) was the editor and Louis Nussbaum the publisher. Stockholders in the company included P. A. Coles, Jack Merritt, Dr. A. B. Cross and B. M. Dorrity of Shreveport.[184]

The *Rice Belt News* appears to have been the *Signal*'s most formidable competitor, possibly because the paper had some strong local backing. At the end of the 1903-1904 fiscal year the *News* was awarded the parish printing by a 7-2 vote of the police jurors; three weeks later the *Signal* lost the city printing to the *News*. The following year the *Signal* got back the parish legals by a narrow two-vote margin over J. L. Craig of the *Rayne Tribune*.[185]

Highlights in the early history of the *Signal* include the paper's first successful community service effort, in 1902; returns of the national election in 1904, and a noteworthy circulation drive in 1913.

The Christmas fund drive of 1902 was staged for the benefit of Crowley's underprivileged families. A total of $316.75 was collected, plus large amounts of groceries, toys, clothing and confections.[186]

Returns of the 1904 national election, received over telegraph and telephone wires, were promulgated in a unique manner by the *Signal*. A stereopticon* was placed on the gallery of the Toler building next to the newspaper office, and bulletins were thrown on a canvas screen stretched between the Lyons building and the *Signal* building. The crowds which had gathered in the streets to watch this pioneer effort at rapid communication cheered when the bulletins showed Teddy Roosevelt ahead for president. Extra entertainment was provided by cartoons drawn by Frank Barry. The cartoons were reproductions of comic characters and caricatures of members of Company F, National Guard.[187]

The *Signal* offered an automobile to the young lady contestant who would bring in the most subscriptions during the circulation drive of 1913. The top prize was won by Marie Picou of Eunice. Esther Toler, in second place, won a Belmore piano. Mrs. Jay Freeland and Katie Regan, in third and fourth places respectively, won diamond rings and Dora Duvall, in fifth place, won a grafonola.[188]

---

* A stereopticon is a highly developed form of the magic lantern.

[183] *Daily Signal*, Aug. 3, 1911; Mar. 8, June 25, 1912

[184] *Ibid*, Feb. 22, 1915

[185] *Rice Belt News*, July 13, 1904; *Daily Signal*, Aug. 4, 1904; July 12, 1905

[186] *Daily Signal*, Dec. 21, 24, 1902

[187] *Crowley Signal*, Nov. 12, 1904

[188] *Daily Signal*, June 2, 1913

Crowley Hospitals, Doctors

Crowley's first hospital was the Crowley Sanitarium, operated by Dr. J. E. Ludeau and Dr. E. M. Ellis. The two-story structure, built in 1901, was located on First Street four blocks east of Parkerson.[189]

Dr. Ludeau opened a second hospital on north Parkerson Avenue in 1902. The hospital, on the west side of the avenue between Eighth and Ninth, was bought in 1907 by Dr. Ellis and Dr. Z. J. Francez. The six-bed hospital had an operating room equipped with up-to-date surgical appliances.[190]

In 1912 a group of Crowley business and professional men bought the old Commercial Hotel in South Crowley for use as a hospital. The stockholders, headed by Dr. Ellis, included Dr. R. B. Raney, Dr. W. Hyde, P. J. Chappuis, J. G. Medlenka, A. Reiber, C. J. Freeland, Dr. D. D. Mims, A. S. Loeb, W. H. Hunter, Dr. M. L. Hoffpauir, T. Simon, P. L. Lawrence, J. H. Lewis, W. W. Duson and Martin Guidry.[191]

The hospital, located at the corner of Parkerson and 16th, opened in November of 1912. Mrs. B. A. Ballew was matron and Emma Cook head nurse.[192]

Barely a year later a gasoline stove exploded in the diet kitchen. The resulting blaze left the hospital a mass of smoking ruins. Five patients in the hospital were brought to safety, and additional drama was provided by the fact that Dr. Ellis was performing an operation when the fire broke out. The old hospital building on north Parkerson, then the property of W. W. Duson, was offered by Duson for use as a hospital until a permanent structure could be built.[193]

Ground was cleared during the summer of 1915 for a new hospital, at Avenue K and Seventh Street. The hospital, known as Crowley Sanitarium, opened January 15, 1916.[194] Several months later the hospital was leased to Dr. Ellis for five years. Dr. J. W. Faulk, Dr. Ellis' associate, was first assistant and had charge of the laboratory; Dr. A. B. Cross was anesthetist, Dr. R. B. Raney was head of the eye, ear, nose and throat and X-ray departments, and Dr. M. L. Hoffpauir was the hospital consultant for internal medicine.[195]

Crowley's first doctor, Dr. D. P. January, was also the town's first mayor. A native of Mississippi, he had been a surgeon in the Confederate army.[196]

The following, compiled from advertising, news items and random

[189] *Crowley Signal*, Mar. 23, 1901
[190] *Ibid*, Jan. 11, 1902; Feb. 16, Mar. 30, May 25, 1907
[191] *Daily Signal*, May 22, 1912
[192] *Ibid*, Nov. 7, 1912
[193] *Ibid*, Dec. 19, 1913
[194] *Ibid*, July 17, 1915; Jan. 15, 1916
[195] *Ibid*, July 10, 1916
[196] *Ibid*, Mar. 15, 1904

references in Crowley newspapers, lists the names of the town's medical doctors and the approximate year each began practice in Crowley:

Carroll W. Allen, 1901; E. L. Booth, 1903; W. F. Brooks Jr., 1909; L. J. Breaux, 1911; Homer Chachere, 1896; H. L. Cockerham, 1908; A. B. Cross, 1906; E. M. Ellis, 1899; W. T. Ellison, 1903; J. W. Faulk, 1916; A. H. Foreman, 1903; Z. J. Francez, 1906; Felix Guilbeau, 1906; N. B. Hayes, 1899; H. H. Hair, 1909; E. F. Hale, 1909; Dr. M. L. Hoffpauir, 1904; A. C. Hundley, 1907; R. L. Hagaman, 1891; W. R. Lastrapes, 1903; Frank Lewis, 1914; J. E. Ludeau, 1900; M. L. Lyons, 1904; R. R. Lyons, 1887; J. F. Morris, 1900; N. B. Morris, 1900; D. D. Mims, 1900; Ralph Newman, 1915; J. F. Naftel, 1887; L. C. Pulliam, Seely T. Pulliam, 1904; R. B. Raney, 1904; S. M. Scott, 1905; J. G. Thomas, 1887; T. M. Toler, 1906; A. B. Walker, 1900; E. L. Watson, 1904; J. R. Wagner, 1902; T. E. Williams, 1901; Warren G. Young, 1903.

Dentists, Veterinarians, Others

Dentists who practiced in Crowley (1887-1920) include J. A. Hines, W. F. Beatty, C. F. Beatty, Dan Beatty, J. C. Copes, R. L. Carter, A. M. Haas, H. H. Hawsey, J. F. Miller, Hugh Steadman, M. J. Woods.

Veterinarians during the period were George W. Stubbs, Thomas A. Mitchell, J. L. Tyler, H. C. Plapper, H. H. Tucker.

Opticians, osteopaths and therapeutists include Wendell Hyde and his sister, Leslie Hyde, osteopaths from about 1902 to 1906; Minnie I. Faulk, osteopath, 1915-1916; John Hathorn and his sister, Mary Maxwell Hathorn, osteopaths, 1917; H. W. Ingram, optician, 1913; J. Z. Vinsy, therapeutist, 1906.

The Black Community

Racial attitudes in Crowley and Acadia Parish from 1900 to World War I tended to reflect the reactionary feelings that came in the wake of the Reconstruction era. Even with so many of its leaders from the north and midwest the racial climate during Crowley's early history did little to promote better relationships between the races.

The black people were tolerated because they were needed. The first blacks in Crowley were brought in to serve as maids, cooks, nurses, gardeners and common laborers. Later on more were imported to work in the rice mills and as workmen in the construction of the network of irrigation systems. When the production of rice doubled and then quadrupled the help of black field hands at harvest time became a necessity.

By 1900 the growing population of black people in Crowley became a source of concern in some quarters. One published proposal was that the section of town call "Coontown" be abolished and all of its buildings—houses, stores, churches—be moved well outside the corporation limits onto land provided by the town.[197]

There were many inequities. Black persons caught committing the most trifling misdemeanors were held accountable. In 1900 the grand jury found a true bill against a black man charged with stealing 65 cents; a black women, jailed on charges of slandering a white woman, was identified by name in the newspaper; the white woman was not named. A black man was arrested for stealing one banana from a Parkerson Avenue fruit stand and sentenced to 30 days street work in default of a $50 fine.[198]

Despite having to function in this entirely white-oriented society, a number of Crowley's black residents succeeded in business and were able to accumulate sizable estates.

Commercial enterprises by blacks go back to an early date. The list of officers and stockholders of a successful all-black undertaking, the People's Investment Company, chartered in 1902, included the names of established businessmen: James A. Spann, George A. Chapman, H. C. Ross, Marcel Thomas, V. Vallien, Jr., Alfred F. Corbin, Alexander Oliver, A. R. Chargois, Adam and Joseph Glode, E. Gardner, George Wilson, Isaac Bascum, Grant Brown, Sam and George W. Easley, Reuben Gordon, John Mitchell, N. E. A. Jones, Joseph Barker, J. B. Leonard, James Harrison, Isiah Lawson, Peyton and V. Washington, Daniel N. Rhone, Ovide and V. Adams Jr., V. C., John and Stonewall Simon, Luster Barker, Jeff McElroy and S. M. Daniels.[199]

Random references in the newspapers identify several other business persons. William M. "Billy" Jacobs, a former cook at the Crowley House, went into business for himself about 1907; within a few years he had acquired considerable property in Crowley.[200] "Aunt Sally" Bias sold coffee at the courthouse for many years.[201] Early restaurant operators included Alice Thornton, Rebekah Freeman and Lilly Boutte.[202] Marcel Thomas owned a general store, sold coffins and operated a funeral parlor prior to 1905.[203]

Jake Johnson operated a skating rink in Benevolent Hall on west Hutchinson in 1906; George Chapman ran an ice cream stand, George Barker had a store, Alex Johnson was a barber and George Easley had a restaurant.[204]

From its earliest days Crowley had orchestras composed of black

---

[197] *Crowley Signal*, Feb. 10, 1900
[198] *Crowley Signal*, Jan. 20, 1900; *Daily Signal*, Mar. 4, 14, 1904
[199] *Daily Signal*, Aug. 4, 25, 1902
[200] *Crowley Signal*, Nov. 16, 1907; *Daily Signal*, July 12, 1916
[201] *Crowley Signal*, Dec. 16, 1901; *Daily Signal*, Dec. 8, 1906
[202] *Crowley Signal*, Dec. 7, 1901; Apr. 20, Aug. 31, 1907
[203] *Daily Signal*, June 26, 1905
[204] *Ibid*, Apr. 11, 1906; May 16, July 20, Aug. 20, 1912

musicians who augmented their day-time wages by playing for dances at night.[205]

The social life of the black community was usually associated with church activities. A popular exception was a cake walk, in which participants executed intricate dance steps in competition for the prize, a home-made cake. Baseball games were favorite pasttimes; the local team, the Highbinders, played out-of-town teams at Coleman's Driving Park.[206] A Knights of Pythias lodge, with 44 members, was organized in Crowley prior to 1906. H. C. Ross was chancellor commander. Courts of Calanthe, with Mrs. B. E. McClung as worthy counselor, had 25 members. An organization of Odd Fellows was active at the same time.[207]

The first two decades of the 20th century was the era when the black people of Acadia Parish—or of any other area in the nation, for that matter—got their names in the newspapers only when they were involved in crime, violent accidents and fatalities. Some notable exceptions were brief items about successful black farmers, such as, "Alex Briggs, colored farmer who raises poultry, hogs, cattle, horses and general crops, is exhibiting samples of his sugar cane at the *Signal* office . . ." and "Pep

---

[205] *Ibid*, Mar. 7, 1905; June 8, 1914; Jan. 4, 1916
[206] *Crowley Signal*, Aug. 4, 1900; *Daily Signal*, June 2, 1902
[207] *Daily Signal*, Jan. 1, Apr. 5, 1906

Scene in west Crowley about 1898, when E. T. Hoyt photographed these two small boys. A third child is shown peeking shyly around the corner of the house.

Lewis, colored man, brought the *Signal* some roasting ears from his garden."[208]

Black people achieved status in the Crowley community through association with white citizens. For example, death notices for blacks were not published in the newspaper unless there was a connection with a white family. Such an obituary appeared in the newspaper when Mrs. Callie Ball, native of Huntsville, Alabama, a former slave, died at age 72. The death notice included the information that Mrs. Ball was survived by one son, W. T. McClung, and had been employed by Dr. M. L. Hoffpauir's family for 14 years.[209] Another was the obituary for Camille Breaux, "in the service of Col. J. F. Shoemaker for 19 years . . . an antebellum type of Negro noted for faithfulness to his employer . . . an example to younger men of his race."[210]

Black people appeared to have more status in the rural regions. News items submitted by country correspondents such as the following were not uncommon: "An old colored woman, living on the Mallet, mother of Donati and Jeanbar Guillory, aged 107, is quite spry yet." "August Papillon, old and respected mulatto . . . died Tuesday. He had lived so that he gained the respect of the white and colored population around him."[211] "Don Louis Charlot, old, highly esteemed colored citizen and up-to-date farmer of Coulee Croche, reports a record-breaking corn crop."[212]

There were two reported instances during this period when black men received public recognition for heroic acts. In 1905 George Ned of Mermentau rescued Mrs. D. M. Thibodeaux and her two-year-old child from a 30-foot deep well. The child fell in the well, which had about 10 feet of water in it, and the mother jumped in to save the child. Ned heard the mother's screams, slid down the tubing of the well pump, managed to get the mother and child on his shoulders, then climbed the tubing to the surface. The newspaper account stated that Ned had accomplished a "superhuman task;" a difficult feat even without a burden, and that he should be given recognition for his bravery.[213]

The second instance was in 1914 when an aged woman came to Crowley by train from St. Martinville to visit relatives, and was saved from serious injury and possible death by the quick thinking of Sidney McClung, a young Crowley Negro, a long-time employee of A. Kaplan. Mrs. Auzemar Francis spoke only French and did not understand when the destination was called by the conductor. When she realized that she was at Crowley she tried to jump from the moving train. McClung rushed forward and lessened her fall by catching her in his arms.[214]

---

[208] *Ibid*, Oct. 10, 1911; May 19, 1905

[209] *Ibid*, June 29, 1917

[210] *Ibid*, Nov. 19, 1914

[211] *Daily Signal*, May 23, 1904; *Crowley Signal*, Aug. 11, 1900

[212] *Crowley Signal*, July 11, 1903

[213] *Daily Signal*, July 18, 1905

[214] *Ibid*, June 2, 1914

Henry Clay Ross

Considering the situation it is remarkable that any black citizen, regardless of qualifications, could have commanded respect from white contemporaries. That this did happen is a matter of record. The strong leadership qualities of a black educator, H. C. Ross, earned him a standing in the Crowley community which has not yet been equalled by a person of his race.

Henry Clay Ross was born in 1871 on a farm near Thibodaux, La. He

Henry Clay Ross
1871-1945

140

completed the equivalent of a three-year high school course at Howe Institute in New Iberia, passed the state examination for a teaching certificate and began teaching at rural schools. During the summer months he continued his education at Baton Rouge College and Leland College of New Orleans to earn certification as an elementary school principal.[215]

Ross began his long teaching career in Acadia Parish in 1899 when he was employed as principal of the one-room school for blacks located on Avenue C.[216] Later, the school with its 18 pupils and the one teacher-principal was moved to west Hutchinson Avenue. Meanwhile Ross continued his education at the Louisiana institutions and at Hampton Institute in Virginia to qualify for the position of high school principal.[217]

During the early part of his career Ross devoted a great deal of time to crusading for better school houses. He made appeals to the school board for funds for such purposes and spearheaded benefit drives among his people to secure matching funds for building, repairs and rebuilding.[218]

By 1908 the school had become known as "the Ross school." At this time enrollment stood at 256, an exceptionally large enrollment for the times. The pupils attended classes in a new school building, secured mainly through Ross' efforts.[219]

Names of graduates appeared in the newspaper for the first time in 1911. The commencement program was held in Morning Star Baptist Church; the class motto was "Not How Much, But How Well." The four graduates were Agnes B. Blackwell, Celia B. Mouton, Beatrice Lemons and Walter J. Barker.[220] Notices of graduation exercises appeared each year in the newspaper, but in only one other instance was a graduate's name listed: at the 1912 commencement, held in Israelite Baptist Church, when Rachel L. Allison was graduated.[221]

About this time (1911) the school principal's name began to appear in the newspaper with the title of professor. From that time he was called Professor Ross by people of both races. The school had continued to grow; Ross had four assistants, an experimental farm, conducted by R. U. Clark, was added for boy students to learn modern farming methods, and the girl students were being taught cooking and household hygiene. Later sewing, needlework, basketry and cooking were added to the school's curriculum, and at the 1915 Acadia Parish Fair the school captured nine first places in the category "Premiums for Colored Schools."[222]

---

[215] Family history, Jeannette Ross May, 1978
[216] *Crowley Signal*, Sept. 16, 1899
[217] Family history, Jeannette Ross May, 1978
[218] *Crowley Signal*, Oct. 13, Dec. 15, 1900
[219] *Ibid*, June 6, 1908
[220] *Daily Signal*, May 17, 1911
[221] *Ibid*, May 23, 1912
[222] *Ibid*, Aug. 31, Sept. 25, 29, 1911; Nov. 1, 1915

Ross was often cited by the Crowley press for his efforts in educating his people. The wording of the citations indicates that the black leader was a conformist, or appeared to be. This is shown by the following, abstracted from a 1909 editorial: ". . . Prof. Ross teaches the colored youth . . . that good citizenship is more important than book learning . . . Leaders . . . of the Ross type are doing much to counteract the vicious tendencies of their race and to nullify the evil influence of the educated negroes who call themselves 'Afro-Americans' and strive for the impossible social equality."[223]

It was clear that Ross was dedicated to the betterment of his people. He was also an intelligent and literate man, wise enough to realize that his efforts could not possibly meet with success unless he conformed to the established order.

One editorial tribute, paid to Ross in 1919, indicates that his achievements were responsible for the lowering of some hitherto unsurmountable racial barriers. After labeling Ross "a credit to the community" the editor felt called upon to explain such unprecedented praise: "We lose sight of the color in this instance, because the man is laboring hard in a worthy endeavor and the respect he receives is due."[224]

Ross was described in the newspaper as "a man of high character and strong influence . . . (his) standing and abilities . . . are recognized and appreciated by all who know him." He was also identified editorially as "the local Booker T. Washington."[225]

A religious man, Ross also devoted time to studying for the ministry and in 1910 became pastor of Morning Star Baptist Church. His civic achievements were many; in 1902 he was one of the organizers of the People's Investment Company, which continues to function at present (1979). Each of the original stockholders in the company put up $1.65 for a share of stock in the company, which for many years was the only source of funds available to residents of the black community for buying land, building homes and sending children to college.[226]

A street, a branch library, a civic center and two educational institutions in Crowley which presently (1979) bear Ross' name are testimonials to the high position he held in the community.

The public school for blacks has been identified with the name of Ross since the early years of Ross' teaching career. The only other school for black children was a private institution operated by D. N. Rhone which functioned for some time around 1909.[227]

---

[223] *Ibid*, Dec. 16, 1909
[224] *Ibid*, Sept. 10, 1919
[225] *Ibid*, Nov. 22, 1911; Apr. 15, 1913
[226] *Daily Signal*, Aug. 4, 25, 1902; Jeannette Ross May
[227] *Daily Signal*, Oct. 1, 1909; Jeannette R. May

Military Service

Crowley's black community provided an example of patriotism in 1917 when a Home Guard unit, composed of all black residents, was organized. Black leaders coordinated their efforts to help their country at war. A massive patriotic meeting called for November 28, 1917 took place at Morning Star Baptist Church when Dr. J. S. Clark, president of Southern University, addressed the gathering. Members of the War Savings committee, Dr. W. H. Ennis, Marcel Thomas, W. M. Jacob and H. C. Ross, held patriotic meetings around the parish to promote the sale of Liberty Bonds and War Savings Stamps. Maceo Lodge No. 22 Knights of Pythias set an example by buying $50 of the stamps.[228]

The first contingent of men to leave Acadia Parish for World War I service was a group of 29 black draftees. Preston Vallien was in charge of the soldiers, who left October 7, 1917 for Camp Pike, Arkansas for training. Arrangements for a patriotic send-off were made by Dr. W. H. Ennis, chairman; S. M. McClung, Ollie Blackwell, Harvey Jacob, Joseph Mahoney, R. U. Clark, A. G. Thomas and East Richard. The farewell program included a reception at a hall in Promised Land and talks by Dr. Ennis, Rev. Eli Jones and Rev. H. C. Ross.[229]

The soldiers were Willie Hall, Gus Cotton, Isadore White, Oscar Brown, Lloyd Lewis, Felix Dugas, Levy Landry, Oscar Henry, Paul Sinclare, Julian Cormier, Bascome Lyons and Vorice Nelson, all of Crowley; Cleveland Washington, Joe Benjamin and Ernest Mouton of Rayne; Ernest Harmon, Joseph Melancon and Joseph Edwards of Maxie; Louis Shilo, Oscar Jauden, Iota; Ofa Duplechein, Arthur Papillion, Avarare Richard, Church Point; Hany Cary, Willie Green, John Carrier, Mowata; Willie Minkin and Joseph Minkin, Egan; Edmond Guillory, Basile.[230]

In June of 1919 George Pier of Crowley was notified of the death of his son, Joe Pier, who died from wounds received in action in France. Another of Pier's sons, Wilfred, was also in service.[231]

"Coontown"

Use of the word Coontown to designate the section of Crowley populated by black residents continued in the Crowley press throughout the period under study, despite some strongly worded protests registered by black leaders. The Negro Home Guard, organized at the onset of America's participation in the war, took the lead in protesting the use of the epithet. Singing the statement of protest, which was published in the

---

[228] *Daily Signal*, Apr. 10, 17, 27, Nov. 24, 1917; June 19, 1918
[229] *Ibid*, Oct. 2, 8, 1917
[230] *Ibid*
[231] *Ibid*, June 4, 1919

Daily Signal of May 30, 1917, were Dr. W. H. Ennis, J. A. Spann, Rev. C. N. Williams, W. M. Jacob, William Shields, H. C. Ross, A. R. Chargois and R. U. Clark.

Historic Highlight

A highlight of black history in Crowley was on April 14, 1915, when Dr. Booker T. Washington visited the city. Elaborate preparations were made at a series of meetings which began six weeks in advance of the noted educator's visit.[232]

Dr. Washington spent four hours in Crowley, from train arrival time shortly after noon until five o'clock, when he was escorted back to the train depot. Lunch was served in the school house by the domestic science department girls, directed by Miss Adelle Landry. Dr. W. H. Ennis was toastmaster.

The official program was presented in the park. Dr. Washington explained his mission in Louisiana: to study conditions among his people and to try to offer some plan for the betterment of such conditions, also to work for a better relationship between the races. The distinguished guest was accompanied by a number of prominent black educators.

H. C. Ross was master of ceremonies. Others on the program included Rev. Eli Jones, Jeanette E. Ross and Arline Mitchell, R. U. Clark, Rev. A. C. Mitchell, Rev. James Patin. Others serving on the various committees were George W. Chatman, Marcel Thomas, D. N. Rhone, J. A. Spann, J. W. Hardy, George Barker, A. R. Chargois. Music was furnished by the Colored Brass Band, Prof. J. Oger, bandmaster.[233]

Several doctors practiced medicine in Crowley's black community between 1900 and 1920. Newspaper references identify Dr. J. C. Chapman, Dr. H. W. Robertson and Dr. W. H. Ennis.[234] Marcel Thomas dispensed patent medicines for many years to a large clientele composed of both blacks and whites.[235]

A civic organization with a beginning membership of 65 was formed in 1919. Projects undertaken by the Crowley Negro Civic League included the improvement of Duson Square, the public park in west Crowley; better lighting, drainage and water facilities for the western sector of the city. One of the first actions of the league was to request city authorities to curb gambling and crap shooting by young blacks. Leaders of the organization were Dr. W. H. Ennis, president; D. N. Rhone, J. A. Spann, W. M. Jacobs, H. C. Ross, G. W. Easley, George W. Barker, A. R. Chargois and Marcel Thomas.[236]

---

[232] *Ibid*, Feb. 25, 1915
[233] *Ibid*, Apr. 9, 14, 1915
[234] *Ibid*, Oct. 18, 1900; Oct. 1, 1902; Apr. 11, 1916
[235] Interview, James Pete Sr., 1978
[236] *Daily Signal*, Apr. 1, 1919

Churches of the Black Community

Seven churches for blacks were founded in Crowley between 1889 and 1920. The first was the historic Morning Star Baptist Church, organized in 1889 with Rev. Joseph Barker as first pastor. W. W. Duson donated two lots to the church in 1892. The church building, located at the corner of Third Street and Avenue B, was severely damaged by a storm in 1902. The church was active in community affairs; in 1900 Pastor Barker took the lead in collecting funds for victims of the Galveston storm.[237]

Mt. Siniah Baptist was first mentioned in the Crowley newspaper in 1900. The pastor was listed as Rev. Henry Bowles, also as Boles.[238] Other than several references in newspapers during the early years of the century information on this religious institution is non-existent.

Israelite Baptist Church was founded in 1901 by Rev. A. Oliver, the first pastor. D. N. Rhone and T. J. Williams were the first clerks. In February of 1901 it was reported that a new church building was under construction alongside the old church on west Fifth street.[239]

St. Joseph Baptist Church was founded in 1901 by Rev. J. W. Wilkins, the first pastor. Jerusalem Baptist, founded in 1902, had Rev. James Mean as first pastor and I. H. Webster as clerk. The church was first known as Little Jerusalem Church.[240]

The sixth Baptist church to be organized during the period under study was Mt. Zion, founded about 1918 by Rev. J. J. Wilson.[241]

Bethel C. M. E. Church, founded August 28, 1904, had for first pastor Rev. C. L. Davis. Presiding elder was Rev. J. C. Philips, and trustees were Henry Cooper, Henry Jones, James Young, Lewis Lyons and Jess Simpson.[242]

The Colored Protestant Cemetery Association was chartered in 1914. Charter members were H. C. Ross, J. W. Wilkins, R. U. Clark, W. T. McClung, W. M. Jacobs, D. H. Rhone, George W. Chatman, G. W. Barker, Alex Riggs, Walter Green, Elias Spincer, Joe Grogen, Van Robinson, Joe Thomas and William M. Mabry. Of the 15 charter members only two signed with an "x."[243]

The "Medlenka River" Project

A one-man crusade to make his home town an inland port was mounted in 1904 by a Crowley attorney and civic leader, J. G. Medlenka.

---

237 Fontenot and Freeland, *Acadia Parish*, 311; interview, Rev. Thomas Phillips, 1978; *Daily Signal*, Oct. 18, 1900; Apr. 14, 1902.
238 *Crowley Signal*, Apr. 21, 1900
239 Interview, James Pete Sr.; *Crowley Signal*, Feb. 2, 1901
240 Interview, James Pete Sr.; *Daily Signal*, July 19, 1906
241 Interview, Sherman Wilson, 1978
242 Cornerstone inscription, Bethel C.M.E. Church, copied by Helen Wilkins
243 *Daily Signal*, Sept. 22, 1914

A native of Houston, Texas, Medlenka came to Crowley in 1887 as the town's first railroad agent. After five years in this position he opened a mercantile business. He began studying law with P. J. Chappuis in 1896, after he was elected justice of the peace, and in 1899 was admitted to the Louisiana Bar. He was one of the organizers and the lifetime manager of the Crowley Building and Loan Company.[244]

Medlenka conceived the idea when he attended a meeting in Lake Charles of the Interstate Inland Waterway League, an organization which promoted the construction of the Intracoastal Canal.[245] Medlenka's plan was to connect Crowley to the trade markets of the world by making Plaquemine Brulee, the bayou which runs north of Crowley, a navigable stream.

A successful professional and business man, Medlenka was not a visionary. His idea of converting the bayou into an inland waterway was both feasible and practical, even more so than the artificially constructed Intracoastal Canal then being successfully promoted by Henri L. Gueydan.

Medlenka worked at the project for almost 12 years. Eventually his efforts met with a measure of success, but by the time the success was realized the forward surge of progress had diminished its value.

A 1907 published review of Corps of Engineers records (no doubt assembled by Medlenka) showed that in 1891 Bayou Plaquemine Brulee had been navigable for some 20 miles from its mouth. In 1896 the Nezpique, obstructed by snags, had been cleared and made navigable for 21 miles at a cost of $2,000. By 1907 Plaquemine Brulee was navigable only from its mouth to a point just west of Estherwood, a distance of less than half that of 1891.[246]

The published review included steamboat shipping statistics on the Mermentau from July, 1906, to July, 1907: an impressive total of 63,230 tons of rice, cotton, other farm products, lumber, cattle, hides, furs, fuel oil, logs, machinery, fertilizer and merchandise.[247]

Medlenka's first objective was to get the government to dredge out the bayou. He attended Corps of Engineers' meetings in Galveston, sessions of the Rivers and Harbors Committee in Washington, D.C. He arranged a survey trip down the bayou for the special benefit of one of the government's engineers. They travelled the route by skiff from the Roller pumping plant, thence down the bayou to Estherwood where they boarded a gasoline launch for the remainder of the trip to the headwaters of the Mermentau.[248]

The engineer agreed that the bayou was broad enough and deep

[244] *Crowley Signal*, Apr. 1, 1899; interview, Leonie Medlenka Gueno, 1978
[245] *Daily Signal*, June 4, 1915
[246] *Crowley Signal*, Sept. 21, Dec. 21, 1907
[247] *Ibid*, Dec. 21, 1907
[248] *Daily Signal*, Dec. 4, 1906; *Crowley Signal*, Dec. 21, 1907

enough for commercial shipping. He said that all that would be required was to remove the obstacles that had clogged the stream. The engineer's report confirmed that the Roller canal, about one mile west of Crowley, could be easily converted into an access waterway from Crowley to the bayou, at an estimated cost of about $22,000.[249]

In the face of apparent lack of public interest and indifference on the part of public officials, in the spring of 1908 Medlenka arranged another waterway survey, hoping to demonstrate the feasibility of the proposed improvement. A party of 12, in two skiffs, was towed from the Estherwood pumping plant to Mermentau. It was found that from Mermentau to just above the Frank Quebedeaux bridge the stream was navigable for vessels "of largest draft." From the Quebedeaux bridge to the pumping plant at Estherwood the stream was about 100 or more feet wide, narrowing at some points to 50-60 feet. The minimum depth at low water was about 25 feet. It was found that at any point the stream had sufficient depth and width for steamers like the *Olive* to navigate, provided obstructions such as logs, snags and fallen trees were removed. Between Estherwood and Crowley the stream was found to be narrower and shallower, and with more obstructions. It was estimated that the modest sum of $10,000 would pay for the necessary dredging and clearing, plus the cost of a turning basin at Crowley.[250]

A year and a half elapsed, and nothing was done. Late in 1909 Medlenka attended another inland waterway meeting in Corpus Christi and returned with renewed interest and enthusiasm. Crowley, he reported, would reap great benefit from the proposed facility. Rice, at the time being shipped by boat and barge only as far as Mermentau, would come on in to Crowley to take advantage of the three railroads there.[251]

The waterway fever died down again. Early the following year the federal government appropriated $10,000 for improvements in Vermilion Bay, the Mermentau River and Bayou Plaquemine Brulee.[252] The sum appropriated, obstensibly to be divided three ways, was woefully inadequate.

A small clamor arose that spring that could have added some impetus to the proposal. The canal companies with pumping plants on the bayou complained that they could not get fuel oil shipped in by barge, because the Southern Pacific railroad had obstructed the waterway by driving pilings in the channel. Even so action was slow in coming. A full year went by before the railroad company and the parish were officially notified that all bridges spanning the stream must be equipped with draws to allow dredge boats to pass, half of the $10,000 appropriation was ear-

[249] *Crowley Signal*, Dec. 21, 1907
[250] *Ibid*, May 2, 1908
[251] *Daily Signal*, Nov. 1, 1909
[252] *Crowley Signal*, Feb. 19, 1910

Clearing work on Bayou Plaquemine Brulee was completed in 1915 and the "Medlenka River" was opened to boat traffic. Photo above shows the snag boat near Crowley in the turning basin, where the stream was 70 feet wide and eight feet deep. (Photo courtesy C. C. Caldwell)

marked for the Medlenka project, and the Corps of Engineers agreed to another inspection tour. At long last clearing was to begin—from the mouth of the bayou above Mermentau to the Roller pumping plant, a distance of about 30 miles. Plans called for making Plaquemine Brulee navigable for vessels 130 feet and 30 feet deep, which would give Crowley connections with the Gulf of Mexico, the Intracoastal Canal and the main tributaries of the Mermentau, Bayous des Cannes and Nezpique.[253]

By October the government dredge *Delatour* had progressed to a point about half a mile above the railroad bridge at Midland. Then the funds gave out. Dredging was resumed during the spring of 1913, but frequent delays kept the work at a snail's pace.[254]

After one of the long time lags Medlenka took the engineers on another inspection tour. The party, which included P. S. and George Lovell, L. A. Williams and an unidentified newspaper reporter, made the trip from Mermentau on the *Hyacinth*, a government boat. It was a slow trip. There were still too many curves in the stream, and the channel narrowed sharply at some points, indicating the need for more work.[255]

The government boat *Grosse Tete* came down to do additional clearing in May of 1914, but got stranded at Mermentau. The dredge, said to be "the finest boat ever seen" in the area, stuck when partly through the

[253] *Crowley Signal*, Apr. 30, 1910; *Daily Signal*, Mar. 10, 1911
[254] *Daily Signal*, July 5, Oct. 30, 1911; May 28, 1913
[255] *Ibid*, Mar. 17, 24, 1914

148

An advertisement in the *Daily Signal* of June 19, 1915 announced the schedule of the *Abil,* a gasoline-powered pleasure boat piloted by Captain Atyole Quebodeaux. The *Abil* made two trips a week between Crowley and Lake Arthur.

railroad drawbridge, halting railroad traffic for a time. The government ordered the railroad to widen the bridge at once. [256]

The first tow boat to go above the Estherwood bridge was the G. B. Zigler Company's tug the *Lee,* which in mid-May of 1914 delivered 15,000 barrels of fuel oil to the Union Relift on Bayou Plaquemine three miles west of Crowley. That fall an additional $9,000 was appropriated for more clearing work.[257]

Meanwhile some shipping had been going on. The Louisiana Irrigation and Mill Company had fuel oil delivered; 5,000 pounds of oysters in the shell, the first shipment direct from the oyster beds of the Gulf, was unloaded at the Union Relift dock and hauled into Crowley markets. The stream was christened "Medlenka River."[258]

In the interim Medlenka had not been idle. As president of the Crowley Board of Trade he continued to boost the advantages of the "Medlenka River" and to solicit support for the project. "If Crowley wants more trade, we must get out and get it," he declared. He wanted a booster group to make the waterway trip and help him convince the government how badly navigation was needed. He compiled an estimate of tonnage

[256] *Ibid,* May 1, 1914
[257] *Ibid,* May 15, 1914; Oct. 20, 1914
[258] *Ibid,* June 16, Nov. 12, 1914

and value for the Corps of Engineers to determine the advisability of future appropriations. His estimates amounted to a total of 24,500 tons of rice, oil, wood, lumber, sand and shells, merchandise, fruit, fish and game valued at more than three quarters of a million dollars. At this time construction on a canal to connect Crowley to the main waterway was nearing completion.[259]

Matters accelerated somewhat at the end of March, 1915 when the first steamboat, the *Hyacinth*, reached the turning basin near Crowley. At an enthusiastic booster meeting, June 3 was set for the opening of the canal which would connect Crowley to the bayou, the name of which had been changed to "Medlenka River.[260]

Pleasure boats and commercial craft began operations on the bayou that summer. A weekend excursion on a launch owned by Captain Graham Meyers took off from Medlenka Landing at 6 p.m. and reached Lake Arthur at 1 a.m. Captain Albert Carron, piloting the sternwheeler *Lillian B.*, came in from Melville preparatory to entering into the river trade.[261]

The *Abil*, a gasoline powered pleasure boat owned by Captain Aytole Quebodeaux, advertised regular twice-a-week runs from Crowley to Lake Arthur, beginning June 24, 1915. The boat could accommodate 30 seated passengers. Fares were $1 for adults, 50 cents for children. The *Abil* left from a temporary wharf (built on land donated by A. B. Longengaugh) for the five hour trip to Lake Arthur. Passengers could take advantage of William Riley's auto service, which conveyed customers from the courthouse to the landing for 25 cents round trips.[262]

The organization of a wharf company was the next step in the development of the facility. The Crowley Wharf Company was formed by T. B. Freeland, H. M. Bone, F. M. Milliken, Dan J. Feitel and J. G. Medlenka, with capital stock set at $5,000. The company planned to put up a wharf and warehouses, and to install adequate loading devices for rice and other commodities. Plans included the establishment of a barge line by G. B. Zigler, one of the stockholders.[263]

The increase in the use of motorized vehicles for long distance hauling and improved roads helped to nullify the usefulness of the waterway. This, plus the collapse of the rice market after World War I account for the short life of "Medlenka River."

---

[259] *Ibid*, Mar. 20, 29, 1915
[260] *Ibid*, Mar. 30, Apr. 1, 1915
[261] *Ibid*, May 28, June 16, 1915
[262] *Ibid*, Apr. 1, June 9, 23, 1915
[263] *Ibid*, Aug. 5, 1916

Rayne

When Acadia was carved out of St. Landry in 1886 Rayne was the only incorporated town in the new parish. An old settlement, Rayne was first known as Queue Tortue, then as Poupeville. When the Louisiana Western railroad came through in 1880 the Poupeville settlement was by-passed by approximately one mile. The three merchants and the priest of Poupeville moved their business houses and the church north to locations nearer the railroad depot, known as Rayne Station. The town was laid out in 1880 by its founder, Dr. William H. Cunningham, and was incorporated in 1883.[1]

At the time of parish division the six-year-old town of Rayne had become the main shipping point for the southwestern portion of the mother parish. Had it not been for the pressures of politics and the activities of a group of land speculators Rayne would have become the parish seat.[2]

Crowley's founding and subsequent promotion by the land company plus its selection as parish seat of Acadia caused the new town to move ahead of the old town in growth and development. By 1900 the 13-year-old Crowley claimed 4,214 inhabitants, while Rayne, which had begun as a settlement as least 50 years earlier, could count but 1,007 residents.[3]

There are no contemporary sources of information on Rayne's reaction to the loss of the courthouse. According to local tradition some Rayne residents, among them Mervine Kahn, at that time the town's leading merchant, blamed Rayne leaders, not Crowley's promoters. Kahn said it had been an accepted fact that Rayne would get the courthouse, but at the most crucial point Rayne's civic leaders could not agree on a location for the public building. One faction wanted it located on the north side of town, while the other faction argued for the south side. Before the local leaders could settle their differences the town of Crowley was founded and had started its successful campaign to become the seat of parish government.[4]

Although Rayne was moved down to second place in the parish, it did not degenerate into a second-rate town. The Rayne community was at no time static or in a state of retrogression. The town maintained a steady rate of growth, keeping pace with other towns of its size in matters of civic improvement and population increases.

At one time Rayne forged ahead of Crowley in the degree of population increase. The 1910 census shows the town with a population of 2,247,

[1] Fontenot and Freeland, *Acadia Parish*, 111, 123, 124
[2] *Ibid*, 255-277
[3] *Louisiana Almanac*, 1973-74
[4] Interviews, Leo H. Kahn, Emile Daboval III, 1976

Dr. W. H. Cunningham
(Photo courtesy Cunningham family)

a gain of 1,240 for the 10-year period, while Crowley's population of 5,099 represented a gain of only 885 for the same period.[5]

The first hotel in the Acadia Parish area was the Stranger's Home in Rayne, operated by Mrs. George Bourdier. The parish's first rice mill, the Acadia, was built in Rayne in 1888. The first newspaper in the parish, the *Rayne Signal*, began publication in Rayne in March, 1886.[6]

Merchants and tradesmen of Rayne who were established before or shortly after parish division included J. D. Bernard, Matthias Arenas, Francois Crouchet, A. S. Chappuis, Mervine Kahn, Moise Dupuis, M. L. Melancon, Thomas P. Bowden, G. J. Malone, George Lagroue, M. Brien, L. A. Keller, Paul Caillouet, Columbus Hoffpauir, Ernest Capel, E. O. Bruner, R. T. Clark. Drug stores were operated by L. A. Duclos, Dr. J. F. Morris, Dr. M. P. Young and Dr. A. W. Harrington. Duson Brothers and R. J. C. Bull were real estate agents; the three saloons were operated by Donat Pucheu, Louis Deputy and McBride and Stephens.[7]

In addition there was established in the town a number of professional people and tradesmen such as physicians, dentists, contractors, painters, surveyors and the like. Rayne was, as much as any town of its size and place in time, a viable, self-sufficient community.

Other than advertisements and brief references in parish newspapers of the period there are no sources of information on other businesses established in Rayne prior to 1910. Business advertisements appearing in the available issues of the *Rayne Tribune* (from November 28, 1903 to October 28, 1905) include:

The Ida Rice Mill; the Acme Saloon, owned by Joseph Schutten and managed by Joseph Schaffhausen; Rayne Brick Co.; Silk Hat Saloon and Restaurant, J. H. Evans; Broussard & Broussard (L. L. and Alcibiades); Derouen's Opera House; Gaston Servat store; Jacques Weil gin; A. E. Richmond, jeweler; Patterson Bros. jewelry; Commercial Hotel; Valverde Hotel; Smith Hardware;

J. B. Richard, meat; Henri Blanc, groceries; F. Clavery, sewing machine repair; O. Broussard, druggist; G. A. Kennedy; John Marks; Bert Case; High Life Saloon, J. Howard Andrus; Stamm-Scheele; Crandall Bros. & Carver, well drillers; Amede Petitjean, butcher; Elite Moving Pictures, S. Hebert; Commercial Bank; R. C. Holt, insurance; Rayne Rice Mill; Rayne Ice Co.; Rayne State Bank;

The Surprise Store, Melancon & Mudd; The Fair, Levy & Weil; Acadia Cash Emporium, David Levy; Adonis Guidry, tonsorial artist; L. Douglas, clothier; Jacques Weil, Boudreaux & Leger; Stewart, Lewis & Taylor, lumber; Chappuis Hardware; Rayne Pharmacy, J. C. Caillouet;

[5] *Daily Signal*, Dec. 27, 1911
[6] *Crowley Signal*, Aug. 25, 1888
[7] *Ibid*

The McBride hardware store on Adams Avenue was one of Rayne's early business places. Here in front of the store are W. S. McBride, the proprietor; his young daughter, Ella; Corinne Mouton (infant in baby carriage), daughter of a pioneer Rayne physician, Dr. G. C. Mouton, and her nursemaid. (Photo courtesy Mrs. A. E. Raymond Jr.)

J. H. Evans Billard Hall; L. A. Duclos, druggist; Rayne Bakery, A. J. Hains; New Orleans Bakery, H. Privat; H. Louis Mersch, groceries, fish, oysters; Live and Let Live Saloon; Miss Josephine Rencurel, ladies clothing, groceries, E. Eleazar, manager.

Earlier, in a section titled "Business Directory and Guide," the *Crowley Signal* listed the following Rayne advertisers: Bruner Bros., buggies, carriages; O. Broussard, druggist; L. A. Duclos, druggist; Crandall & Robinson, lumber; Aug. L. Chappuis, hardware, implements; Rayne Ginning Co.; J. C. Besse, furniture; H. Louis Mersch, grocery; B. Guyral, manufacturer's agent; Pearce and Irion, wheelwrights.[8] Charles Oudin and A. C. Poulet were also in the lumber business in Rayne.[9]

---

[8] *Ibid*, Feb. 16, 1901
[9] *Ibid*, Oct. 27, 1894

Rayne got its second railroad line in 1907, when the long-awaited Opelousas, Gulf & Northeastern went through. The town had supported the movement to get another railroad by voting a five mill tax to run for 10 years.[10]

The coming of the new railroad appears to have been the catalyst for a renewal of interest in civic development in the town. In the Christmas edition of the Crowley newspaper Rayne proudly listed its assets: two railroads, a cotton oil mill, four cotton gins, two rice mills, two machine shops, one grist mill, two lumber yards, a brick plant, two pop factories and an ice plant; two churches, three schools, two banks, a waterworks and light plant, a military company and a fire company. Included were five fraternal organizations: Catholic Knights, which owned its two-story meeting hall; Knights of Pythias, Masons, Woodmen of the World, and Odd Fellows.

Included in the Christmas write-up was some background history on Rayne business firms:

A cold storage plant was being constructed by Jacques Weil, Boudreaux and Leger; the Mathilde Cotton Gin was owned by Jacques Weil, Edmond Weil and S. Morales.

Officers and directors of Rayne State Bank, which had been organized in 1894, were Mervine Kahn, David Levy, L. A. Duclos, L. J. Delaune and R. R. Richard. Principal officers of the Commercial Bank, organized in 1902, were O. Broussard, David Levy, R. C. Holt Jr. and L. M. Milligan.

The Rayne Cotton Oil Co., established in 1904, had for its officers J. P. Suberville, H. L. Smith, P. E. Bergerie and C. C. C. Carlisle. The plant cost $30,000 and had a daily capacity of 35 tons of cotton seed. Its output consisted of cooking oils, cotton seed, cake and meal, fertilizers, laundry soap and mixed feed. John H. Carlisle was engineer for the plant, which employed 26 persons.

Stamm, Scheele & Co. was established in 1902. Herbert C. Irion was foreman. The company specialized in machine shop work and putting down deep wells.

The Acadia Cotton Co. was headed by F. J. Bernard, president and manager; J. Chappuis, vice president and treasurer, and R. Duhon, secretary. Six men were employed by the plant. S. Boudreaux had the grist mill; two other cotton gins were owned by S. Rayon and O. Bailleux (sic, probably Baillio), and Auguste Perres had a machine shop.''[11]

Random references in the Crowley newspaper identify A. B. Theunissen as a Rayne merchant, Miss Ora Kelley as a milliner, and Mrs. Ernest Beslin of St. Martinville as having leased the Crouchet Hotel on Texas Avenue as a boarding house.[12]

---

[10] Minutes, Rayne Town Council, Apr. 19, 1905
[11] *Crowley Signal*, Dec. 14, 1907
[12] *Crowley Signal*, Dec. 21, 1907: *Daily Signal*, Jan. 21, Mar. 1, 1909

Maurice Heymann, who later became the founder of Lafayette's Oil Center, was in business in Rayne in 1909. Heymann operated a moving picture show and a dime store in the Acadia Parish town. In January of 1909 he sold his interest in the Arcade Theater to G. Derouen and took over (or established) the Victor Theater. Two months later Heymann, known in Rayne as "*Dix Sous*" (Ten Cents) closed his dime store and moved to Thibodaux. Heymann was described as "an asset to the town . . . an energetic man and good fellow . . . Rayne loses a valuable citizen. Adieu, Dix Sous!"[13]

A grocery store, established by Anthony "Tony" Plattsmier about 1898, was a long-time Rayne business place.[14]

Additional newspaper items reveal that in the spring of 1909 G. A. Kennedy had set the opening of his new "magnificent glass front store," and that the A. S. Chappuis firm had a brick yard north of town and a new warehouse on the south side of the track near the *Tribune* office.[15]

By 1910 Stamm-Scheele had expanded the firm's services to include the installation of rice irrigation machinery in Arkansas and Texas, and "picture shows" were fast becoming the most popular form of entertainment. Rayne movie houses advertising in the Crowley newspaper were the Elite Moving Picture Theater and the Dreamland Picture Show.[16]

Minutes of the town council after 1910 identify the town's barroom operators. All applications for permits to operate bars within the corporate limits of the town required official sanction by the council. The first such action granted permits to Martin Petitjean, John Servat, Cesaire Hebert and Sol Kahn. Permits later went to Nemour Miguez, Delma and Theoville Hanks, Amede Petitjean and Charles Fauroux. The Hanks saloon was later sold to Oneil Comeaux and Calice LeBlanc, and the Amede Petitjean place was bought by E. U. Boudreaux and Louis Dupin.[17]

Privat Bros. was established in 1913, when Louis Privat bought the lumber business from H. E. Lewis of Crowley. Prior to going into the lumber business Privat operated a bakery in Rayne.[18]

A new moving picture show, the Crystal, opened in August of 1914. The theater was housed in the building formerly occupied by Boudreaux, Leger and Weil, and its first performance drew a large crowd. P. A. Preddy was manager of the new entertainment center. One of the main attractions was a local talent show titled "Dangers of the Day." Playing leading roles were Edna Petitjean, Jeanne Besse, Paul Fremaux and Robert Bull.[19]

---

[13] *Daily Signal*, Jan. 21, 28, Mar. 11, Dec. 4, 1909: interview Leo H. Kahn, 1977
[14] Interview, Antonia Plattsmier Andrus, Leo H. Kahn, 1978
[15] *Daily Signal*, Feb. 4, Mar. 1, 1909
[16] *Crowley Signal*, Feb. 5, 12, 1910: *Daily Signal*, Jan. 12, 1911
[17] Minutes, Rayne Town Council, Dec. 16, 1910: Jan. 3, 28, July 8, 1911: Jan. 2, 1912: Jan. 6, Dec. 30, 1914
[18] *Signal*, 50th Anniv. Ed., 41: interview, Louis Privat, 1978
[19] *Daily Signal*, Aug. 1, Dec. 10, 1914

The surrey with the fringe on top was still in use when this picture was taken. The occupants are, from left, Joe Petitjean, George K. Bradford, W. J. McBride, and Etta Stamm Sweeney. (Photo courtesy Mrs. A. E. Raymond Jr.)

A newspaper item of 1914 reported the establishment of Rayne's first service station: "A gasoline supply tank has been placed opposite Stephens' confectionery by Anthony Raymond of Gulf Refining Co."[20]

A new railroad depot and improved train boarding facilities came about as the result of a delegation of Rayne citizens appearing before the Louisiana Railroad Commission in 1915. The Southern Pacific agreed to build a new passenger depot on the north side of the main line opposite the old freight depot. The town donated a strip 17 by 240 feet for the railroad company to build a larger building. The citizens' delegation in-

[20] *Ibid*, Nov. 19, 1914

157

cluded Howard Bruner, Ben H. Bailey, Dr. J. D. Hunter, P. F. Besse, Dr. M. Stagg, O. P. Bonin, J. L. Chappuis and Joseph Gossen.[21]

Jacques and Edmond Weil were proprietors of "Le Moulin Rouge," a theater in Rayne in 1916. A new opera house had been built the year before on Texas Avenue by J. S. Craig.[22]

The first civic organization in Rayne was the Progressive Union, formed in 1903. The roster of officers and directors provides a fair identification of the community's leaders: E. L. Chappuis, G. V. W. Lyman, O. Broussard, A. J. Duclos, C. W. Lyman, Jacques Weil, F. J. Bernard, A. S. Chappuis, R. J. C. Bull, Ben Melancon, Joseph Schaffhausen, John Taylor, Mervine Kahn, H. S. Kopmier, J. C. Valverde, Oneil Comeaux, E. O. Bruner, J. F. Stamm, August L. Chappuis, R. C. Webb, John P. Mauboules, Joseph Gossen, G. N. Reynolds, R. C. Holt Jr., N. C. Crandall, Dr. M. A. Young, E. Daboval Jr., Jonas Weil, Dr. J. P. Mauboules, E. L. Crandall, George K. Bradford, H. C. Irion, J. L. Crandall, O. E. Cammill, George Parker. The 35 directors paid a fee of $5 a month; the 70 members paid $1 per month.[23]

The first project undertaken by the Union was to improve the town hall. An appropriation of $500 was made for this purpose. C. W. Lyman was secretary for the organization; through his efforts a weather bureau station was secured for the town. Signal flags indicating the type of weather to be expected were hoisted on a 62-foot high pole. Another Progressive Union project was the Pleasure Pavilion, which opened in July, 1903. C. W. Lyman was the speaker and about 1,000 persons attended.[24]

The Rayne Building and Loan Co. was organized in 1900. Directors were Dr. R. C. Webb, John Taylor, M. A. Robinson, O. Broussard, I. Lehmann, J. Schwartz, Mervine Kahn and A. S. Chappuis. J. G. Medlenka, Crowley's pioneer in the home loan field, organized the Rayne company.[25]

A military company was organized in Rayne in 1904. Company E, Louisiana State National Guard, First Battalion of Infantry, was mustered May 1, 1904 by Adj. Gen. Allen Jumel. Capt. Eugene L. Crandall was commanding officer; Gus Bienvenu and Rufus Hoffpauir were first and second lieutenants respectively. The company had 22 members.[26]

In February of 1907, the year the new railroad line went into operation, a town lot sale was held. Property in the vicinity of the OG & NE depot, totaling 150 lots, was sold at $60 to $110 per lot. The sale brought a total of $15,000. A large amount of the property offered was reportedly

[21] *Ibid*, Feb. 24, 1915: May 5, 1916
[22] *Ibid*, Sept. 16, 1916: Mar. 12, 1915
[23] *Daily Signal*, Feb. 23, 1903: *Crowley Signal*, Sept. 12, 1903
[24] *Daily Signal*, Feb. 23, 1903: *Crowley Signal*, Apr. 25, July 25, 1903
[25] *Crowley Signal*, May 12, 1900
[26] *Daily Signal*, Apr. 30, May 2, 1904

bought by O. R. Hopson, a Lafayette lumberman, who planned to operate a branch lumber yard near the depot.[27]

The year 1907 was a good one for Rayne banks. The Rayne State Bank increased its capital stock from $15,000 to $60,000 and declared a 300 per cent dividend. The bank's financial statement showed a surplus of $45,000. The bank was second in the state that year in profits earned. Officers and directors of the Commercial Bank in 1907 were O. Broussard, president; David Levy, vice president; R. C. Holt Jr., cashier; Dr. R. C. Webb, J. D. Bernard, W. B. Milligan, Joseph Gossen, J. F. Fulton and I. M. Lichtenstein, directors. David Levy, the vice president, was also vice president of the Rayne State Bank; one of the new directors, Joseph Gossen, owned and operated the ice plant.[28]

The Frog Industry

The same topographical conditions that led to the cultivation of rice in Acadia created another food industry in the parish. This was the frog shipping business which, like providence rice, thrived because of the numerous ponds, *coulees* and *marais* which dotted the flat prairie lands before land reclamation and drainage projects were begun.[29]

Shipments of frogs from Rayne to New Orleans were reported as early as 1887. Donat Pucheu was probably the first resident of Acadia Parish to engage in the business of shipping frogs. A native of France, Pucheu settled with his family in Rayne in 1887. Like his fellow countrymen, he considered frog legs a gourmet food and got into the business of shipping live frogs to restaurants in New Orleans.[30]

It remained for another native of France, Jacques Weil, to expand the unique industry into gigantic proportions—shipping out as much as 10,000 pounds of frog legs in a week. Jacques Weil and his brothers, Edmond and Gontran, came to Rayne from Paris about 1901. Jacques became the senior partner in the firm of Jacques Weil, Boudreaux and Leger. The firm shipped frogs, poultry, eggs and produce to New Orleans and other large cities.[31]

The frog shipping season began as early as the last week in February and reached a peak in April. During the 1908 season the Rayne firm shipped out more than 100,000 frogs. The industry grew at such a rate that there was talk of getting a frog experiment station for Rayne.[32]

[27] *Crowley Signal*, Feb. 2, 1907

[28] *Ibid*, Jan. 19, Nov. 2, 1907; interview, Laurent Boudreaux, 1978

[29] Interview, Wiltz Chatelain, 1978

[30] *Acadia Sentinel*, Feb. 12, 1887; Fleming, Estelle Bonin, "Rayne Frog Industry Dates Back to 1880," supplement, *Rayne Acadian-Tribune*, Aug. 30, 1973

[31] *Daily Signal*, Feb. 26, Mar. 1, 1909; Apr. 21, 1914; Craig, Myrta Fair, "Three Weil Brothers Bring Rayne Fame as 'Frog Capital of the World'" supplement *Rayne Acadian-Tribune*, Aug. 30, 1973

[32] *Daily Signal*, Mar. 1, May 28, 1909

ene in the Dressing Department. Filling a 50,000 Frog Order for Chica

Peak season at the Jacques Weil frog dressing department, about 1903. A crew of five to six frog skinners was kept busy day and night preparing the frogs for shipment. (Photo courtesy *Rayne Acadian Tribute*)

Many heads of families supplemented their income by hunting frogs; some full time hunters supported their families with their earnings, young men found frog hunting a handy way to get pocket money. During the first balmy nights of spring the hunters would walk along the coulees or other shallow waterways with lighted lanterns and burlap sacks. The light of the lantern immobilized the frog by temporarily blinding it; it was an easy matter then to capture the frog by hand and pop it into the sack.

Occasional references in the Crowley newspaper show that frog hunting was a popular sport throughout the parish. Ebenezer and the coulees in the Mallet Switch section were two favorite hunting grounds for frogs. The night's catch was usually kept in a sack in a cool place until enough frogs were caught to justify a trip to the Rayne market.[33]

During March and April, the prime time of year for the frog business, the Rayne company's premises presented a remarkable sight: as many as 15,000 live frogs were kept in large wire netting coops, and a half dozen

---

[33] *Daily Signal*, Mar. 25, 1909; interview, Roland Fontenot, 1978

employees were kept busy preparing the frog legs for shipment. During peak years of the industry the shipments were figured in tons.[34]

Because of the uniqueness of the business he headed for more than 40 years Jacques Weil achieved a rare status: he became a legend in his own time. His whimsical sense of humor is best revealed by a story which has been in circulation since the early years of the frog shipping business:

During the rush season, when many thousands of frogs were being processed, at night the cooped-up live frogs tended to pile up in the corners of the cages; consequently those on the bottom were sometimes suffocated. It was common practice to dress the suffocated frogs first, then butcher and skin the live ones later. As the story goes, first thing each morning Jacques Weil reminded his crew. "Kill the dead ones first!"[35]

There was considerable activity in the frog business elsewhere in the parish. The *Signal* correspondent for the Redlich community reported that Ben Johnson had made a trip to Iota to ship a load of frogs, E. D. Fruge was known as the Mermentau "frog man," and large shipments were going to Houston from Crowley. Shipments of the dressed frogs brought $1,500 in a two-week period, with about a thousand pounds a day leaving Crowley for the Texas market.[36]

Frog hides were a by-product of the industry. As the frogs were butchered and skinned, the hides were thrown into barrels and sprinkled with salt, then sent to tanneries to be made into purses and other leather goods for women.[37]

The rapid growth of the frog industry in Acadia Parish was viewed with alarm in some quarters. In the summer of 1906 the Crowley newspaper reported that 9,000 pounds of frog skins, taken from 64,854 frogs, had been shipped from Crowley, in addition to some 4,000 frogs sent live to New Orleans and large quantities shipped from other points. This decimation of the frog population was thought to pose a threat to the rice industry. "This may upset the balance of nature," the editor wrote. "Frogs eat insects; if they become extinct, perhaps some new insect could cause damage to the rice."[38]

A story in the *Daily Signal* of May 5, 1916 demonstrates the ability of the bullfrog to survive out of water for long period of time. A frog, believed to have escaped from a Parkerson Avenue store in Crowley where frogs were bought and sold, took refuge beneath the walls of an adjacent building, a drug store. The creature apparently was imprisoned beneath the brick wall, and at the time the incident was reported had been there

---

[34] *Daily Signal*, Mar. 25, 1909; interview Wiltz Chatelain, 1978
[35] Interview, Roland Fontenot, John "Moustique" Pleasant, 1978
[36] *Daily Signal*, Apr. 4, 12, 1906; May 8, 1912
[37] *Ibid*, Apr. 4, 1906
[38] *Ibid*, June 22, 1906

Among Acadia Parish bullfrog shippers was John P. Hoyt of Estherwood, shown here with three jumbo specimens. Hoyt, a justice of the peace for many years, was known as Judge Hoyt. (Freeland Collection, Dupre Library, USL)

for three years, doubtless subsisting on whatever insects came its way. The presence of the frog was detected because of its nightly bellowing:

> At any rate, for the past three years, ever since the day when froggy first sought refuge beneath the walls which proved for him a prison house, he has given nightly concerts in a deep bass voice, the tones of which have grown ever deeper and louder with the passing years, until now visitors to the store are frequently greeted by a bass voiced solo which can proceed from the throat of nothing less hearty than a full lunged, mature and perfectly developed bullfrog.
>
> While at the first these concerts proved somewhat disconcerting to proprietors and clerks at the store, they have now become so accustomed to his singing that does his frogship omit his concert for but a single day, a sense of loneliness and depression pervades the spirit of the store, while many regular customers of the place congregate nightly to listen to the warbling of the deep throated melody of the lonely but not disheartened prisoner.

Municipal Officers

Highlights of the administrations of the five mayors who served from 1900 to 1920 will be considered briefly here, following a resume of municipal officers from 1883.

Prior to 1900 eight mayors served the town of Rayne: J. D. Bernard, 1883; B. H. Harmon, 1886; R. J. C. Bull, 1887; Thomas P. Bowden, 1889; Louis A. Keller, 1890; James Webb, 1891; Emile Daboval Jr., 1895; Oliver Broussard, 1898.

Aldermen prior to 1900 included B. H. Harmon, A. L. Chappuis, L. R. Deputy, M. Arenas, J. F. Morris, M.D., Thomas P. Bowden, R. T. Clark, H. W. Anding, J. D. Bernard, R. C. Webb, M.D., G. C. Mouton, M.D., Mervine Kahn, L. A. Keller, Armas Gillard, G. J. Maloné, E. O. Bruner, W. C. Chevis, J. C. Sanguinette, Ernest Capel, R. H. Bagley, W. F. Perkins, W. S. McBride, J. C. Caillouet, D. Levy, Auguste Perres, Emile Daboval Jr., O. Broussard, J. B. Richard, W. B. St. John, P. F. Besse, M. A. Young, M.D., Jonas Weil. Town marshals during this period were J. E. Wimberley, P. O. Trahan, O. P. Guilbeau, A. V. Lyons and Elias Deputy.[39]

The only controversy recorded in the minutes of the town council during this earlier period was during the Bowden administration in 1890,

---

[39] Minutes, Rayne Town Council, 1883-1900

Municipal affairs were handled in this neat building on Louisiana Avenue. The frame structure served as Rayne's town hall for half a century.

when the council rescinded a previous action making the *Acadia Sentinel* the official journal of the town. The wording (in part) of the resolution, adopted unanimously by the council on August 20, 1890, is as follows:

"Whereas, the *Acadia Sentinel* is constantly abusing some of the town officials without cause and constantly condemning their actions without justification, which is calculated to cause people who are not acquainted with the gang that runs the paper to form a bad opinion of members . . . also calculated to retard the progress of our town . . .

"Whereas, the *Acadia Sentinel* is not being run in the interests of good works. . . fair-minded people know that (we have) better drains, better worked streets, and one of the finest and best furnished school houses in southwest Louisiana . . .

"Whereas, the Acadia Sentinel is not being run in the interests of Rayne and its people. . . ."

The next "whereas" stipulated that the town would no long pay the newspaper $50 a year to publish the minutes of the town council meetings. Instead, the minutes would be posted on the door of the town hall.

The owner of the *Sentinel* at that time was Oscar L. Alpha, who had bought the newspaper earlier that year from its founder, George K. Bradford.[40]

An apparent difference between two religious factions claimed the attention of the council in 1898. The mayor and aldermen reviewed a petition asking that the colored Baptists be prohibited from building a church near the colored Methodist Episcopal church "or anywhere north of the railroad" on the grounds that "they (the Baptists) are a disagreeable crowd" and would cause "great confusion in that part of town." No action was taken on the matter.[41]

Olivier Broussard served the longest term of any of Rayne's early mayors, from 1898 to 1908. Aldermen during Broussard's 10-year tenure included David Levy, Jonas Weil, A. L. Chappuis, G. O. Besse, Emile Daboval Jr., R. C. Holt Jr., Dr. R. C. Webb, John Taylor, John F. Stamm, J. B. Richard and Howard Hoffpauir. Town marshals were J. E. Wimberley and Lyman L. Clark.[42]

The first woman employee of the Town of Rayne was L. Bertha Webb, who served as town treasurer during the Broussard administration.[43]

Two major civic improvements were initiated in the early years of the Broussard administration. In 1901 the town granted a franchise to operate the Cumberland Telephone and Telegraph Co., and a year later took steps to secure an electric light and water plant for the community. At a special

---

[40] Fontenot and Freeland, *Acadia Parish, etc.*, 316
[41] Minutes, Mar. 7, 1898
[42] *Ibid*, 1900 to 1908
[43] *Ibid*, Dec. 3, 1899: all further references to municipal affairs will be from this same source unless otherwise noted

election held May 20, 1902 taxpayers approved a proposition to levy a five mill tax for 30 years to pay off the indebtedness of the $20,000 bond issue to finance construction of the utilities system.

The light and water plant began operations September 23, 1903 with 26 residence lights, 224 commercial lights and one water connection. By December the figures had increased to 482 lights, residential and commercial, and 11 water connections. At the time the operation and maintenance of the plant was more of a public service than a source of revenue to the town. The November report, submitted by the plant superinten-

Construction of a municipally-owned utility plant was authorized by the town in 1902. The plant was put into operation September 23, 1903.

dent, S. B. Harmon, showed a revenue of $218.35. Subtracting the cost of the fuel necessary to run the plant left a cash balance of $9.32. Harmon ended his report with a reminder: "As the nights grow longer the lights are bound to be run longer and cause an increase in fuel bills."

Gambling was an issue that came before the town council from time to time. In April of 1900 the mayor and council adopted an ordinance prohibiting slot machines in the town. The gambling devices were termed "a nuisance and demoralizing to the youth of the community." Later the council debated another gambling matter. A citizens' petition asking for an anti-gambling ordinance was laid over for six months, at which time action on the matter was postponed indefinitely.

Meters were installed at the utility plant in 1907. Fifty customers were reported on a meter basis. For the first time the plant superintendent's report showed no deficit.

A new town employee was added in 1907 when A. M. Servat became the first night marshal.

A large number of citizens petitioned the council to call a special election for the purpose of financing a new school building. The proposition was defeated at the polls on February 19, 1908. The popular vote was 43 for, 79 against; assessments for, $72,728, and assessments against, $126,210.

Largest assessments voted against the school tax were Mervine Kahn, $39,865, and August S. Chappuis, $12,360. Largest amounts voted for were R. C. Webb, $11,887 and O. Broussard, $10,695. Supporters of the school tax included five taxpayers of the German colony: A. B. Theunissen, John F. Stamm, J. W. Ohlenforst, Joseph Knipping and Joseph Gossen. Not any of the names of the German residents appeared in the list of those who voted against the school tax.

A year later, in 1909, under the administration of Mayor Eugene L. Crandall, a similar proposal was approved by voters. The 94 signatures on the petition presented to the council included several who had fought the issue the year before, such as Kahn and Chappuis. The new proposition called for a bond issue of $25,000, of which $20,000 would be used for the new school building and $5,000 for an extension of the water works and to pay off the existing bond issue. Results of the election, held July 13, 1909, were 47 for, three against; assessments of $160,589 for, $3,820 against. The Mervine Kahn assessment, voted for the proposal, was $55,506.50; Chappuis, also voted for, $13,330.

The construction of concrete sidewalks had been considered by the council in 1906, but no action was taken on the matter. An ordinance requiring all property owners to put down plank sidewalks was passed in 1908. Specifications on the construction of the walks were given in the ordinance. An anti-gambling ordinance was passed by Mayor Crandall and the council in 1909.

Prior to the Crandall administration Rayne mayors and aldermen

166

appeared to be in complete accord on all matters concerning municipal government. The minute books show no dissenting votes on actions taken by the council. The first vote that was not unanimous took place at the meeting of April 8, 1910. A resolution was introduced to allow Dr. G. C. Mouton and Dr. J. D. Hunter $75 each for services rendered during the smallpox epidemic. Two of the four aldermen present voted for the resolution, the other two voted against it. Mayor Crandall broke the tie by voting against the measure.

Aldermen serving with Crandall were H. E. Bruner, A. J. Duclos, J. P. Mauboules Jr., John B. Richard, J. F. Stamm, A. S. Chappuis, Martin Petitjean, Alfred Kahn and A. C. Chappuis.

Crandall had no opposition in the 1910 election. A total of 59 votes was cast for Crandall's ticket, which included Aldermen Richard, Stamm, Kahn, Chappuis and Petitjean, and Clark for marshal.

Less than a month after the election Crandall resigned the office and Dr. John D. Hunter was appointed mayor by the governor.

Crandall's reason for resigning his position is not known. Although he had had no opposition in the 1910 election, he had narrowly won the 1908 election over Dr. R. C. Webb. This (the 1908 election) was one of the few times during Rayne's early history when there were two tickets in the running for municipal offices. The Crandall ticket included Duclos, Dr. Mauboules, Richard, Martin Petitjean and Howard Bruner, and Lyman Clark for police chief. Dr. Webb's running mates were John Stamm, John Taylor, Dr. Hunter, A. A. Hains and Romer Duhon for council, and William Burke for chief of police. Crandall received 117 votes, a margin of 11 over Dr. Webb. One of the Webb ticket candidates, John Stamm, was elected to the council.[44]

Dr. Hunter was mayor for three terms of two years each. Actions taken by the council during his first term of office included setting a youth curfew and an auto speed limit. Youths under the age of 16 were affected by the curfew, which was 9 p.m. in summer and 8 p.m. during the winter months. The speed limit for automobiles was set at eight miles per hour within the city limits; this was later amended to 12 miles an hour. A. C. Chappuis had cast the only dissenting vote when the speed limit measure was first brought up in May, 1910. It was probably through his influence that the speed limit was reset at a more realistic figure.

During the summer of 1910 the town called an election proposing an additional two and a half mills tax for the schools. Taxpayers approved the measure almost unanimously, 35 to 4.

New names on the council during Dr. Hunter's administration included F. B. Melancon, L. J. Chappuis, O. P. Bonin, Joseph Gossen, J. M. Marshall, M. Stagg and Dermas Petitjean.

Strong support for education is shown in proceedings of the town

[44] *Crowley Signal*, Oct. 27, 1907; Feb. 1, 1908

council during Mayor Hunter's tenure. At the meeting of November 5, 1912, the mayor was authorized to buy "the necessary furniture and fixtures to complete the equipment of the public school for the establishment of a high school." When parish school funds ran low the town stepped in and appropriated funds to extend the school term to a full nine months. At one time as much as $2,100—a sizable sum for the times— was appropriated for Rayne High School. The town also gave money to Prof. R. U. Clark to extend the school term for black children.

Civic improvements inaugurated during the Hunter administration included the purchase of a new engine for the light and water plant, construction of concrete sidewalks and the purchase of a street grader.

O. P. Bonin (spelled Bonnin in the town records) went in as mayor in 1916. Serving with him were Aldermen E. J. Latour, Larkin Hoffpauir, Homer Comeaux, Forest Richard and Herbert Kahn. (The name of Herbert Kahn is not listed in the official records of the Louisiana Department of State. His name does appear in returns of the April 18, 1916 election, written into the proceedings of the Rayne Town Council of April 22, 1916)

Main action undertaken during Mayor Bonin's two years in office was to order major improvements and expansion of services of the light and water plant.

Abner C. Chappuis, another long-term mayor, went into office in 1918. Aldermen were J. H. Johnson, E. J. Lacour, Herbert Kahn, Felix Perres and Sylvestre Boudreaux. When Chappuis was re-elected for his second term in 1920 the councilmen were R. D. Daboval, A. E. Raymond, R. O. Besse, Kahn and Boudreaux.

A. M. Servat, long time Rayne peace officer, served under the five mayors whose careers were reviewed here. He went in as night marshal during Mayor Boudreaux's regime, was elected town marshal in 1910, holding this office until 1918 when B. H. Bailey became town marshal.

Hard surfacing of Rayne streets was inaugurated during Mayor Chappuis' first term of office. Several ordinances provided for the graveling of principal streets in the town.

Three years earlier Rayne had the distinction of having the first graveled street in the parish, when Mervine Kahn donated gravel for an unspecified length of Polk street. The street work was done in accordance with state highway engineers' plans governing such work; the street was graveled to a width of 18 feet with gravel mixed with clay, well tamped and rolled, and finished with a coat of washed river gravel.[45]

Kahn was a long-time treasurer for the town. He came to Rayne in 1884 and established the store which bears his name, was also the organizer and first president of Rayne State Bank, and owned a large rice warehouse.[46]

---

[45] *Daily Signal*, Mar. 12, 1915
[46] Interview, Leo H. Kahn

Medical History—to 1920

Dr. William Harris Cunningham, Rayne's founder, was also the town's first physician, although it is doubtful that he practiced his profession in the town he established. Two of his sons, Robert Edward and J. Marvin, became doctors and practiced medicine in Acadia Parish.

Dr. Robert Edward Cunningham served in the Spanish-American War and taught school before following his father and grandfather into the medical profession. He married Grace Hunter, an Acadia Parish school teacher and was a member of the parish school board. Both he and his brother, Dr. J. Marvin Cunningham, lived in the Castille community northeast of Rayne and practiced in the Rayne area.[47]

Dr. J. F. Morris was probably the first doctor to practice in Rayne. He bought lots on Texas Avenue when Dr. Cunningham held the first town lot sale in 1880, and erected the first business building, a drug store, in the town. After Acadia was created Dr. Morris moved his drug store to Crowley.[48]

The St. Landry Parish register of physicians and surgeons practicing in Rayne in 1886 listed Dr. Morris, Dr. G. C. Mouton, Dr. F. L. Licht, Dr. A. W. Harrington and Dr. Rufus C. Webb. Dr. A. J. Hooker was also a Rayne physician, practicing there for an undetermined length of time until he was fatally shot in 1883.[49]

Dr. J. P. Mauboules, a member of one of Rayne's pioneer families, graduated from Tennessee University medical school in 1889. The Mauboules family came to Rayne in 1883. Dr. Mauboules was also a successful business man and civic leader in the Rayne community, and was president of Rayne State Bank.[50]

Dr. John D. Hunter received his medical degree from Memphis Hospital medical school. He came to Rayne in 1889 and practiced medicine there for 33 years. He served two terms as mayor and two terms as state representative.[51]

Dr. Mike Lyons Clark came to Rayne shortly after he completed a graduate course in medicine from Tulane University in 1919. He received his medical degree from the University of Louisville and began practice at Ridge. He married Solange Daboval of Rayne in July, 1913.[52]

Four members of a distinguished family of Vermilion Parish doctors practiced medicine in Rayne at various times. The first was Dr. Francis D. Young, father of five sons and four daughters. The five sons became physicians and one of the daughters married a doctor, Dr. C. J. Edwards.

---

[47] Supplement, *Rayne Independent*, Apr. 3, 1969
[48] Fontenot-Freeland, *Acadia Parish*, 123, 127
[49] *Rayne Signal*, Apr. 3, 1886; *Opelousas Courier*, Oct. 30, 1883
[50] Supplement, *Rayne Independent*, Apr. 3, 1969
[51] *Ibid*
[52] *Ibid*

Three of the five sons practiced medicine in Rayne: Dr. Warren Young, Dr. Marion A. Young and Dr. Lawrence Young.[53]

There were six physicians practicing in Rayne in 1903: Dr. G. R. Harris, Dr. H. C. Webb, Dr. G. Clinton Mouton, Dr. J. P. Mauboules, Dr. M. A. Young and Dr. J. D. Hunter.[54]

Dr. G. R. Harris, a brother of the noted Louisiana educator, T. H. Harris, began practice in Rayne in 1902. He married Mayme Pucheu, daughter of a Rayne pioneer, Donat Pucheu. He died in Rayne of typhoid fever in 1904.[55]

Dr. George Clinton Mouton practiced in Rayne for some 25 years. The son of Alexandre Mouton, former governor of Louisiana, he was graduated in medicine from Louisiana State University in 1881 and moved to Rayne when the village was just building up. He served the parish as coroner and health officer.[56]

Dr. Rufus C. Webb Sr. was the grandson of John Webb, native of England, who settled at Mermentau Cove in 1827. Dr. Webb married Susan Clark, daughter of Dr. Bennett E. Clark, a pioneer physician of St. Landry and Acadia. He started practice in Rayne in 1885. His only son, Rufus Clyde Webb Jr., was a Rayne physician; his brother, Dr. H. C. Webb, practiced in both Rayne and Crowley.[57]

Dr. R. C. Webb Jr., a graduate of Tulane University, received his medical degree in 1912. He was associated with his father in the practice of medicine in Rayne, and succeeded his father as owner of the first hospital in Rayne, Rayne Sanitarium, completed in 1914.[58]

Dentists

Newspaper references, advertisements and oral history identify dentists who practiced in Rayne between 1883 and 1920: J. N. Laney, Dr. H. A. Steadman, Dr. J. W. Bourdier, Dr. Marcel Stagg and Dr. E. L. Bercier, Sr.[59]

Churches, Schools

Rayne's first religious edifice, the historic St. Joseph's Catholic Church, was constructed by the Jesuits of Grand Coteau in the Poupe-

---

[53] Interview, Mathilde Edwards, b. 1892, granddaughter Dr. Francis D. Young

[54] *Rayne Tribune*, Dec. 4, 1903 advertisements

[55] *Rayne Tribune*, Aug. 6, 1904: supplement, *Rayne Independent*, Apr. 3, 1969

[56] *Daily Signal*, Oct. 26, 1911

[57] Supplement, *Rayne Independent*, Apr. 3, 1969; Fontenot and Freeland, *Acadia*, etc. 166: *Daily Signal*, July 6, 1914

[58] Supplement, *Rayne Independent*, Apr. 3, 1969: *Daily Signal*, Feb. 6, 1914

[59] Fontenot and Freeland, *Acadia*, 139: *Crowley Signal*, Aug. 8, 1900: Apr. 25, 1903: Aug. 13, 1910

ville settlement about 1877. Rev. Joseph Anthonioz, S.J., the first resident pastor, had the church building hauled up to the Rayne location in 1882.[60]

For the first 50 years of its history St. Joseph's was served by three pastors, all natives of France: Father Anthonioz, to 1891; Rev. Blaise Branche, 1892-1899; Rt. Rev. A. S. Doutre, 1899-1928.[61]

Prior to his death in August of 1891 Father Anthonioz had invited the Sisters of Mt. Carmel to open a school in Rayne. Three of the nuns arrived in Rayne on December 16, 1891: Mother M. Faustine, Sisters Xavier and Philomene. During the time the sisters' home was under construction they slept on the floor at the rectory and the pastor lived at the Henry Anding home.[62]

Some important parochial construction took place during Father Branche's pastorate. In addition to the home for the sisters and a convent school a two-story rectory was built in 1894, and a new and larger church was built in 1899. The drive for funds for the new church was begun in 1893, when the first contribution was received. Among the first donations was 38 sacks of rice, given by August Chappuis and Frank J. Bernard, which brought $92.28 for the building fund. In 1910, during Father Doutre's administration, the church was enlarged by adding wings at each side.[63]

Early church organizations included St. Joseph's Society and Ladies' Altar Society, both formed during Father Branche's pastorate, and the Catholic Knights of America, which admitted both men and women members.* Rayne Council No. 867, Catholic Knights of America had 29 members; officers were O. Broussard, president; Mrs. Rosa H. Poulet, first vice president; Mrs. Justine Manouvrier, second vice president; Romer Duhon, recording secretary-treasurer; F. J. Bernard, financial secretary; J. E. Hains, George Besse and Henri Blanc, trustees; Oneal Comeau, sgt.-at-arms; J. H. Carlin, sentinel.[64]

St. Joseph's cemetery, adjacent to the church and rectory, for many years enjoyed a unique distinction. It was the only known Christian cemetery where the graves are placed in a north-south position lengthwise. According to ancient Christian custom graves are positioned east-west, so that the bodies of the dead lie facing the rising sun, the symbol of Christ's resurrection. No one knows why the Rayne cemetery does not follow the old tradition.[65]

The three priests from France had several of their own countrymen

* Not to be confused with the Knights of Columbus, an organization for Catholic men only, established later in Rayne

[60] Fontenot and Freeman, *Acadia*, 118, 224
[61] Booklet, St. Joseph's School Golden Jubilee, 1891-1941
[62] *Ibid*
[63] *Ibid*
[64] *Crowley Signal*, Apr. 20, 1901
[65] Interviews, Rev. Gene Tremie, Jan Lewis, 1978

The first Catholic school in Acadia Parish was Mt. Carmel convent, constructed in 1892. The first teaching nuns arrived in Rayne in December, 1891. (Reproduced from the *Crowley Signal,* Oct. 27, 1894)

for company in Rayne. Rayne families with direct connections with France (not those of Acadian-French descent) included the Chappuis, Duclos, Daboval, Petitjean, Privat, Eleazer, to name a few. The Weil brothers, Jacques, Edmond and Gontran, came from Paris and located in Rayne at the urging of their friend, Father Doutre.[66]

Father Doutre began an unusual experiment in 1905. Some years earlier Father Zarn, the priest at St. Leo's in nearby Robert's Cove had established a so-called "factory for making syrup" (a cane syrup mill) and found a market for the product. So successful was the project that many gallons of the syrup were being shipped from Rayne annually. Encouraged by this success Father Doutre ordered a press to extract the juice from pears grown in his own orchard. It was his plan to set up a factory to make a beverage called *poire,* said to have been popular in Europe at the time.[67]

The Sisters of Mt. Carmel conducted separate schools for girls and boys for a number of years. The girls' school, known as Mt. Carmel Convent, was also a boarding school. The boys attended St. Aloysius Boys' College. Classes for boys were held in the original church building, which had been moved to one side when the larger church was constructed. The schools were later consolidated under the name of St.

[66] Craig, Myrta Fair, "Weil Brothers, etc." *Rayne Acadian-Tribune,* Aug. 30, 1973
[67] *Crowley Signal,* Sept. 16, 1905

172

Joseph High School. The first graduate was Alma Duclos, only member of the class of 1917.[68]

Rayne's Methodist congregation is as old as the town itself. Services were first held in the home of Dr. W. H. Cunningham, the town's founder, for the Cunningham, Johnston and the Dunshie families. The city block, on which the Methodist church stands, was donated by Dr. Cunningham's widow.

The first concrete step taken towards building a church came in 1883 when Rev. Christian Keener, presiding elder of the Opelousas District introduced a resolution at the conference which provided for a building committee for a church in Rayne.

Members of the building committee were B. H. Harmon, B. Faulk, Walton Faulk, W. B. Clark, Starcus Hoffpauir, M. L. Lyons, Dr. R. R. Lyons, M. Hoffpauir, W. W. Duson and Lewis A. Reed. The committee met May 30, 1883 and drew up plans for a building 80 feet by 50 by 30, together with complete specifications.

Construction began in the spring of 1884. Workmen were boarded at the Cunningham home at no cost other than the furnishing of their food. Mrs. Cunningham collected funds from members, friends and neighbors to purchase the church bell. William F. Johnston was in charge of painting the building.

The year 1884 marked the 100th year of the establishment of Methodist Episcopal Church, South, and the Rayne church was given the name Centenary Methodist Church in honor of the anniversary. Bishop Keener, father of Rev. Christian Keener, officiated at the church dedication June 29, 1884. A Sunday School was organized that same year.

Pastors of the church, 1884 to 1920, were Revs. M. C. Manley, T. S. Keener, H. O. White, L. H. McClendon, R. M. Blocker, H. Armstrong, T. L. Randle, J. S. Sanders, I. T. Reams, R. C. Grace, Martin Hebert, N. H. Brown, W. D. Kleinschmidt, F. M. Freeman, A. F. Vaughan, W. L. Doss Jr., B. T. Crews, A. A. Bernard, John Scholars, C. E. Fike, E. C. Gunn.

The first adult missionary society was organized by Rev. Manley between 1884 and 1886 and was known as the Home and Parsonage Society. The name was later changed to the Woman's Missionary Society.[69]

Starlight Baptist Church dates its organization to 1881, under the leadership of the Rev. Henry C. Roy. First officers of the church were P. A. Kingston, who also served as church clerk; Bun Moore, David Brown, J. M. Robinson and Rudolph Wilridge.

---

[68] *Daily Signal*, Sept. 6, 1906: Sept. 2, 1909: St. Joseph's Golden Jubilee booklet
[69] Cunningham, James M., "History of Centenary Methodist Church," paper, prepared from records kept by Mrs. W. F. Johnston

Only two pastors served Starlight Church from 1881 to 1920: Rev. Roy and Rev. V. B. Bryant.[70]

Cunningham C. M. E. Church was founded July 26, 1887. Prior to this date colored Methodists attended services at the church at Plaquemine Brulee (Branch). Bishop Elias Cottrell of the New Orleans Conference authorized the founding of the Rayne church. The first pastor was Rev. Johnson S. Witherspoon. Other pastors, to 1920, were Revs. Alexander, H. C. Harrison, R. B. Martin, J. D. Jones, Eli Jones, C. L. Jones, A. Kinnon, James Brillo Sr., J. C. Heard. The church was rebuilt about 1910 at its original location, 300 west Harrop street.

The church was named for Mrs. Mary Cunningham, widow of the town's founder, who donated one lot of ground to the church, then sold the church a second lot for the nominal sum of one dollar.[71]

It has been established that the Rayne community had a public school as early as 1878. The school, for white students, was located near the Bernard store in the Poupeville settlement.[72]

By 1885 the new town at Rayne Station was reported to have two schools, a public and a private school.[73] The public school grew rapidly; for the 1899-1900 session Samuel S. Landoc was the lone teacher. By 1906 the faculty had increased to 10.[74]

In 1900 Danny Terry was appointed to replace Landoc and Nellie Cunningham was added to the teaching staff. The following year a third teacher, Grace Hunter, was appointed.[75]

The faculty for 1902-1903 consisted of T. H. McGregor, principal; Nellie Cunningham and Grace Hunter. T. L. Story, long-time principal of the Rayne school, was first appointed in 1904. Other members of the faculty that year were Anna McGregor, Nellie Cunningham and Grace Hunter.[76]

Three students at Rayne High School received diplomas in 1910 at what is believed to have been the first graduation program. The graduates were Kathleen Johnston, Mabel Fleming and Clyde Bruner.[77]

It has been previously noted that Rayne citizens were strongly supportive of education. This was corroborated by the final report of J. H. Lewis, superintendent of schools of Acadia Parish from 1908 to 1913. In his report Lewis made the following statement:

> The city of Rayne in the past seven years has, perhaps, shown the greatest improvement of any town in Louisiana. Seven years ago Rayne

---

[70] Akols, Annie L., historian, Starlight Baptist Church
[71] Dugas, Beatrice, historian, Cunningham C. M. E. Church
[72] *Opelousas Courier*, Sept. 28, 1978
[73] *Ibid*, Mar. 21, 1885
[74] *Crowley Signal*, Sept. 16, 1899; *Daily Signal*, July 2, 1913
[75] *Crowley Signal*, Sept. 8, 1900; Sept. 14, 1901
[76] *Daily Signal*, Sept. 3, 1902; May 16, 1904
[77] *Crowley Signal*, June 4, 1910

had four teachers, which number has now been increased to ten teachers, with the request for two more for another year. Seven years ago Rayne had an old wooden structure in a dilapidated condition. She now has one of the most beautiful brick buildings in the state, equipped from bottom to top. Rayne has taken advanced standing in demanding the best teachers; no teacher being permitted to teach unless he or she has a college degree.[78]

Two individuals stand out as educators and leaders of the black community of Rayne. They are Mary Ella Louisa Armstrong and R. U. Clark.

Mrs. Armstrong was the first black teacher in Acadia Parish. A native of New Orleans and daughter of a former slave, she taught in parish schools for 46 years. Her first teaching job was in Crowley in 1891; later she taught classes in the Cunningham C.M.E. Church of Rayne. She organized fund raising projects to buy land for Rayne's first school for black children. Mrs. Armstrong taught in Rayne for 27 years.[79]

R. U. Clark, born in Lecompte, La. in 1881, was graduated from Leland College in Baker, La., and studied at Hampton and Tuskegee Institute.[80]

Clark was sent to Acadia Parish by the president of the Anna T. Jeanes Foundation. The fund was set aside by the founder for the instruction of Negroes in the industrial and agricultural field. His salary was paid by the foundation, but his work was coordinated by the Acadia Parish School Board. He directed courses at schools at Crowley, Rayne, Church Point, Iota and Gassler.[81]

Clark was principal of Acadia Parish Training School for 33 years, beginning in 1915, except for 14 months military service in France during World War I.[82]

Disastrous Fires

Six major fires caused damage and destruction to valuable property in Rayne between 1900 and 1920. During the summer of 1902 five commercial buildings were burned down: Bruner Bros. general merchandise store, the George Oudin saloon, Chappuis implement building, the Postal Telegraph office and a barber shop.[83]

Rayne suffered an estimated $40,000 fire loss in 1903 when an entire business block went up in flames. Destroyed were the Donat Pucheu saloon, the Valverde saloon; R. J. C. Bull's drug store and livery, a build-

[78] *Daily Signal*, July 2, 1913
[79] Interview, Lolette H. Fowler, 1978
[80] Interview, Alberdia Clark Smith, 1978
[81] *Crowley Signal*, Jan. 8, Feb. 26, 1910
[82] *Daily Signal*, July 19, 1911; interview, Alberdia Clark Smith, 1978
[83] *Daily Signal*, June 9, 1902

Mrs. M. E. L. Armstrong
(Photo courtesy Lolette Helen Fowler)

ing owned by A. S. Chappuis, the H. L. Mersch store and residence; Charles Donzler's restaurant, and the Hebert and Comeaux drug store. Fire losses included damage to the Chappuis hardware stock and the Stewart, Lewis and Taylor lumber stock. Crowley firemen made a valiant effort to assist. They raced to the railroad depot through mud and slush with fire fighting equipment, only to be refused permission to load the equipment. They then jumped on boxcars for the ride to Rayne, arriving in time to help the exhausted Rayne firemen put out the blaze.[84]

An early morning fire in the fall of 1903 caused a loss of $22,000. Destroyed were the Ben Harrell and Bourdier livery stable on Polk Street, the F. G. Cole general merchandise store, H. S. Kopmier's grocery, the J. H. Andrus saloon and four buildings owned by August L. Chappuis. The flames spread across the street to the G. A. Kennedy store; firemen saved the building but some of the stock was destroyed. The blaze threatened the Kahn block and stores on Main Street; the Mervine Kahn and Kopmier residences were badly scorched.[85]

Rayne had only frame buildings until 1901, when Mervine Kahn put up the first brick structure to house Rayne State Bank adjacent to the Kahn store. Other early brick buildings include the Commercial Bank, Levy and Weil building and Chappuis hardware, all constructed in 1902.[86] As more and more fire-resistant buildings replaced the frame structure, damage from fire decreased proportionately.

The most disastrous fire of the decade was in 1908, when the Ida rice mill and the Mervine Kahn warehouse were burned. Total loss was estimated at $100,000. The fire started in the rice mill about one o'clock in the morning; the mill watchman fired a pistol to give the alarm. The flames spread to the Kahn warehouse east of the mill.[87]

The mill was not rebuilt. Mervine Kahn replaced the burned warehouse with an all-brick building, 80 by 240, with a galvanized iron roof. The building, constructed at a cost of $13,000, was said to have been virtually fireproof and "one of the most substantial warehouses in the state."[88]

The David Levy department store was destroyed by fire for the second time in 1909. Levy, one of the town's business and civic leaders, had been in business for 18 years. In the first fire, in 1895, he had lost his store and its contents. The fire loss in 1909 was estimated at $80,000, with approximately half covered by insurance. An immediate offer of help came from a fellow townsman: Emile Daboval Jr., who owned the Valverde Hotel at that time, offered the use of the two-story brick structure free of charge until Levy could rebuild. (After Levy's death the business

[84] Ibid, Feb. 3, 1903
[85] Crowley Signal, Oct. 24, 1903
[86] Crowley Signal, Jan. 5, 1901; Daily Signal, July 7, 1902
[87] Crowley Signal, Dec. 26, 1908
[88] Daily Signal, May 5, 1909; interview, Lee H. Kahn

was taken over (1911) by a company composed of J. D. Hunter, D. Petit-jean, Albert McNeal, R. Levy, Dorris Andrus and P. E. Voorhies).[89]

A gasoline explosion in 1917 started the fire which destroyed another Rayne landmark, the Valverde Hotel. The large brick structure, located near the railroad track, housed a hotel on the second floor, a restaurant and a tailor shop on the ground floor.[90]

The history of Rayne's fire company goes back to pre-parish division days. The town had a hook and ladder company and fire fighting equipment in 1886.[91] In 1905 the town assumed the responsibility for providing fire protection for the community when the council voted to buy equipment owned by the Rayne Fire Association for $300, and appropriated $100 to pay bills owed by the association.[92]

Cotton

For many years cotton vied with rice as the main money crop of the Rayne countryside. During the period covered by this work there were two large ginning companies and several smaller operations in Rayne. The large gins were operated by August L. Chappuis and Jacques Weil; others were owned by S. Rayon and O. Bailleux. A cotton oil company was in operation there for some years.[93]

Chappuis, who headed the Rayne Gin Co., appeared to have been one of the town's most progressive businessmen. The latest innovation in cotton baling—equipment to make round bales of 250 pounds each—was installed at the gin in 1901. Capacity of the plant was 80 bales in 12 hours. The Chappuis gin was the second in the state to use oil for fuel: a large storage tank near the boiler room held 10,000 gallons of oil, which was transmitted from the storage tank to the furnaces. The high-speed engine, 130 horsepower, was oiled automatically: the oil was filtered and returned for re-use.

The Chappuis gin was the mechanical marvel of its time. A suction pipe brought the cotton from the storage rooms below up to the gin, where machinery separated the seed from the cotton. With the seed and lint removed the cotton went to the compress, while a conveyor belt brought the seed 75 feet to the seed house. The cotton, hauled to the gin in wagons, was forced into storage houses through a system of discharge pipes.[94]

During the 1903-1904 season the Rayne Ginning Company paid out

---

[89] *Daily Signal*, June 23, 24, 1909; Aug. 8, 1911
[90] *Ibid*, May 5, 1917
[91] Fontenot and Freeland, *Acadia*, 130, 288
[92] Minutes, Rayne Town Council, Apr. 4, 1905
[93] *Crowley Signal*, Dec. 14, 1907
[94] *Ibid*, Sept. 28, 1901

This rare old photo was reproduced by John Stephan from a fungus-damaged glass negative in the Freeland Collection, Dupre Library, University of Southwestern Louisiana. The business shown was a combined operation of rice milling and cotton ginning.

almost a quarter million dollars for cotton, which was then selling at 15 cents a pound, the highest price in 35 years.[95]

The gin company initiated a lively harvest time competition which was reported for the first time in 1904. Gold pieces were offered for the first cotton delivered to the gin. Contestants had to race from the city limits to the gin after midnight on August 26. By 10 p.m. twelve contestants were lined up, their wagons loaded with cotton; at the stroke of midnight all made a dash for the gin while a large crowd cheered and applauded. Bero Breaux, the first to reach the gin, won first prize of a $10 gold piece. Nathan Stutes was second and received $5 in gold. Olivier Chiasson won $5 for the heaviest bale.[96]

Chappuis was also in the brick making business. His plant was the largest in the south with a capacity of 100,000 bricks a day. The company kept one million bricks on hand. Material for the bricks was said to consist of an "inexhaustible supply of clay of excellent quality." Chappuis' other business enterprises were a large hardware store, banking interests and manufacturing stock feed. The feed was made of the entire ear of corn—cob, kernel, husk—ground up together.[97]

Jacques Weil, who was to become widely known as a shipper of bull

95 *Ibid*, Jan. 9, 23, 1904
96 *Ibid*, Sept. 3, 1904
97 *Ibid*, Apr. 25, Dec. 5, 1903

frogs, built the Mathilde cotton gin in 1903 and named it for his wife, the former Mathilde Lagneau. The gin was located east of Rayne and south of the Southern Pacific railroad tracks, on what is now Highway 90. The gin was put into operation in 1904 and by mid-November had ginned 1,000 bales, none of which weighed less than 500 pounds.[98]

Rayne Politicians

The important role played by George K. Bradford in the formation of Acadia Parish was revealed for the first time in 1907, more than 20 years after the parish was created. The information was published in the *Crowley Signal* of November 9, 1907, at which time Bradford was a candidate for state representative.

The article read, in part:

"It was Bradford who organized and led the movement for the formation of the parish of Acadia. He drew up the original bill under the authority of which the parish was carved out of St. Landry, and he spent the entire session of 1886 in Baton Rouge working for the bill."

The biographical sketch in the newspaper included the following: Bradford was a native of the old parish, born at Bellevue south of Opelousas, but had lived in New Orleans until 1885, when he settled at Rayne. He was a son-in-law of Gov. Francis T. Nicholls and was "connected by birth and marriage to some of the best families in the state."

The article made no mention of Bradford's activities in Rayne as a surveyor, real estate agent and newspaper man, or his appointment by President Grover Cleveland as agent for the detection of fraudulent entries of public lands.[99]

The incumbent and successful candidate for the post sought by Bradford was E. O. Bruner, who had moved to Rayne in 1883 and established a hotel and livery business. A native of Plaquemine Brulee (Branch) he had been tutored as a youth by Capt. John M. Taylor. Like Bradford he had supported and worked for the creation of the new parish. He had won the office of representative without opposition in 1906, to fill the unexpired term of H. W. Carver, resigned. His legislative record shows that he also was an advocate of partition of Calcasieu and St. Landy (the creation of Jefferson Davis and Evangeline Parishes) and that he was instrumental in securing the Rice Experiment Station for Acadia Parish.[100]

In 1911 Bruner was appointed commissioner of agriculture by Gov. J. Y. Sanders to fill an unexpired term. He was re-elected to the office in

---

[98] *Crowley Signal*, Nov. 19, 1904: Craig, Myrta Fair, "Three Weil Brothers, etc." *Rayne Acadian-Tribune*, Aug. 30, 1973

[99] *Abbeville Meridional*, May 21, 1887

[100] *Crowley Signal*, Dec. 14, 1907: *Daily Signal*, May 1, 1911

1912 and served a four-year term. He was defeated by Harry D. Wilson by a narrow margin in the 1916 state election.[101]

One of the strongest political figures in the early history of Acadia was James Webb, 1833-1904, who spent the last 15 years of his life as a resident of Rayne. The son of John Webb of Mermentau Cove he was a veteran of the Civil War, having served for two and a half years with Brent's Cavalry. After the war he operated a mercantile business at Plaquemine Brulee (Branch) and there became highly influential in the political and business lives of two nephews, C. C. and W. W. Duson. His political career included justice of the peace, 14 years, St. Landry Parish; mayor of Rayne, state representative and state senator. He was the father of two prominent Acadia Parish physicians, Dr. R. C. Webb and Dr. H. C. Webb.[102]

The most colorful figure in the political history of Acadia was a resident of the Rayne area. This was Prosper Caruthers, who created a sensation in 1907 when he ran for sheriff against Louis Fontenot, one of the most successful politicians in the history of the parish.

Caruthers appears to have been an uneducated Acadian with an Anglo name. He was born on the Mermentau River about 1861 but had lived some four miles northeast of Rayne since he was four. He claimed that his paternal grandfather Caruthers was a native of West Virginia who had been a well known sheriff in his native state.

Hampden Story, a prominent Crowley attorney, was reported to be Caruthers' political mentor. It is difficult to tell from the newspaper announcement if the news writer was serious or trying to pull off some sort of political joke. Since Lawyer Story's name was mentioned but once in connection with Caruthers, the conjecture is that the matter did start out as a joke. In the light of subsequent developments it is easy to deduce that the only person who took Caruthers' candidacy seriously was the candidate himself.

Caruthers was cruelly ridiculed in the press. He was, the *Signal* reported, seeking the Democratic nomination for "the important and lucrative office of sheriff and tax collector . . . like his distinguished sponsor, Caruthers is as frank as living sunlight, as free from guile as a hired hand when the dinner gong sounds. He is frankly out for the office, and assured the *Signal* that if he 'catches it' he will do something about it, yes. . . . He will not be haughty and aloof from the plain people if he is elect, but he will shake hands with all men, him. . . ."[103]

The writer opined that Caruthers' candidacy "would not detract from the picturesqueness of the campagn," as indeed it did not. Caruthers provided copy for southwest Louisiana newspapers for some seven months, both before and after the campaign.

---

[101] *Daily Signal*, May 1, 1911: Feb. 22, 1917

[102] *Crowley Signal*, Dec. 10, 1904: Fontenot and Freeland, *Acadia*, 215, 225

[103] *Crowley Signal*, Aug. 10, 1907

When Caruthers spoke at a political rally in Rayne the *Signal* devoted almost an entire column to lampooning him: ". . . a large and enthusiastic meeting at Rayne indicates strong support . . . some eggs were thrown, but this could have been making fun of Rayne, 'the Egg City'. . . ."[104]

Caruthers was even invited to speak outside the parish, in Opelousas, Eunice and Gueydan, where he drew large crowds and more newspaper ridicule. He appeared to have been oblivious to the fact that he was considered a *paillasse* (comic figure), and that the only reason he was invited to make speeches was to entertain the crowd.

Reporting on his speech-making in Opelousas, the *Clarion* stated: "He is not a rhetorician, neither is he a Demosthenes. . . . He speaks the English language as she is spoken by the distinguished Caruthers *pere* when he was sheriff of Virginia. Prosper stirs things; he is hot stuff and the sparks fly when he rattles the bones of robber office holders."[105]

Undaunted by his defeat (he received seven votes in the January 28, 1908 election), Caruthers, called "The Colonel of Marais Bullard" by the newspapers, announced a new campaign—to secure a night school. He said he was "determined to get an education."[106]

Sports

The Rayne area has long been associated with horse racing and cock fights, two types of sporting events which usually go along with lively betting. As late as 1915 cock fights were being staged in the heart of the town. A customer, R. Duhon, went into Kennedy's store and couldn't find a clerk to wait on him. The store employees were all in the alley watching a fight between "a grade Brahma and a one-eyed Plymouth Rock."[107]

Early horse races took place at the Theo Broussard race track where the Louisiana Derby was a special two-day event. There were 11 entries in the 1906 Derby, among them "Limber Jim," owned by L. S. Cornett of Crowley; "Fly," owned by J. Melancon of Rayne, and Theo Broussard's "Gito." A purse of $240 was offered for the quarter mile for two-year-olds. These races drew large crowds; special trains were run from Lake Charles, Lafourche and other points.[108]

Rayne Farmers

The Rayne community had a large share of the more progressive

[104] *Ibid*, Sept. 7, 14, 1907
[105] *Ibid*, Nov. 2, 1907
[106] *Ibid*, Feb. 15, 1908
[107] *Daily Signal*, Dec. 7, 1915
[108] *Daily Signal*, Mar. 10, 1906; *Crowley Signal*, June 1, 1907

farmers of Acadia Parish. Among the best known were the Hains brothers and Martin Petitjean.

Albert and Guilford Hains had a highly diversified farm operation years before the outbreak of World War I. The Hains raised rice, corn, cotton, sugar cane, yams, garden produce. They also specialized in thoroughbred horses, registered swine, high grade cattle and poultry, and raised their own alfalfa and lespedeza.[109]

Martin Petitjean, termed one of the parish's most progressive farmers, was also a leader in the civic, business and religious life of the community. As a farmer he was largely interested in the production of rice and cattle. One of the highlights of the year at "La Campagne," the Petitjean plantation, was branding day, when as many as 250 head of cattle would be marked and workers and visitors alike treated to a barbecue meal.[110]

Bastille Day

A most colorful part of Rayne's past history was the annual celebration of Bastille Day on July 14, the anniversary of French Independence.

The first published account of the unique celebration was in 1899; the last available printed reference to the event appeared in the *Daily Signal* of June 11, 1914: "The 14th of July (*Prise de la Bastille*) will be celebrated in Rayne in the usual manner by the French element."

The originator of the celebration, believed to have been the first of its kind in southwest Louisiana, was Eugene Eleazar, native of St. Esprit, France, who came to the Rayne area in 1888. The observance began on the Eleazar farm near Rayne, then was taken up by the townspeople, a number of whom were French immigrants or descendants of French immigrants. The Eleazar family moved to Kaplan about 1907 and a second Bastille Day celebration was begun by Eleazar in the Vermilion Parish town, where it has been continued to the present, 1978.[111]

The 1899 celebration featured a parade, a picnic, ball game and a dance. The morning parade was led by Mayor O. Broussard riding a handsome horse bedecked with bright ribbons and streamers. Marching music was provided by the Rayne Silver Cornet Band. Parade chairmen were Emile Daboval Jr. and Leon Eleazar.

Seven floats made up the parade. The Mervine Kahn float, a representation of the Statue of Liberty, was described as "an elaborate piece of work." The republics of France and the United States were saluted by the Levy and Weil float, with the United States represented by Uncle Sam in full costume and France by "a young lady surrounded by soldiers and little girls."

[109] *Crowley Signal*, Oct. 31, 1908; *Daily Signal*, July 8, 1911; July 29, 1914
[110] *Daily Signal*, Apr. 1, 6, 1911
[111] *Rayne Tribune*, Jan. 10, 1904; interview, Paul E. Eleazar, Myrta Fair Craig, 1977

Plattsmier's grocery entered a float titled "Innocence." A wagon completely covered in white was filled with little girls dressed in white. The L. A. Duclos float was a representation of the interior of his drug store.

O. Broussard's drug store float, decorated with bunting, carried a figure of justice with balanced scales. Residents of the German colony at Robert's Cove near Rayne provided a float and a cavalcade of horseback riders. The float, described as "novel and beautiful," portrayed Cleopatra. Float riders were Joseph Schaffhausen, Joseph Knipping and David Levy.

The seventh float, entered by Rayne area farmers, was loaded with agricultural products grown around Rayne. Six parade marshals rode alongside the floats.

A picnic in the park took place after the parade. The ball game ended with a tight score of Rayne, 4, and Crowley, 3. Ball players of both teams were entertained at supper at the Commercial Hotel. A dance at the Opera House concluded the program.[112]

The July 14 celebrations at Rayne were briefly noted in the Crowley newspaper in 1907, 1909 and 1914. The 1909 celebration, which featured a parade and horse races, was sponsored by the Rayne firemen.[113]

The First Daboval

Emile Daboval Jr., whose name was so long associated with the parish's first rice mill, was a man of many interests. In addition to rice milling and rice brokerage, Daboval was also interested in oil, real estate, drainage projects and inventions. He bored the first oil well in the Evangeline field on the Houssiere-Latrielle tract when oil was first discovered in Louisiana in 1901.[114]

In 1914 Daboval promoted a plan for clearing Bayou Queue de Tortue so as to create a navigable stream from the Intracoastal Canal to a point northeast of Rayne. He felt that this clearing project would provide perfect drainage for the Rayne section and also give the town competing freight rates.[115]

Some years earlier, when Rayne was known as "Egg City" because of the large shipments of eggs originating there, Daboval invented an egg carrier. The contrivance was described as "a series of molds made of cheap straw or wood pulp, each mold holding an egg and protecting it from injury. The molds are in sheets of a dozen or half dozen and are convenient for transporting eggs in any quantity."[116]

[112] *Crowley Signal*, July 22, 1899
[113] *Crowley Signal*, July 20, 1907: *Daily Signal*, July 9, 1909: June 11, 1914
[114] *Daily Signal*, Dec. 14, 1907: Jan. 16, 1909
[115] *Ibid*, Feb. 6, 1914
[116] *Crowley Signal*, Dec. 5, 1908

Poupeville-Rayne Post Office

The history of Rayne's post office goes back to the Poupeville settlement. Octave P. Bonin was appointed postmaster at Poupeville August 5, 1858. Bonin was succeeded by D. Bernard, John H. Hoffpauir and Mrs. Scholastie Sittig. The post office was discontinued January 24, 1870 then re-established eight years later, on October 24, 1878, with Joseph D. Bernard as postmaster.

The name of the post office was changed to Rayne on May 21, 1881. Other early postmasters (1883-1920) were Nicholas Young, Alphonse Duclos, C. Poulet, Michael D. Coleman, Blaise A. Chappuis, Romanta T. Hart, Charles W. Lyman and Joseph Abadie.[117]

Rayne Newspapers

Acadia's first newspaper, the *Rayne Signal*, began publication March 13, 1886. The proprietors were C. W. Felter and George Addison. Six months later W. W. Duson bought the paper. A second newspaper, the *Acadia Sentinel*, edited and published by George K. Bradford, began publication September 14, 1886.[118]

Several other newspapers were begun in Rayne during the mid-1890s. Three—the *Rayne Ranger*, *Rayne Herald* and *Rayne News*, lasted but a short while. A fourth, the *Rayne Tribune*, was more durable.[119]

The *Rayne Tribune* was established in November of 1894. R. N. May, formerly with the *Chicago Tribune*, was the first editor.[120]

Other early editors were W. B. Hardwick and W. A. Henslee. Henslee took over in April of 1901, and apparently remained until May of 1903 when S. G. Watkins took over the editorship.[121]

Watkins was replaced in May of 1904 by Misses Blanche M. Jesse and Cora L. Kraemer as editors and managers. The two women came to Rayne from Kinder, where they had published the *Kinder Times*. George K. Bradford directed the editorial policy of the newspaper, and Charles W. Lyman was president of the Tribune Publishing Co.[122]

The newspaper changed hands again in the fall of 1904. J. L. Craig, formerly of the *Tyler County News*, Tyler, Texas, bought the paper from the Misses Jesse and Kraemer.[123]

---

[117] Register of Postmasters, National Archives and Records Service
[118] Fontenot and Freeland, *Acadia*, 128, 130
[119] *Ibid*, 316
[120] *Crowley Signal*, Oct. 13, 1894: *Rayne Tribune*, Dec. 4, 1903
[121] *Crowley Signal*, Apr. 6, 1901: May 2, 1903
[122] *Rayne Tribune*, May 7, 1904: *Daily Signal*, May 10, 1904
[123] *Crowley Signal*, Sept. 10, 1904

Church Point

Church Point, a predominantly Acadian-French Catholic community in the northeast corner of Acadia, is the second oldest settlement in the parish, dating from the early 1840s.

The first Catholic church in the area that was to become the civil parish of Acadia was established in Church Point in 1848. A small building, to be used for a chapel, was secured by the Daigle brothers, Joseph E. and Theodule. The chapel building was hauled into the embryo town and placed on land that had been bought by the Jesuits of Grand Coteau. The church acquired additional land in 1854 when the Daigles donated five arpents for use as a cemetery.[1]

A new church, built partly from interest-free funds loaned by Jean Barousse, was dedicated April 21, 1885.

Two resident pastors, both natives of France, served the Church Point church during the period under study. They were Rev. Auguste Eby, who took over from the Jesuits in 1883, and Rev. Auguste F. Roger, 1902-1928.

A Catholic school opened in the fall of 1914 with an enrollment of 140. The Sisters of the Immaculate Conception had charge of the school. Earlier, during Father Eby's administration, a small school had functioned for three years, from 1891 to 1894. Two lay teachers were employed.[2]

An unusual event for the times, a mass of thanksgiving for a bountiful harvest, now a common practice in south Louisiana, took place in Church Point in 1904. The solemn high mass was celebrated with a full choir assisted by an orchestra. A capacity crowd attended the mass, held in late February.[3]

Church affairs dominate published information about Church Point during the early years of the century. The interior of the large church (seating capacity, 1,450) was painted in 1905 by A. W. Guidry, contractor, and a crew of men. A new altar, costing $700 with the names of the donors inscribed on it, was installed in 1906.[4]

The most prestigious gathering that took place in Church Point's early history was in the summer of 1905, when Archbishop Placide L. Chapelle, head of the New Orleans archdiocese and apostolic delegate to Cuba, visited the town while on a confirmation tour of southwestern Louisiana.

A company of 100 men welcomed the church dignitary. Mounted on

---

[1] Guidry, Anita G., *La Pointe de l'Eglise*, 4, 9

[2] Baudier, Roger, "Dedication of the New Church of Our Lady of the Sacred Heart," booklet, 1954

[3] *Crowley Signal*, Feb. 27, 1904

[4] *Daily Signal*, May 26, 1905: Jan. 20, 1906

Jean Barousse, patriarch of one of Church Point's earliest families. A native of France, Barousse came to the area in 1840. (Photo courtesy Mary Leola Barousse Harmon)

decorated horses and armed with double-barrelled shotguns the caval-cade met the archbishop at a point about midway between Church Point and Sunset. When the entourage entered the town limits a cannon was fired, the brass band played and the church bell rang. The music and bell ringing continued until the archbishop reached the church, where he con-firmed 355 persons and heard a welcome address delivered by Dr. C. V. Richard. Following the ceremonies the cannon roared again, the band played and the company of mounted men fired a 100-gun salute.[5] (The confirmation ceremony in Church Point could have been the archbishop's last pastoral act. The remainder of his tour was cancelled because of the yellow fever epidemic. He returned to New Orleans, contracted the dis-ease and died on August 9, 1905, less than three weeks after the celebra-tion in Church Point.)

The first Acadia Parish resident to enter the Catholic priesthood was a Church Point native, Rev. Alfred Latiolais, who was accepted into the Jesuit novitiate September 14, 1889 and ordained in 1897.[6]

The Methodist congregation of Church Point acquired land on which to build a church in the spring of 1891. One arpent of land was sold by V. C. Breaux to W. S. Evins, president of the board of trustees, for $150. The description of the property located it "north by land of vendor . . . to begin at a gum tree near Breaux's gully, running north 64 yards with the street known as Bridge Street." An additional strip was sold to the church in 1902 when Jerry Wimberly, representing the church, bought 10 feet by 192 feet from Albert Breaux for $25.[7]

A post office was established at Church Point in 1873 with Jules David as first postmaster. Other postmasters and postmistresses (1877-1920) were Charles S. Perrodin, 1877; P. L. Guidry, 1881; Laurent Barousse, 1900; Emile Daigle, 1900; Linda M. Hargroder, 1913; Moise Bellard, 1919-1923.[8]

The post office was at several locations during the early years. At one time it was in a saddle shop near the P. L. Guidry home, then was moved in 1900 to the J. E. Daigle and Son store.[9]

Although the town was not incorporated until 1899, records show that Homer Barousse was the first mayor, serving from March 11, 1893 to February 1, 1895. He was succeeded by Dr. L. B. Arceneaux.

J. David was appointed mayor in 1897. Serving with him was a five-member board of aldermen composed of Homer Barousse, T. Guidry, H. D. McBride, Albert Olivier and Albert Breaux, all appointed. The same officials were re-appointed in 1899, and A. Higginbotham was named town marshal.[10]

[5] *Ibid*, July 21, 1905
[6] Jesuit Archives, Grand Coteau, La.
[7] Conveyance Books F, #3233, 200; C-2, #20408, 560, Acad. Par.
[8] Register of Postmasters, National Archives and Records Service
[9] *Daily Signal*, Sept. 11, 1900
[10] Louisiana Department of State

The first post-incorporation town election took place in 1900, when the incumbent officials, except Albert Breaux, were elected. E. A. Henry was appointed to the council in July of 1900.[11]

In 1902 the five seats on the council were reduced to three. John D. Murrel was elected mayor and council members were Edward Daigle, Maurice Barousse and Edmond Deville. R. W. Davis was elected marshal.[12]

Murrel continued in office until 1909. Other officials serving with him included Hubert J. David, alderman; C. L. Lyons and Treville O. Guidry, marshals.[13]

Laurent Barousse, a son of the first mayor, began a 16-year tenure in 1908. Council members during the Barousse regime included Theo Daigle, John Horecky, John D. Murrel, Lloyd Franques, R. B. Boeltcher, Ben Daigle and Albert Breaux. Marshals during this period were Elash McBride and T. O. Guidry.[14]

There was virtually no opposition to Democratic nominees for municipal posts during the early years. Random news reports show that the office of town marshal was contested in two elections: in 1902 R. W. Davis was opposed by P. D. McBride; Davis won with 16 votes to McBride 10. In 1908 T. O. Guidry squeaked by Alcee Sonnier by a one-vote plurality. The 1910 election was summed up thus: ". . . a victory for the Democratic ticket, which was the only one in the field;" it was further noted that the vote was "very light."[15]

Commerce

From its earliest years Church Point was a trade center for a wide area, but population-wise, the town itself showed little growth. The 1900 population of 278 residents had increased to 481 by 1910, but the next decade showed a decline in population. The 1920 census gives the town 393 inhabitants.[16]

Pioneer merchants and tradespeople include Jean Barousse, L. Schnerb, Leonard Franques, P. L. Guidry, J. B. David, Thelesmar Guidry, Etienne Latiolais, H. D. McBride and Moses Landry. The assets of the town, prior to 1900, included the two churches, one of the larger public schools of the parish, attendance-wise; several cotton gins and two resident physicians.[17]

Church Point was the heart of Acadia's cotton industry for more than

[11] *Ibid*

[12] *Ibid*

[13] *Ibid*

[14] *Ibid*

[15] *Daily Signal*, Apr. 24, 1902; *Crowley Signal*, Feb. 15, 1908; Apr. 23, 1910

[16] *Louisiana Almanac*, 1975-1976; *Daily Signal*, Dec. 27, 1911

[17] Fontenot and Freeland, *Acadia Parish, a History to 1900*, 153, 154

The People's Cotton Gin handled large amounts of cotton when this photo was taken in 1907. Cotton was the main money crop of the Church Point area at the time.

half a century. As many as four cotton gins were in operation there at one time.[18]

Many of Church Point's leading businessmen were involved with cotton in one way or another. Names of investors in cotton gins, taken from charters filed during the time period being considered, include Homer, Laurent, Bertrand and J. A. Barousse; Theodore, H. J. and Edward Daigle; D. and Albert Breaux; Polite, Dupre and Theogene Richard; M. A., Willie and Arthur L. Harmon; E. H. Richard, Mrs. H. P. Richard, Dr. L. B. Arceneaux, Oralian Thibodeaux, A. J. Jagneaux, Charles J. Bourque, Gaston d'Augereaux, Lawrence Young, L. D. Bellard, William B. Brisco, Sidney Savoy, Lloyd Franques, Joseph Beaugh, J. C. Wimberley, F. E. Lyons, Homer David, J. B. A. Bergeron, J. M. Davis, J. B. Gardiner, J. C. Chachere, A. T. Smith, J. T. Leger and Francois Ledoux. The first cotton gin was owned and operated by Valentin Breaux.[19]

After the cotton boll weevil brought discouragement and demoralization, cotton planters turned to raising corn, cane and rice. Early in the 1909 season the sale of corn had increased from 10,000 to 25,000 barrels, which was estimated to have put an additional $25,000 into circulation in Church Point.[20]

---

[18] *Daily Signal*, Feb. 16, 1917
[19] Guidry, Anita G., *La Pointe*, 40
[20] *Daily Signal*, Nov. 30, 1909

Merchants and tradesmen of Church Point could offer customers a respectable variety of merchandise and services by 1901. J. E. Daigle and Son ran a general store and cotton gin: David and Breaux were dealers in general merchandise. T. Guidry's diversified interests offered hardware, groceries, implements and wagons. Guidry also manufactured shoes, harness and saddles, and operated a barber shop.[21]

Homer Barousse sold general merchandise, hardware and implements and operated a cotton gin. L. Franques sold groceries, hardware and notions: Rudolph David handled wines, liquors and cigars.[22]

Edmond Deville had an iron works, E. M. Richard did carpentry, made barrels, cisterns and coffins: A. W. Guidry was the town's painter and paperhanger and James Stakes was a bricklayer.[23] Deville's blacksmith and wheelwright shop was located near the Guidry hardware store. Deville's specialties included made-to-order peddling hacks. Richard's specialty was making coffins. During the summer of 1899 the Church Point "coffin factory" was reported running full time, with extra workmen put on at night.[24]

Deville's iron works was chartered in 1901 as the Church Point Manufacturing Company. Officers and directors were Homer Barousse, T. Guidry, L. Broussard, H. J. David, Edmond Deville, J. D. Murrel and George Jagneaux. At that time a feed and livery business was being operated by P. D. McBride and R. W. Davis, Mrs. Albert Breaux kept the ladies supplied with stylish millinery, and Theodore Daigle ran the Klondike Saloon.[25]

The town's first restaurant, operated by Albert Olivier and Rudolph David, opened for business on Main Street July 1, 1900.[26]

Church Point's first bank, the Commercial State Bank, with capital stock of $15,000, was organized in 1902. Officers and directors were Homer Barousse, Edward Daigle, Dr. R. C. Webb, I. M. Lichtenstein and W. M. Smith of New Orleans, Abrom and Henry Kaplan. The firm of Castain and Russell was awarded the contract for the bank building, Church Point's first brick structure.[27]

New construction during 1902-1903 included the new Homer Barousse store: the John Horecky warehouse, built near the Horecky store: a second livery stable, built by James Bourgeois, a racket (novelty) store, opened by Joseph Barousse and Willie Hornsby, and Mrs. Jules David's new hotel building.[28]

[21] *Crowley Signal*, Feb. 16, 1901
[22] *Ibid*
[23] *Ibid*
[24] *Ibid*, Mar. 10, 1900; July 22, 1899
[25] *Ibid*, Feb. 2, Sept. 21, Dec. 21, 1901; Jan. 4, 1902
[26] *Ibid*, June 30, 1900
[27] *Crowley Signal*, Feb. 22, 1902: *Daily Signal*, Jan. 30, 1903
[28] *Daily Signal*, July 4, 1902: *Crowley Signal*, Feb. 1, 1902: Apr. 18, Oct. 10, 1903

Business notes of 1904 included a new post office building, occupied by Postmaster Emile Daigle: Victor Brunet, who made and repaired shoes, saddles and harness, also sold tobacco and soft drinks. The J. E. Daigle and Son business was expanded. A larger store, a two-story building, was constructed that summer. The old store building was moved to another lot nearer the post office to make way for the new building.[29]

The P. D. McBride livery stable was destroyed by fire during the winter of 1905, causing damage estimated at $2,000. The horses were saved, but 14 buggies, stored supplies and feed were lost. The fire was caused by a gasoline explosion; an employee lit a match to see if the faucet on a barrel of gasoline stored in the building had been left open. The building was ablaze within minutes after the resulting explosion.[30]

A lesser disaster that year involved the I. O. Guidry livery stable. The upper floor of the building, where 200 barrels of corn were stored, gave way and crashed. Fortunately the hostlers had just vacated the building.[31]

The year 1905 brought some new businesses, several changes and some improvements. Arsene Langley of Iota opened a racket store on the corner of Main and Plaquemine, Mrs. H. D. McBride's new casket store was opened for business, the Pleasant Resort Saloon, run by Maurice Barousse and Felix A. Dejean, occupied a new building and R. David opened a restaurant in the old saloon building. The old Schnerb store building, owned by Homer Barousse, was torn down, and John Horecky brought ice to Church Point. He built a cold storage plant with a capacity up to 5,000 pounds.[32]

Efforts to develop the town were begun in 1905 by Thelesmar Guidry, a self-made tradesman. Born at Church Point April 10, 1856, Guidry grew up as an illiterate farm boy. In 1897 he married Hermina Daigle, who taught him to read and write in both English and French. Guidry learned from the columns of the Opelousas newspaper, printed in both English and French at the time.[33]

Guidry learned the shoemaker's trade and in 1882 set up his own business with tools supplied by Jean Barousse. He soon expanded the business to include saddlery and barbering. By 1903 he had a well-stocked store, office, a handsome residence and owned 120 acres within the corporation limits. He was a community leader, having served on the town council, as a trustee of the Catholic church, a school director and member of the Democratic committee.[34]

Guidry promoted two sales of town lots. The first was December 19, 1905, when 120 lots were auctioned. Six of the lots were given for public

[29] *Crowley Signal*, Feb. 27, 1904: *Daily Signal*, July 21, 28, 1904
[30] *Daily Signal*, Jan. 23, 1905
[31] *Ibid*, June 23, 1905
[32] *Daily Signal*, May 1, 26, July 21, 1905: *Crowley Signal*, Oct. 28, 1905
[33] *Daily Signal*, Feb. 20, 1903
[34] *Ibid*

school use. Entertainment was provided by the Church Point and Breaux Bridge bands. The second lot sale took place January 11, 1908, after the Opelousas, Gulf and Northeastern railroad was completed to Church Point. The promotion plans included an excursion from Melville at reduced rates, band music, and the auctioning of 150 lots in the T. Guidry addition. A listing of the town's assets, published as part of the lot sale promotion, included "18 to 20 residences."[35]

Meanwhile other improvements had come about. The town's telephone exchange began operations in May of 1906. Bertha Landry was the

---

[35] *Crowley Signal*, Dec. 16, 1905: Jan. 4, 1908

These photos were reproduced from the 1907 Christmas edition of the *Daily Signal*. Thelesmar Guidry, shown with the orange tree, initiated town development when the railroad came through. The Commercial Bank was the town's first brick structure. The view of the church is the only known photo which shows the large crucifix in front of the church.

first operator. A fine three-story hotel, costing $6,000, was built near the OG depot by T. Guidry. The town band, known as the Guidry band, was re-organized with A. W. Guidry as leader. Members in 1906 were Joe Hoffman, Maurice and Vorice Wimberly, M. D. Murrel, Lawrence Thibodeaux, Gilbert David, Jules Richard, Eddie Hodd, Ignace, Charles, Benjamin, John and Joseph L. Guidry.[36]

A soda pop factory, begun by Alcee Sonnier, was bought by Pierre Guidry, son of Thelesmar, in 1906. Pierre's brother, Theodule, a blacksmith and wheelwright, invented a hay baler which he had patented.[37]

Business changes and additions during the time of railroad construction included:

H. J. David took over the David and Breaux mercantile, and Albert Breaux opened his own general store. A bakery, operated by Alia Battershell and Jake Fontenot, offered "excellent bread, delicious cakes and jellyroll."[38]

A. W. Guidry and Joseph Hoffpauir opened a tin shop, George Jagneaux started a blacksmith and wheelwright business and Dr. L. B. Arceneaux, Wimberley and Richard sold their livery to Donovan Brothers. J. D. Murrel and Brother built a new hardware store and Ralph David opened a soda fountain in his father's restaurant.[39]

With Church Point's first rail connection with the outside world about to become a reality the quiet little village literally hummed with activity. By the end of 1907 a total of $50,000 had been spent on new construction. On the south side of the $2,500 OG&NE depot the improvements included the Guidry Hotel, a printing office, the J. B. Gardiner store; new homes for families of Jack Wimberley, Emile Daigle, Mrs. Oscar Breaux, Ernest Hundley, Sidney Savoy, Arras Guidry, Charles Guidry, Joseph Beaugh, Mrs. Frank Bergeron, E. A. Henry, John Labbe, Adolphe Guidry and Miss Eugenia Thibodeaux; home additions by Pierre Guidry, Joseph Lejeune, T. O. Guidry; the Murrel warehouse, Farmer's Warehouse Company warehouse and office and Adolphe Guidry's blacksmith shop.[40]

On the north side of the depot new construction included the P. D. McBride livery, A. G. Guidry barber shop, the Langley store, Daigle warehouse; additions to the Franques store, Rudolph David's Pearl Restaurant, Donovan's livery; sheds and a new office at People's Lumber firm; Dr. L. B. Arceneaux's new office; homes for Ben Daigle, Dr. J. B. Parrott and Dr. W. A. Jenkins.[41]

The railroad track reached Church Point on April 19, 1907. The event

[36] *Daily Signal*, May 15, Dec. 15, 1906
[37] *Daily Signal*, May 4, 1906: *Crowley Signal*, Oct. 17, 1908
[38] *Daily Signal*, Jan. 20, 1906
[39] *Daily Signal*, Feb. 8, May 29, July 1, 1906: *Crowley Signal*, Feb. 16, 1907
[40] *Ibid*, supplement Dec. 14, 1907
[41] *Ibid*

The three-story Guidry Hotel, built in anticipation of business to be brought in by Church Point's first railroad, the Opelousas, Gueydan and Northeastern. The hotel was one of the Thelesmar Guidry enterprises. (Freeland Archives photo, Acadia Parish Library)

was celebrated with music by the band and firing the town's cannon, the Flying Molly.[42]

The OG established two new place names in Acadia along its track between Church Point and Crowley, Clarksdale and Soileau. The between stations were Branch, Clarksdale, Soileau and Rayne. The run from Church Point to Branch took 14 minutes; Branch to Clarksdale, 10 minutes; Clarksdale to Soileau, 8 minutes; Soileau to Rayne, 5 minutes; Rayne to Crowley, 15 minutes.[43]

The firm of Theo Daigle and Bros. was organized in 1910 by three of Ernest Daigle's sons, J. E. Daigle Jr., Theodore and Emilien Daigle. Another son, Ben Daigle, bought out J. E. and Emilien in 1917. The older firm of J. E. Daigle and Sons Ltd. was founded by the father, Ernest Daigle, and continued by another son, Edward Daigle.[44]

Early bakeries in Church Point were operated by Ben Franques, Felix Barousse, Dennis Keller and Arthur David.[45]

Church Point's first druggist was Constant Bries. When Bries and his family left Church Point in 1900 to live in Brussels, Belgium, the drug

[42] *Ibid*, May 4, 1907
[43] *Daily Signal*, Mar. 1, 1909
[44] Guidry, *La Pointe*, 68, 71
[45] *Ibid*, 60

store was bought by Dr. L. B. Arceneaux and Theodore Daigle. Other druggists (to 1920) were Oscar Martin and A. L. Gaudet.[46]

Church Point was the first community in the parish to get rural free mail delivery. Delivery began June 1, 1911. Moise Bellard was the first rural mail carrier.[47]

A new store, owned by M. A. Hargroder, opened in 1912. The business, located near the Guidry Hotel, offered general merchandise, cold storage and meats. That same year Laurent Thibodeaux, owner of two cars, brought Church Point residents a new service, an automobile transfer line.[48]

The town got concrete sidewalks and its first movie theater in 1913. Brooks and Chachere brought a traveling moving picture show to town. The nightly entertainments were well attended, which resulted in the show being held over another week. The first permanent movie house was the Bijou, opened in 1915 by Laurent Thibodeaux and Dr. C. J. Alleman.[49]

A vegetable and fruit canning plant, set up in 1913, was reported a success after one season's operation. The factory processed 40,000 cans of blackberries, figs, tomatoes, sweet potatoes and cane syrup. All except the syrup was sold before the 1914 planting season began.[50]

Hypolite Richard, one of the largest landowners in the section, a successful farmer and stockholder in a Church Point lumber company and cotton gin, was co-owner with his son Ernest of the H. P. Richard and Son Saloon.[51]

A major development of 1914 was the construction of the large John Horecky warehouse on Third Street. The building, on a brick foundation, had a galvanized iron frame and roof. Horecky came to America from his native Austria-Hungary in 1886 and settled in Church Point about 1890. In 1892 he married a Church Point girl, Julia McBride. He started out as a chicken and egg peddler, peddling his wares by walking from house to house. He progressed from this to a peddling hack, then to owning his own store. The next step was the purchase of a wholesale grocery company, which had been organized earlier by Leo Franques and Emile Daigle.[52]

People's Lumber Company is Church Point's oldest lumber firm.

[46] Ibid, 64: Crowley Signal, July 14, 1900: Daily Signal, Mar. 3, 1911: La Pointe, 103
[47] Daily Signal, Mar. 3, 1911: Guidry, La Pointe, 103
[48] Daily Signal, July 12, Sept. 26, 1912
[49] Daily Signal, May 8, June 20, 1913: Guidry, La Pointe, 54
[50] Daily Signal, Mar. 9, 1914
[51] Ibid, Aug. 14, 1913
[52] Daily Signal, Feb. 14, 1914: Guidry, La Pointe, 65. From that small beginning Horecky expanded the business into the largest independent wholesale grocery company in the south, a business that had a major influence in the economy of the community and parish.

Theodore Daigle bought the company from A. C. Skiles of Opelousas in 1907.[53]

The first meat market was owned by Ernest Daigle, son of Joseph E. Daigle, one of the founders of the town. The market, which opened for business about 1870, was expanded during the 1880s into the general merchandising store.[54]

Church Point residents had their pictures taken by itinerant photographers Ira Kohler and E. H. Risher, who came to town to work at different times between 1901 and 1906.[55]

There were several syrup mills in Church Point and vicinity during the early years. These were operated by Walter Briscoe, Willie Higginbotham, Theobert Venable, Clifford Lyons and Eddie Jagneaux.[56]

Gaston Barrilleaux had a store in Church Point in 1916, and the Leo Harmon general store opened for business in 1917. By this time the principal streets in the town had been graveled.[57]

A second bank for the town, Farmer's Bank and Trust Company, was organized in 1919 by Edward Daigle.[58]

Doctors and Dentists

Dr. J. A. McMillan, Dr. W. A. Jenkins and Dr. L. B. Arceneaux were the three best known pioneer physicians of the Church Point area. Dr. McMillan first located in Church Point in 1870 and practiced there for some 20 years before moving to Bourque Point near Crowley.[59]

Dr. Jenkins, physician and surgeon, began a 40-year medical practice in Church Point in 1887. He married Mattie Hundley of Church Point, and the couple raised a large family of adopted children. Dr. C. E. Hamilton joined Dr. Jenkins in practice for a short while after World War II, in 1919.[60]

Dr. Arceneaux started practice in Acadia at Pointe-aux-Loups in 1891, but shortly thereafter moved to Church Point. He married Mary Amy Vautrot in 1895, the year he became mayor of Church Point. Dr. Arceneaux kept his medical knowledge up-to-date, and was a strong believer in new techniques in the treatment of disease, especially in the

---

[53] Guidry, *La Pointe*, 69

[54] *Ibid*, 22

[55] *Crowley Signal*, Aug. 17, 1901; *Daily Signal*, Sept. 25, 1906

[56] Guidry, *La Pointe*, 40

[57] *Daily Signal*, Feb. 3, 1916; Mar. 2, 1917; Guidry, *La Pointe*, 66

[58] Guidry, *La Pointe*, 70

[59] Perrin, W. H., *SW. La. Biographical and Historical*, Part II, 268; *Crowley Signal*, Sept. 21, 1889

[60] Guidry, *La Pointe*, 43

use of anti-toxin for diphtheria, the dread killer of young children. It was his boast that in six years he had lost but two diphtheria cases.[61]

Dr. A. B. Childs started medical practice in Church Point in 1907, then moved to Eunice.[62]

Although not a resident of Church Point Dr. Frank Savoy, a graduate of Tulane Medical School, practiced in rural Church Point for many years. He died of tuberculosis July 18, 1908.[63]

Other early physicians were Dr. George Lessley, Dr. Knox, Dr. Donovan, Dr. L. Mason, who occupied an office on the second floor of the David building in 1904,[64] and a Dr. Stephens.

Other than the names, no information on these early professional men survives, except for Dr. Stephens, an eccentric recluse who became a legendary figure in Church Point. When Dr. Stephens died in the spring of 1905 Pierre Guidry, the *Signal*'s Church Point correspondent, wrote as follows:

> Old Dr. Stephens, of near Church Point, died on last Monday, age about 70 years. He was noted as one of the queerest old men on earth. For the last 37 years he had lived three miles from town in an old hut. He had plenty of money at his command and a well-read man as well as a fine physician, but would very seldom treat a patient. When he felt disposed he would go if called. No one could ever find out from him where he was from. Living in the edge of the wood with his cattle, it seemed to be his greatest desire to pet his cattle. He was a Mason and was buried in the wood near an oak tree where he always asked to be buried.[65]

Dr. Clay V. Richard was Church Point's first dentist. A native of Grand Coteau, Dr. Richard came to Church Point in 1902 and practiced about 10 years. His office was in the home of Mrs. Henry McBride on Main Street. Dr. C. J. Alleman began a lifetime dental practice in Church Point in May of 1906. Other early dentists were Dr. Lonnie Childs and a Dr. Hines. Dr. E. A. Hundley was a Church Point optometrist for many years, beginning in 1917.[66]

Newspapers

Church Point's first newspaper was the *Advocate*, published in 1894-1895 by T. C. Lewis with financial backing by Homer Barousse.[67] It is not known how long the paper remained in publication.

A 1902 news item reported that Church Point was "going to have a paper to replace the *Advocate*," but it was not until mid-February of 1903

[61] *Crowley Signal*, Apr. 4, 1903

[62] *Ibid*, Dec. 14, 1907

[63] *Ibid*, July 25, 1908

[64] Guidry, *La Pointe*, 43, 44: *Daily Signal*, July 28, 1904

[65] *Daily Signal*, Mar. 7, 1905

[66] Guidry, *La Pointe*, 46: *Daily Signal*, May 15, 1906

[67] Fontenot and Freeland, *Acadia*, 316

that the *Church Point Post* made its appearance.[68] The publication was apparently short-lived.

More is known of the town's third newspaper, the *Church Point Democrat*, which began publication August 1, 1907. E. Z. Hart, the editor, occupied an office in a $350 building put up by T. Guidry in his addition south of the depot. M. I. Ramsey took over as editor in 1908.[69] At an undetermined time between 1909 and 1911 L. J. V. Breaux was the editor. The *Democrat* was printed in Church Point; there are several published references to a printing office, and Cleveland Murrel was identified as the typesetter. Publication of the *Democrat* was suspended in February of 1911.[70]

Politics

Church Point was Acadia's political problem child during the pioneer years of parish organization. Stubbornly opposed to division of the mother parish, Church Point voters had cast 200 out of 228 ballots against the proposal in the 1886 referendum.[71] Once the issue was decided, the rebellious sibling grabbed for the reins of power. Within the first decade of Acadia's existence Church Point justified the old adage:

"Rayne wanted the courthouse, Crowley got it, Church Point runs it."

The man primarily responsible for the belief that Church Point "ran the courthouse" was Homer Barousse, the most powerful political figure in the history of Acadia Parish to date (1978).

Because of his family connections and position in the community Barousse was a power in politics even before Acadia was carved from St. Landry. This was demonstrated when he was named to the five-member police jury in the first action of parish organization, November 3, 1886.[72]

Barousse scored his first significant political victory in the summer of 1887. A supporter of Francis T. Nicholls for governor, Barousse was elected chairman of the parish Democratic Executive Committee over strong opposition put up by the Duson-McEnery faction.[73]

In 1893 he became Church Point's first mayor, serving one two-year term. He no doubt would have continued as mayor except for the fact that in 1894 he was elected state senator, winning over Gus Fontenot in a hotly contested race.[74] He served two years, was re-elected in 1900 and held

---

[68] *Daily Signal*, May 15, 1902; Feb. 18, 1903
[69] *Crowley Signal*, Dec. 14, 1907; Oct. 17, 1908
[70] *Daily Signal*, June 7, 1909; Feb. 2, 11, 15, 1911
[71] Fontenot and Freeland, *Acadia*, 247, 254
[72] *Ibid*, 258
[73] *Ibid*, 292-293
[74] *Crowley Signal*, Apr. 14, 1894

the post until he retired in 1932. He was seldom opposed for the office.[75]

Because he rarely spoke on the floor of the state legislature, Barousse earned the title of "The Sphinx of the Louisiana Senate." Nonetheless he was recognized as one of the most influential leaders of south Louisiana. He was respected by his colleagues and feared by his political enemies.[76]

A 1911 pre-election editorial in the *Daily Signal*, written in support of Barousse's candidacy for the senate seat, reads, in part, as follows:

> "That man from Acadia is not much on the gab, but he has been in the Senate so long he knows the state business thoroughly, he is absolutely conscientious, does what he thinks is right, and when he passes his word it is as good as a government bond. He comes pretty near my ideal of a Senator."
>
> That was said of Senator Barousse of Acadia by a man who has for years had an intimate knowledge of the men who shape affairs at Baton Rouge. It is a pretty fair estimate of the man and of the Senator. Even the men who do not agree with him and who would refuse to subscribe to the opinion that Barousse is an "ideal Senator" will tell you that the Church Point man's word passes current like a gold dollar, that he does what he thinks is right, no matter who thinks otherwise, and his record supports the statement that he is his own man—a conscientious man and not one who is led.

Barousse was a member of the Acadia Parish Police Jury for 10 years, also served on the Church Point town council. His business enterprises included expanding his father's general merchandising business, banking, cotton ginning, cotton buying and operating large farms in the Church Point vicinity.[77]

Homer Barousse was born September 25, 1849, the son of Jean Barousse and Caroline Fontenot. He was educated at a private school in Washington, La., and in 1869 married Emelie Daigle, daughter of Theodule Daigle, one of the founders of Church Point. The couple had 10 children: Oscar, Homer, Maurice, Laurent, Philipe, Bertrand, Fernando, Joseph, Ledia and Lily.[78]

Edward Daigle, son of J. E. Daigle, was the top man in the 1912 race for state legislature. Commenting editorially on the candidate for representative the *Daily Signal* editor wrote: "Like another distinguished citizen of Church Point, Mr. Daigle is not very loquacious."[79]

Church Point furnished a number of officials for parish posts, including two sheriffs, J. L. Murrel and Louis Fontenot, during the period under study.

---

[75] *Daily Signal*, Feb. 11, 1903; Dec. 14, 1907; Guidry, *La Pointe*, 24

[76] *Daily Signal*, Mar. 16, 1911; Lavergne, Gary, "Homer Barousse, etc." *Attakapas Gazette*, Vol. XI, No. 2, 59

[77] *Daily Signal*, Feb. 11, 1903; Dec. 14, 1907

[78] *Ibid*, Lavergne, "Homer Barousse, Portrait of an Acadia Parish Politician," *Attakapas Gazette*, Vol. XI, No. 2

[79] *Daily Signal*, Jan. 24, 26, 1912; July 13, 1911

Fires

Only three disastrous fires resulted in loss of life and property in Church Point between 1900 and 1920. The first was the previously reported fire, resulting from a gasoline explosion, which destroyed the P. D. McBride livery in 1905.

During the winter of 1911 the Homer Barousse store and warehouse burned, causing a loss estimated at between $30,000 and $40,000. The business, one of the first in the town, had been started by Homer's father, Jean, a native of France who came to Church Point in 1840.[80]

Two inmates of the town jail died in a fire which destroyed the jail in December of 1912. One of the victims was a man named William Collier; the other was unknown. The jail was located on the outskirts of the town, isolated from other buildings. It was believed that the prisoners started the fire,[81] perhaps in an attempt to keep warm.

A fire-fighting company, Hope Hook and Ladder Company, was established in April of 1899. The fire house was on church property, at the corner of Main and Church Streets, and the church bell sounded the fire alarm. Officers of the 40-member company were H. J. David, C. C. Chandezon, Joseph Bourque Jr., Edmond Deville, Edward Daigle and Laurent Barousse.[82]

Schools

The first school in what is now Acadia Parish was established at Church Point in 1856. The school, which accommodated 12 pupils, was domiciled in one room adjoining the Catholic chapel.[83]

A new school building was put up by Homer Barousse and J. E. Daigle in 1875. The school was on property owned by Valentin Breaux, a tract which was later sold to the Methodist church.[84]

By 1902 the enrollment had reached 98 and the faculty was increased to two. Paul S. Lauve was principal, assisted by Evelina Daigle.[85]

Miss Luna Fitch of Washington was principal from 1903 to 1906. Her assistants during this time were L. E. Lacombe, then Lillian Lafleur of Eunice.[86]

A new four-room school, costing $4,000, was built in the Guidry addition in 1906. The faculty of three consisted of R. W. Eggleston, prin-

---

[80] *Daily Signal*, Nov. 15, 1911
[81] *Ibid*, Dec. 3, 1912
[82] Guidry, *La Pointe*, 51; *Crowley Signal*, July 22, 1899
[83] Guidry, *La Pointe*, 15
[84] *Ibid*
[85] *Daily Signal*, Sept. 3, 1902; Jan. 30, 1903
[86] *Crowley Signal*, Oct. 10, 1903; Oct. 14, 1905

cipal, Luna Fitch and Lillian Lafleur.[87] Within a year, with an enrollment of 150 and a faculty of four, the school was filled to capacity. The teachers were Margaret Smith, principal; Claudia Pardue, Eliza Arnett and Mrs. George Vidrine.[88]

Earlier teachers included Louisa Davis, 1899-1900; Lillian Hardey, 1900-1901; Maud Latta, 1901-1902.[89]

Albert Longuemare was a home tutor and private school teacher in Church Point for many years. He died in 1914. Another private school was conducted by Mrs. William Young.[90]

A school house for black children was built in 1906.[91] The location of the school and the names of the early teachers are not known.

Sidelights

One of the more interesting facets of Church Point history concerns a cannon called "Flying Molly." Believed to have been a souvenir of the Civil War, the four-inch gun was fired on festive occasions, such as 4th of July celebrations, and when the archbishop visited Church Point in 1905.

An exercise employing the cannon was scheduled for the July 4th celebration of 1900. The program included a basket picnic, demonstrations by Hope Hook and Ladder Company, music by the Jolly Boys Brass Band; bicycle, balky mule, sack and frog races; *jeu de ciseaux* (scissors game), and "an artillery exercise by Capt. D. D. Goss and his troops, who manage 'Flying Molly' with all competence."[92]

Plans for the 1903 Independence Day observance called for the "little monster to belch forth its three pounds of powder."[93]

Subsequent July 4th notices made no mention of "Flying Molly."

The published program of the 1906 July 4th celebration contained an interesting but cryptic feature: Dr. Clay V. Richard delivered his annual oration "at Bourbeux Hill on Bayou Plaquemine Brulee in Acadia Parish" and also "explained why it was necessary to retire all controversies pertaining to the boundary lines of Bourbeux Hill."[94]

Great excitement prevailed in Church Point in 1901 when 20 of the town's most prominent citizens formed a company to mine gold near the town.

[87] *Daily Signal*, Dec. 15, 1906
[88] *Ibid*, Dec. 14, 1907
[89] *Crowley Signal*, Sept. 16, 1899; Sept. 8, 1900; Sept. 14, 1901
[90] Guidry, *La Pointe*, 17; *Crowley Signal*, June 9, 1900
[91] *Daily Signal*, Oct. 9, 1906
[92] *Crowley Signal*, June 9, July 7, 1900. The celebration was not held because of the death of Albert Olivier, member of the town council.
[93] *Ibid*, June 27, 1903
[94] *Daily Signal*, July 1, 1906

The organization of the mining company was effected after a substance, found earlier on one of the Homer Barousse farms, was analyzed as gold. About the time of the Civil War a well had been dug on the property; at about 28 feet down a substance resembling slate laced with something that appeared to be gold, had been brought up. Apparently the substance had been kept until 1901, when it was analyzed and declared to be gold.[95]

Officers and stockholders of the Church Point Gold Mining Company were Albert Breaux, T. Guidry, Edward Daigle, Homer Barousse, Dr. L. B. Arceneaux, Oscar Martin, H. J. David, H. D. McBride, R. W. Davis, E. A. Henry, P. D. McBride, J. D. Murrel, D. Breaux, T. Daigle, E. Deville, Maurice, Laurent and Felix Barousse, Pierre Guidry and Emile Daigle. The company issued 20 shares of stock at $100 a share.[96]

The well where the substance was found was boarded up and armed guards posted around it day and night. Despite some scoffing editorial comments in several southwest Louisiana newspapers, the investors evidently had faith in the mine. Two weeks after the analysis report T. Guidry refused a ten-to-one offer for his one share.[97]

Subsequent news reports from Church Point made no mention of the gold find. The conjecture is that the analysis may have been made by some unqualified person who may have acted in good faith; obviously the caliber of the men involved precludes any sort of fraud or confidence game.

One news item that may have had some relation to the so-called discovery: A dance held at Pride's Hall had music provided by "The Gold Bugs."[98]

An unusual Christmas gift changed hands in 1901. Theodore Daigle received a young tiger as a present from his uncle, H. J. Daigle. The tiger cub was put on exhibition at the Klondike Saloon.[99]

One section of Church Point (or an area in the vicinity of the town) was known as "Promised Land." According to local legend treasure had been buried there during the Civil War, and people were constantly digging up the area in search of treasure.[100]

One night in 1903 Theodule Guidry disguised himself as a ghost and quietly presented himself to a group of searchers. The spectre so frightened the prospectors that they fled in all directions, tearing down a panel of barbed wire fence in their wild panic. Theodule, described as "the only

---

[95] *Crowley Signal*, May 4, 1901
[96] *Ibid*
[97] *Ibid*, May 18, 1901
[98] *Ibid*, May 11, 1901
[99] *Ibid*, Jan. 4, 1902
[100] *Ibid*, Sept. 26, 1903

joker in town," returned with some "treasure" that had been left at the scene: a double-barrelled shotgun, two revolvers, a divining rod and three hats.[101]

Cigarettes, called "coffin nails" by the old timers, figured in a 1903 news item. Edmond Deville, said to have been "a slave to cigarettes," decided to stop smoking. Within 60 days he had increased in weight from 130 to 157 pounds, a weight gain of 27 pounds.[102]

In the Acadian tradition weddings, *boucheries* and Mardi Gras were occasions of feasting and fun in the Church Point countryside. When Ida Bellard and Wesley O'Pry were married November 29, 1905 in the Church Point Catholic church, the event was appropriately celebrated that evening with a *bal de noce* (wedding dance) at Martin Lejeune's hall at Pointe Noire.[103]

A double wedding was an event of January 29, 1906, when Eveline and Celise Blanchard, daughters of Valmont Blanchard, were married to Theobert Jeanis and Angelas Matt respectively. Rev. A. Roger officiated at the double rites.[104]

The biggest boucherie of the 1905 season was held at Francois Savoy's place, when a hog weighing 750 pounds was butchered. The porker yielded 42 gallons of lard.[105]

During the fall of 1908 Maurice Barousse was appointed the first game warden of Acadia Parish, and Pierre Guidry had an unusual exhibit at the Acadia Fair in Crowley: a three-legged calf and a four-legged duck.[106]

An article of unusual historical interest appeared in the *Crowley Signal* of December 26, 1908. The article reviewed the background of J. F. Shoemaker, one of the northerners who became a well-known farmer and rice miller of Acadia Parish. Shoemaker told how his step-father, Daniel O'Neill, had come to Louisiana in 1809, accompanied by William Butler. The two settled on Bayou Wykoff south of Church Point. During the five years they stayed there they built a brick house, the first brick structure in southwest Louisiana. The house was situated on Bayou Wykoff, opposite the Pelton place.* O'Neill made the bricks himself, burning oyster shells

---

* A home built by John Pelton in the 1880s on the immense William Wykoff Spanish land grant. Wykoff and Daniel O'Neill were contemporaries; a wealthy landowner and cattleman, Wykoff may have employed O'Neill and Butler to build the house and gin.

[101] *Ibid*

[102] *Ibid*, Apr. 18, 1903

[103] *Ibid*, Dec. 9, 1905

[104] *Daily Signal*, Jan. 31, 1906

[105] *Crowley Signal*, Nov. 18, 1905

[106] *Ibid*. Oct. 24, 31, 1908

for lime. Butler and O'Neill also built the first cotton gin in old St. Landry,** one of the pioneer gins of the state. The men left the area in 1814 to return to the north, each with $2,500 in gold. Shoemaker, the article stated, was able to identify the site of the house and cotton gin built by his step-father. The foundations of the house were still standing at the time.

Information on two perennially popular Acadian sports—horse racing and cock fighting—is virtually non-existent for the Church Point area.

During the early years of the century Dr. Clay V. Richard, a Church Point dentist, was reported to be the owner of "the fastest horse in the state," also "the best fighting rooster within 30 miles."[107]

Some years earlier, in 1886, horse racing was the main feature of the three-day fair staged to raise funds for the Catholic church. The feature race was between a horse owned by the pastor, Father Eby, and one raised and trained by Jean Barousse.[108]

It is safe to assume that Church Point was not without its own Cajun straightaway, although only one published reference to a race track was found: the Daigle and Fux track, which was in operation in 1909.[109]

The first reported Mardi Gras celebration in Church Point was in 1903, when the merrymakers elected to celebrate ahead of time. They staged a successful "*courir Mardi Gras*" on the Sunday before Shrove Tuesday, and held the masked ball on Monday night.[110]

A fraternal organization, the Woodmen of the World, and a debating society were formed in Church Point in 1909. First officers of the WOW were Laurent Barousse, R. B. Boettcher, Jerry Higginbotham, L. J. V. Breaux, C. L. Harmon, E. A. Hundley, Fred Barousse, Oscar Landry, Dr. A. B. Childs, Adam A. Reed, Ralph David, Ben Daigle and A. C. Gardiner.[111]

One of the intriguing subjects debated by the Church Point Literary and Debating Society was "Resolved: That woman has more influence over man than money." Taking the affirmative were Leo Franques and M. I. Ramsey; on the negative side were Emile Daigle and W. T. Harrison.[112]

Church Point residents had difficulty indentifying a strange animal in 1910: Newton Barousse found his mule colt killed and partly devoured.

** At that time St. Landry Parish covered a vast area: from the Atchafalaya River west to the Sabine, and south from the Rapides district to the Gulf of Mexico.

[107] *Daily Signal*, Aug. 6, 1902; *Crowley Signal*, Nov. 19, 1904
[108] *Opelousas Courier*, Dec. 18, 1886
[109] *Daily Signal*, Jan. 27, 1909
[110] *Ibid*, Feb. 26, 1903
[111] *Ibid*, Feb. 4, 1909
[112] *Ibid*, Feb. 25, 1909

He let the carcass lay, and waited. An animal that he took to be a dog appeared; Barousse shot and wounded the beast.

The following day J. E. Daigle looked at the animal and said it was a cross between a wolf and a dog. Others said it was a wolf. The animal was described as red-greyish-black in color, about four feet long, one and a half feet high and six inches lower at the hind quarters, giving the animal the appearance of sloping toward the back, a characteristic of the hyena. The six-inch tail was thick. The animal had a bulky head, long nose, small straight, erect ears. Its neck, shoulders and forelegs were developed to double the proportions of the hind quarters. A growth of hair about three inches long was on the neck and shoulders, and running along the back was a streak of stiff hair like a hog's bristles.[113]

A 1915 obituary paid special tribute to an old resident of Church Point. Francois Ledoux, 75, died December 12, 1915. He was termed "one of the best known men of Church Point, where he spent the greater part of his life doing good for those whose condition in life was not as fortunate as his own."

A rabid animal claimed a victim in Church Point in 1917. Valentine Daigle had to go to New Orleans to take the Pasteur treatment for hydrophobia.[114]

---

[113] *Crowley Signal*, May 21, 1910
[114] *Daily Signal*, June 29, 1917

H. J. David

Senator H. Barousse

Plaquemine Brulee-Branch, Gum Point

Branch, Acadia's oldest settlement, was known as Plaquemine Brulee for almost a hundred years. At one time the name Plaquemine Brulee applied to all locations along the length of the bayou by the same name, from Church Point in the northeast corner of the parish to the waterway's juncture with Bayou des Cannes above Mermentau.[1] Eventually the name came to designate the specific area now known as Branch.

The name of the post office at Plaquemine Brulee was changed to Branch in 1890, but published references to the place as Plaquemine Brulee continued to appear for 10 or more years.[2]

The Plaquemine Brulee post office was established in 1838. Early postmasters (1838-1920) included Joseph Clark, Jesse B. Clark, Orsamus Hayes, Joseph E. Andrus, Dallas B. Hayes, George J. Rose, Colbert W. Foreman, Edmund L. Harmon, Edgar Barousse, Joseph A. Barousse, Olive Parrott, William H. Hornsby, Howard A. Hudson, Homer P. Barousse, Leo Franques and Robert E. Guilbeau.[3]

At the start of the century Edgar Barousse, owner and operator of a large general store and cotton gin, was the settlement's only businessman. The business was expanded in 1903 when Willie and Branch Hayes began operating a grist mill at the Barousse store.[4]

Edgar Barousse died in 1905. His son, Joseph A. Barousse, took over the management of the estate. At this time promotion of the construction of the Opelousas, Gulf and Northeastern railroad through Branch was at its height: Barousse gave 10 acres of land for railroad development and plans were made to lay out a town site.[5]

Construction of the railroad and talk of town building generated plans for a newspaper, to be named the *Branch Times*. H. A. Hudson, an Acadia Parish school teacher and businessman, and J. A. Barousse were to manage the publication,[6] which apparently did not get beyond the planning stage.

Interest in community development reached a high point in 1907. Dr. J. B. Parrott, a practicing physician and newcomer to Branch, had the town plotted and sold a number of lots at $50 to $150 each. The town was laid out by Fred W. Haralson, a Rayne surveyor. By the end of the year the town had three stores and promise of a fourth; a cotton gin, drug store, barber shop and a cane mill.[7]

[1] Fontenot and Freeland, *Acadia Parish, a History to 1900*, 94

[2] Register of Postmasters, National Archives and Records Service; *Crowley Signal*, June 8, 1901

[3] Register of Postmasters, etc.

[4] *Crowley Signal*, Sept. 26, 1903; Feb. 27, 1904; *Daily Signal*, Jan. 21, 1903

[5] *Signal* Christmas supplement, Dec. 16, 1905

[6] *Daily Signal*, Aug. 13, 1906; *Crowley Signal*, Feb. 9, 1907

[7] *Signal*, Christmas supplement, Dec. 14, 1907; interview Winston Barousse, 1978

The Edgar Barousse store at Branch. From left are Hollis Hayes, Joseph A. "Bob" Barousse and Homer P. Barousse. (Photo courtesy Homer Barousse)

J. W. Webb and Company was one of the new firms. Webb, a new arrival from Sabine Parish, and Dr. Parrott put up a new store building, 24 by 90 feet, at a cost of $1,200 and stocked it with up-to-date merchandise.[8]

H. A. Hudson, the school principal and deputy postmaster, was also a Branch merchant. The post office was located in the Hudson store. Hudson operated the Branch Mercantile until 1916 when he sold to Leo Franques of Church Point. At the time of the sale the store stock was valued at $50,000.[9]

The third store had for its proprietor B. H. Hayes, who had previously operated a business in Prairie Hayes. His Branch store was a block

---

[8] *Signal*, Christmas supplement, Dec. 14, 1907
[9] *Ibid*, Aug. 23, 1916

from the depot. Charles Smith, who had a store on the bayou about a mile from the depot, moved his business into town.[10]

Jack Fortner was the town's first barber, plying his trade in a newly constructed building. Dr. Parrott operated a drug store in connection with his office. Felix Barousse managed the cotton gin and Golbert Barousse was connected with the Webb store.[11]

A 1907 map of Branch shows a town plat of 12 blocks. Streets were named as follows: Plaquemine, Western, Eastern, Haralson, Barousse, Lyons, Hudson, Andrus, Hayes and Commercial.

Churches, Schools

The first religious edifice built in the Acadia Parish area was at Plaquemine Brulee. This was the Methodist church built in 1819 by Rev. Daniel Devinne.[12]

The historic church remained in the same location until 1896 when it was moved onto a square acre of land given by W. W. Duson. The land, located about a mile northeast of the first church site, was accepted by the church's trustees, E. L. Harmon, W. F. Lyons, Orsamus Hayes and Eugene W. Harmon.[13]

In 1917 the church, represented by J. S. Bruner, Camron Andrus and A. A. Lyons, bought 1.85 acres of land from Claude Boudreaux at a price of $96. The land, one mile west of Branch, was used for an addition to the old Plaquemine Brulee cemetery.[14]

Land for Elizabeth Memorial Baptist Church was purchased in 1915. The four-acre tract, priced at $200, was bought from Edwin Wyatt. Church trustees negotiating the land sale were J. M. Davis, Adam Richard and T. J. Merritt.[15]

Branch can also claim the first church for black people built in the Acadia Parish area. Maryland Christian Methodist Episcopal church was built near the Plaquemine Brulee settlement in 1870, on land given by Mrs. Jesse Clark. Representatives of the church bought a half acre of land in 1917 for use as a cemetery. The land, described as located one mile northwest of Branch, was sold to the church for $25 by T. P. Andrus. Vorice Vallery and Philip "Pleg" Gibson represented the church in the land transaction.[16]

Mt. Calvary Baptist Church of Branch acquired land in purchases made in 1911 and 1917. The first property, 50 by 100 feet, was bought from Henderson Byars for $40. Ralph Yokum and Lixie Wilridge rep-

[10] *Crowley Signal*, Aug. 10, Dec. 14, 1907
[11] *Ibid*, Dec. 14, 1907
[12] Fontenot and Freeland, *Acadia Parish*, 95
[13] Conveyance Book P, #10479½, 267, Acadia Par.
[14] Conveyance Book C-3, #45027-28, 383, 384, Acad. Par.
[15] Conveyance Book C-3, #45085, 409, Acad. Par.
[16] Fontenot and Freeland, *Acadia*, 102: Conveyance Book C-3, #45632, 537, Acad. Par.

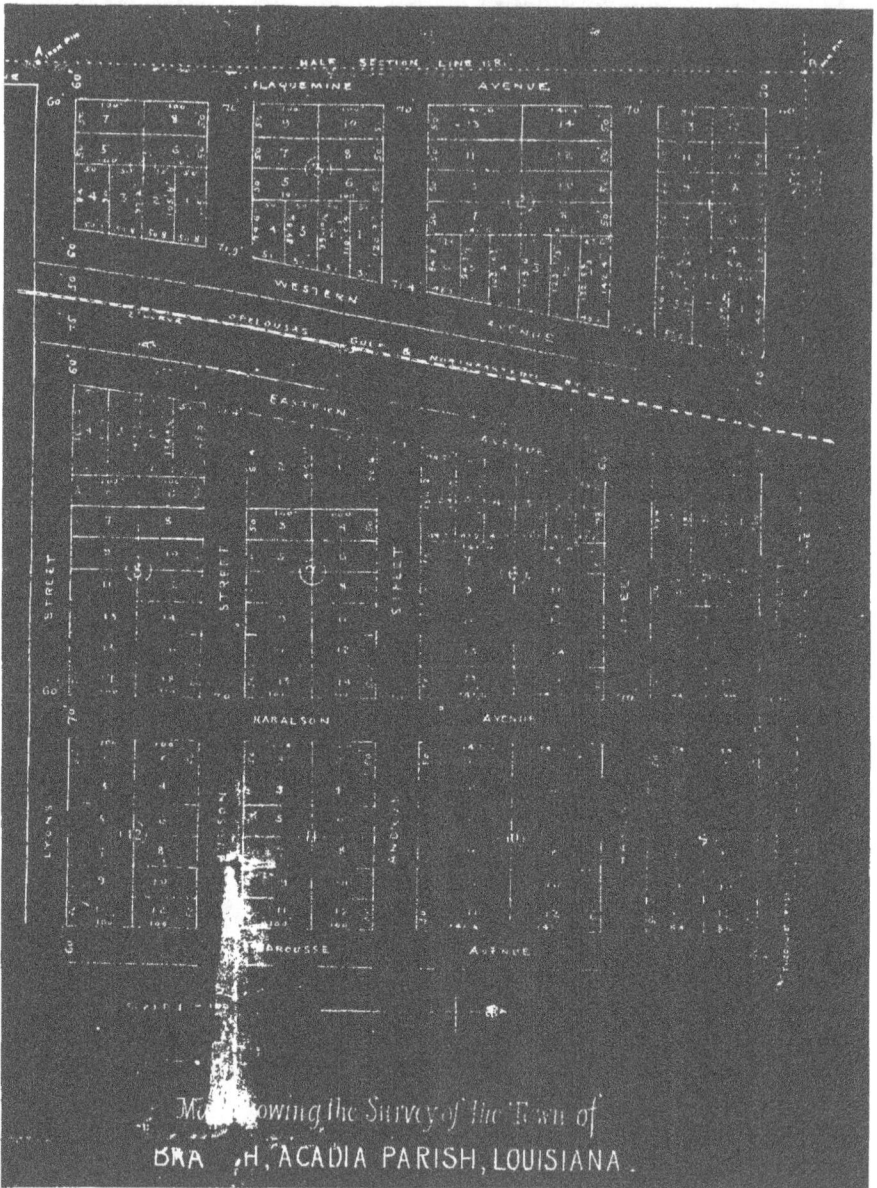

A 1907 town plat of Branch showing the five avenues and five streets in relation to the Opelousas, Gulf and Northeastern railroad track. Fred W. Haralson, a Rayne surveyor, laid out the town. (Map reproduction courtesy of Clyde Bibb)

resented the church. A second land transaction involved buying a tract 100 by 50 feet from H. C. Bruner for $25. Church trustees were Ralph Yokum, Alex C. and Raymond Wilridge.[17]

_____
[17] Conveyance Books U-2, #35785, 15: E-3, #46501, 46, Acad. Par.

Public schools for both white and black pupils were in operation at Plaquemine Brulee for 10 or more years before parish division. During the early years of the 20th century teachers at Branch schools included Carrie Hively, Lizzie Beauchamp, Margaret Bovell, Orion Kirkpatrick, Mrs. M. E. L. Armstrong and W. H. Simmons. Mrs. Armstrong and Simmons were the teachers at the school for black children in 1901 and 1906, respectively.[18]

Branch Brevities

One of the show places of the parish was lost in 1900 when the $5,000 John E. Pelton residence, Linden Grove, went up in flames. The place was located about a mile east of Branch on the William Wikoff land grant. The contents of the house, including a library which had cost between $1,500 and $2,000, were also destroyed.[19]

Reports of wild animal sightings in the Branch area were frequent in the early years. In 1900 one of Ted Lyons' dogs was severely mangled by a bear. Lyons chased the bear into the cane brake, shot at it six times, but missed. On another occasion some boys were coon hunting in the Lyons cane brake and flushed out a large bear. Tom Fortner shot eight times before he could kill the animal.[20]

Another animal incident involved William Meche, son of Leovar Meche. Driving in a buggy near Branch, Meche was attacked by a panther; with difficulty he managed to beat the beast off. The panther sprang from the roadside and struck the dashboard of the buggy. The animal's tracks were found in the road next morning. Other reports told of a large yellow animal having been seen between Robert's Cove and Church Point; hunting parties were organized, but failed to find the animal.[21]

A death notice published in 1901 reported the death of Mrs. Eugene Holloway, at age 105. Mrs. Holloway, a native of St. John Parish, had lived at Branch for 50 years. A second report of Mrs. Holloway's death gave her age as 115.[22]

Branch Leaders

Leading citizens of Branch during the period under study were Edgar Barousse and Dr. Joseph Bowers Parrott.

---

[18] Fontenot and Freeland, *Acadia*, 106; *Crowley Signal*, Sept. 16, 1899; Sept. 8, 1900; Sept. 14, 1901; Oct. 19, 1903; *Daily Signal*, Sept. 3, 1902; May 16, 1904; July 10, 1906
[19] Interview, Roy Andrus, 1974
[20] *Crowley Signal*, Jan. 20, 1900; *Daily Signal*, Aug. 22, 1905
[21] *Crowley Signal*, Mar. 12, 26, 1910
[22] *Ibid*, Feb. 23, Mar. 2, 1901

Dr. Joseph B. Parrott and his wife, the former Olive Miller, shortly after their wedding in 1902. The picture was taken May 5, 1902 when the Parrotts were at the St. Charles Hotel, New Orleans, on their honeymoon. (Photo courtesy Sybil Parrott Andrus)

Barousse, son of Jean Barousse, was born in Church Point January 15, 1854. He opened a general merchandise store in Branch in 1888 and was postmaster there for 14 years.[23] Dr. Parrott, a graduate of Tulane University, practiced medicine and farmed at Branch for some 20 years, from 1907 until 1927 when he moved to Church Point.[24]

Plaquemine Brulee (Branch) produced several of the pioneer Acadia Parish leaders, including Dr. Bennett E. Clark, Raymond T. Clark, John Crawford Lyons, W. W. Duson, Dallas B. Hayes and Elridge Lyons.

Dr. Clark, son of Valentine Clark and Fanny McClelland, belonged to two of the long-established families of the region. He was first president of the Acadia Parish Police Jury and served for 18 years, from 1886 to 1904. Prior to parish division he was president of the St. Landry Police Jury for nine years.[25]

Raymond T. Clark, a brother of Dr. Clark, was the first Acadia Parish clerk of court, serving for 17 years. He married Laura Duson, a sister of W. W. and C. C. Duson.[26]

John Crawford Lyons was elected to the Louisiana Legislature in 1880 and served two terms. He introduced the bill that created Acadia Parish.[27]

Dallas B. Hayes, a Confederate veteran, was postmaster and justice of the peace at Branch until his appointment as chief deputy clerk and recorder of Acadia Parish, a post he held for 17 years. He served one term as state senator and in 1904 was elected Crowley city judge.[28]

Elridge Lyons was the first sheriff of Acadia Parish.

Gum Point

Gum Point was in use as a place name of Acadia Parish in the Branch area as early as 1900.[29]

In 1901 the citizens and patrons of the Thibodeaux school in Ward 2 petitioned the school board to move the school house one mile north to land donated by Portalis Fuselier. This was done, and the school was thereafter known as the Gum Point school.[30]

A new school house was built in 1907. Jack Merritt, Victor Richard and S. A. Going had charge of construction. School patrons raised 60 per cent of the cost of the building. Among early teachers at Gum Point were Ella Hazelwood and Ernest Rush.[31]

---

[23] *Ibid*, Apr. 11, 1903
[24] *Rayne Independent*, supplement, Apr. 3, 1969
[25] *Ibid*; *Daily Signal*, June 15, 1904
[26] *Daily Signal*, Sept. 16, 1911
[27] *Crowley Signal*, Dec. 23, 1905
[28] *Ibid*, Jan. 2, 1904; Nov. 17, 1907
[29] *Ibid*, Apr. 21, 1900
[30] *Ibid*, Dec. 14, 1901
[31] *Crowley Signal*, Oct. 19, 1907; Sept. 16, 1899; *Daily Signal*, Sept. 3, 1902

Prairie Hayes

Prairie Hayes, named for a colonial landowner, Bosman Hayes, was once described as "bounded by Bayou Plaquemine Brulee on the south, Bayou des Cannes on the west, and Bayou Mallet on the north."[1] These limits encompass the middle half of the parish.

As time went by scattered settlements developed in this vast expanse of land: Jonas Cove, later known as Egan; Long Point, the Maxie-Ellis area; Cole's Point, Richard (also known as Thrailkill and Coe), Pointe Noire, Hundley and Pitreville. When railroads went through the prairie in 1894 and 1906 other place names were created: Iota, Trilby (Gassler, Frey), Rhineland, Mowata, Rork and Rorkdell. Until these names came into use "Prairie Hays" was the accepted designation for everything that lay within the above described boundaries.

One of the early businesses in the prairie was a tannery, operated by W. B. Mitchell. Twelve kinds of leather were made at the tannery.[2]

Peddlers brought their wares to the scattered farmsteads of Prairie Hayes. Among these horse-and-buggy salesmen were Sam Hornsby, Felix McBride and V. Barras. Hornsby and McBride, from the Church Point vicinity, sold household goods and food staples. Barras, who lived in the Patassa section of the parish south of Eunice, sold and repaired sewing machines over a wide territory which took in all of Prairie Hayes and Prairie Mamou.[3]

There were at least two cotton gins in the prairie during the early years of the century. The gins were owned by Franz Brinkman and P. J. Scanlan.[4]

The T. & O. store, established in 1915, was a Prairie Hayes landmark for many years. The business was owned by Terville Guidry and his son Oscar. The large store, located seven miles northwest of Church Point, was stocked with hardware, clothing, piece goods, groceries and notions.[5]

Grass fires plagued Prairie Hayes farmers in the early days. In December of 1903 grass fires went out of control across both Prairie Hayes and Prairie Mamou, threatening property and setting the Nezpique woods on fire.[6]

Wild animals roamed the prairie and preyed on livestock until about 1908, when the predators were hunted down and killed by parish sportsmen. Leaders in the wild animal hunts were Dr. Hines C. Webb, Dr.

---

[1] *Crowley Signal*, Aug. 25, 1888
[2] *Ibid*, July 15, 1899
[3] *Ibid*, July 22, 1899; May 19, 1900; interview, Garland D. Barras, Winston Atteberry, 1978
[4] *Crowley Signal*, Oct. 5, 1901; *Daily Signal*, Sept. 9, 1902
[5] *Daily Signal*, 50th Anniv. Ed., 1949, 188
[6] *Crowley Signal*, Dec. 15, 1903

Prairie Hayes merchant and politician Oscar Guidry in a photo taken before World War I. Guidry and his father owned and operated the T. & O. store for many years.

H. H. Hair and Mack Robinson. The hunting parties, with packs of dogs, tracked down and killed a number of animals known at that time as catamounts. On one such hunt the mounted men and dogs tracked and killed a catamount (a cougar or a lynx) after a run of nine miles over the prairie. At another time a 50-pound catamount was killed near Mack Robinson's place.[7]

One of the folkways observed by the Acadian population of Prairie Hayes was "running the Mardi Gras." Country correspondents for the Crowley newspaper reported: "In accordance with an old custom here, the Creoles, dressed in masquerade . . . and at night gave a grand masque ball," and, "the Mardi Gras rode as usual, and from the racket they made, had a good time."[8] The countryside was especially lively on Shrove Tuesday of 1907, when the Mardi Gras revelers were out in force. One band came from Bayou des Cannes west of Eunice, another from

[7] *Ibid*, May 30, 1908; Mar. 12, 1910
[8] *Ibid*, Feb. 15, 1903; Feb. 27, 1904

around Bayou Mallet, and a third group was made up of Negro merry-makers from the Eunice area. All "begged" for chickens, money and other provisions, and concluded the day's frolic at a masked ball.[9]

Richard—Baptist Academy—Coe—Light and Tie

About midway between Church Point and Eunice in Prairie Hayes are two settlements known as Richard and Baptist Academy. Both place names stem from schools: Richard, from the Richard school built on land given by Theogene Richard, and Baptist Academy from the school of the same name which opened in 1917.

Richard and Baptist Academy are little more than a half mile apart. A third settlement, situated one and a half miles southeast of Baptist Academy, was once known as Light and Tie.[10]

At the Richard school D. R. Ross was the teacher from 1899 to 1901. In 1901 the faculty was increased to two, with teachers Charles J. Johnson and Agnes Stagg. In 1904 Robert O. Hardey took over as principal with Stella Aleman as assistant. Also in the neighborhood was the Hornsby school, where Estelle Cole was the teacher from 1903 to 1905. At the Light and Tie school some of the early teachers were Dora Jenkins, Miss B. Griffin and Zena Young.[11]

A landmark institution of the Richard-Baptist Academy section is Pilgrim's Rest Baptist Church, organized in 1870. The church became a full time church with regular Sunday services in 1899. Pastors, from 1897 to 1924, include R. A. Watson, B. H. Mitchell, W. L. Stagg Sr., H. W. Ford, W. J. Westberry, J. B. Herndon.[12]

Land for a cemetery was purchased in 1897. The church, represented by William J. Hazelwood and William H. Huckaby, deacons, bought an acre from Theogene Richard for $20. The deed specifies that the land was to be used for a cemetery.[13]

The name Baptist Academy did not come into use until after the school was built in 1917. Ten acres of land was sold to Pilgrim's Rest church by Hubert Jeanis in November of 1917. Representing the church in the transaction were Rev. W. J. Hazelwood, Rev. W. J. Westberry, Sam McManus, W. H. Eastwood, J. W. Young and James Stagg. The price paid was $650, and the deed stipulated that the property would be used "to build a school." Less than a year afterwards the church bought an additional 10 acres from Sam McManus for $585. The land use was not specified.[14]

---

[9] *Ibid*, Feb. 16, 1907

[10] Interview, Mrs. Edgar Bieber, 1978

[11] *Crowley Signal*, Sept. 16, 1899; Sept. 8, 1900; Sept. 14, 1901; Oct. 10, 1903; *Daily Signal*, May 16, 1904

[12] Prather, Mrs. Ulric, "Baptist Church in Richard, etc." *Signal*, Anniv. Ed., 1949, 21

[13] Conveyance Book P, #10725, 574 Acad. Par.

[14] Conveyance Books C-3, #45107, 693; E-3, #47757, 515, Acad. Par.

Acadia Baptist Academy, for years a landmark in the northeast portion of Acadia Parish. This first school house, a frame building, was constructed in 1917. (Photo courtesy Bessie Richard Courville)

Acadia Baptist Academy
NEAR A FINE OLD COUNTRY CHURCH
Between Eunice and Church Point in Acadia Parish.

Under the Auspices of Louisiana Baptist and the Home Mission Board of the Southern Baptist convention. Has five instructors, and offers a high school course with music, lessons in the Bible and in Christian Work.

Gives special attention to English among French speaking pupils

Advocates education for character, and open Bible and complete religious liberty. The only expense is a small incidental fee. Enrollment the first year one hundred and sixty-six.

SECOND SESSION OPENS SEPTEMBER 16, 1918.

A new modern dormitory for girls, board in homes for boys. For catalog write Principal,

J. H. STROTHER, -- Route 1, Church Point, La.

At the start of 1918-1919 school year this display advertisement was used in the *Crowley Signal.* At the time the school had a faculty of five and offered some dormitory and boarding facilities.

Baptist Academy opened in December of 1917 with two teachers instructing 54 pupils. By May of 1918 the school had a faculty of four, including Rev. J. H. Strother, the principal, and an enrollment of 165.[15]

A post office was established in Prairie Hayes in 1888, in the general area of Richard-Light and Tie. The office was named Thrailkill, for the first postmaster, William F. Thrailkill. In 1895 David H. Dobbs became postmaster and the name was changed to Coe. The Thrailkill-Coe post office functioned for 26 years; the office was discontinued April 30, 1914 and the mail sent to Mowata. Other postmasters serving the Coe office were Louis T. Tully, 1898, and Frank C. Robinson, 1902.[16]

The approximate location of the Light and Tie settlement was near the northwest quarter of Section 36, Township 7 South, Rayne 1 East, where Benjamin G. Merritt owned property in 1879.[17]

Sam McManus was perhaps the best known farmer-merchant of the Coe neighborhood of Prairie Hayes. During this time McManus, in addition to farming, operated a rice-grist mill, livery stable, syrup mill, sawmill, blacksmith shop, barber shop and general store. The second floor of his store, used as a meeting room by the Woodmen of the World, was also

---

[15] *Daily Signal*, May 22, 1918. The school was closed in 1973 after almost 56 years of successful operation.

[16] Register of Postmasters, National Archives and Records Service

[17] Interview, Henry Bieber

the first telephone exchange for that particular rural area. Miss Mattie Merritt was the telephone operator.[18]

Other businesses in the general vicinity were run by L. H. Harmon, John Wesley Young and Valmont Blanchard. Harmon and Young owned general stores and Blanchard had a corn mill and cotton gin. A well known justice of the peace who served the Coe area many years was O. K. Brunson, known as Judge Brunson.[19]

Pointe Noire

One portion of Prairie Hayes, a few miles due west of Church Point, was known as *Pointe Noire*, or Black Point. The place name is quite old, and its origin is obscure.

In 1905 a young man named Cleophas C. Sonnier was the Pointe Noire correspondent for the Crowley newspaper. He described his home area as "one vast prairie" where once large herds of wild cattle grazed "as far as the eye could reach." The prairie was dotted with large ponds where the traveler could see "large cranes leisurely wading, and others slowly flying," and hear "the weird notes of the killdeer." Sonnier found the scattered Acadian cabins of Pointe Noire "in harmony with the surroundings." He wrote that the numerous herds of Creole ponies that once grazed the prairie were no longer to be seen, nor were the *vacheros*, who once branded the calves and colts in the springtime.[20]

Cole's Point

Cole's Point, a specific location in the large land area known as Prairie Hayes, was a name in use in Acadia Parish until the Frisco (Missouri-Pacific) railroad, Eunice to Crowley, bisected the parish in 1908. The place was near Cole's Gully about two miles east of Maxie or Long Point.

A post office was established at Cole's Point May 10, 1899, with Lyman L. Clark as postmaster. The post office, known as Star, was located in Clark's store at Cole's Point.[21]

Willie Higginbotham had a syrup mill at Cole's Point in 1899; Charles Dischler farmed there until 1906, when he moved his family to the home he had built in the Patassa area southeast of Eunice.[22]

The Star post office was moved to Maxie on the Frisco railroad in 1908. The name was changed to Maxie post office.

[18] *Crowley Signal*, Dec. 14, 1907; Dec. 17, 1910; interviews, Hazel McManus Randel, Henry Bieber, 1978

[19] *Crowley Signal*, Oct. 10, Nov. 14, 1903; *Daily Signal*, July 3, 1906; Jan. 14, 1911

[20] *Daily Signal*, July 20, 1905

[21] Register of Postmasters; *Crowley Signal*, Apr. 15, 1899

[22] *Crowley Signal*, Dec. 2, 1899; *Daily Signal*, Jan. 19, 1906

Coulee Croche—Castille—
Marais Bouleur—Point Wikoff

The Castille settlement, some three and a half miles northeast of Rayne (as the crow flies) was one of the early voting precincts of Acadia Parish. The place was sometimes referred to as Coulee Croche, a land area and coulee located just over the line in St. Landry Parish. Castille-Coulee Croche country was part of a larger land area called Marais Bouleur which extended several miles south from what later became the Higginbotham settlement. The designation Marais Bouleur appears to have been a general term for anything located northeast of Rayne.[1]

Ernest Higginbotham ran a store at Coulee Croche in 1904.[2] One of the earliest references to Coulee Croche as a place name of Acadia Parish may be found in Donations Book No. 1, Acadia Parish courthouse, dated February 2, 1888, when Lorenzo I. Tansey sold two arpents of land to a Methodist congregation represented by William N. Milton, W. H. Ramsey and T. A. Spears.

The name Castille appears to have supplanted that of Coulee Croche about 1900, although both place names occur in the early history of the parish.

In 1900 the voting poll at Castille was located at the Deshotels and Dejean store. A syrup mill, run by Homer Arceneaux was in operation at Castille in 1903. Among prominent residents of the place were Moise and Sidney Arceneaux. There was woodland in the area; in 1903 a wildcat was found in the Moise Arceneaux woods while some tree cutting was being done.[3]

One of the early schools, the Dejean School, is believed to have been located in the Castille area. Some of the early teachers were Daisy White, 1899; Maggie Hunter, 1901; Marvin Cunningham, 1902.[4]

A short-lived post office, named Dejean for the postmaster, Adolph Dejean, was probably located near Castille. The Dejean post office, established March 11, 1902, was ordered closed 15 days later, on March 26, 1902.[5]

Castille residents received their mail at Rayne until February of 1902 when the Castille post office was established with Louis Castille postmaster. Alexandre Castille became postmaster in August of 1902 and served for 12 years. He was replaced in 1914 by Marie L. Castille, who held the

---

[1] Interview, Elton Arceneaux, 1978
[2] *Crowley Signal*, Sept. 10, 1904
[3] *Crowley Signal*, Sept. 8, 1900; Sept. 5, Nov. 28, 1903; *Daily Signal*, June 22, 1904
[4] *Ibid*,Sept. 16, 1899; Sept. 14, 1901; *Ibid*, Sept. 3, 1902
[5] Register of Postmasters, National Archives and Records Service

position until 1932 when the office was discontinued and the mail sent to Rayne.[6]

Newspaper references identify Castille as Marais Bouleur, also as the settlement which later came to be known as Mier (Mire). The historic first church of Rayne (Poupeville), built in 1878, was dismantled in 1922 and moved to "Marais Boulard."[7]

There is an old tradition that the name Marais Bouleur originated from that of an early landowner, an immigrant from Germany named Buhler. The land was low and swampy, hence the "marais." The name Buhler was eventually transcribed in court and church records as Buller and pronounced "Bouleur" by the Acadians, therefore became "Marais Bouleur."[8]

Some inhabitants of Marais Bouleur had the kind of reputation that caused the more timid and non-aggressive individuals to keep a safe distance. The rough riding young blades of Marais Bouleur liked nothing better than an excuse to fight, and many were the brawls and cutting scrapes that went on at dances at Marais Bouleur.

All participants respected the time-honored method of settling a feud. This was the *grand rond*, when friends of both parties formed a ring around the combatants, who were thoroughly searched for concealed weapons such as sticks or brass knuckles. No interference was permitted during the fight. The agreement was that relatives of the loser would not prosecute the winner, no matter what the consequences.[9]

One reported incident that caused quite a stir in Marais Bouleur had nothing to do with fighting and settling a grudge. This was in 1907 when Alexandre Mire found an infant abandoned in his barn lot. The foundling was taken in by the Emile Royer family while the sheriff conducted an investigation and efforts were made to find the baby's parents.[10]

Point Wikoff

Point Wikoff, virtually unknown as a place name of Acadia Parish, is identified as such in an 1882 legal document. That year Louis August Richard sold a portion of land containing one and a half arpents to a group of farmers who lived in the vicinity of Point Wikoff. The land was to be used for a graveyard "for the benefit of the persons within the vicinity . . . and for no other use."

The price paid for the land was $15. Present and accepting the land for the purpose specified were Jean Trahan, Joe Trahan, Valerien

---

[6] *Ibid*
[7] *Daily Signal*, Oct. 5, 1916; *Rayne Tribune*, May 2, 1929
[8] Interview, George Buller, 1975
[9] *Daily Signal*, Apr. 23, 1906; interview, Elton Arceneaux
[10] *Crowley Signal*, July 13, 1907

Richard, Orilien Arceneaux, Sidgni Arceneaux, Ben Arceneaux, Jean Mouton, Charles Melancon, Raymond Richard, Joseph C. Guidry, Olivier Alouet, Ozolin Gotrot, Telesport Gaspard.[11]

Names of these landowners locate Point Wikoff north of Rayne on Bayou Wikoff, a tributary of Bayou Plaquemine Brulee.

---

[11] Conveyance Book M-2, #21737, St. Landry Par.

Prudhomme City and Pitreville

Prudhomme, located six miles east of Eunice near Bayou Mallet as that waterway enters St. Landry, is another Acadia place name that existed before the parish was created. The name owes its origin to Michel Prudhomme Sr. and Michel Prudhomme Jr., both of whom owned large land acreage by Spanish grant.[1]

For many years the name was written in its original form, *Prud'homme*, a French word meaning skillful artisan or an upright, honest man. The apostrophe was dropped about 1904. The settlement was also known as Prudhomme City.[2]

Prudhomme's school history goes back to the 1870s. Names of the first teachers are not known. Ottie Longmire and J. O. Brunson were among the teachers at Prudhomme school between 1884 and 1901.[3]

The Prudhomme post office, established in 1873, functioned until 1881 at which time the mail was sent to Church Point. Postmasters for this period were Spotswood H. Sanders, T. C. Chachere, Etienne Stagg, J. O. Brunson and Raymond Chachere. The post office was re-opened in 1886 with T. C. Chachere as postmaster.[4]

Methodist Episcopal Church (South) was established at Prudhomme City in 1894. Mrs. Annie Prudhomme deeded one acre of land to the church for $10. Representing the church were William Seidel, C. J. Hundley Jr., and Claude Sloan.[5]

A pioneer Acadia Parish physician, Dr. W. T. Jenkins, and his wife celebrated their 50th wedding anniversary at Prudhomme City on April 15, 1902. Another well known member of the medical profession, Dr. T. C. Chachere, was a resident of Prudhomme City. Two other physicians, Dr. W. A. Jenkins and Dr. Harry Jenkins, began practice in their native area of Prudhomme City, then moved to Church Point and Eunice respectively.[6]

Pitreville

Pitreville is an Acadia Parish community located in the northeast corner of the parish on the boundary between Acadia and St. Landry. The name was created in the early 1900s when a post office was named Pitre-

---

[1] Fontenot and Freeland, *Acadia Parish*, 189-192

[2] *Daily Signal*, June 2, Sept. 15, 1902; July 9, 1904

[3] Fontenot and Freeland, *Acadia*, 190, 192; *Crowley Signal*, Sept. 16, 1899; Sept. 8, 1900

[4] Register of Postmasters

[5] Conveyance Book L, #7678, 445, Acad. Par.

[6] *Daily Signal*, Apr. 2, 1902; May 20, 1904; *Crowley Signal*, Jan. 8, 1910; Perrin, *SW La., Biographical and Historical*, Part II, 266

ville for the first postmaster, Edgar Pitre. The post office was in the Pitre store just across the parish line in St. Landry. Raymond McManus, clerk in the Pitre store, helped with the mail and Hortsfield Brunson was the mail rider.[7]

Other early merchants of the Pitreville area were Paul Darbonne, Visca T. Delarue and Michael W. Scanlan. Darbonne was in business in 1902; Delarue and Scanlan started a general merchandise store in 1904.[8]

Pitreville's best known early resident was Michael Scanlan. Known familiarly as "Mike," Scanlan began a long career as a public figure in southwest Louisiana in 1916, when he was nominated for the police jury from Ward 3 by the highest vote cast for any of the candidates.[9]

---

[7] *Daily Signal*, June 18, 1902; Mar. 23, 1904
[8] *Ibid*, Oct. 13, 1902; *Crowley Signal*, Oct. 8, 1904
[9] *Daily Signal*, Feb. 2, 1916

Bayou Blanc and Long Bridge

Two small settlements near Crowley, Bayou Blanc and Long Bridge, are all but forgotten place names of Acadia Parish.

Bayou Blanc settlement takes its name from the bayou of the same name, a small tributary of Bayou Plaquemine Brulee that flows south and southwest of Crowley. The bayou was named for the first landowner, Antoine Blanc, whose Spanish land grant takes in the western part of Crowley.

The settlement was called Coulee Blanc in 1857 when a post office was established there, with James Miers as postmaster. Miers, one of the parish's earliest settlers, was living there in the 1820s. Two of the families living at Bayou Blanc in the early 1900s were the Felix Guillorys and Mr. and Mrs. Ulysse Mier, whose daughter, Odel, was married to Willie Lee at her parent's home in 1906.[1]

The Long Bridge settlement was near the bridge of the same name which spanned Bayou Plaquemine Brulee about two miles north of Crowley. The first bridge over the bayou was built in 1886 as a preliminary to the founding of Crowley, and was known as the Duson bridge. The bridge was re-built in 1888 by the Acadia Parish Police Jury. The new 1,815-foot

---

[1] Register of Postmasters; *Crowley Signal*, Aug. 25, 1888; May 16, 1903; *Daily Signal*, Sept. 5, 1906

Bayou Blanc bridge, circa 1898. The picture is from the Edward T. Hoyt photo album, preserved by his daughter, Mrs. N. Smith Hoffpauir.

bridge, said to have been "the longest bridge in southwest Louisiana," was thereafter known as Long Bridge.[2]

A merchant named Charles E. Schwall (or Schwab) had a store near Long Bridge in 1902. W. A. Eastwood, who ran a store at Long Bridge in 1906, renamed the place Tannerville, for B. F. Tanner, but the name was shortlived. The Sam Elrich and Bro. store at Long Bridge was sold in 1916 to Tim Linscomb.[3]

Long Bridge was in the news in 1901. A black bear, weighing 235 pounds, was killed on the E. A. Wellman farm just across the bridge. The carcass was loaded onto a wagon and brought to Crowley to sell to a butcher, but the butcher wouldn't meet the price asked. The animal was brought back to the Wellman place where it was skinned and dressed, the meat given to friends and neighbors and the hide given to Mrs. Wellman for a rug.[4]

---

[2] Fontenot and Freeland, *Acadia*, 251, 346-347
[3] *Crowley Signal*, Mar. 8, 1902; *Daily Signal*, Mar. 9, 23, 1906; Oct. 27, 1916
[4] *Crowley Signal*, Apr. 27, May 25, 1901

The German Colonies

Fabacher—Trilby—Gassler—Frey

The first settlement of German people in the Acadia Parish area, other than a few scattered families, took place in 1870 when Joseph Fabacher and Zeno Huber started a colony in Prairie Faquetaique, the land area that lies between Bayous des Cannes and Mallet southwest of Eunice. Within the year Fabacher and Huber had induced some 60 persons to settle in the area.[1]

The coming of the Germans brought about the establishment of a post office, known as Faquetaique. Joseph Chenier was appointed postmaster at Faquetaique on May 5, 1873. Some five weeks later, on June 18, 1873, Chenier was replaced as postmaster by Joseph Fabacher, founder of the colony. Fabacher continued to serve in that capacity until December 15, 1873, when the Faquetaique post office was discontinued.[2]*

The curious fact here is that on June 11, 1873, exactly one week before Fabacher was appointed postmaster at Faquetaique, he was appointed postmaster of an office shown in government records as Fabacher. This indicates that he was postmaster for both the Faquetaique and Fabacher post offices for the six months that the Faquetaique post office was in operation. One explanation offered is that Fabacher's son, Joseph H. Fabacher, was one of the postmasters. However, the official record shows only Joseph Fabacher. Also, Joseph H., the son, was only 15 years of age in 1873. Possibly the best explanation of the dual office holdings is that Joseph Fabacher was the only available person who could qualify to handle government business for the two post offices.

The Fabacher post office was in operation for 24 years. Zeno Huber replaced Fabacher as postmaster in 1878 and held the post until 1890. Joseph Kopps and Calvin Heath were short-term postmasters (1890-1891), then Huber was re-appointed and served another six years until the office was discontinued.[3]

Old (pre-1900) maps of Acadia show the Fabacher settlement (or post office) located on or near the Joseph Fabacher land holdings in the north-

---

* The Faquetaique post office, after being closed for seven years, was re-opened February 17, 1880, with Edward Dardeau as postmaster. The office was closed nine months later, on November 18, 1880, according to the National Archives and Records Service. Because the region known as Prairie Faquetaique extends north past the Acadia-St. Landry boundary, the re-established Faquetaique post office is believed to have been located in St. Landry, probably in that part of the parish which later became Evangeline Parish. Another clue to the location is the name of the postmaster. The name Dardeau belongs to a pioneer family usually identified with the Evangeline Parish area.

[1] Fontenot and Freeland, *Acadia Parish, etc.* 177-179
[2] Register of Postmasters, National Archives and Records Service
[3] *Ibid*

227

east quarter of Section 21, Township 7 South, Range 1 West. After the Midland-Eunice railroad was constructed in 1894 Fabacher began to lose its identity as a place name. The railroad company built a station on the line six miles northeast of Iota (about a mile and a half southeast of Fabacher, on the south side of Bayou Mallet). The railroad station was named Trilby. Shortly thereafter a post office was opened at Trilby. The post office was named Santo, and John Frey became the first postmaster.[4]

Different names for the railroad station and the post office, both located at an embryonic dot on the map, created confusion. In 1906 the name Trilby was changed to Gassler, in honor of Rev. F. L. Gassler, and the government agreed to change the name of the post office to conform with the station name. This remained the status quo for six years; in 1912 the name of the settlement and post office was changed to Frey, for John Frey, the first postmaster and one of the original German settlers.[5]

The post office at Frey was in operation until July 31, 1919, when the mail was sent to Iota. Other postmasters who served at Santo-Trilby-Gassler-Frey were F. J. Klein, Mina Mayer, Joseph A. Klein, John M. LeBoeuf and Annie Rearson.[6]

Families brought over by Fabacher and Huber included those of Klein, Ruppert, Linden, Zenter, Wilfert, Flash, Meyers, Frey, Krayter and Schamber. All were successful rice farmers; four were businessmen and two were politicians as well as farmers, and a fifth, Christian Ruppert, invested heavily in real estate in the new St. Landry town of Eunice.[7] Businessmen and politicians of the colony were Joseph H. Fabacher, son of the founder, who had a general store and rice warehouse at Trilby in 1894; F. J. Klein, merchant and member of the police jury; Louis F. Schamber, postmaster at Basile and member of the school board; John Frey, postmaster and merchant.

The stock of the Fabacher store included dry goods, hats, caps, boots, shoes, drugs and farm implements.

Franz Joseph Klein first entered the mercantile business at Trilby in 1896 with John Frey, under the firm name of Frey and Klein. In 1900 Klein bought out Frey's interest in the store. The Klein store was a polling place in 1900. Election officials who served for the 1900 referendum were Zeno Huber, Joseph Frey, L. O. Bertrand and George Lotz.[8]

A drive for funds to build a Catholic church at Trilby, instigated by Rev. F. L. Gassler of the Iota church, was kicked off in 1905 when John Frey canvassed the parish for donations. The church building, 50 by 90 feet, was completed in 1906 and named St. Lawrence for Lawrence Fabacher, who gave the land. The church and rectory were destroyed by

---

[4] *Ibid; Crowley Signal*, Dec. 14, 1907
[5] *Daily Signal*, Dec. 14, 1907; June 13, 1912
[6] Register of Postmasters
[7] Fontenot and Freeland, *Acadia*, 177
[8] *Crowley Signal*, Feb. 16, 1901; Sept. 19, Nov. 28, 1903; Mar. 31, 1900

fire on June 25, 1908. Two statues, a crucifix and the holy sacrament were saved. The $10,000 loss was partially covered by insurance.[9]

The one reported event that took place in the first St. Lawrence church before it was destroyed was the wedding on August 22, 1906 of Lena Christ and Iva E. Miller.[10]

The church was rebuilt in the same location. Construction was completed in the spring of 1909. One of the more important functions held in the church was in 1911 when Bishop Cornelius Van de Ven of Alexandria visited the church on a confirmation tour. For the occasion the church tower and steeple were decked with flags of five nations, representing the different nationalities of the congregation. These and other elaborate decorations were done by Mr. and Mrs. F. J. Klein and Lawrence and Joseph Zaunbrecher. The bishop, after administering the sacrament to 140, spoke in both French and English to a crowd that overflowed into the church yard.[11]

Priests who served the Gassler-Frey church during the period under study were Rev. Adrian Van der Broek, Rev. Adrian Loots and Rev. J. V. Monteillard.[12]

One of the special occasions at the second church was on June 27, 1914 when Mr. and Mrs. Dautrive Miller celebrated their golden wedding at high mass. They were attended by Mr. and Mrs. Homer J. Daigle, who had celebrated their 50th wedding anniversary in December of 1913.[13]

Before the Gassler church was built the large Catholic population of the area was served by churches at Iota and Eunice. An item in the Fabacher news column of the *Signal* reported a double wedding held at the Eunice church in 1904 which united two prominent families of the section: Sidney Sittig was married to Julia Goss, and John Goss was wed to Maude Sittig. The double nuptials were reported by George Lotz, long time reporter for Fabacher to the Crowley newspaper.[14]

At one time Trilby-Gassler was an important shipping point for rice, with some 40,000 sacks a year shipped out to mills to Eunice and Crowley. By 1907 there were three large warehouses; Lawrence Fabacher ran his father's 50 by 100 foot warehouse; the Zaunbrecher brothers operated a warehouse 50 by 75 feet, and F. J. Klein had a 50 by 150 warehouse on the railroad switch.[15]

One of the early enterprises in the Frey area was a so-called "chair factory," which was in operation in 1910.[16] The kind of chairs made at the "factory" and the identity of the manufacturer are not known but in all

[9] *Daily Signal*, June 23, 1905; *Crowley Signal*, Dec. 14, 1907, June 27, 1908
[10] *Daily Signal*, Aug. 29, 1906
[11] *Ibid*, Feb. 17, 1909; June 28, 1911
[12] *Crowley Signal*, Dec. 14, 1907; *Daily Signal*, June 28, 1911; Mar. 16, 1916
[13] *Daily Signal*, June 30, 1914
[14] *Crowley Signal*, Nov. 26, 1904
[15] *Ibid*, Dec. 14, 1907
[16] *Ibid*, June 25, 1910

probability the product was the hand-made rawhide bottom chairs in common use at the time.

One of the problems faced by the early settlers were the depredations of wild animals that lived in the dense woodlands along the two bayous. In 1902, after farmers had lost a large number of sheep to the predators, a hunting party was organized which killed five wild cats. Some years later a wolf attacked dogs in the vicinity and ate the pups. Two of the dogs, hurt by the beast, had to be shot because they developed hydrophobia.[17]

A newsworthy event of 1912 was the 50th wedding anniversary on January 29 of Mr. and Mrs. Peter Klein Sr., two of the original German settlers. The celebration began with high mass read by Father Loots, assisted by Father Gassler of New Orleans and Father Celestine Chambon of Eunice. Father Gassler preached the sermon in German. A few months earlier, on July 23, 1911, Peter Klein Sr. had celebrated his 80th birthday. After mass and communion at the church he had spent the day at home with family and friends some of whom were reported to have "walked to Faquetaique to visit the octogenarian."[18]

There are indications that some of the customs practiced by their French-Acadian neighbors were absorbed into the German culture at an early date. For example, the Louisiana French traditions of cleaning and decorating graves on All Saints' Day, November 1, and the celebration of Shrove Tuesday, or Mardi Gras. As early as 1901 the country Mardi Gras masqueraders were reported "out in force, begging for chickens and eggs to make gumbo and tarts."[19]

Two of the early teachers at the Fabacher school were Cornelius Scully, 1900-1901, and Viola McMillan, 1902-1903.[20] A school for black children was established in 1906. The Acadia Parish School Board granted a petition to build a school house on an acre of land donated by the petitioners. Early teachers were Edwarter L. Norris and L. B. Barker.[21]

Robert's Cove

A second settlement of German families was begun in 1880 by a New Orleans priest, Rev. Peter Leonhard Thevis. The approximate center of the settlement was about five miles northwest of Rayne at Robert's Cove.

The place, also called Prairie Robert or *l'Anse Robert*, takes its name from Benjamin Robert, the original owner of a Spanish land grant on Bayou Plaquemine Brulee's south side.[22]

[17] *Crowley Signal*, Mar. 1, 1902; *Daily Signal*, Mar. 15, 1911

[18] *Daily Signal*, July 27, 1911

[19] *Crowley Signal*, Nov. 7, 1903; Feb. 23, 1901

[20] *Crowley Signal*, Sept. 8, 1900; *Daily Signal*, Sept. 3, 1902

[21] *Daily Signal*, Apr. 9, July 10, 1906; *Crowley Signal*, July 13, 1907

[22] Fontenot and Freeland, *Acadia Parish*, 42

The first German immigrant to acquire property in the Cove was Peter J. Thevis, who bought land from Emma L. Clark. R. J. C. Bull, a Rayne notary public and real estate man, handled the transaction. The land sale is recorded in Alienation Book No. 2, 504-505, March 28, 1881, St. Landry Parish.

The colony grew rapidly. St. Landry Parish records show purchases of land early in January of 1882 by Peter Gossen, Frantz Reiners, Christian J. Hensgens and Hubert Wirtz. Xavier Morell of New Orleans was the agent handling the sales. Gossen, Hensgens and Wirtz acquired 100 acres each; Reiners bought 50 acres—40 acres of prairie land and 10 acres of woodland. Prices ranged from $4.50 to $6.25 per acre.[23] Later additions to the settlement included the families of Grein, Vondenstein, Leonards, Achten, Schlicher, Zaunbrecher, Gielen, Theunissen, Scheufens, Spaetgens, Jacob, Heinen, Dischler, Schaffhausen, Ohlenforst, Habetz, Dorr,

---

[23] Conveyance Book L-2, 443-444, St. Landry Par.

The first Catholic church building at Robert's Cove, constructed in 1893. The wooden structure, built at a cost of $550, was in use for more than sixty years. (Photo courtesy Clara Habetz)

Pastor and teacher, Rev. Leo Schwab and Peter Schneider, pose with pupils of St. Leo's School, Robert's Cove. The thirty-two boys and girls are children of the German immigrants who settled the area in the 1880s. (Photo courtesy Clara Habetz)

Kloor, Dommert, Stamm, Klumpp, Olinger, Cramer, Bollich, Ronkartz, Schneider, Neu, Schatzle, Bischoff, Meier, Berken, Huesers, Kopmeir, Koch, and Jabusch.[24]

The German settlers, all devout Catholics, established their own congregation in 1883. Rev. Aegittius Hennemann, a Benedictine priest, was the first pastor. Other pastors (to 1920) included Revs. Silvan Buschor, Jacobus Zienenfuss, Felix Rumpf, Placidus Zarn and Leo Schwab.[25]

---

[24] Fontenot and Freeland, *Acadia*, 180; St. Leo's Church and School Directory, booklet, 1903-04; St. Leo's Church records; interview, Etta Stamm Sweeney, 1978
[25] St. Leo's Church records; *Rayne Acadian-Tribune*, Mar. 2, 1929

St. Leo's convent at Robert's Cove. This home for the Sisters was built during the second pastorate of Rev. Felix Rumpf, 1893-1897. (Photo courtesy Clara Habetz)

Father Rumpf was pastor of St. Leo's for seven years, from 1888 to 1890, then from 1893 to 1897. During his second time as pastor the first church building was constructed (1893), followed by the construction of a school, cemetery and convent.[26]

The German immigrants were gradually drawn into the mainstream of life in Acadia Parish, although they maintained their language and customs longer than most. The first concerted effort to preserve the Germanic heritage, initiated by Louis Kloor, took place in December, 1909. A meeting to organize a German society was held at the Crowley Knights of Columbus hall.[27]

The *Crowley Signal*, editorializing in its issue of January 5, 1910, had words of praise and high commendation for the organization, *Die Deutsche Gesellschaft,* its aims and objectives:

> The German Society of Acadia Parish, organized on Sunday by representative citizens of the parish of German birth or descent, starts

[26] *Rayne Acadian-Tribune*, July 12, 1956
[27] *Daily Signal*, Dec. 10, 1909

233

out with nearly 50 members from every section of the parish and with good prospects for a useful existence. Its objects are entirely commendable. It seeks to build up the prestige of those citizens of Louisiana who are of German extraction; to foster in the hearts of German-Americans a love for the language and literature of the German Fatherland; to assist the worthy German immigrant by good counsel, and by substantial assistance where it is necessary; to promote social intercourse among those of German blood and to foster the best ideals of citizenship.

The United States has no better citizens than the Germans, taken as a body, and the Germans of this parish are among its best citizens. The German is thrifty, industrious, intelligent, law-abiding, honest and above all a home builder. Intensely patriotic, he cherishes always a tender love for the land that gave him birth—"The Fatherland," he calls it—but he is always loyal to the land of his adoption. Loyalty is a characteristic German trait. Not only are Germans loyal to country, but they are loyal to their private associations. German friendship is strong and dependable friendship. The German is a respecter of his word. He is reliable under every condition. He is slow to act, but he moves when he does move in straight lines. The German is a home body. He is a lover of wife and children and generally his sturdy sons and rosy-cheeked daughters are many. He is a monogamist, and the marriage relation is sacred to him. He seldom figures in the divorce courts and illegitimacy is rare in a German community. He is a lover of the soil, a home-maker. As a tiller of the soil he has no superior. This is because he is industrious, frugal, patient, intelligent. The German is God-fearing. He upholds the church and is a pillar of the state. He believes in schools. Where is the German who can neither read nor write? He is enlightened and progressive. He reads and thinks. He takes a wholesome interest in the government of parish, state and nation, but he is no politician.

The German is a good citizen, and the organization of the German Society of Acadia Parish is calculated to increase his usefulness and to promote his type of citizenship. The organization is in no sense local and is devoted not to the interests of a class or a section, but of a people. Therefore it is entitled to and will be accorded recognition. . . .

The first publicized event planned by the society—a July 4th picnic on Joe Leonards' property at Anding's Lake—was rained out, and the meeting was held in the Crowley Knights of Columbus hall. The program included a talk, in English, by Rev. A. F. Isenberg, pastor of St. Michael's Catholic Church of Crowley; talks in German by Pastor Meibohm of the German Lutheran Church of Crowley, and Prof. Schneider, a teacher at the Catholic school of Robert's Cove.[28]

A second July 4th program was scheduled for 1911. A German flag was raised at the Crowley courthouse, and a brief speech was delivered by Karl Hetzel, president of the German Society. A German *Volksfest* was held at Mowata.[29]

Nothing concerning the society appeared in the Crowley newspaper for more than three years, until after Germany became embroiled in

---

[28] *Crowley Signal*, July 29, 1910
[29] *Daily Signal*, July 3, 5, 1911

World War I. A meeting of the German Society was called at the Crowley Fire Hall. The meeting notice, in both German and English, appeared on the front page of the *Daily Signal* of October 31, 1914. Invited to the meeting were "all members, all Germans, Austrians and sympathizers."

This was the final public mention of *Die Deutsche Gessellschaft*. At any rate the organization could not have survived the "spy hunt" of 1917 and 1918. However, until the United States became involved in the war German residents of Acadia openly expressed pro-German sentiments. Several were quoted in the Crowley newspaper:

Karl Hetzel, ". . . progressive and prosperous German resident of Prairie Hayes, expresses the belief that the fatherland will ultimately win out and vindicate the position taken by that government."[30]

Otto Mayer and his wife, the former Minna Feitel, visiting the J. Kollitz family in Estherwood after a trip to Germany, said that "German guns and soldiers were far superior to those of the allies."[31]

Conrad Hensgens, "substantial German farmer," said he had eleven first cousins at the front, and "predicts victory for Germany."[32]

This neutral climate changed rapidly in the spring of 1917, when the national epidemic of "German spy fever" spread to Acadia Parish. The first local incident happened at Iota, when two unidentified persons, of unspecified nationality, accused of interfering with a recruiting officer and insulting the flag, were reported to have been "severely dealt with" by Jesse Reed. Another incident involved Louis Kloor, first president of the German Society. A veteran official of the Crowley Fire Department, Kloor was accused of refusing to display the American flag at the fire station.[33]

Kloor was fully exonerated but the contagion spread. Scare headlines, such as "What to Do to Catch Spies," and hideous caricatures of the Kaiser appeared in the *Signal*. A near panic resulted when a craft, thought to be a German raider, was reported seen taking soundings in the Mermentau River.[34] All persons with German connections became suspect.

A few newspaper reports, pointing up the loyalty and patriotism of several of the local German-Americans, may have helped to alleviate the situation. One such story, concerning sons of Joe Knipping, was headlined "Crowley Man Gives Two Sons to U.S. Cause," and sub-headed, "by the way, he's German." A later issue carried photos of the two Knipping boys, Henry, with Company B, and W. Joseph, in the United States Navy, and also a story about George Kloor's service in American aviation. A third report said that Will Heinen had sold $20,000 in war

---

[30] *Ibid*, Jan. 13, 1914
[31] *Ibid*, Oct. 12, 1914
[32] *Ibid*, Jan. 8, 1915
[33] *Ibid*, Apr. 5, 11, 1917
[34] *Ibid*, Apr. 13, 1917

savings stamps and certificates to people of German extraction in his neighborhood.[35]

A proclamation issued by Sheriff Louis Fontenot notified foreign-born residents that "they will be protected in the ownership of their property and money" and "will be free from personal molestation so long as they obey the laws of the country."

The proclamation stated that enemy aliens who had not been implicated in anti-American plots had nothing to fear, so long as they refrained from public discussion of questions involved in the war crisis. The sheriff urged the citizenry to maintain "a calm and considerate attitude toward all, without regard to nationality," and cautioned against rash interpretation of the phrase "enemy alien," so as "not to confound or mistake the intention and construe it to apply to foreign-born Germans, or others, who are naturalized residents and part of our best citizenship."[36]

Unfortunately, the headlines and placement given the sheriff's news release as the front page lead story in the *Signal* stressed the "warning to aliens" angle.

The matter climaxed during the summer of 1918 when a United States marshal arrested three German-Americans, Joseph Schaffhausen of Rayne, Ferdinand Olinger of Robert's Cove and John Frey Jr. of Gassler-Frey.[37]

The three were alleged to have made disloyal and treasonable utterances. They were taken to Jennings for a hearing before a United States district attorney.[38] The men were released after the hearing and returned to their homes the same day they were arrested.[39]

Although the newspaper account of the arrests included a request that people suspend judgment until the allegations were proven, the paper did not carry a follow-up story concerning the immediate release of the three men. Damage had been done. Families of the men felt ostracized, their children were shunned at school. The reaction of the German people was to withdraw from their non-German neighbors, and to refrain from using the German language except in the privacy of their homes. They invested in war bonds and stamps to demonstrate loyalty to their adopted country.[40]

Robert's Cove, because of the Germans, their church and school, acquired a distinctively German-Catholic character. However, not all residents of the area were German, or Catholic. Property owners included Anglo-Protestants and Acadian Catholics. Robert's Cove Methodists at-

[35] *Ibid*, July 19, 1917; Jan. 7, June 28, 1918
[36] *Ibid*, Apr. 13, 1917
[37] *Ibid*, July 6, 1918
[38] *Ibid*
[39] Interview, Elizabeth Schaffhausen, 1978
[40] *Daily Signal*, July 9, 1918; interview, Elizabeth and Ann Schaffhausen

tended services at Branch, and those of the Baptist congregation travelled to Pilgrim's Rest in Prairie Hayes.[41]

The Christian Church bought property in Robert's Cove in 1917, but it has not been established that a church was built on the land. Records of the land transaction indicate that there was a Christian church congregation, however. Joseph L. Istre sold three and one eighth arpents of land to the Christian Church of Robert's Cove, represented by Louis Ancelet, J. Prather, Simonet LeBlanc, Marcus Smith and Andrew Laughlin. Price paid was $100.[42]

There was also a public school in the Cove. Among early teachers were Maggie Hunter, Lilly F. Van Valkenburg and Bertha Griffin.[43]

Among the non-German pioneer families of Robert's Cove were the Robinsons. In 1915 Mr. and Mrs. S. B. Robinson, aged 94 and 90 respectively, were said to be the oldest native-born couple in Acadia Parish.[44]

Mowata

During the period under consideration (1900-1920) a number of first generation German-Americans of the Robert's Cove colony acquired land in Prairie Hayes, in the vicinity of Mowata and Frey, thereby linking the two German settlements of Robert's Cove and Fabacher-Frey.

Meanwhile a third colony, composed of several German-Protestant families, had come in to add to the German population in the same general area.

Like the earlier immigrants these settlers also became successful rice farmers. Within a few years they had established their own church, the Mowata German Baptist Church.

Charter members of the church were Mr. and Mrs. Friedrich Loewer, Mr. and Mrs. David Loewer, Mr. and Mrs. Carl Casselmann, Mr. and Mrs. Heinrich Bieber, Gustaf Casselmann, Elise Goebel, Albert Bollinger, Marie Loewer Virnau and Jakob Bieber.[45]

All of the families were related by blood or connected by marriage. First member of the Loewer family to come to Acadia Parish was Henry Loewer, who became a Crowley businessman in the 1890s, later located in Iota.[46]

The first of the families to locate in the Mowata area were the Casselmanns, who arrived about 1901. The Biebers and the other members of

---

[41] Interview, Myrta Fair Craig, 1978

[42] Conveyance Book C-3, #45403, 491, Acad. Par.

[43] *Crowley Signal*, Sept. 16, 1899; Sept. 14, 1901; *Daily Signal*, May 16, 1904

[44] *Daily Signal*, Nov. 11, 1915

[45] Letter from F. D. Loëwer to Walter Grotefend, Nov. 7, 1977

[46] Interview, Mrs. Edgar Bieber, 1978

the Loewer family arrived in 1905, followed shortly thereafter by the others.[47]

The church, built in 1907 on land given by Heinrich Bieber, was served by traveling missionaries who lived with the families of the congregation. Church services were conducted in the German language. The first marriage ceremony performed united Albert Bollinger and Marie Loewer, widow of Carl Virnau.[48]

Members of the church were active in Baptist affairs outside their congregation. In 1916 the Acadia Parish delegation to a Baptist conference in Kyle, Texas, was made up of Mr. and Mrs. Friedrich Loewer, their daughter Emma and son, Fred Jr., Mrs. Carl Casselmann and Carl Goebel.[49]

In time the church acquired property for a cemetery. The half acre of land, located about a half mile from the church, was sold by Fred Loewer to representatives of the church Henry Bieber and August R. Loewer.[50]

Mowata became a place name about 1907 when the Frisco (Colorado Southern) railroad was built from Eunice to Crowley. The name was given the train station by Winston Jones and T. T. Atteberry. Jones, one of the largest rice planters in the early part of the century, was the guiding hand behind the immense Jones Brothers holdings, covering seven sections, in the northern part of Acadia Parish. Atteberry managed the sprawling rice farm.[51]

In the initial process of railroad construction Jones granted a right-of-way across three sections of his land. The three years prior to completion of the line were extremely dry years; it became necessary for Jones to put down 14 new water wells and install machinery to operate them, in order to provide sufficient irrigation for the rice fields.[52]

After the track was laid and the station locations determined, the Frisco company asked Jones to suggest a name for the station. After a consultation, Jones and Atteberry decided to submit the name "Morewater," because of the continuing need for more irrigation. The name was accepted, but when it appeared on the depot it was spelled Mowata.[53]

While the Eunice-Crowley railroad line was being laid the name Morewater appeared in print several times. In May of 1907 the side track at Morewater was reported completed and the railroad camps moved to that location.[54]

---

[47] *Ibid*

[48] *Ibid*. Church services in the German language were continued until 1958, when the younger members of the congregation found it difficult to follow the mother tongue of their elders.

[49] *Daily Signal*, July 11, 1916

[50] Conveyance Book N-3, #50602-03, 188-189, Acad. Par.

[51] Interview, Winston Atteberry, 1977

[52] *Ibid*

[53] *Ibid*. The Mowata spelling led to a belief that the name was of Indian origin.

[54] *Crowley Signal*, May 4, 1907

A *Crowley Signal* release of June 1, 1907 revealed that the new town of Morewater, in the vicinity of the Jones farm, had elected municipal officers. The town officials were H. J. Lambert, mayor; M. G. Johnson, chief of police, tax collector and street commissioner; B. B. McClelland, C. Kilbeaux, W. F. Anding, J. W. McAlpen and W. E. Morrison, aldermen; A. S. Wright, attorney; W. K. Andrews, clerk; Harry Anding, president board of health; T. T. Atteberry, secretary. The names of the officials do not appear in records of the Louisiana Department of State.

A post office was established at Mowata in 1911. Ivie E. Miller, the first postmaster, served for 10 years. Benjamin F. Harrell was postmaster for about a year, then the post office was closed and the mail sent to Eunice.[55]

The post office was located on Louis Frey property, in a general store operated by Postmaster Miller. Mail was delivered from the Mowata office by buggy to the Richard community and other points.[56]

A private school, also located on the Frey property, was taught by Mrs. Maurice Miller. After public schools in the area were consolidated the children were taken to schools in Eunice and Iota in buses driven by I. E. Miller and Meus Blanchard.[57]

Rhineland, a whistlestop on the Frisco railroad about halfway between Crowley and Eunice, endured as a place name until World War I when the name was changed to Judd because of anti-German feelings generated by the war. Conrad Hensgens, one of the original German immigrants in the Robert's Cove area, acquired property at Rhineland in 1907. Hensgens' residence in the area, along with that of other German families, accounts for the original name of Rhineland.[58]

Another place name in the northern half of the parish was Mallet Switch, a railroad switch on Bayou Mallet at Rork, between Mowata and Eunice.[59]

Rorkdell and Rork

Rorkdell and Rork, both named for the same individual, were whistle-stops on two different railroad lines and were located three quarters of a mile apart.

Rorkdell, on the Southern Pacific branch line from Midland to Eunice, located just south of the Bayou Mallet woods about three miles south of Eunice, was on the north side of a 1,100-acre farm owned by

[55] Register of Postmasters, National Archives and Records Service
[56] *Signal*, 50th Anniv. Ed., 65
[57] *Ibid*
[58] Fontenot, "Le Bon Vieux Temps," *Crowley Post-Signal*, Nov. 13, 1977
[59] *Daily Signal*, Mar. 15, 1906

W. J. Rork. The Rorks owned this farm when the Frisco line was built, and there is about a mile of Frisco railroad right-of-way across the farm. The Frisco company put in a switch track and a whistle-stop and named it Rork.[60]

For a brief time Rorkdell had a post office. The facility was established April 6, 1904, but the order was rescinded June 25, 1904. The short-term postmaster was Dr. W. T. Patterson, who later practiced medicine in Crowley and Morse.[61]

Another post office in the general area between Mowata and Eunice by the name of Jelks was established in 1910 with Clifton Tubre as postmaster. William E. Jelks was named postmaster in 1911. The Jelks post office was discontinued in 1912 and the mail sent to Eunice.[62]

---

[60] Interview, Winston Atteberry, 1977

[61] Register of Postmasters

[62] *Ibid.* There are no clues to the locations of two early Acadia Parish post offices shown in the official record except the names of the postmasters: Redtop post office, 1891 to 1894, postmasters James A. McMillan and Louis McMillan; Beulah post office, postmaster James L. Murphy, established September 18, 1908, discontinued December 15, 1909.

Long Point—Star—Maxie—Ellis

Another portion of Prairie Hayes which has undergone several name changes is the Maxie-Ellis area, situated in the approximate center of the parish.

The early name for the area was Long Point, stemming from the nearest stream, Long Point Gully, a tributary of Bayou Plaquemine Brulee. A post office, named Star, was established in the vicinity in 1899, with Lyman L. Clark as postmaster. Rupert V. Sloane became Star postmaster in 1903.[1]

Long Point kept its identity until 1907 when construction of the Frisco (Colorado Southern) railroad from Eunice to Crowley was completed. The railroad company located so called stations at six points between Crowley and Eunice: at Lawson, four miles north of Crowley; at Ellis, eight miles; Maxie, 10 miles; Rhineland, 12 miles; Mowata, 14 miles; Jones Spur, 16 miles; Rork, 17 miles.[2]

The Lawson station was a spur track on the W. E. Lawson farm. Rhineland was also a spur track, located on the Conrad Hensgens farm. During harvest season box cars were placed there for the farmers of the vicinity to ship their rice to the mills. The Jones Spur was on the Jones Brothers farm between Mowata and Eunice.[3]

Only three of the six place names created by the railroad have endured: Ellis, Maxie and Mowata. Ellis was named for W. E. Ellis, a Crowley banker, and Maxie for Maxwell Duson, son of W. W. Duson.[4]

The name of Star post office was changed to Maxie in 1908. Postmasters included Rupert V. Sloane, Bryan J. Sloane, Ivy A. Sweeney and Milton Andrus. Another post office in the Maxie-Ellis vicinity was the Echo office, established in 1890 with Henry A. Abney as postmaster. Avery Tobey and James E. Andrus also served as postmasters. The Echo post office was terminated in 1892 and the mail sent to Crowley. Ellis had its own post office from 1908 to 1927. Postmasters were Robert J. Black, Alfred T. Moore and Charlie C. Martin.[5]

Some of the early teachers at the Long Point school were Maud Latta, J. A. Patten, J. W. Jones and Felton W. Young.[6]

The Daigle school house was described as located "north of Long Point." The site of this school, which was one of the oldest in the parish, has been pin-pointed exactly: two miles north of Maxie, and one mile

[1] Register of Postmasters, National Archives and Records Service
[2] *Crowley Signal*, Dec. 14, 1907
[3] Interview, Winston Atteberry, 1978
[4] Fontenot-Freeland, *Acadia Parish, etc.* 196
[5] Register of Postmasters; the Maxie and Ellis post offices were closed in 1926 and 1927 respectively, and the mail in each case sent to Crowley
[6] *Crowley Signal*, Sept. 16, 1899; Sept. 8, 1900; Sept. 14, 1901; Sept. 3, 1902

west of the Conrad Hensgens home place at the Rhineland spur. The older children in the Hensgen family attended this school.[7]

A private school functioned in the vicinity around the turn of the century. In June of 1899 the Daigle school house was the scene of an "exhibition" by St. Ignatius school. The program included an examination of pupils and an ice cream festival, followed by the closing exercises and a dance. Dancing was in an open pavillion decorated with Japanese lanterns, and music was furnished by four violin and two guitar players. Lillian Hardy, the teacher at the Daigle school, was also the teacher at St. Ignatius School.[8]

The religious character of the Maxie-Ellis neighborhood has always been predominantly Protestant. Several Protestant congregations were organized and flourished in the section during the early years.

The Long Point Methodist Episcopal Church (South) was the first house of worship established. A four-acre tract of land was given the church by Southwestern Louisiana Land Company, represented by W. W. Duson, in 1892. Church trustees making the transaction were Isaac Hayes, George P. Abney, Henry A. Abney, William A. Higginbotham and Jefferson Murphy.[9]

The church acquired more land in 1914 when A. Kaplan donated a square acre. Jacob J. Stewart represented the church in the transaction.[10]

Maxie's oldest landmark is the cemetery which adjoins the church yard. Family names noted on the older tombs in the cemetery include Amos, Amy, Anding, Andrus, Childs, Clark, Cole, Darphin, Harmon, Hayes, Hornsby, Jelks, Kerr, Lambert, Laughlin, McClelland, McNeil, Milner, Miller, Muller, Murff, Rasberry, Rue, Robertson, Robison, Sloane, Robinson, Stakes, Steen, Stewart and Tobey.

Early families of Maxie include those of B. M. Lambert, R. V. Sloane, N. W. Robinson, Norris Sloane, Truman Stakes, Glen Stakes, Jim Stakes, Beecher Stakes, Colan Daigle, Henry Mosley, W. A. Higginbotham. In the Ellis area were James McCain, William McCain, Alphonse Wirtz, E. J. Kerr, Herbert Kerr, J. O. Stewart, Madison Amy, E. C. Hayes, Arthur Humble, Sam Henderson, Mack Robinson, Jack Amy and Elihue Henderson.[11]

A Christian church at Long Point, established at an unspecified time, was destroyed by fire in 1903.[12]

In 1910 Samuel W. Tobey donated land to the United Brethren in Christ Church of the Ellis charge. The property consisted of the northeast quarter of the northwest quarter of Section 6, T9SR1E. The act of dona-

---

[7] *Ibid*, June 17, 1899; interview, Kate and Marie Hensgens, 1978

[8] *Crowley Signal*, June 17, 1899

[9] Hebert, Betty Henderson, historian, Maxie Methodist Church

[10] Conveyance Book V-2, #39302, 598, Acad. Par.

[11] Jabusch, Willa Duhon, unpub. research

[12] *Crowley Signal*, Nov. 14, 1903

tion stipulated that the land be used for a church house. The church was dedicated in the spring of 1911.[13]

Some three years later, in 1914, the Pentacostal Church of the Nazarene bought property from the United Brethren Church for $200. By 1916 the church, also called the Ellis Apostolic church, had acquired a large following, with many Crowley people driving out to attend nightly services in the summertime.[14]

In 1907, when the coming of the railroad had set off dreams of town building, Maxie was described as "a new town." Its assets included a neat depot, three section houses, two other dwellings, the Methodist Church and the Rupert V. Sloane store, where the post office was located.[15]

The Maxie Mercantile company was formed in 1908. Owned by a group of farmers, the store was managed by Rupert Sloane, the merchant-postmaster of the Star Post Office. The incorporators were Lewis Robinson, Octave Amy, Rupert V. Sloane, John T. Andrus, W. A. Higginbotham, Robert B. Sloane, Bryan J. Sloane and John W. Davis. Capital stock in the business was increased from $10,000 to $20,000 in 1916. New stockholders were B. H. Laughlin, M. D. Sloane, C. E. Faulk and Merton Andrus.[16]

Ellis had at least one merchant—A. T. Moore, who operated a store there for many years.[17]

News notes in the *Daily Signal* identify two Maxie residents as doctors: Dr. R. H. Fisher and Dr. G. H. McGuffey.[18] It is believed that both were medical doctors, but it is not known that they were practicing physicians at the time.

The dense woodlands west of Long Point-Star-Maxie at one time harbored a variety of wild animals. Professional trappers lived in the area during the winter months. The trappers lived in tents in the woods and set traps for fur-bearing animals such as raccoons. One of the regular trappers was Frank Broussard. Panthers howled around the Methodist cemetery at night, and posses with hounds hunted the predators around Mallet Switch after calves and other young domestic animals were found killed and eaten.[19]

---

[13] Conveyance Book O-2, #33210, 753 Acad. Par.; *Daily Signal*, Mar. 31, 1911
[14] Conveyance Book Y-2, #41872, 702, Acad. Par.; *Daily Signal*, Aug. 4, 1916
[15] *Crowley Signal*, Aug. 24, 1907
[16] *Crowley Signal*, Feb. 15, 1908; *Daily Signal*, May 12, 1916
[17] *Daily Signal*, Mar. 20, 1913; Anniv. Ed., 1949, 77
[18] Sept. 15, Oct. 27, 1911; May 22, 1912
[19] *Crowley Signal*, Nov. 25, Dec. 9, 1905; *Daily Signal*, Aug. 3, 1906

Jonas Cove—Regan—Canal Switch—Abbott—Egan

Egan, a town two and one half miles north of Midland near Bayou Jonas, was first known as Jonas Cove. The public school that served the area was called the Jonas Cove school. The Acadia Parish School Board made an appropriation of $200 in 1901 to build a new school house at Jonas Cove; at the time Mrs. Eunice Kleinpeter was the only teacher. A second teacher, Lucile Seitz, was added to the staff in 1902. In 1904 when the name of the school was changed to Egan, Nettie and Maggie Tuite were the teachers.[1]

Three post offices were established in the Egan area before 1900. Regan post office, named for John Regan the first postmaster, began operations in 1888. Thomas D. Schrock, appointed postmaster in 1890, served until 1891 when the post office was discontinued and the mail sent to Crowley.[2]

Canal post office was established in 1890 with Joseph H. Fabacher as postmaster. The office was closed in 1892 and the mail sent to Crowley. The third post office was the Abbott, which functioned from December, 1900 to August 3, 1903, when the name of the place and post office was changed to Egan. Postmasters (to 1922) were Joseph Rose, 1900; Andrew J. Davis, 1901; John W. Smith, 1902; Clyde C. Bell, 1904; Margaret Dixon, 1907; Elmire Truax, 1907; Andrew J. Davis, 1912; Frank M. Scanlan, 1915; Fern Richey, 1922.[3]

The Jonas Cove settlement acquired the name Canal Switch in 1899 when the Abbott-Duson canal people built a warehouse for the convenience of rice farmers in the area. The Southern Pacific railroad ran a switch there to handle shipping, hence the name Canal Switch. The Abbott post office was named for Miron Abbott, pioneer in rice irrigation.[4]

The final name change was in honor of William M. Egan, president of the company that built the rice mill at Egan and developed the town. In the spring of 1903 Egan and two merchants of the settlement, John W. Smith and Frank Scanlan, bought 600 acres of land from W. W. Duson for about $30,000. The purchase took in virtually all of the town lots of the place. At the time plans to build the rice mill had been finalized, and the railroad company had agreed to build a depot.[5]

Smith and Scanlan owned a general merchandise store at Egan.

[1] *Crowley Signal*, July 20, 1901; *Daily Signal*, Sept. 3, 1902; May 16, 1904
[2] Register of Postmasters, National Archives and Records Service
[3] *Ibid*
[4] Leeper, Clare d'Artois, quoting T. J. Carruth in *Louisiana Places*, Baton Rouge, 1976, 86
[5] *Crowley Signal*, May 2, 1903

Smith, a former railroad engineer from New York, had come to Acadia Parish in 1898 as an engineer for the Abbott-Duson canal. He had also managed the Key Stone Ranch in Prairie Hayes. He went into business with the firm of J. Laughlin and Scanlan in 1901. The firm owned the Black Diamond Farm, formerly called the Blind Mule Ranch.[6]

Frank M. Scanlan, born in 1877 at Plaquemine Ridge, was the son of Mike Scanlan, a rice and potato farmer of the northeast corner of the parish. Scanlan started in business as part owner of a cotton gin, then speculated in rice lands, buying at $5 an acre and selling three years later for $45 an acre.[7]

Laughlin retired from the firm in 1903 and the store became known as the Smith and Scanlan store, handling general merchandise, farm implements, grain and feed. In February of 1904 the store was destroyed in a fire, and was not rebuilt.[8]

The Smith and Scanlan store was not the first business firm in Egan. In 1901 a general store was operated by the firm of A. Rose and Son.[9]

Other pioneer businessmen of Egan were the Truax brothers, G. E., Joe, E. D. and Frank, who came from Michigan with a sawmill before 1900. Their first venture was the sawmill, which handled pine and cypress lumber.[10]

Truax Brothers general store was in operation in 1902. A dance hall and saloon were located in the store building. Later the business was separated into two stores, run by G. E. and E. D. Truax respectively. In 1909 the post office was located in the E. D. Truax store.[11]

Other businesses in operation before World War I were the J. J. Regan store and warehouse; J. N. and Dominique Leger's warehouse and feed company; the Egan branch of Farmer's Mercantile, run by Armas Bourgeois, F. A. Roy and Aurelien Hebert.[12]

Manuel Bossley was the village blacksmith, and his wife ran a rooming house in Egan. Bossley was a brother to Henry G. Bossley, who homesteaded land near Egan in 1900. The Bossley brothers married daughters of Mr. and Mrs. R. M. Wainwright, a pioneer family of Acadia. Manuel Bossley was also the coffin maker for the Egan community.[13]

Dr. E. A. Kleinpeter of New Orleans located in Egan in 1904,[14] but it is not known how long he practiced medicine there.

Egan's first church was constructed in 1906. The United Brethren in

[6] *Ibid*, Oct. 23, 1903
[7] *Ibid*, Apr. 11, 1903
[8] *Ibid*, Dec. 21, 1901; Apr. 11, 1903; Feb. 20, 1904; interview, Steve Truax, 1978
[9] *Crowley Signal*, Apr. 13, 1901
[10] Interviews, Steve and Grant Truax, 1978
[11] *Daily Signal*, June 24, 1902; Nov. 30, 1909; interview, Steve Truax, 1978
[12] *Daily Signal*, Nov. 20, 1917; interviews, Steve Truax, Verbie Regan Truax, Magdalen Bossley Ziegler, 1978
[13] *Crowley Signal*, May 16, 1903; interviews, Magdalen Bossley Ziegler, Steve Truax
[14] *Daily Signal*, Jan. 16, Mar. 1, 1904

Christ Church bought Lots 1 and 2 in Block 3 from P. B. Lang and F. M. Scanlan for $200. Representing the church in the land transaction were James A. Hook, Charles J. Kilmer and John Laughlin. The church was built in the summer of 1906. James Akers was the building contractor.[15]

Catholics of the community attended religious services at the Iota church six miles north of Egan. An event of significance to the Catholic congregation of Egan took place in 1917, when Chapel St. Paul, "the only church on wheels in the South," was brought to Egan for a week.[16]

The specially equipped railroad car, weighing 134,000 pounds, was built of steel with a copper roof at a cost of $30,000. The interior was of Cuban mahogany, Gothic design. The equipment included both gas and electrical lighting systems, private quarters for the chaplain, a Redemptorist priest, and a kitchen. The traveling church, donated by an Ohio family, was operated by the Catholic Extension Society.

When the chapel car arrived in Egan a delegation of Catholic men formed a welcome committee at the depot: John Regan, J. J. Regan, Tom Regan, F. A. Roy, J. N. Leger, Arcade Pousson, H. S. Bossley and Noah Sensat.

The chapel car, which seated 100 persons, could not accommodate the large crowds that came for evening services, so the Woodmen of the World hall was used at night and the chapel car for morning Mass.[17]

Egan was never incorporated. Whatever civic projects undertaken during the early years were left to the school to initiate. An example of such a project was Arbor Day of 1906, when the school children planted trees about the town.[18]

Two of the more interesting news items originating at Egan during the early years concerned animals. In 1907 a cow on the Paul Trumps farm lived for 15 days without water. Cattle had eaten a hole in the rice straw stack on the farm, and the stack toppled on top of one of the animals. Trumps thought the cow was dead, and did not attempt to dig it out. Fifteen days afterwards the herd of cattle literally ate the cow to freedom—as the animals ate the straw the imprisoned cow, still alive, was freed. Dehyrated and emaciated, the animal was able to eat and drink and recovered completely.[19]

The second news story concerned a wild animal hunt. George Abbott and a party of young men and dogs bagged a 50-pound catamount (panther) in the spring of 1909, while out hunting 'coons and 'possums. The dogs chased the animal for four hours, from the David Gow farm to the Abbott farm, then from the woods to a rice field. The cat put up quite a

---

[15] Conveyance Book S-2, #33780, 155, Acad. Par.; *Daily Signal*, Aug. 2, 1906
[16] *Daily Signal*, Jan. 25, Feb. 9, 1917
[17] *Ibid*
[18] *Ibid*, Jan. 13, 1906
[19] *Crowley Signal*, Mar. 16, 1907

fight, and laid out a number of the hounds before the dogs finally killed it. The pelt was given Mrs. Martin Abbott for a rug.[20]

The worst disaster in Egan's history struck on May 6, 1915, when a cyclone killed two residents, injured 10 others, demolished homes, barns and business buildings. The storm, which had also left casualties and destruction at Mermentau, killed Mrs. Leanna Woolridge and her eight-year-old son Stephen. The injured included Mr. and Mrs. Charles Rutledge, Johanna Regan, Mr. and Mrs. James Akers, Mrs. Jack McClelland, Mr. and Mrs. John Mayfield.

The Truax and J. J. Regan warehouses were leveled. Residences destroyed included those of Charles Rutledge, James Akers, John Rutledge, Mrs. Lindsey, Mrs. Margaret Dixon, L. Micker, N. Meyers, William Bellard, Neal Regan, J. J. Regan and Mike Hession.[21]

Hannah Regan, one of the teachers, sustained a broken arm from flying timber. She had run out of the school building when a frightened child, Wilson Myers, ran from the building and fell into a ditch.[22]

Another teacher, Catherine Johnson, and a 10-year-old school girl, Magdalen Bossley, were blown out of the school house and prevented from re-entering the building by the force of the wind. They clung to a fence to keep from being blown around. Most of the school children crawled under the school for protection. Willie Stafford was injured when struck by a flying chair. A 12-year-old boy, Steve Truax, was wearing a wide brim straw hat tied under his chin. The wind lifted him and carried him a ways. There were several reports of chicken feathers being driven into trees.[23]

---

[20] *Daily Signal*, Jan. 21, 1909
[21] *Ibid*, May 8, 1915
[22] *Ibid*, interviews, Steve Truax, Verbie Regan Truax, Magdalen Bossley Ziegler
[23] Interviews, Truax and Ziegler

Iota

The past history of Iota, another Acadia Parish town created by the railroad, is identified with Pointe-aux-Loups, one of the oldest place names in southwest Louisiana. Pointe-aux-Loups, or Wolf Point, was the location of mineral springs that attracted summer visitors for half a century, beginning about 1858.[1]

The older settlement was located on Bayou des Cannes about two miles west of the present town of Iota. A post office, named Cartville for the first postmaster, Samuel Cart, was established in the vicinity of Pointe-aux-Loups Springs in 1884. Ten years later, in 1894, a railroad branch line, laid from Midland to Eunice, bypassed Cartville by a mile or so. The railroad company built a depot at a point on the line nearest to the Cartville-Pointe-aux-Loups settlements and named it Iota.[2]

The name of the Cartville post office was changed to Iota in 1900. Postmasters to 1920, other than Samuel Cart, were Adolph Baumann, Savinien Cart, Louis Cart, Jesse H. Nordyke, Nellie E. Nordyke, Henry L. Daughenbaugh, Alonzo F. Fruge, Viola M. McMillan, Viola M. Fontenot.[3]

The first postmaster, Samuel Cart, was the son of Antoine B. Cart, first proprietor of Pointe-aux-Loups Springs and progenitor of the Cart family of Acadia. Antoine and his sons, Samuel, Savinien, Louis and Neuville, were influential political figures of the 4th ward.[4]

Adolph Baumann, native of Stuttgart, Germany, was the first station agent in Iota, locating there in 1894 when the railroad was built. He was also a pioneer merchant of Iota. Another of the early postmasters, Jesse H. Nordyke, a native of Ohio, came to Iota in 1899. He was a rice farmer and managed an implement company.[5]

C. C. "Curley" Duson is credited with being the founder of Iota. It was he who promoted the construction of the Southern Pacific line to Eunice, the new town he founded in St. Landry Parish. At the same time, 1894, Duson acquired the land on which Iota now stands, a 160-acre tract which had been homesteaded by Archille Doucet in 1835. Duson divided the land into town lots and sold them.[6] Duson was the prime mover in the establishment of the Acadia Canal Company in the vicinity of Iota, and was president of the rice mill put up in Iota in 1901, the two businesses said to have been responsible for the town's economic development.

[1] Fontenot and Freeland, *Acadia Parish, a History to 1900*, 155-165
[2] *Ibid*
[3] Register of Postmasters, National Archives and Records Service
[4] *Crowley Signal*, May 23, 1903
[5] *Ibid*, Apr. 4, 1903; *Daily Signal*, July 12, 1904
[6] *Crowley Signal*, June 22, 1907; Oct. 31, 1908

Some 12 years after Duson had the town lot sale in Iota, some interesting litigation grew out of the land transaction. When Archille Doucet, the original landowner, died, he left a widow and six children, four of whom were minors. The major heirs sued the widow for a partition of licitation; at the ensuing land sale the widow bought half of the land and W. W. Duson, the remainder. Both the widow and W. W. Duson sold their halves of the land to C. C. Duson, who proceeded with his plan for town development.[7]

In 1906 the Doucet heirs who had been minors in 1894 brought suit to set aside the partition sale made in 1894 and recover their interests. A test case was made against Michael Fenelon, one of the large property owners of Iota. The case went on for two years. The district court judgment was given for the defendant, but the Louisiana Supreme Court reversed the decision of the lower court, re-heard the case and reaffirmed its decision. The effect of the decision was to unsettle all land titles in the town of Iota. The higher court ruled that the partition sale was null and void, and all titles emanating from it were null and void. According to the terms of a compromise the Doucet heirs received 150 lots in Iota in settlement of all claims.[8]

The early 1900s found Iota with an estimated population of 300 and a dozen or so business firms in operation. A parish business directory, published as a weekly feature of the *Crowley Signal*, carried advertisements for 10 Iota firms. These included Adolph Baumann, general merchandise; J. A. Sabatier and Company, general merchandise and implements; E. Barousse, general merchandise; Callahan Manufacturing Company, lumber and building supplies; H. I. Daughenbaugh, general merchandise; R. A. and J. A. Murff, blacksmiths; Fenelon Brothers, warehouse; Menou and Company, grain, feed, lumber; Hayes Pharmacy, in office of Dr. F. N. Hayes, physician and surgeon; Crescent Saloon, Cart and Regan, "jug trade a specialty."

Other firms in business in 1901 included the Brooks and Clark drug store, Dr. George E. Brooks and Dr. L. A. Clark; the Ben F. Toler Lumber Company; Miss Mary Amy's millinery shop, and Eugene Lyons, liveryman.[9]

A hotel was opened in the summer of 1901 by William J. Young who was assisted in running the hotel by his wife and daughter, Rosebud. The hotel was destroyed by fire a few months after it opened for business. A 12-room hotel with two baths replaced the burned structure.[10]

The Crescent Saloon changed hands in 1901. The business was sold at a sheriff's sale "to satisfy the state of Louisiana for the license the gentlemen neglected to take out when they commenced selling liquor."

[7] *Ibid*
[8] *Ibid*
[9] *Ibid*, Aug. 24, Oct. 26, Nov. 23, 1901
[10] *Ibid*, Aug. 17, Dec. 7, 1901; Dec. 14, 1907

Iota's first hotel, owned and operated by Mr. and Mrs. William Young. The first building burned in 1901 and was replaced by the structure shown above. (Reproduced from *Crowley Signal,* 1907)

The saloon was sold to Theodore Daigle and Cornelius Richard, both of Church Point, for $1,300, and the name was changed to the Club Saloon.[11]

The next few years witnessed several new businesses opening in the town. Two barber shops were run by C. Darbonne and Henry Dobson in 1902; Henry Loewer built a large implement warehouse near the depot that year. The Barousse store stock was sold to the Amy brothers, who built a new store building on Duson Avenue; two meat markets were opened by Dave Rasberry and Frank Hayes, and Emile Bourgaux announced plans to build a hardware and implement house on his property facing Point-aux-Loups Avenue.[12]

One of the enterprises begun in 1902 was the publication of a newspaper for Iota. The first issue of the *Iota Weekly Times* came out in April of 1902.[13] It is not known when the newspaper suspended publication; the only other reference appeared in the Iota news column of the *Daily Signal* of July 9, 1902: "The *Iota Weekly Times* will be printed at home from now on." It is believed the newspaper was short lived. In 1904 the Iota news correspondent complained that the town had been "utterly ignored in the Christmas issues of Crowley newspapers" and promised, "just wait 'til

---

[11] *Ibid*, Aug. 3, 1901; Feb. 27, 1904
[12] *Ibid*, Jan. 12, Feb. 8, Apr. 2, Aug. 1, 7, 1902
[13] *Daily Signal*, Apr. 16, 1902

we get a newspaper, you'll see!" indicating the absence of any publication in Iota at the time.[14]

More new businesses for Iota were listed in the Crowley newspaper's business directory of 1903. New firms listed were O. W. Collins, livery; Frank E. and Wynne W. Woodworth, dry goods and notions, doing business as "The Racket Store;" S. A. Going, blacksmithing and repairs; Bourgaux and Reed, implements and buggies; Iota Implement Company, J. H. Nordyke; J. H. Deshotels, general merchandise; I. E. Collins, fruits, confections.[15]

Chris Lejeune ran a barroom in Iota in 1903; H. J. Daigle and son bought out Lejeune that year. The Iota Drug Store was owned by Dr. W. J. Smith.[16]

References to two heretofore unmentioned livery businesses were noted in news briefs of 1904: the Simon and Reed livery, and the G. C. Robert and O. W. Collins livery. These could have been old businesses which had changed hands. J. N. Simon had a new implement store in 1904 and Miss Eliza Cart ran a hat shop.[17]

Three of the older Iota business firms changed hands in 1904 and 1905. H. J. Daigle and Robert McManus bought the stock of the Baumann store and also the store owned by the Amy brothers. The business was carried on in the Amy building under the name of Daigle and McManus. B. F. Toler bought out Jules Menou and consolidated the two lumber yards.[18]

An Iota landmark was demolished in 1905. This was the first warehouse constructed in the town. The building, put up by Philomen Miller, had been used as a store and warehouse by the Sabatier firm.[19]

A business highlight of 1905 was the formation of the Farmers' Mercantile, successor to J. H. Deshotels' store, a new company capitalized at $10,000. The stockholders were all substantial farmers and business men. Jules Menou was president of the company and J. H. Deshotels the secretary-treasurer. Alfred V. Ducote was manager of the store.[20]

Iota's first brick building was Dr. F. N. Hayes' new drug store, constructed in 1906. Another "first" was the Iota Minstrel Band, which was performing in 1904. The next reference to a musical organization was the Doucet Brass Band, led by Remy Doucet.[21]

Other early businesses included the Robert Sittig livery; the Iota Cash Store, Alex Amy, proprietor; the Iota Planing Mill; D. R. Pucheu

[14] *Crowley Signal*, Dec. 31, 1904
[15] *Ibid*, Mar. 21, Oct. 24, 1903
[16] *Ibid*, Nov. 14, 1903; *Daily Signal*, Feb. 26, 1903
[17] *Ibid*, Feb. 27, 1904; *Daily Signal*, Apr. 2, 8, 1904
[18] *Crowley Signal*, Dec. 31, 1904; *Daily Signal*, Feb. 11, 1905
[19] *Crowley Signal*, Oct. 28, 1905
[20] *Ibid*, Oct. 7, 1905
[21] *Daily Signal*, June 21, 1906; *Crowley Signal*, Jan. 2, 1904; Aug. 1, 1908

saloon; Joe Elster's general merchandise, located in the old Baumann store; D. V. Waymire, photographer; J. R. Rodrigue, groceries.[22]

By 1908 Iota had a population of 600, two schools, three churches, a rice mill, several warehouses and a number of substantial businesses. Three sawmills on nearby Bayou des Cannes and the Acadia canal system contributed to the economic welfare of the town. The sawmills, run by Elliott Farley, Dan Fisher and G. M. Parker, employed about 30 men.[23]

The largest stores operating in the town during the early years of the century were the Sabatier company and the Farmers' Mercantile. In 1908 the Sabatier store had five employees: George Wright, the manager; Paul J. Sabatier, Ernest Fruge, Ed Darphin and Willie Fontenot, clerks. The Farmers' Mercantile occupied five buildings; within three years the firm's capital stock of $10,000 had been increased to a paid up capital of $20,000. The store stock included hardware, furniture, buggies, wagons, rice bags and twine. Company officers were Jules Menou, S. B. Andrus and J. H. Deshotels. A. V. Ducote, the manager, was assisted by Max Simar, R. L. Doucet and Louis Cart. During the busy season 12 persons were employed. The firm put up a cotton gin in 1911.[24]

The contract to build the first bank in Iota was let in October of 1912. Principal stockholder in the Bank of Iota was Jules Menou. The facility was later bought by Remy Doucet.[25]

Several residence and business telephones were in use in Iota in 1914. Dr. F. N. Hayes built the line, to serve his drug store and residence. Connected with the Crowley exchange of Cumberland Telephone and Telegraph, the line also served the residences of George D. Wright, Dr. L. A. Clark and the J. A. Sabatier home and store. Two years later Iota had its own telephone exchange with 50 subscribers.[26]

In the spring of 1915 Artelus Roy had a small rice and grist mill in operation. The facility was equipped with a rice huller, a grist mill, a feed crusher and a fanning mill.[27]

About this time the young people of the community were sipping sodas at Cleophas Bourgeois' soda fountain and confectionery, and the ladies of the town could find the latest in Easter bonnets at Anna Bordelais' millinery shop.[28]

A. B. Dore bought out the George Wright store in 1917, about the time Theo Smith, Iota baker, decided to enlarge his baking furnace at his shop on Duson Avenue. A year later the town acquired its first movie house; Emile Bourgaux built the theatre on Duson Avenue and bought his

[22] *Daily Signal*, Feb. 6, 7, Aug. 11, 1906; *Crowley Signal*, Jan. 26, Feb. 23, Sept. 21, Dec. 14, 1907
[23] *Daily Signal*, Dec. 14, 1907
[24] *Ibid*, Dec. 14, 1907; Nov. 8, 1911
[25] *Ibid*, Oct. 4, 1912; interview, Walter Doucet, 1978
[26] *Daily Signal*, May 27, 1914; Nov. 23, 1916
[27] *Ibid*, Mar. 26, 1915
[28] *Ibid*, Sept. 26, 1916; Mar. 6, 1917

own dynamo to run the picture show. Ed Fogleman was the town's first garageman.[29]

Historiettes

Political speeches and July 4th celebrations were at one time the main crowd attractions in Iota. During the campaign of 1912 a political rally drew a record number of people. A speaker's platform had been erected on the east side of the rice mill, and some 500 seats arranged in the open air. Electric and gasoline lights illuminated the area. The seats were filled before the speaking began; many had to stand on the sidelines while others sat in their buggies. Dr. George E. Brooks was master of ceremonies and the Doucet band provided music. The program must have been a lengthy one; the first of the three speakers talked for one and a half hours.[30]

The July 4th observance was an annual affair sponsored by the St. Joseph Society. At the 1912 celebration and picnic Max Simar spoke on behalf of the sponsoring organization, the Doucet band played appropriate selections and the St. Cecilia Choir sang patriotic songs. C. B. Debellevue, candidate for district attorney, delivered speeches in both French and English.[31]

Iota had its share of early automobiles. About 27 residents owned cars in 1916, including a new Buick purchased that spring by P. E. Landry, cashier of the bank.[32]

When the United States entered World War I Iota was one of the first communities to form a home guard unit. Officers of the Iota Home Guard were Dr. H. G. Durio, captain; W. C. Gosling, drillmaster; Max Simar, first lieutenant; Jesse Reed, second lieutenant; Louis H. Andrus, orderly sergeant; Henry Miller, second sergeant; Paul Miller, third sergeant; A. B. Cart, fourth sergeant; D. I. Fisher, first corporal; Buck McNeil, second corporal; E. J. Russell, third corporal; Theo Smith, fourth corporal; Dr. L. A. Clark, surgeon; Asa Sonnier, color bearer.[33]

Despite the 14 officers, the Iota company was not composed of the traditional "too many chiefs and not enough Indians." Recruits for the guard unit who were not officers included Charles Matte, Henry A. Taylor, Joe Roy, A. C. Lavergne, C. Amy, E. J. Ledoux, Leopold Miller, Darvoust Cart, Samuel Cart, Alfred Hebert, L. H. Andrus, A. V.

[29] *Ibid*, Feb. 6, 1917; Aug. 26, 1918; interview, Henry Bourgaux, 1978
[30] *Ibid*, Sept. 21, 1911
[31] *Ibid*, July 12, 1912
[32] *Ibid*, Feb. 2, 1916
[33] *Ibid*, Apr. 24, 1917

Ducote, A. C. Hebert, A. S. Bourgeois, G. A. Pousson, Julius Savant, H. J. Casteran, Ernest Fruge, H. W. Foret Jr., J. A. Dupuy, A. B. Dore, Mathias Pousson, Alex Amy, J. F. Simar, Artheuse Broussard, Jules Menou, Theo Smith, Frank Gravot, Mitchel Miller, Zan Rasberry, John C. Sittig, J. P. Seilhan, James Reed, P. Menou, H. J. Daigle, G. Bordelais, Samuel Cart Jr., Joe Ritter, Eli Ledoux, Cleo Bourgeois, Amos Reed, Louis Cart, Constant Daigle, Tom Sittig, A. V. Smith, Alcide Simar Jr., R. L. Doucet, Theo Miller, Artelus Roy, Raoul Roy, James Pousson, J. B. Gourdin, M. Pousson Jr., Raymond Laughlin, H. G. Fisher.[34]

The guard unit was organized by Captain J. M. Taylor, one of the parish's legendary characters. Captain Taylor was asked to be captain of the military organization, but declined because of his age, which was 78 at the time. A Confederate veteran, Taylor was among the few survivors of the Marshall, Texas, Guards which had surrendered with General Robert E. Lee at Appomattox. Following the war he turned to teaching and journalism. For many years he was Iota correspondent for the *Crowley Signal*.[35]

One of Iota's early merchants served rural customers by means of a peddling hack. A classified ad in the *Crowley Signal* of March 31, 1900 read as follows: WANTED—Man to run peddling hack. Must speak French and English and understand the care of horses. H. I. Daughenbaugh, Cartville, La.

The famed springs at Pointe-aux-Loups continued to be promoted and advertised until 1907. The hotel was remodeled in 1900 and Miss Mamie Fisher was employed by Mrs. G. Miller, the proprietess, to manage the place. The springs began going down in 1901, but efforts were made to keep the resort going. For the summer of 1904 a new reservoir was added and a boiler and pump attached by which the water was conveyed to the bath houses.[36]

Some new information on the springs was published in the *Daily Signal* of May 29, 1905. The story told how Placide Richard and his family camped in the vicinity in 1814, with the additional information that Richard bathed his son, afflicted with scrofula, in the springs on the advice of Attakapas Indians, and the boy was cured. Legends of the times said that the Attakapas Indians had bathed in the waters of the springs, also that Jean Lafitte had visited the springs.

The final advertisement promoting the resort appeared in the summer of 1907. The location of the springs was given as two and a half miles from

---

[34] *Ibid*, Apr. 10, 1917
[35] *Ibid*, 50th Anniv. Ed., 32
[36] *Crowley Signal*, June 9, 1900; *Daily Signal*, July 11, 1904

Iota. Prospective guests were asked to write Mrs. G. Miller, or phone 69, four rings.[37]

The first race track in the Iota area was built by Jean Pierre Seilhan on the Pousson estate and was run by "Tuce" Broussard, about 1915. Jean Pierre Seilhan also ran a race track at a later date.[38]

Before horse races, July 4th celebrations and such Iota's chief entertainment was the annual Catholic church fair, promoted and well publicized by Father Gassler. At the 1904 fair, held in early January when the crops were all in and the farm families had money to spend, one of the attractions at the fair was a local talent play. Titled *La Mariee Perdue*, or "The Lost Bride," the original piece was written in Acadian French, and "this pearl of farces" was guaranteed to bring applause and laughter."[39]

Mardi Gras was another occasion for fun and merriment. The day was observed in the Acadian tradition, with masked and costumed men riding horses around the country begging for food for the feast that night. In 1910 the cavalcade paraded down Iota's main street; in the entourage was a decorated "chariot" carrying the musicians. That night the celebration ended with a dance at the Savinien Cart hall.[40]

During the early years of the century timber was one of the area's most valuable commodities. A notable sale of timber land was made in 1907 when W. W. Duson and Brother sold 1,000 acres of timber land on Bayou des Cannes two miles west of Iota. F. M. Joplin and Miss Sallie Thomas bought the land for $20,000.[41]

Iota Pioneers

In addition to the Carts and Doucets pioneer residents of the Iota area should include Mrs. G. Miller, Matthew Pousson Sr., Louis Simar and Jules Menou.

Mrs. Miller, long time proprietess of the Pointe-aux-Loups hotel, was born in Hanover, Germany, January 21, 1840. She came to Acadia Parish with her brother, Henry J. Fischer.[42]

Matthew Pousson, born in 1826 at Garonne, France, came to the United States at age 29 and settled in what was then St. Landry Parish. He died in 1916 at age 90.[43]

---

[37] *Crowley Signal*, June 29, 1907
[38] Interview, Walter Doucet, Alphonse Doucet, 1978
[39] *Crowley Signal*, Dec. 26, 1903
[40] *Ibid*, Feb. 12, 1910
[41] *Ibid*, Sept. 21, 1907
[42] *Ibid*, July 23, 1910
[43] *Daily Signal*, May 19, 1916

Louis Simar died February 16, 1905 at age 85. He was born two miles south of Iota in the same house where he died.[44]

Jules Menou, a native of Brittany, Cote du Nord, France, came to Pointe-aux-Loups in 1886. He farmed until 1900 when he went into the lumber business and a year later went into buying and selling rice. He was president of Farmer's Mercantile and of the Bank of Iota.[45]

Among the earliest landowners of the Iota section of Acadia Parish were Antoine Hebert, who homesteaded land in 1835, and Alexandre Daigle, whose residence was a voting precinct in 1852.[46]

Doctors, Dentists

Several fine physicians were pioneer practitioners in the Iota area. The best known were Dr. L. A. Clark, Dr. George E. Brooks and Dr. Francis Nathaniel Hayes.

Dr. Clark and Dr. Brooks began practice at Iota in 1893, when the Branch railroad was being built. Dr. Clark, a Tulane medical school graduate, was the son of Dr. Bennett E. Clark of Branch, first president of the Acadia Parish Police Jury. Dr. Clark married Delia Taylor in 1896. Dr. Brooks, from Mississippi, practiced at Port Barre and Millerville before locating in Iota. Dr. Hayes moved his practice from Crowley to Iota in 1901. In addition to his medical practice and drug store he ran a 500-acre farm.[47]

Dr. Walter J. Smith was in Iota in 1902 and 1903.[48] Newspaper references between 1900 and 1904 identify the following: Dr. H. J. Fenelon, Dr. Willie Jones, Dr. A. V. Jones. Of these Dr. Willie Jones is the only one known to have been a medical doctor. He was reported to have left Iota "to practice medicine in Grand Cheniere." His wife was a teacher at the Evangeline school.[49]

During the period under study three dentists located in Iota. They were Dr. O. J. Trappey of Jeanerette, Dr. Charles Culb of Tennessee and Dr. Henry Durio. Dr. Trappey and Dr. Culb came to Iota in 1909. Dr. Durio started a lifetime practice about 1916.[50]

Iota's first contribution to a medicine-related field was in the person of Dr. Dan Robertson. The son of Will Robertson and an honor graduate of Iota High School, he finished at Veterinary College of Kansas City. He served as inspector of horses and mules for the United States Army on the Mexican border during the conflict of 1916.[51]

---

[44] *Ibid*, Feb. 16, 1906

[45] *Crowley Signal*, Oct. 3, 1903; Dec. 14, 1907

[46] Fontenot and Freeland, *Acadia*, 155

[47] *Daily Signal*, Dec. 14, 1907; 50th Anniv. Ed., 68

[48] *Daily Signal*, July 16, 1902; Feb. 26, 1903

[49] *Crowley Signal*, Jan. 27, 1900; May 9, 1903; *Daily Signal*, May 21, June 13, 1904

[50] *Daily Signal*, June 11, Oct. 23, 1909; Sept. 26, 1916

[51] *Ibid*, Sept. 19, 1916

Catholic Church at Iota, La.

St. Joseph's Catholic Church of Iota, built in 1899 during the administration of Rev. F. L. Gassler. The church and adjacent rectory were destroyed by fire in 1936. (Photo courtesy Gerald Wright)

257

Churches, Schools

Catholics of the Iota-Pointe-aux-Loups section were served by Jesuit missionaries from Grand Coteau from about 1867 to 1883. The first St. Joseph's church, dedicated in 1879, was administered by the Jesuits until 1883 when a pastor was appointed.[52]

The list of early pastors include J. Chasles, P. Silvan, O.S.B., A. Thebault, C. Van de Ven, Adolph LeGuilline, Francis L. Gassler and Francis A. Buquet.[53]

Father Gassler, shepherd of the Catholic flock for 15 years, became one of the most popular priests in southwest Louisiana. An aggressive leader, he began his pastorate at the small church of Pointe-aux-Loups in 1895. During the early years of his administration he built a new church at a cost of $8,000. He organized three church societies, planned successful church fairs and civic benefits. A large rectory was built under his supervision in 1904. He was responsible for starting a Catholic school at Iota, and for the erection of churches at the Frey settlement (which was renamed Gassler in his honor), another at a location in Mamou Prairie, and a chapel at Morse.[54]

Sacred Heart School of Iota was staffed by lay teachers. Early teachers included Mary and Elizabeth Duggan, Leonie Raine and Eunice Kleinpeter.[55] The first newspaper reference to the school was in the *Crowley Signal* of October 8, 1904, when the Iota correspondent reported: "The Catholic school opened Monday morning."

As many as 75 pupils, taught by three teachers, were enrolled at the school for the 1906-1907 session. In 1909 the old church building was converted into a convent "for the sisters who will have charge of the parochial school long established here." But Father Gassler's hopes of bringing teaching nuns to Iota did not materialize at that time. A few months later Father Gassler was assigned to a Baton Rouge church and was replaced in Iota by Father Francis Buquet.[56]

The school was continued during Father Buquet's pastorate. Efforts to secure teachers of a religious order were finally successful in 1916. The Sisters of Divine Providence of San Antonio, Texas agreed to staff the Iota school.[57]

A new school building was constructed by Gaudens Pousson, Iota contractor. The building, 85 by 58 feet, contained four classrooms, a hall and a cloak room. The residence for the sisters contained eight rooms, two halls, a dining room and kitchen, and could accommodate eight

[52] Baudier, Roger, *The Catholic Church in Louisiana*, 451
[53] *Signal*, 50th Anniv. Ed., 21
[54] *Crowley Signal*, Feb. 8, 1902; 50th Anniv. Ed., 68; Dec. 14, 1907
[55] *Daily Signal*, Oct. 3, Dec. 15, 1906; interview, Marie Bordelaise Gravot
[56] *Daily Signal*, Oct. 3, Dec. 15, 1906; Aug. 19, Nov. 26, 1909
[57] *Ibid*, Oct. 12, 1911; May 15, 1912; Aug. 3, 1916

boarding students. Student tuition was set at $1 to $1.50 per month, according to grade. The institution, re-christened St. Francis School, opened September 11, 1916 with 114 students enrolled.[58]

When the second session began in the fall of 1917 St. Francis School had an enrollment of 200, with more expected after the crops were laid by.[59]

Another major parochial activity was the completion of a new rectory in 1917.[60]

Six Protestant congregations were formed in Iota between 1900 and 1920—Methodist, Lutheran, United Brethren, Baptist, Church of Christ and Apostolic.

Property on which to build a Methodist church was given to the Iota congregation in 1901 by C. C. Duson. For the consideration of $1, Duson deeded Lots 8 and 9 in Block 39 to the church, represented by Robert B. Sloane, Isaac Hayes and William A. Higginbotham.[61]

The Methodist church was dedicated in 1902.[62] Two years later a historic relic of Acadia Parish was put to use in the church. The old bell from the parish's first courthouse was secured for the church by a committee headed by Mrs. J. H. Nordyke. The installation of the bell in the church was directed by C. H. Pratt.[63]

St. John Lutheran congregation was formed October 6, 1901. The first church building was dedicated April 21, 1902. First members were John Dietz and family, Fritz Rampmaier and family, Michel Muller and family, Karl Rampmaier and family, George, William and Edward Dietz.[64]

Before the church was built, Lutheran services, in the German language, were held in the John Dietz home.[65]

The Baptist congregation began holding services in 1905, but had no church building.[66]

United Brethren had a church in Iota in 1906. Ministers from the Jennings church preached for the Iota congregation.[67]

Mt. Triumph Baptist Church of Iota acquired property in 1913. W. E. Ellis, John Green and L. A. Williams, acting as liquidators for the Crowley State Bank, sold the church Lots 2 and 3 in Block 6, Duson addition,

---

[58] *Ibid*, Aug. 3, 25, 30, Sept. 12, 1916

[59] *Ibid*, Oct. 18, 1917

[60] *Ibid*, June 5, 1917. The rectory was burned in the same fire that destroyed the church in 1936.

[61] Conveyance Book Z, #17661, 315, Acad. Par.

[62] *Daily Signal*, Aug. 28, 1902

[63] *Crowley Signal*, Dec. 31, 1904

[64] *Daily Signal*, May 1, 29, 1902; St. John Lutheran Church 75th Anniv. booklet, Oct. 31, 1976

[65] *Crowley Signal*, Apr. 7, 1900

[66] *Daily Signal*, June 13, 1905; July 13, 1906

[67] *Ibid*, Feb. 6, 1906

for $25. Rev. M. T. Gilbert, pastor, represented the church in the transaction.[68]

The Church of Christ, represented by Samuel W. Tobey, bought a lot in Iota in 1915. The property, Lot 9 in Block 25, was purchased from William G. Robertson for $40.[69]

Members of the Apostolic religion held services in a tent in Iota in 1915, with Rev. Sam Henderson in charge.[70]

Iota acquired a public school in 1901. Prior to that time the school was located at nearby Pointe-aux-Loups. Mrs. M. Brooks was the teacher for the 1899-1900 session.[71]

The school house, built on a block of ground given by C. C. Duson, was completed during the summer of 1901. A summer storm blew the building off its foundation; the school board, at the request of H. J. Fisher, chairman of the building committee, appropriated $100 to repair and replace the building.[72]

Iota's pioneer educators include James A. Patton, the first teacher at the new school house in the village; Lizzie Hazen, Mary Torrance, Martha Andrus, Maud A. Duroy, W. B. Greer, Howard Nordyke.[73]

---

[68] Conveyance Book X-2, #38176, 47, Acad. Par.
[69] Conveyance Book Z-2, #41929, 362, Acad. Par.
[70] *Daily Signal*, Nov. 18, 1915
[71] *Crowley Signal*, Sept. 16, 1899; July 20, 1901
[72] *Ibid*, July 20, 1901; Feb. 23, 1907
[73] *Ibid*, Sept. 14, 1901; Oct. 3, 1903; Oct. 8, 1904; *Daily Signal*, Sept. 3, 1902

Seven school transfers, 1918 vintage, with drivers at the wheels, are shown lined up at Iota High School. This type of motorized school bus replaced the wagonette, or horse-drawn bus, used earlier in the century. (Photo courtesy Frank Bacon Jr.)

Graduates of Iota High School, class of 1910, were from left, seated, Mollie Hayes, Bertha Brooks, Martha Robertson, Miss Mary Lena White, the teacher; Curtis Pemble and Mary Amy; standing, Albert Brooks, Daniel Robertson, Eugene Miller, Day Farley, Nathaniel Amy, and (not shown) Anne Stagg. (Photo courtesy Hazel Brooks)

By 1904 the enrollment justified the addition of a new classroom and increasing the faculty to three. By 1906 a faculty of four—A. V. Smith, Mrs. J. R. Hazen, Mary Lena White and Martha Andrus—was instructing 170 pupils in the four room school.[74]

A proposition to levy a four mill school tax for 10 years was narrowly passed by fourth ward voters in 1907, due to some strong opposition to the tax. Property assessment voted for the tax was $95,385; against, $87,777. The popular vote was 103 for, 98 against. The opposing faction was composed of Catholic school supporters, who felt that it was unfair that they be taxed for public schools when they had their own school to maintain.[75]

Public school patrons began planning for a new building by the end of 1907. The school had been enlarged to five rooms to accommodate an enrollment of 200.[76]

An attempt to form an organization of parents and teachers in 1908 encountered some communication problems. The news correspondent for the Crowley paper reported a large attendance of mothers had attended a meeting at the school for the purpose of getting to know the teachers and

[74] *Crowley Signal*, Oct. 8, 1904; *Daily Signal*, Dec. 15, 1906
[75] *Crowley Signal*, Aug. 31, Sept. 7, 1907; Jan. 4, 1908
[76] *Ibid*, Dec. 14, 1907

261

each other: "Some spoke French, some spoke German, some spoke English, and some spoke nothing."[77]

The language barrier did not hamper activities of Arbor Day in 1909. Iota residents got together and went in wagons to the woods for trees. Seventy young oaks were planted on the school grounds.[78]

First graduates of Iota High School were Morris Hazen, James Robertson and Clifton Pemble. High school diplomas were presented in May, 1909. Pemble was valedictorian, Hazen salutatorian and Robertson class historian.[79]

During the summer of 1909 the contract to build a new school was awarded to Ernest Miller of Eunice on a bid of $13,375. Plans for the building were drawn by R. A. Nockton of Crowley.[80]

The new school was dedicated June 10, 1910, after commencement exercises for the 10 graduates of the class of 1910. Receiving diplomas were Annie Stagg, Eugene Miller, Mollie Hayes, Bertha Brooks, Curtis Pemble, Day Farley, Mary Amy, Dan Robertson, Martha Robertson and Nathaniel Amy. When the program was over the graduates of 1910 got together with the graduates of 1909 and formed an alumni association.[81]

Iota's black citizens pooled their resources about 1905, bought land and built a school for their children. The Acadia Parish School Board accepted the donation of the building and the land in January of 1906. E. L. Norris was one of the early teachers. The school took part in the parish agricultural program of 1910 which had been instigated by R. U. Clark. An acre of land was set aside for the students to cultivate.[82]

Municipal Affairs

Six mayors served Iota between 1902 and 1920. Of the six only two were elected to more than one term.

Iota was incorporated as a village in 1902. Preliminaries to the incorporation were begun at a meeting held at the Clark and Brooks drug store some four months earlier. Dr. G. E. Brooks acted as chairman for the meeting and Ben F. Toler was secretary. A committee of five was named to draft plans: Emile Bourgaux, Henry Fenelon, J. R. Hazen, Joseph Bergeron and Dr. L. A. Clark. Louis Cart was appointed to take a census within the proposed limits of the village.[83]

First officials, named at a mass meeting held about two months later, were Dr. Brooks, mayor; Ben F. Toler, H. J. Daigle, J. A. Sabatier,

[77] *Ibid*, Apr. 4, 1908
[78] *Daily Signal*, Jan. 29, 1909
[79] *Ibid*, May 13, 1909
[80] *Ibid*, May 21, July 12, 1909
[81] *Crowley Signal*, June 14, 1910
[82] *Daily Signal*, Jan. 10, 1906; *Crowley Signal*, July 13, 1907; Jan. 29, 1910
[83] *Crowley Signal*, Jan. 11, 1902

aldermen, and Jules McGee, marshal. These officers were formally appointed by the governor on May 23, 1902, the date of incorporation.[84]

Early ordinances passed by the village council includes those governing police regulations, sidewalk construction and obstructions, animals at large, Sunday closings, the speed of trains, shooting fireworks, business and professional licenses, carrying concealed weapons and levying a 5-mill property tax.[85]

Attention was given to fire prevention. At the August meeting of 1903 the council approved an ordinance providing that only brick or galvanized iron flues could be used when buildings were within 150 feet of each other.[86] At the time many chimneys were of the *bousillage*, or mud-and-moss construction, which increased the threat of fire damage.

Jules McGee resigned his marshal job after serving about 15 months. James Milner was appointed to the post, but he resigned shortly afterward and Frank Hayes, known as "Red Frank" was named marshal.[87]

The appointed officials were elected to the same offices in the 1904 election. The 1906 election resulted in two new aldermen on the village board: J. H. Deshotels and George D. Wright, replacing Sabatier and Daigle. Dr. Brooks was re-elected mayor, Ben F. Toler to the council, and Jules McGee won for marshal. There is little information on details of the campaign. A comment in the newspaper, "at Iota the result was close," indicates that another ticket was in the race, but the particulars were not published. One of the new aldermen, George D. Wright, had served as village treasurer; he was replaced in that position by Robert McManus.[88]

The office of marshal changed hands twice before the next election. J. G. Burleigh, former Crowley policeman, was appointed October 8, 1906, to replace McGee, resigned. Six months later Burleigh resigned to return to Crowley and Robert McManus was named marshal. Dr. Brooks resigned as mayor in June of 1907 and Louis Cart was appointed to the position.[89]

Ben F. Toler served one term as mayor, elected in 1908. On the board of aldermen were George Wright, Dr. L. A. Clark and Samuel Cart. Bertrand Simar was marshal.[90]

One of the actions taken by this council was the purchase of land for a public cemetery. The village bought three acres from Mrs. C. Singletary in November, 1909.[91]

With the exception of Samuel Cart, all of the officials elected in 1910

---

[84] *Daily Signal*, Mar. 26, 1902; Louisiana Department of State
[85] Iota town records
[86] *Crowley Signal*, Aug. 8, 1903
[87] *Crowley Signal*, Sept. 12, 1903
[88] *Daily Signal*, Apr. 18, May 21, 1906
[89] *Crowley Signal*, June 8, 1907; Louisiana Department of State
[90] Louisiana Department of State
[91] *Daily Signal*, Nov. 13, 1909

were new. They were A. V. Smith, mayor; E. J. Bourgaux, marshal; Edmund Darphin and F. L. Crabtree on the council with Cart.[92]

Samuel Cart began his first term as mayor in 1912. Councilmen were S. B. Andrus, W. H. Wade and F. L. Crabtree. James Bihm was elected marshal. George Wright was returned to the council by appointment in April of 1913.[93]

Officials elected in 1914 were S. B. Andrus, mayor; George D. Wright, Louis Bernard and Dan I. Fisher, aldermen, and John Sittig, marshal. Sittig won the marshal post over James Bihm by one vote.[94]

W. C. Gosling, appointed mayor in November, 1914, was elected to the office in 1916. Wright, Bernard and Fisher were returned to the council and Sittig re-elected marshal. Wright died in August of 1916 and was replaced on the council by Max Simar.[95]

Several civic measures went into effect during the Gosling administration. Ordinance No. 31, introduced by D. I. Fisher November 26, 1916, made it unlawful for any member of the negro population to rent or occupy a house or dwelling "except in that part of the village designated as the north part of McMillan Gulley."[96]

Two other ordinances of approximately the same period are indicative of the changing times:

Ordinance No. 28 granted privileges to the Iota Gun Club to operate shooting grounds on the property of the Planter's Warehouse for trap shooting clay pigeons. Ordinance No. 32 prohibited the running of gasoline or kerosene engines (tractors) on Duson Avenue.[97]

In January of 1917 Mayor Gosling and Marshal Sittig celebrated Arbor Day by planting several more oaks in the town park, located between the depot and Iota rice mill. The mayor announced plans to build a fence around the park, and to gravel Duson Avenue.[98]

Samuel Cart began a second term as mayor in 1918 and was re-elected to a third term in 1920. Aldermen elected to serve with him were Buck McNeil, A. V. Smith, Dr. H. G. Durio. Marshal Sittig was returned to office in 1918 and 1920. In July, 1920 the council was expanded to five members; Remy L. Doucet and Davoust Cart were appointed to the new seats on the board of aldermen.[99]

During Mayor Cart's third administration the council took steps to secure a waterworks and electric light plant for the town. A bond issue totaling $29,500 was voted for the civic improvements.[100]

Among Iota citizens serving in appointive positions (to 1920) were Ben F. Toler, Louis Bernard, Buck McNeil, town clerks; J. A. Sabatier, George Wright and Robert McManus, town treasurers.

---

[92] Louisiana Department of State
[93] Ibid
[94] Daily Signal, May 4, 1914
[95] Louisiana Department of State
[96] Iota town records
[97] Ibid
[98] Daily Signal, Jan. 23, 1917
[99] Louisiana Department of State
[100] Iota town records

Prairie Mamou

Evangeline, Millerville, Nezpique, Redlich, Basile

Prairie Mamou, the land area between Bayous des Cannes and Nezpique in the western portion of Acadia, extends northward from the confluence of the two bayous, across the parish line and the St. Landry Parish "sleeve" into Evangeline Parish.

The lower part of the prairie is called *Tee Mamou*, a contraction of *Petit Mamou*, French for Little Mamou. The upper part is Grand Mamou, or Big Mamou. On old maps the place name appears *Prairie Mammouth*, French for Mammoth Prairie. The dropping of the "th" in the modern spelling is attributed to the fact that the "th" sound is not pronounced in French.

Early settlements in Prairie Mamou include Evangeline, Millerville, Nezpique, Redlich and Basile.

A story of buried treasure in Prairie Mamou came to light in 1903. A Crowley resident, Louis Deputy, exhibited a half dollar, minted in 1834, part of a cache buried at the beginning of the Civil War by an aged negro named Prien.

Prien owned a small farm in upper Mamou in an area of Acadia Parish known as Prien Noir Cove, named for the landowner. Prien had managed, after years of hard work, to save about $450. When the war came in 1861 he buried the money under the barn. Some years later, during Prien's last illness, he refused to reveal the hiding place of the money because of activities of the Jayhawkers, and the secret died with him.

The old barn was eventually torn down and a corn field made on the spot. A grandson of Prien's, while plowing, unearthed a small stone jar which was found to contain $460.25 in gold and silver. Prien's wife, at the time almost a century old, was placed in possession of her husband's life savings, which had been buried for more than 40 years.[1]

A well-known landmark of Mamou Prairie is the Lantz house, built in 1854 by Jacob Lantz, a pre-Civil War resident of the Acadia Parish area.*

Evangeline

One of the older place names of Acadia Parish, Evangeline has an unusual background of religious history. The first Lutheran congregation

---

* The Hayes Pousson family of Iota bought the old Lantz place in 1951. The house has been renovated, but many of the original features have been retained.

[1] *Crowley Signal*, Aug. 8, 1903

in southwest Louisiana was established there in 1873 by Rev. H. Gellert, and an organization of Quakers flourished there for a time.[2]

Dr. Andrew D. Tomlinson, leader of the Society of Friends (Quakers), was Evangeline's first postmaster, appointed in 1887. Other early postmasters and postmistresses (to 1920) were Miles T. Tomlinson, Mrs. Susan G. Hines, Arthur Latreille, Elizabeth E. Trubshaw, Bob W. R. Lawton, Golda Aylsworth Lawton, Mrs. Elsie E. Baker and Georgie J. Hefferman.[3]

Situated in the lower end of Mamou Prairie the settlement remained static until 1901 when the oil field was established. The discovery brought oil field workers and tradespeople to the scene and for a time the village gave promise of developing into a boom town.

Large headlines in the *Daily Signal* of August 19, 1904 reflected the excitement and ambitious planning which the discovery of oil, the first in Louisiana, generated at the time: "Another Flourishing Commercial Center Will Be Founded in Acadia in Center of Oil District; Alba Heywood Prepares to Father the New Town . . . The Townsite Has Been Completed."

The account in the newspaper read as follows:

> The new town of Evangeline, which is to be located at the oil field in the western part of Acadia Parish, promises to be one of the most interesting municipalities in the United States.
>
> The town site is owned by the Jennings-Heywood Oil Syndicate, of which Alba Heywood, former comedian, musician and present oil magnate and promoter, is president. The townsite is but a few hundred yards from the proven district of the Mamou oil field, the greatest field in the south.
>
> The post office at Evangeline is an old one, while the little French settlement of Evangeline existed long ere Crowley or Jennings were founded. With the discovery of oil on the Jules Clement tract of land some three years ago, the Evangeline prairie grew into a village and from a village it has grown into a town of several hundred people. That is the old town of Evangeline, now known as the oil field. But the new town will be laid out with parks, drive-ways and wide streets, different strips being laid out for public buildings.
>
> There will be 140 lots sold. Most of the lots are 50 by 145 feet and the town site is the highest and best drained section of the Evangeline country.
>
> Alba Heywood, who is founding the new town, struck upon a unique and original idea in naming his streets and avenues, taking names from characters in Longfellow's famous poem, "Evangeline."
>
> The avenues are named Longfellow, Evangeline and Grand Pre, and the streets are named Benedict, Basil, Bellefontaine, Acadia, Gabriel, Michael and Felician.
>
> The new town of Evangeline promises to become one of the most important points in this section of the state. As the oil field develops the

---

[2] Fontenot and Freeland, *Acadia*, 197

[3] Register of Postmasters, National Archives and Records Service

town will naturally enjoy a good substantial growth and as the residents of that section are almost all connected with the development of the field, and are parties with means, an effort will be made to make Evangeline "A Model City."

The name and history of the early settlement of Evangeline will always be interesting, for it is claimed by many of the oldest French inhabitants of the section that Longfellow's original characters once resided there, and that there are many ways of substantiating it. However, this is disputed by the residents of the Teche country in St. Martin and Iberia parishes, who claim that Longfellow resided in New Iberia while Evangeline was written, while there are those in St. Martinville who are ready to point out to you the grave of the original Evangeline.

Mr. Heywood says that he has not decided whether he will have any public sale of lots or whether the syndicate will sell them privately.

During the summer of 1903 a weekly newspaper, *The Rotary*, circulated its first issue. The paper, devoted exclusively to the oil field and "published within the shadow of the oil derricks at Mamou," was edited by John A. Schmink, formerly of the *Jennings Daily News*.[4]

Some of the early teachers at Evangeline (1899-1904) were J. Lee Hereford, Mae Beals and Mrs. J. W. Jones. A school for black children and a school in the oil field were in operation in 1904. Della Nowlan was teacher at the oil field school.[5]

In 1907 the schools at Evangeline, Riverside and the oil field were consolidated. Two hack lines brought the rural children to Evangeline, where two teachers instructed 125 pupils.[6]

A new five-room school was built at the oil field in 1913, at a cost of $2,600. Each of the three largest oil companies gave $100 for the school; the remaining $2,300 was subscribed by the oil field workers. W. D. Hughart was president of the local board of education.[7]

A Catholic church was built in the Evangeline-Millerville neighborhood in 1909, on land donated by Ursin Daigle. The church was built during the pastorate of Rev. F. L. Gassler of the Iota Catholic church. On the building committee were Ursin Daigle, Jules Clement, Leon Hebert Jr., Andrew Meredith and Homer Fruge. Gaudens Pousson was awarded the contract to build the church.[8]

An unusual political situation in Evangeline claimed attention in 1912. Citizens of the town and those living west of Bayou des Cannes and north of the south boundary of Ward 3 got together and decided they wanted to be annexed by Jeff Davis Parish. The entire community was reported to have pledged support to the movement to secede from Acadia, on the promise that they would receive badly needed roads and

---

[4] *Crowley Signal*, June 13, 1903
[5] *Crowley Signal*, Sept. 16, 1899; Sept. 8, 1900; *Daily Signal*, Sept. 3, 1902; Sept. 16, 1904
[6] *Crowley Signal*, Nov. 2, 1907
[7] *Daily Signal*, Sept. 30, 1913
[8] *Ibid*, Jan. 8, 29, 1909

bridges.[9] No background for the movement was given, no names were mentioned, nor did any follow-up newspaper story report the outcome.

Evangeline remained unincorporated. There are indications that there may have been plans for incorporation in 1915; a *Daily Signal* news item referred to William Gamble as "mayor" of Evangeline.[10]

Random references in the Crowley paper identify several Mamou Prairie residents as doctors. The first was Dr. J. S. Branch, who was in the area around 1900-1902.[11] Others were Dr. Will Johnson of Mamou Prairie, Dr. A. J. Foreman of Evangeline,[12] and Dr. J. A. Broussard, who was in the area in 1916.[13]

Redlich

Redlich was an official place name of Acadia Parish for 14 years, from 1903 until 1917. A post office, established in 1896, was first named Genais for the postmaster, Rene Genais. William I. Case succeeded Genais as postmaster until 1897, when Julia Redlich was appointed. The name of the post office was changed to Redlich in 1903. The post office was discontinued in 1917 and the mail sent to Basile.[14]

The settlement, located in the northwest corner of the parish in Prairie Mamou about eight miles north of Millerville, was also identified with the Ben Johnson election poll. The school house, which also served as a voting place, was known as the Ben Johnson school. Serving as officials for the 1900 election at the Ben Johnson poll were Jesse Young, Miguel Johnson, L. F. Schamber and H. B. Redlich.[15]

In 1903 the school board granted a petition to move the Ben Johnson school house onto an acre of land donated by Henry B. Redlich, one of the early teachers at the school.[16]

Another school in the general vicinity of the Redlich settlement was the Neville Reed school. Viola McMillan was one of the pioneer teachers at the Neville Reed school. The school house was replaced in 1903 by a new building, constructed by Raymond Reed and Ernest Hebert.[17]

Brief references in the Crowley newspaper locate two early stores at Redlich: the Johnson Brothers store, and the H. B. Redlich store.[18]

Among the settlers in the Redlich-Genais area was Joe Klumpp, a rice farmer who had an unusual experience putting down a deep well. In

[9] *Ibid*, Aug. 26, 1912
[10] *Ibid*, May 7, 1915
[11] *Crowley Signal*, Mar. 17, 1900; *Daily Signal*, Nov. 5, 1902
[12] *Daily Signal*, Oct. 18, 26, 1909
[13] *Ibid*, Feb. 18, 1916; Sept. 11, 1918
[14] Register of Postmasters, National Archives and Records Service
[15] *Daily Signal*, Apr. 23, 1902; *Crowley Signal*, Mar. 31, 1900
[16] *Crowley Signal*, Sept. 16, 1899; Oct. 10, 1903
[17] *Ibid*, Sept. 16, 1899; Sept. 26, 1903
[18] *Daily Signal*, Nov. 13, 1902; *Crowley Signal*, Mar. 23, 1907

the spring of 1902 Klumpp completed the well after some difficulty. At a depth of 222 feet the drill struck a cypress log which could not be cut through, so the well casing was drawn to that depth.[19]

Tales of buried money brought treasure hunters to the area in 1905. Riclobert Declouet, an aged mulatto, lived alone near the Nezpique woods. Known to his Acadian neighbors as "Broin," Declouet had acquired a reputation as a miser. After his death treasure hunters began digging up the woods around his place.[20]

There was also a report of a haunted house in the area. Although no ghosts were seen, queer noises were heard at night in the J. M. Deuran (Doiron?) house, and the occupants moved away.[21]

Millerville-Nezpique

Millerville is one of the older place names of Acadia Parish. Located on Bayou Nezpique 12 miles north of Mermentau (the Louis Chachere Spanish land grant), Millerville was a major shipping outlet in the 1880s. Large amounts of rice, lumber, eggs, chickens and wool were shipped by boat on the Nezpique to Mermentau, thence by rail to market.[22]

Millerville got its name from the first merchant and postmaster, Dennis Miller, who owned a general store and a sawmill. The place had the potential of a town in 1888; at that time Millerville boasted two general stores, a saloon, a hotel, a blacksmith shop and a school.[23] The identities of the other business people of Millerville are not known. There is one newspaper reference to "the Daigle store" at Millerville, also a reference in 1908 to the E. C. Quirk warehouse at Millerville.[24] Another item identifies John Klumpp as "a prominent planter and merchant of Mamou Prairie" who lived near the Nezpique post office.[25] Election officials at the Millerville poll in 1900 were H. C. Wilkins, J. R. Myers, I. G. Jarvis and Fernest Reed.[26]

Millerville changed its identity three times between 1887 and 1904. It was Millerville in 1887 when Dennis Miller was postmaster. In 1890 the post office was re-named Lodi, then in 1899 changed again to Whitehouse. The post office was discontinued in 1904 and the mail sent to Evangeline. Other postmasters were Leon Viterbo, Walter S. Cocke, John B. David, Mary P. Figueron, Hannah Beals and Anna B. Jarvis.[27]

---

[19] *Daily Signal*, Apr. 5, 1902
[20] *Ibid*, July 10, 20, 1905
[21] *Crowley Signal*, Sept. 23, 1905
[22] Fontenot and Freeland, *Acadia*, 176
[23] *Crowley Signal*, Aug. 25, 1888
[24] *Ibid*, Mar. 31, 1900; Feb. 15, 1908
[25] *Daily Signal*, June 29, 1909
[26] *Daily Signal*, Mar. 31, 1900
[27] Register of Postmasters

A post office named Miller was in operation for six months, from February to August of 1892. It is believed that this post office was quite near Millerville, as the postmaster, Isaac G. Jarvis, was identified with Millerville-Whitehouse. The mail was sent to Millerville when the Miller post office was terminated. Another nearby post office was at Nezpique, about three miles north of Millerville-Lodi-Whitehouse. Leon Hebert Jr. was the first and only postmaster, serving from March 20, 1900, to August 31, 1917, when the post office was discontinued and the mail sent to Evangeline. Postmaster Hebert was a merchant; the post office was located in his store.[28]

The Dennis Miller store and pumping plant at Millerville were destroyed by fire of unknown origin in 1903. Within a month the store was rebuilt and open for business.[29]

Teachers at the Millerville school from 1899 to 1902 were Margaret Dickson, Laura Wright and Mabel M. Merritt.[30]

The Millerville-Nezpique area had two resident doctors in the early years. They were Dr. W. H. Stagg of Millerville and Dr. H. E. Martin of Nezpique.[31]

One of the pioneers of the area was Joseph Langley, who was born near Millerville in 1833. His father, from Connecticut, had settled in that portion of old St. Landry early in the 19th century and had married into another pioneer family, the Millers.[32]

Basile

The Basile settlement belonged to Acadia Parish until 1907, when the Colorado Southern railroad was completed. Located in the northwest corner of the parish, the original settlement had a post office, a sugar mill, at least one store and a school.[33]

The place was first known as Schamber, for the first postmaster, Louis F. Schamber, appointed April 14, 1888. The name of the post office was changed to Basile in 1889 when Frank E. Garrould was made postmaster. Schamber was again appointed in 1893[34] and held the position until 1907 when the post office was re-located at the new town site.

Basile's first postmaster, Louis F. Schamber, was an influential figure in his ward and in the parish. The son of Louis Schamber, native of Strasbourg, both father and son were in the first contingent of Germans

[28] *Ibid; Daily Signal,* Apr. 28, 1900
[29] *Crowley Signal,* Apr. 25, May 23, 1903
[30] *Ibid,* Sept. 16, 1899; Sept. 8, 1900; Sept. 14, 1901
[31] *Crowley Signal,* July 22, 1899; *Daily Signal,* Apr. 16, 1904
[32] *Crowley Signal,* Mar. 14, 1908
[33] *Ibid,* Oct. 10, Nov. 28, 1903
[34] Register of Postmasters

brought to Acadia Parish in 1870 by Joseph Fabacher and Zenon Huber. Schamber was a notary public, a sheriff's deputy, long time correspondent for the Crowley newspaper and member of the school board for four years.[35]

The new town of Basile, just over the line in what was then St. Landry Parish, was laid out on land bought from Gerasin Miller. Founders of the town were Gus Fuselier and James J. Lewis of Eunice, and Louis S. Burke (or Berg).[36]

The original plan was to name the town St. Louis, for Judge Thomas E. Lewis, the man who did most to promote the construction of the new railroad line. A private sale of town lots took place March 16, 1907; the post office was moved from the Schamber property in Acadia to the Thomas H. Lewis Jr. store in the new town.[37] The familiar name of the old post office, Basile, was retained, and Acadia lost a community—another example of a settlement being relocated for what was at the time a sound and practical reason—the convenience of a railroad for traveling and marketing.

---

[35] *Crowley Signal*, June 6, 1903; Jan. 2, 1904
[36] *Ibid*, Aug. 15, 1908; 50th Anniv. Ed., 75
[37] *Daily Signal*, May 22, 1906; *Crowley Signal*, Mar. 9, May 18, 1907

Lyons' Point, Ebenezer, Other Place Names

Two rural settlements of southeast Acadia, situated in relatively close proximity, are representative of the predominate cultures of the area: Lyons' Point, peopled mainly by French-Acadian Catholics, and Ebenezer, settled by Anglo-Saxon Protestants.

Both communities have retained their original names and identities. Lyons' Point, located seven miles directly south of Crowley, is named for John Lyons, colonial settler who bought land on nearby Bayou Queue de Tortue from the Attakapas Indians. Jesuit missionaries from Grand Coteau began visitation work at Lyons' Point in the early 1850s.[1]

A Catholic chapel, St. John the Baptist, was established at Lyons' Point in 1908. The chapel was served by priests from Crowley. One of the memorable occasions was the first confirmation, held in May of 1908. Archbishop Blenk of New Orleans administered the sacrament. He was assisted by a young priest, Rev. Jules Jeanmard, who was destined to become a historic figure in southwest Louisiana—the first bishop of the Lafayette Diocese, established in 1918.[2]

There was a public school at Lyons' Point in 1902, with Cornelius Scully as teacher.[3] The school was either discontinued or given another name as it does not reappear in school lists during the early years of the century.

The Crowley newspaper carried very little news originating from Lyons' Point. The few items published during the period under study included the previously cited information about the church and several news items about individuals. Three of the four items abstracted concern members of the Broussard family:

Anastasie Comeaux Broussard, widow of Augustin Broussard, died May 19, 1903 at her home at Lyons' Point, leaving 117 descendants.[4]

Joe Broussard of Lyons' Point, while digging at his place, found $18,000 that had been buried there. He had been searching for the money for many years and came across it by accident.[5]

Ben Broussard of Lyons' Point was a long-time peace officer. By 1903 he had served 16 years—as constable for 12 years, and sheriff's deputy for four.[6]

The home of Valin Primeaux of Lyons' Point was the setting for

---

[1] *American State Papers, Public Lands, Vol. III*, 97; Baudier, "History of Our Lady of the Sacred Heart Church," booklet, 47

[2] *Crowley Signal*, May 30, Dec. 19, 1908

[3] *Daily Signal*, Sept. 3, 1902

[4] *Crowley Signal*, May 30, 1903

[5] *Ibid*, June 27, 1903

[6] *Ibid*, Dec. 26, 1903

Catholic religious services in 1909. Rev. J. V. Monteillard said mass in the Primeaux home, and before the mass the priest "blessed the marriages of five couples." Most of these were said to have lived together under civil contracts "and through hard circumstances had delayed to have their union made holy by the church."[7]

Ebenezer, about four miles southeast of Crowley, is roughly the same distance from Lyons' Point. The settlement takes its name from the first Protestant church established in the vicinity. The Ebenezer Methodist Church, of the northern branch of Methodism, was organized September 1, 1889 by Rev. W. H. Cline. The church was founded by Walter Faulk and Rev. William Shepherd. Land on which to build a parsonage was bought in 1897. Benjamin Faulk sold the land to the church, represented by George Faulk, for $30.[8]

Summer revivals, known as "camp meetings," conducted by the Ebenezer Methodist Church, became as well-known and popular as the summer religious services held at Lake Arthur.

The camp meetings, of 10 days duration, were started before 1900. Families brought bedding and provisions and pitched tents on the campgrounds near the church. Open air preaching took place nightly under a tent, later under a shelter called a tabernacle. As the attendance increased more facilities were added; a dining hall was put up for those desiring to board; another convenience was a ladies' dormitory, occupants of which were expected to bring quilts, pillows and mosquito bars.[9]

A new church building was dedicated in 1913. Bishop Wilber P. Thirkield of New Orleans officiated at the ceremonies, held June 29.[10]

The camp meetings continued, but in a different location. In 1915 the Acadia Holiness Association, represented by Seward Phillips, president, and Otis Faulk, secretary, bought two acres of land from David Boudreaux for $70.[11] The land, located on Bayou Queue de Tortue near Faulk Bridge, about two and a half miles south of the church, was ideally suited for the purpose.

Among early pastors of the Ebenezer church were Rev. Lastie Hoffpauir, Rev. J. T. James and Rev. J. A. Carruth.[12]

Shortly after the first church was built, in 1891, a post office was established at Ebenezer. The post office was operated for 29 years, until 1920, when it was discontinued. Only two postmasters served: Charles W. Faulk and Haughton Faulk.[13]

[7] *Daily Signal*, May 24, 1909
[8] *Ibid*, 50th Anniv. Ed., 12; Conveyance Book P, #10434, 215, Acad. Par.
[9] *Crowley Signal*, July 21, 1900; June 27, Aug. 8, 1903; June 23, 1906; June 20, 1908
[10] *Daily Signal*, June 28, 1913
[11] Conveyance Book, C-3, #44904, 351, Acad. Par.
[12] *Crowley Signal*, Mar. 10, 1900; Feb. 8, 1902; June 27, 1903
[13] Register of Postmasters, National Archives and Records Service

The William Sarver homestead, south of Ebenezer. With the parents (shown at center) are sons and daughters, from left, O'Neal, Claude, Laura, Clara, Alice and Cora; Cora's husband, Ed Smith. Boys in the foreground are grandsons, Frank and Levi. (Photo courtesy Theresa Smith LaSabe)

William Morgan, Ebenezer's first merchant, traded chickens and country produce in Crowley for staple goods to supply his country store, which was in operation before 1900. A second grocery was opened in 1901 by F. D. Meaux.[14]

Members of the southern branch of Methodism also had a church in the general vicinity of Ebenezer. This was the Hebron Methodist Church, about two and a half miles south of Ebenezer church. The church, built about 1900, was a branch of the Methodist Episcopal Church South at Indian Bayou, just across the line of Lafayette Parish, and was served by

[14] *Crowley Signal*, May 5, 1900; Feb. 16, 1901

274

ministers from the Indian Bayou church. Pioneer families which lived nearest the church and belonged to the congregation were the Joe Morgans, the Raymond Sarvers and the Joe Atkinsons.[15]

Residents of the Ebenezer-Hebron section appear to have been literate and education-minded. As early as 1899 the Ebenezer school had two teachers, Miss Inglis Fraser, principal, and Miss Roberta Baker, assistant. Three other schools were located within a four-mile radius of the Ebenezer school. These were Comeaux school, three miles north; Hoffpauir school, three and a half miles northeast, and Perry Point, two and a half miles south. Teachers at these schools in 1899 were Eula Milton at Comeaux; Lacie Windsor at Hoffpauir; S. R. Ellis, Perry Point. Another school in the vicinity was Stutes' Cove school.[16]

The Ebenezer area schools were among the first in the parish to be consolidated. By 1906 the Hoffpauir and Comeaux schools were consolidated with Ebenezer, and a wagonette was provided to transport the children to school.[17]

More progress was noted in 1911. The Ebenezer school was one of 17 in the state selected for agricultural experimentation, and the first commencement took place.

A five-acre tract of land was bought by the parish for the experimental farm and a building put up for the storage of tools and implements, also to serve as a stable for the farm animals. The state contributed $1,400 to the project that first year. Directed by P. L. Guilbeau, the students raised a mouth-watering list of vegetables, including potatoes, corn, cow peas, velvet beans, German millet, muskmelon, watermelon, yams, beans, cabbage, peppers, soy beans, peas, eggplants, beets, sorghum, radishes and lettuce. Students taking agriculture courses were trained in practical botany and the study of plant diseases.[18]

Three graduates received high school diplomas at the commencement. They were Eliza Faulk, Iva Little and Elbert Hoffpauir.[19]

A course in instrumental music was added to the school curriculum in 1912, taught by Miss Bertha Doty. D. M. Brewer was principal at the time.[20]

By 1913 the school had become fourth largest in the parish with a faculty of seven and three transfers bringing children in from three different directions. An approved high school, Ebenezer had a domestic science department and the agriculture school. This brought the school about $2,000 per year in state funds.[21]

---

[15] *Crowley Signal*, July 8, 1899; *Daily Signal*, Apr. 18, 1902; Aug. 23, 1906; interview, Marilyn Morgan Hebert, 1978
[16] *Crowley Signal*, Sept. 10, 1899; Sept. 8, 1900
[17] *Daily Signal*, Sept. 19, 1906
[18] *Ibid*, May 24, 1911
[19] *Ibid*, June 2, 1911
[20] *Ibid*, Sept. 7, 1912
[21] *Ibid*, July 2, 1913, final report of J. H. Lewis, retiring superintendent of schools

Early teachers at Ebenezer include S. R. Ellis, Lily Van Valkenburgh, Rev. J. T. James, Margaret Bovell, Sadie Hamilton and Celeste Barry.[22]

The school at Perry Point was one of the one-teacher schools that survived longer than most. Perry Point was on the parish school list as late as 1916. Miss Juliette Atkinson was the best remembered teacher.[23]

Perry Point, the school location, and Hebron, site of the church (Methodist South), sometime appear to have been two names for the same locality. Individuals identified as being from Perry Point were at other times said to be from Hebron, and vice versa.[24]

The people who lived in the Ebenezer-Hebron-Perry Point vicinity were gregarious and sociable. Reports of neighboring families visiting each other, church socials, crop and weather news appeared regularly in the Crowley newspaper. One of the popular diversions for the young people was singing. One of the favorite places for "a singing" was the H. M. Pitre home; the singers who gathered at the Pitre home included Limond, Jane and Robert Sarver; Edna and Ada Pitre; Mancell Hoffpauir; Mattie, Daisy and John Sarver.[25]

Queue Tortue

The place name Queue Tortue or Queue de Tortue, originally applied to the Poupeville-Rayne area, appears to have followed settlers as they occupied lands in a westerly direction along the bayou of the same name. The name was in use as late as 1918. Following are abstracts from the Crowley newspaper, 1900 to 1918, which mention Queue Tortue:

1900: Ernest Leleux and John Abshire, "merchants of Queue Tortue;" Abner Hoffpauir of Queue Tortue . . .[26]

1903: ". . . roads between Crowley and the Queue Tortue country are almost impassable . . . farmers are going to experience no little difficulty in hauling their grain to market . . . Queue Tortue is one of the most prominent rice sections in southwest Louisiana . . ."[27]

1904: Pierre Bertrand, J. D. Guidry of Queue Tortue . . .[28]

1906: Neuville Abshire of Bayou Queue de Tortue vicinity . . . Columbus Abshire of "QT."[29]

1915: Claude Stelly, prominent farmer of Queue de Tortue section . . .[30]

---

[22] *Crowley Signal*, Sept. 8, 1900; *Daily Signal*, May 1, Sept. 3, 1902; May 16, 1904
[23] *Daily Signal*, Feb. 1, 1916; interview, Marilyn Morgan Hebert
[24] *Ibid*, Aug. 24, 31, 1904
[25] *Ibid*, Mar. 20, 1905
[26] *Crowley Signal*, Apr. 4, Oct. 6, 1900
[27] *Ibid*, Sept. 5, 1903
[28] *Daily Signal*, June 11, 1904
[29] *Ibid*, May 26, 1906
[30] *Ibid*, Mar. 30, 1915

1916: Emile Pleasance of Queue de Tortue was in Crowley with a supply of gumbo *filé** for which he has an enviable reputation.[31]

1918: Mr. and Mrs. James Daily of Queue de Tortue . . .[32]

Other names designating places in the south part of the parish (south of Bayou Plaquemine Brulee) which have lost their identity include:

Mouton *Vacherie*, one mile north of Rayne. Meaning the Mouton cattle ranch, the name stems from the property owned by Antoine Mouton which was purchased by Dr. W. H. Cunningham as a town site for Rayne.[33]

Prairie Gregg, believed to have been in the vicinity of Ebenezer and Perry Point.[34]

Crooked Bridge, nine miles south of Crowley, derived from a crooked bridge over Bayou Queue de Tortue. The "crooked bridge" was replaced by a new bridge in 1904[35] but the name remained in use for many years.

Stutes' Cove is believed to have been on Bayou Queue de Tortue near a bridge. A half school at Stutes' Cove was maintained by the Acadia Parish School Board in 1900 with Roberta Baker as teacher. Schools designated as half schools were near parish boundary lines and attended by students from two parishes, with maintenance costs shared by the two participating parishes, hence the "half school."[36]

Point Francois, in the vicinity of Morse. Mrs. Johnson Hanks, mother of Joseph Hanks, a Morse merchant, lived at Point Francois until 1909.[37]

Leger's Point, eight miles southwest of Estherwood. Jennie Gault taught at a public school there in 1904; three years later the school was consolidated with Morse, Evangeline and Riverside schools.[38] After the school was discontinued the place lost its identity. The location is believed to have been the Michel Leger Spanish land grant on the bayou some three miles west of Morse.

Tasso Point, *l'Anse Hibou* (Owl Cove) were other names for, or specific places in, the general area known as Mermentau Cove.[39]

Quaint place names of long ago located on the north side of Bayou Plaquemine Brulee included:

---

* *Filé*: Dried and ground leaves of the sassafras tree, used as a flavoring agent in gumbo, a thick Acadian soup.

[31] *Ibid*, Sept. 14, 1916
[32] *Crowley Signal*, Nov. 16, 1918
[33] *Daily Signal*, Apr. 25, 1906; Conveyance Books G-2, I-2, St. Landry Par.
[34] *Daily Signal*, Mar. 19, 1904
[35] *Crowley Signal*, Oct. 1, 1904
[36] *Ibid*, Sept. 8, 1900; Sept. 14, 1901
[37] *Daily Signal*, Jan. 21, 1909
[38] *Crowley Signal*, Apr. 13, 1907; *Daily Signal*, May 16, 1904
[39] *Daily Signal*, Jan. 26, 1909; July 29, 1915

Faquetaique, designated as the location of lands owned in 1917 by Joseph Christ, Tony and Andrew Wilfert and Peter Klein, in Township 7 South Range 1 West.[40]

Pointe au Fiere, site of a cemetery six miles southwest of Eunice.[41]

L'Anse aux Vaches (Cow Cove), mentioned in Basile news column.[42]

Pointe-au-Tigre (Tiger Point), mentioned in Branch news column in 1907. Oscar Brunson was a resident of *Pointe-au-Tigre*.[43]

Pleasantview: an area near the farms of C. J. and T. B. Freeland in Prairie Hayes was known by this name in 1899.[44]

Haw Point, an area north of Church Point, in both Acadia and St. Landry Parishes.[45]

---

[40] *Crowley Signal*, Dec. 15, 1917, legal notice
[41] *Daily Signal*, Sept. 3, 1914
[42] *Crowley Signal*, Aug. 11, 1900
[43] *Ibid*, Jan. 12, 1907
[44] *Ibid*, May 6, 1899
[45] *Ibid*, July 20, 1901

Estherwood

Like other towns created by the coming of the trains, Estherwood was named by, and probably for, a railroad official or member of his family. There are several stories about how Estherwood got its name. One is that the word Estherwood is a combination of two names, the result of a compromise made to end a controversy over whether to name the place Wood, for a Dr. Wood, or Esther, for the wife of the section foreman of the railroad. Another version explains the "wood" part as follows: the station was a re-fueling point for the early wood-burning engines, and the name was derived from the large quantities of wood which were stored near the station.[1]

Before the railroad came through the place was known as Coulee Trieve (Trive, Trief), so named for an early settler, Jean Baptiste Trieve who had built a cabin on the coulee about 1816. A mysterious and sinister figure, Trieve was believed to have been a pirate.[2]

Jacob Kollitz and A. D. LeBlanc are credited with having provided the nucleus of a village when they established individual businesses near the site of the Trieve cabin about 1891. Kollitz also owned a 15-room hotel which was managed by others on a rental basis. Those who operated the hotel included Mrs. E. B. Holbrook, in 1899; F. L. Feray and S. G. Watkins.[3]

The Estherwood Hotel was closed down sometime before the end of 1907, and apparently was not re-opened. In its Christmas edition that year the *Signal* noted that the Estherwood postmistress, Mrs. Mary H. Coles, "also serves meals to the traveling public since the hotel went out of business."

A post office was established at Estherwood in 1881 with Joseph Roy as first postmaster. Other early postmasters were Eugene D. Roy, Sam H. Goldberg, Dupre LeBlanc Jr., Thomas E. Lewis and J. J. Aulds. Mrs. Coles, appointed April 23, 1898, was postmistress for more than 33 years.[4]

The establishment of two enterprises connected with the rice industry appears to have been the reason for a spurt in growth and development in Estherwood during the early years of the century. These were the Miller-Morris canal, one of the first and largest rice irrigation systems constructed in Acadia, and the Eureka rice mill, which began operations in 1900.

At this time there were several thriving business places in the village,

---

[1] *Signal*, Anniv. Ed., 64, 65

[2] *Ibid*, 64

[3] *Ibid; Daily Signal*, Apr. 17, 1902; *Crowley Signal*, Oct. 28, 1899; Jan. 27, 1900; Feb. 16, 1901; Sept. 19, 1903

[4] Register of Postmasters, National Archives and Records Service

Estherwood's first business establishment, Jacob Kollitz's Estherwood Emporium. Customers could buy dry goods, shoes, hats, groceries, hardware, saddles and notions at the store, which was located on what is now Highway 90.

in addition to those previously mentioned. These included the David Balshaw general store, opened in 1891; Alcee L. Gaidry's store and Maitre Mack's grocery and fruit store, in business since 1899; Caldwell Bros. general store, established in 1900. S. V. Guidry operated a livery stable and C. Hiller sold fruits.[5]

By the spring of 1900 some 30 new residences had been constructed, the streets were well graded and drained, and sidewalks had been put down. The Hoyt brothers, W. M. and E. T., opened a lumber yard and constructed a large warehouse, in addition to operating a merchandise business. Dr. R. Trezevant, the town physician and surgeon, also sold drugs.[6]

The village acquired more tradespeople in 1901. Lyons and Kelly were blacksmiths and wheelrights, W. H. Fleshman and P. E. Coles had a livery and feed store, V. Roussell and son ran a general store. Adam Alvarado opened a barber shop and the third Hoyt brother, John P., established himself as a justice of the peace and notary public. The Caldwell store had changed hands; it was now Estherwood Mercantile, owned by J. H. and P. B. Lewis.[7]

About this time A. Kaplan, who owned the canal and rice mill, took steps to promote the town. He bought a half interest in building lots owned by J. Kollitz; the lots were improved and plans made for two

---

[5] *Crowley Signal*, Apr. 28, Mar. 17, Aug. 4, 1900; Oct. 3, 1903; Dec. 14, 1907
[6] *Ibid*, Mar. 7, Oct. 13, 1900; Feb. 16, 1901
[7] *Ibid*, Feb. 16, 1901; Dec. 14, 1907

additions to the town. The Estherwood Development Co. was organized with Kaplan, Kollitz and M. J. Barnett as officers. In addition to the town property the company owned 1,000 acres of rice and timberland in the vicinity of Estherwood.[8]

Two town lot sales were held, but there is no information about the first, and little about the second, which took place in May, 1902. It was reported that 1,000 persons came by train from points such as Washington and Abbeville for the sale, but other details are lacking. Presumably the property offered for sale at the auction was owned by the Estherwood Development Co.[9]

Estherwood's Commercial Bank was established in 1902. Officers were Henry Kaplan, president; J. Kollitz, vice president; Sam Michaels, cashier. Others on the board of directors were William Mason Smith and I. M. Lichtenstein of New Orleans, A. Kaplan, Crowley, and David Roy, Estherwood.[10]

Few changes took place in Estherwood during the next few years. In 1904 Miss Emma Henry clerked at Kollitz' Emporium and the post office was domiciled in a Second street building. By 1908 P. E. Coles had bought out W. H. Fleshman's interest in the livery and had added a dray and transfer line to the business; school children could buy their textbooks from the Gaidry store, and residents needing notarial services could consult Joseph H. Lumpkin or J. P. Hoyt. Henry Feitel managed the Kollitz store, assisted by Emile Myers and Tom Hoffpauir, and J. O. Faulk was head clerk at Estherwood Mercantile.[11]

Estherwood's pioneer store, Kollitz' Emporium, was bought by Hoffpauir Mercantile in 1915. That same year Allen C. Hoffpauir established a bakery to serve Estherwood, Midland, Mermentau and Morse. A baker from France named Richard was hired to operate the bakery.[12]

Newspaper references show that there were several other businesses operating in Estherwood between 1910 and 1915. Those mentioned were Istre Brothers and Faulk store, E. P. Myers' livery barn, the Bouttee Restaurant and Dr. Francez's drugstore.[13]

Municipal Affairs

Estherwood was incorporated as a village March 12, 1901. The corporation boundaries were set as follows:

> Beginning at the southeast corner of Section 15, Township 10 South, Range 1 West, Louisiana Meridian, thence west following the section

[8] *Ibid*, Dec. 21, 1901; Dec. 14, 1907
[9] *Daily Signal*, May 29, 1902
[10] *Ibid*
[11] *Ibid*, Mar. 14, Apr. 2, 1904; Dec. 14, 1907
[12] *Ibid*, June 24, July 30, 1916
[13] *Crowley Signal*, Oct. 15, 1910; *Daily Signal*, Oct. 29, 1914

line dividing sections 15 and 22, and 16 and 21 to the southwest corner of Section 16; thence directly north to the crossing over Louisiana Western railroad back to Bayou Plaquemine; thence following said bayou to a point directly north of the beginning; thence south to the point of beginning.

The first town officials, selected at a mass meeting held January 15, 1901 and ratified by gubernatorial appointment, were Henry Feitel, mayor; Jacob Kollitz, Dupre LeBlanc and E. T. Hoyt, aldermen; Henry Myers, marshal. The village claimed a population of 300.[14]

Feitel was retained as mayor at the regular election held in April, 1902. Kollitz and Hoyt was returned to their council seats and David Roy replaced Dupre LeBlanc for the third alderman position. The newly elected marshal, William Myers (Miers) resigned his office shortly after the election and was replaced by his brother, Henry Myers.[15]

An unusual political wrangle developed in 1903. The story, as best it can be pieced together from contemporary accounts, is as follows:

Henry Feitel moved to Beaumont, leaving the mayor's office apparently vacant. Henry Myers, the marshal, moved from the ward. The citizens petitioned the governor to appoint replacements for the two offices; David Balshaw was named mayor and Arthur Heinsz marshal. Feitel returned from Beaumont and claimed his office, and suddenly the village had two mayors. Dr. R. Trezevant, the town treasurer, went to Crowley for legal advice; he said he didn't know which of the two mayors he was supposed to obey when warrants were drawn.[16]

Gov. W. W. Heard gave some consideration to the matter, said he may have acted too hastily on the petition asking for a new set of officers, and that he might revoke the commission issued to Balshaw and Heinsz. Whereupon Mayor Feitel called a council meeting. Councilmen Kollitz and Roy attended, but E. T. Hoyt refused to condone the action; he said he would stand by Balshaw's appointment, which had been made in response to the petition circulated when Feitel moved to Texas.[17]

The next development was the resignation of Dr. Trezevant as treasurer, and Heinsz as marshal. A. L. Gaidry was named to replace Dr. Trezevant. At the request of the governor P. S. Pugh, a Crowley attorney (and probably attorney for the village) investigated the matter. Pugh reported that he had no solution to the problem of what to do about two mayors and two marshals.[18]

The final newspaper report on the matter stated that Gov. Heard had re-instated Feitel as mayor, since he (Feitel) had been absent only temporarily, and that Heinsz, although unqualified, was the marshal.[19] The

[14] *Crowley Signal*, Jan. 19, Feb. 16, Mar. 23, 1901; La. Dept. of State
[15] *Crowley Signal*, Jan. 19, Feb. 6, 1901
[16] *Daily Signal*, Jan. 14, 19, 1903
[17] *Ibid*, Jan. 21, 31, 1903
[18] *Ibid*, Feb. 4, 6, 1903
[19] *Ibid*, Feb. 10, 1903

governor's action evidently did not resolve the matter, as Feitel's name as mayor does not appear in the official record for this period. Records of the Louisiana Department of State show Balshaw mayor and James T. McGary replacing Heinsz as marshal.

An even more bizarre and complex situation grew out of the 1904 municipal election campaign.

About a month before the election an opposition ticket to the Balshaw faction was nominated at a mass meeting held in Feray's Hall. Leaders were Ellis Hoffpauir, J. T. McGary, E. W. Harrington, E. M. Feray, J. Kollitz, E. D. Roy and Andrew Wise. Nominated were T. C. Tinker, for mayor; J. T. McGary, P. B. Lewis and S. V. Guidry, aldermen; Ovey Roy, marshal.[20]

Balshaw's running mates were E. T. Hoyt, J. L. Trahan and A. L. Heinsz, for aldermen; Henry Myers, for marshal. The results of the election showed Balshaw the winner—by two votes. Elected aldermen were two from the Balshaw ticket: Hoyt and Trahan, and S. V. Guidry of the opposition. Ovey Roy won for marshal.[21]

The defeated candidates contested the election—not on the basis of the narrow margin of victory, but on the legality of the voting procedures.

An explanation of what had gone on is contained in a front page story in the *Daily Signal* of April 21, 1904:

> It develops that there has been a queer muddle in the municipal election at Estherwood, owing to the use of an independent ticket, printed at Crowley, besides the official ticket issued by the secretary of state from Baton Rouge, resulting in the election of David Balshaw for mayor by a majority of two votes over Thos. C. Tinker, and a contest of the election by the defeated candidates.
>
> The facts in the case are that when the Tinker ticket was nominated in convention, it was sent to Baton Rouge as the only ticket to be used and the official ticket accordingly came back with one set of candidates.
>
> This did not meet with unanimous approval, and a number of citizens nominated David Balshaw for mayor, with a full set of aldermen and a marshal, had their ticket printed in a Crowley job office and offered it to the voters.
>
> The commissioners of election, William Hoyt, Clemsey LeBlanc, Ellis Hoffpauir and David Roy, agreed that both tickets should be used, and the election proceeded accordingly, until three o'clock in the afternoon, when, in response to an inquiry, a telegram was received from Secretary of State Michel, instructing the commissioners to allow the use of only the official ticket.
>
> When the votes were counted, Mr. Balshaw's ticket was found to have a majority of two votes. The defeated candidates are contesting the election, and the opinion of some of Crowley's leading attorneys has already been invoked. One of the lawyers consulted thought the election legal, but another opined that the law would not permit the use of any but official ballots and that the election of the Balshaw ticket would be

---

[20] *Crowley Signal*, Feb. 27, 1904
[21] Louisiana Dept. of State

declared invalid, only one ticket having been voted under the law—that of the Tinker faction, adding he felt confident his confrere would take the same view in the case and recognize his error in thinking the election of the Balshaw ticket valid.

The newspaper story elicited a lengthy rebuttal from Tinker, the defeated candidate. His letter to the editor sheds more light on what came to be known as "The Estherwood Election Muddle" and is also a prime example of the type of politely sarcastic invective used by politicians of that period:

> The attention of the candidates on the Democratic ticket at the recent village election, having been called to your recent article under the heading "Election Muddle of Estherwood," the opinion was expressed that you had either been misinformed or that you had got "the facts in the case" as badly mixed as is our election, and believing that were your array of "facts in the case" unchallenged, it might be inferred that sharp practice, or some snide game had been played on the opposition that is not consistent with fair dealing, or gentlemanly conduct.
>
> On behalf of Messrs. P. B. Lewis, S. V. Guidry, Jas. T. McGarry, Ovey Roy and myself, I propose to state, not only "the facts in the case," but the truth. You say the facts in the case are that when the Tinker ticket was nominated in convention it was sent to Baton Rouge as the only ticket to be used, and the official ticket accordingly came back with only one set of candidates. The fact is "that when the Tinker ticket was nominated in convention" the nominees qualified as candidates as provided by law, and the ticket was then sent to Baton Rouge—not as the only ticket to be used—but to be printed on the official ballot. That the Balshaw ticket was not printed on the official ballot is manifestly because they failed to qualify. Does that imply sharp practice on the part of the Democratic nominees as your statement of "facts in the case" would lead the public to infer, or is it not a plain exhibit of ignorance of the law on the part of the Balshaw ticket? That is their misfortune, not our fault. We have yet to learn that it was any part of our duty, as candidates, to make inquiry or to manifest great anxiety lest "the other fellow" fail to qualify.
>
> Again you say: "This did not meet with unanimous approval, and a number of the citizens nominated David Balshaw for mayor, with a full set of aldermen and a marshal, had their ticket printed in a Crowley job shop and offered it to the voters." This seems to imply that the Balshaw ticket is a creature of very recent growth, but that is not the case. On the contrary, during last December, a mass meeting was called at LeBlanc's Hall, at which David Balshaw was nominated for mayor, and Messrs. E. T. Hoyt, A. L. Heinsz and Joseph L. Trahan for aldermen, and Henry Miers for town marshal, and was published as the "Ticket of the People's Party." It is a well known fact in Estherwood that Mr. Balshaw has long had the mayoralty "bee in his bonnet." (Witness the fiasco of the winter of 1902-1903, when by questionable tactics, he endeavored to oust Mayor Feitel) The people of the village, however, seemed content to accept the ticket, knowing that in E. T. Hoyt and "Joe" Trahan there were two good and true men on the ticket and notwithstanding some expressed fear that later they might become a mere tail to the kite of Messrs. LeBlanc, Balshaw, Miers and Co.
>
> The people, as I say seemed content with the Balshaw ticket. Later

on, however, the public report that Mr. Balshaw had declared his hostility to the village high school, and again in a street row, wherein one of the participants—one Miers—"pulled a gun" on his opponent and was not arrested therefor, for the simple reason that he is "couzan" to the present acting and would-be future marshal—Henry Miers.

Then the progressive and law abiding element of the people of our village saw that it behooved them to bestir themselves or be saddled with an incubus, a reactionary "Old Man of the Sea." In March a meeting was called at which a majority of the voters of the town were in attendance, and the Democratic ticket, as printed on the official ballot was nominated; you further state that the commissioners of election—Wm. Hoyt, Clesmay LeBlanc, Ellis Hoffpauir and David Roy—agreed that both tickets should be used. David Roy finally acquiesed in that, but Ellis Hoffpauir protested, reserving his rights to the last.

At three o'clock when the telegram from Secretary of State Michel was shown the commissioners instructing them to only use the official ballot, then, and only then, did Messrs. Hoyt, LeBlanc and Roy decide that the voters might use which ballot they liked. Mr. Hoffpauir still protesting that the official ballot was the only legal ballot.

But it was at night when the votes were to be counted that the fun began. There was "racing and chasing"—not over Netherly Lea, but over the Estherwood-Crowley road, and the Balshaw people brought an attorney—a lawyer on the field, Mr. Pugh of that ilk, a counselor learned in the law—A Legal Luminary (a large "L" please) whose bulging brain contains a complete epitome of all law, divine, human or otherwise, who at once gave an exhibition of his acumen or acuteness by protesting that the official ballot should not be counted. He sprang the 2,500 inhabitant clause and under that the official ballot was illegal. But since then some forgotten or darkened page of the epitome of the law has been enlightened and Mr. Pugh doubtless knows more of the election law today then he did on the night of Tuesday, April 19, 1904. There are later clauses than that of "2,000 inhabitants." Mermentau with a less number of voters than Estherwood used only the official ballot.

Thanking you for your kindness in permitting me to lay "the facts in the case" before your readers,

I have the honor to be, yours truly,

Thomas C. Tinker[22]

The outcome of the controversy was not reported, but state department records show that Balshaw kept his seat.

Two tickets were in the running for the 1906 election. Candidates were David Balshaw, the incumbent, and Ellis Hoffpauir for mayor; Ovey Roy and U. V. Young, marshal; P. B. Lewis, A. L. Gaidry, Joseph L. Trahan and S. V. Guidry for the three seats on the council. Again the Balshaw ticket went in.[23]

Ellis Hoffpauir was appointed mayor and E. F. Myers alderman in September of 1907.[24] Reasons for the appointments, whether to fill vacancies created by death or resignation, are not known.

[22] *Daily Signal*, Apr. 26, 1903; verbatim except for shortening paragraphs to improve readibility

[23] *Ibid*, Mar. 6, Apr. 18, 1906

[24] La. Dept. of State

F. J. Barnett was elected mayor in 1908. Council members were Euphrosin Myers, Adam Myers and Joseph L. Trahan. Ovey Roy began another term as town marshal. Less than a year later, in January of 1909, Ellis Hoffpauir again served as interim mayor. Some months later Joseph L. Trahan resigned his alderman seat and Sam Michaels was appointed to replace him.[25]

Ellis Hoffpauir, who had served two part-terms as mayor by appointment, was elected to the office April 19, 1910. His councilmen were J. W. Embry, James Otis Faulk and Sam Michael. Marshal Ovey Roy was the only candidate with opposition—Jules Myers ran against him but was defeated by the veteran law officer. The candidates had been named at a mass meeting held in the D. Roy hall with Dr. Z. J. Francez acting as chairman and J. P. Hoyt as secretary. The newspaper account of the meeting indicated that political strife in the village was at an end, at least for the time being:

> The meeting was well attended and harmonious and all pledged themselves for good government and the upbuilding of the town and section. Good roads and drainage were brought up and the matter of advertising the best interests of the town. It was brought out that the schools, churches and general improvements are 100 per cent ahead of five years ago, and that we are living in the garden patch of ideal soil for all crops in Louisiana.[26]

Alderman Embry resigned after serving about six months and was replaced by E. D. Roy. Jacob Kollitz became a member of the council by appointment in 1911.[27]

Prior to the 1912 referendum Mayor Hoffpauir announced that he would not seek re-election. The nominees were James Otis Faulk and Monroe P. Spell for mayor; Kollitz, Joseph L. Veanan (*sic*), Adam Myers and James A. Leighton, aldermen; David Roy and Ovey Roy for marshal. Elected were Faulk, Kollitz, Myers and Leighton, mayor and council members, and Ovey Roy marshal. Adam Roy became marshal in 1913, by appointment.[28]

A lively campaign developed prior to the 1914 election with an unprecedented number of candidates in the running: three for mayor, five for the three council seats, and four for marshal. The slate of candidates included P. H. Boutte, Marvin Spell and Thomas B. Hoffpauir for mayor; J. Kollitz, Gerard Hoffpauir, Willie Lee, Ovey Roy and Adam Myers, aldermen; Adam Roy, Eugene Roy, Sezar Simon, Tenus Lejeune for marshal.[29]

The victors were Thomas B. Hoffpauir, J. Kollitz, Gerard Hoffpauir,

---

[25] *Daily Signal*, June 5, July 19, 1909
[26] *Crowley Signal*, Mar. 19, 1910
[27] *Ibid*, Nov. 19, 1910; La. Dept. State
[28] *Daily Signal*, Mar. 14, 1912; La. Dept. of State
[29] *Ibid*, Mar. 5, Apr. 21, 1914

Ovey Roy and Sezar Simon. Before the end of the year Dominique Leleux had replaced Simon as marshal, by appointment. Another between-elections appointment was that of David Roy Sr., alderman.[30]

Only one change resulted from the election of 1916—Mayo Broussard replaced Gerard Hoffpauir on the council. Mayor Hoffpauir and Leleux, the marshal, resigned in August of 1917 and were replaced by Columbus Spell as mayor and Adam Roy, marshal.[31]

Mayor Spell was returned to office at the 1917 election along with Marshal Adam Roy and Councilmen Kollitz and Broussard. Will Lee replaced Ovey Roy on the council then resigned in May, 1919 and was himself replaced by Victor C. Coles.[32]

Re-elected in 1920 were Mayor Spell, Marshal Adam Roy and Alderman Kollitz. New aldermen were Willie Roy and O. Lejeune.[33]

Reports on actions taken by the Estherwood council were not published in the Crowley newspaper on a regular basis. The few published reports are important, being the only record available of the proceedings of the town council for the period under consideration.

The following, given in chronological order, is a compilation of other bits of information about Estherwood found in the newspaper files from 1907 to 1917:

J. P. Hoyt replaced Sam Michaels as town clerk in 1907; the town authorized construction of a bridge over Coulee Boeuf in 1909.[34]

A 1910 ordinance prohibited children up to 14 from lounging or playing on or near the railroad. Cypress sidewalks in the village were authorized by the council in 1911.[35]

At the December, 1911 meeting the council accepted the application of Willie Roy for a retail liquor license for 1912, the business to be conducted in the Dupre LeBlanc building. In other actions the council adopted an ordinance prohibiting fire works on Main Street. Violators were to be fined a maximum of $25 or 25 days in jail—or both, at the discretion of the mayor.[36]

A full report on a council meeting was carried in the *Daily Signal* of June 6, 1912:

> Mayor James O. Faulk and the new city aldermen held their first session Tuesday night in the town hall with much business and several ordinances of importance introduced by James A. Leighton. J. P. Hoyt was retained as clerk, elected by the aldermen; Philip H. Boutte as treasurer with $1,500 bond. The board of health was composed of Dr. Z. J. Francez, Walter H. Fleshman and Ellis Hoffpauir. Adam Myers

---

[30] La. Dept. of State
[31] La. Dept. of State; *Daily Signal*, Aug. 9, 1917
[32] La. Dept. of State; *Daily Signal*, May 29, 1919
[33] La. Dept. of State
[34] *Crowley Signal*, July 6, 1907; *Daily Signal*, June 26, 1909
[35] *Crowley Signal*, Aug. 6, 1910; *Daily Signal*, Jan. 18, 1911
[36] *Daily Signal*, Dec. 11, 1911

and J. A. Leighton are on the street, sidewalk and bridge committee; Jacob Kollitz and J. A. Leighton were named to the finance committee. The city council elected Smith and Carmouche for the coming year as city attorneys at $25 per annum.

Preston B. Lewis Jr., was elected principal of the Estherwood high school for the next session. Mr. Lewis was raised here and is highly recommended.

The stock ordinances of the town were amended, so that there is a penalty not to exceed $10 for not keeping up town stock at night.

For fire protection a deep well was ordered dug and to be given to the lowest bidder.

Mr. Leighton introduced a playground ordinance to be centrally located and put in good shape, to be used only week days. No horse racing, base ball games or anything of that kind will be allowed on Sunday, also making it a misdemeanor for boys to play games for gain or pleasure in streets or any public buildings under a fine or imprisonment. No marble playing for keeps will be allowed, also no children under 15 years will be allowed to roam around after 8 o'clock at night and $25 will be the penalty for anyone throwing at buildings, wires, cars or anything of that kind.

During Mayor Faulks's regime steps were taken to install electric lights in the village, at a cost of $1,000. On the night of July 4, 1913, Estherwood residents watched proudly as 47 electric lights were turned on for the first time. Gerard Hoffpauir was manager of the light plant.[37]

The village did its part to further the good road movement in 1914, which came about because of the increased use of automobiles for transportation. The council appropriated $250 to help build what was called the "Transcontinental Highway" (Hwy. 90) at that time under construction.[38]

When Mayor Thomas B. Hoffpauir went into office in 1914 L. P. Hoffpauir was town clerk and treasurer, and Mrs. J. Kollitz was appointed tax collector.[39]

Autos speeding through the town in 1915 resulted in the council setting a speed limit of 10 miles per hour; two years later the limit was upped to 15 miles per hour. A youth curfew ordinance, adopted in 1917, prohibited boys under 14 from being on the streets after 9 p.m.[40]

Churches, Schools

Construction on Estherwood's first church, the Methodist Northern, was begun in the fall of 1900. Situated in the western part of town on property donated by E. T. and W. M. Hoyt, the building was put up at a

---

[37] *Ibid*, Mar. 6, July 3, 1913; May 10, 1914
[38] *Ibid*, Mar. 5, 1914
[39] *Ibid*, May 10, 1914
[40] *Ibid*, Apr. 16, 1915; Aug. 9, 1917

cost of $1,000. Accepting the donation of property on behalf of the church were the church trustees, W. F. Lyons, C. H. Cowen, Roy Culver and the Hoyts. The deed to the property is dated April 2, 1901. A regular pastor (unidentified) was assigned to the church, also known as Central Methodist, in December of 1901.[41]

Methodist and Baptist services for black people were being conducted in Estherwood as early as 1902. In March of 1902 the Estherwood Development Company donated Lot 16 on the north side of the Southern Pacific track to the Methodist church, colored, represented by the church trustees, Mansul Bias and Henry Brunt. The church building, if one was built, also may have been used by the Baptist congregation. The Estherwood news correspondent for the *Signal* reported the following in 1902: "The camp meeting of colored Baptists is still in progress. Quite a party of white people went last evening, but three or four young white men on the outside misbehaved so badly that they all went home before the service was concluded. The officers should not allow the colored people to be disturbed in their worship." In 1912 the Baptist congregation bought Lot 39 in Block 19 from the Estherwood Development Company for $25.[42] It is presumed that a church was built on the lot.

A church for the Estherwood congregation of Methodist Episcopal Church South was dedicated May 21, 1905, with Rev. J. T. Sawyer of Crowley officiating. A belfry and steeple were added to the church in 1906. The Estherwood news reporter, John P. Hoyt, took note of the installation of the bell: ". . . that evening the sound of the bell calling the people to church was heard for the first time." Rev. Ivy Hoffpauir was one of the early pastors.[43]

The church was wrecked by a storm in the spring of 1917. The former Dupre LeBlanc saloon building was moved to another location and remodeled for use as a church. The building had been first sold to Charles Wright, then to Ellis Hoffpauir, who donated it to the church.[44]

The Baptist congregation's first church in Estherwood was built in 1906. Two lots were purchased from W. M. and E. T. Hoyt for $25. Representing the church in the land deal were Thomas Wiggins and John Gill, deacon and trustees. A parsonage had already been secured for the pastor, Rev. R. M. Wise. News items about revivals and baptizings in the Morris Canal indicate that services were continued on a regular basis for a number of years.[45]

Catholic services were first held in the village in 1904 when Mass was celebrated once a month on Saturdays in the home of Mr. and Mrs.

[41] *Crowley Signal*, Oct. 13, 1900; Dec. 21, 1901; *Daily Signal*, Dec. 15, 1906
[42] Donations Book I, Acad. Par.; *Daily Signal*, May 30, 1902; Conveyance Book U-2, #36892, 369, Acad. Par.
[43] *Daily Signal*, May 20, 1905; Feb. 7, Dec. 15, 1906
[44] *Ibid*, Apr. 4, 1917; Feb. 21, 1918; interview, Lucille Hoyt Hoffpauir, 1977
[45] Conveyance Book J-2, #26862, 311, Acad. Par.; *Daily Signal*, Aug. 16, 1906; Mar. 30, 1912; *Crowley Signal*, June 13, 20, 1908

St. Margaret's Catholic Church of Estherwood, built in 1910, was named in honor of Mrs. Adricole LeBlanc, in whose home Mass was first celebrated in Estherwood. (Photo courtesy Margaret Fontenot)

Adricole LeBlanc. Plans to build a Catholic chapel were formulated in 1909, and the structure was in use by the spring of 1910. Prior to the construction of the chapel services had been held in the David Roy hall and on the upper floor of the Dupre LeBlanc saloon.[46]

The Estherwood chapel, a mission of St. John the Evangelist Church of Mermentau, was served by Rev. Bartholomew Fontaine, pastor of the Mermentau church 1908-1917. The land for the church was bought by the Diocese of New Orleans, represented by Father Fontaine, from Ovey Roy and Augustin Fruge for a consideration of $250 on December 14, 1909.[47]

In 1900 Estherwood children attended classes in a new school house, erected on the south side of the railroad on land purchased from the Hoyt brothers. Funds for the new building, 20 by 40 feet, had been appropriated during the summer of that year. The new teacher, who replaced Miss Bertha Pratt, was Miss Stella Blackburn.[48]

Some of the early teachers were Nathaniel D. Stephenson, Fannie B.

---

[46] Diocese of Lafayette archives; *Daily Signal*, Oct. 22, 1909; *Crowley Signal*, Feb. 4, 1910

[47] Conveyance Book 0-2, #32890, 635, Acad. Par.

[48] *Crowley Signal*, Sept. 16, 1899; Aug. 11, Sept. 29, 1900

Two-room school, built in 1900. After the new brick school was constructed in 1910, this building was moved to another location to serve as a school house for black children. Some years later it was moved again—to a location midway between Estherwood and Midland. (Reproduced from Edward T. Hoyt photo, circa 1900)

Porter, Eula L. Bean, Fannie Bean, Lola Pritchard, Mr. and Mrs. W. P. Arnette, Inez Dalton and Genevieve Smith.[49]

Members of Estherwood's board of school trustees were Henry Feitel, T. C. Tinker and P. B. Lewis.[50]

A fine brick school building went up in 1908, at a cost of $7,000. The plans, drawn by R. A. Nockton, called for six classrooms and a large hallway. The location was a block of ground in the center of town, donated by A. Kaplan and J. Kollitz.[51]

Six members of the senior class of 1918 were the first graduates of Estherwood High School. They were Winnie, Lucille and Myrtle Hoffpauir, Smith Hoffpauir, Laurie Barnett and Ellis Istre. Smith Hoffpauir was class valedictorian.[52]

First classes for black children of Estherwood were conducted in the Negro Baptist Church during the summer of 1906. In response to a petition the school board appropriated $60 for the operation of school. Mrs. H. C. Ross applied for the summer teaching job.[53]

---

[49] *Crowley Signal*, Sept. 14, 1901; Apr. 18, Oct. 10, 1903; Dec. 14, 1907; *Daily Signal*, Sept. 3, 1902
[50] *Crowley Signal*, Apr. 18, 1903
[51] *Ibid*, Jan. 4, 1908; Dec. 14, 1908
[52] *Daily Signal*, May 23, 31, 1918
[53] *Ibid*, Apr. 9, 1906

Mary Rhodes Hoyt, wife of Edward T. Hoyt, was one of the early music teachers of Acadia Parish. She taught music in Estherwood and Morse for about 20 years. (Reproduced from Edward T. Hoyt photo, circa 1900)

In 1911 the board gave the old south elementary school house to the black people. The building was moved to another location and was known as North Estherwood School.[54]

A few years later, in 1916, the school was re-located about midway between Estherwood and Midland to accommodate children from both communities.[55]

The Hoyts

Estherwood's most prominent pioneers were the Hoyts, who settled in Acadia Parish in 1886. The father, D. W. Hoyt, brought his family down from Pennsylvania and located on a farm two miles west of Estherwood. D. W. Hoyt was the first superintendent of schools for Acadia Parish.

Hoyt's three sons, Edward T., William M., and John P., were leaders in the religious, civic, business and political life of the village and parish.[56]

---

[54] *Ibid*, June 2, 1911
[55] *Ibid*, Nov. 9, 1916
[56] *Crowley Signal*, Dec. 21, 1901; May 16, 1903

Doctors

Estherwood's first resident physician was Dr. R. L. Trezevant who started medical practice in the village in 1900. The doctor was also a registered pharmacist and carried a line of drugs at his office on Main street. After three years in Estherwood the doctor and his family moved to Morgan City; two years later they returned to Estherwood.[57]

A Dr. Lewis was practicing in the Estherwood vicinity in 1902. An item in the Crowley newspaper revealed: "Dr. Lewis of Estherwood was on horseback answering a call when the animal lost its footing and fell on the doctor's leg, breaking it above the ankle." Some months later, shortly after Dr. Trezevant left for Morgan City, it was announced that Dr. J. W. Nolan of Louisville, Ky., and Dr. Lewis, at the time taking a surgical course in Louisville, planned to open an office and drug store in the Kollitz Hotel building. There were no further references to the medical partnership, but evidently Dr. Nolan did practice for a time in Estherwood: six months after the announcement of his plans he spoke on "The Medical Profession" at a parish convention of Women's Christian Temperance Union held in Estherwood.[58]

In 1904, about a year before Dr. Trezevant returned to Estherwood, Dr. W. T. Ellison fitted up an office in the Estherwood Hotel, and a new druggist, L. S. Shirley of Glasgow, Ky., opened a drug store in the Kollitz building.[59]

Dr. Z. J. Francez, Acadia coroner for many years, began practice in the parish at Estherwood in 1909. Both Dr. Trezevant and Dr. Francez were active in civic affairs of the village. Dr. Trezevant served as village treasurer during the early years and Dr. Francez was chairman of the board of health, serving with Walter H. Fleshman and Ellis Hoffpauir.[60]

The first dentist to locate in Estherwood was Dr. F. F. Lewis of New Orleans who came in 1914. He shared an office with Dr. Francez.[61]

Fires

Only two major fires took place in Estherwood between 1910 and 1920. On the night of October 13, 1910 fire started in the Istre Brothers and Faulk store, spread to the Kollitz residence and Dupre LeBlanc store. The loss was estimated at $10,000. The villagers fought the flames and managed to save the Kollitz store.[62]

---

[57] *Crowley Signal*, March 17, 1900; May 9, 1903; *Daily Signal*, Aug. 30, 1905

[58] *Daily Signal*, Nov. 18, 1902; *Crowley Signal*, June 20, Dec. 5, 1903

[59] *Daily Signal*, May 14, 1904

[60] *Crowley Signal*, Mar. 19, 1910; *Daily Signal*, Jan. 19, 1903; Oct. 30, 1909; June 6, 1912

[61] *Daily Signal*, Aug. 3, 1914

[62] *Crowley Signal*, Oct. 15, 1910

Three buildings went up in flames in the fall of 1914. Destroyed were the E. P. Meyers livery barn, the Boutte restaurant and Dr. Z. J. Francez' drug store. The nearby Hoffpauir Mercantile store was saved.[63]

Dance Halls

For at least two decades dance halls played an important part in the social and political life of Estherwood. Fun-loving Acadians from miles around came to town to attend the regular *fais-do-dos* (colloquial term for Acadian dances, the term believed to be a corruption of *fete de Dieu*, or religious festival), wedding dances and Mardi Gras balls. The dance halls also provided places for political rallies and public entertainments.

The first such place was operated by F. L. Feray, beginning in 1900. The Feray hall was the setting for the annual Mardi Gras celebration, and was also used extensively for wedding dances, called *bal de noce* by the Acadians who originated the custom. The first reported wedding dance was given April 20, 1904 for Placide Landry and Sidonia Miers, who were wed earlier that day.[64]

A second dance hall went into operation in 1901. The proprietor was Dupre LeBlanc, who operated a barroom and restaurant on the ground floor of his two-story building, and ''an opera house and ballroom'' on the second floor.[65]

In later years the David Roy dance hall was the scene for Mardi Gras and wedding celebrations as well as political gatherings. On Mardi Gras day of 1911 more than 600 people took part in the annual merriment. Most of the revelers wore carnival costumes and masks, and all ended up at the dance in Roy's hall that night.[66]

Organizations

The earliest known organization in Estherwood was the Circle Seven of Progressive Women of America, which was active in 1900. The club held two meetings a month, one business and one social. The club roster listed Mesdames J. Kollitz, N. E. Cowen, A. Sigur, B. E. Kollitz, J. P. Hoyt; Misses Hattie Feitel and M. Feitel.[67]

Estherwood Lodge No. 123, Independent Order of Odd Fellows, with 24 members, was formed in 1907. Officers were Sam Michael, P. B.

---

[63] *Daily Signal*, Oct. 29, 1914
[64] *Crowley Signal*, Jan. 27, 1900; Sept. 19, 1903; Feb. 6, 1904; *Daily Signal*, Apr. 23, 1904
[65] *Crowley Signal*, June 15, Dec. 21, 1901
[66] *Daily Signal*, Mar. 2, 1911
[67] *Crowley Signal*, June 30, 1900

Lewis, J. O. Fremaux, R. Trezevant, Henry Feitel, J. Kollitz, Ellis Hoffpauir, Frank Giozza, E. G. Baumgarten, Ovey Roy, H. C. Mourain, W. F. Lyons, H. H. Powell, J. W. Gill and P. E. Coles.[68]

Woodmen of the World, Fig Lodge of Estherwood, was organized in 1911 by A. M. Hargroder of Church Point. James A. Leighton was first council commander.[69]

The WOW sponsored debates on timely topics. The subject of one such debate was "Resolved: That a Traction Engine Is Better to Farm Rice Than a Mule Team." P. B. Lewis and O. Roy were on the affirmative side, while J. O. Faulk and J. L. Myers debated for the negative, which was judged the winner.[70]

Horse Racing

Horse racing in Estherwood was an attraction in 1911. On July 4 of that year some 500 people gathered at the race track at the north end of town for a picnic, races and riding wild horses. The races were held the following July 4th and attracted a large crowd.[71]

Parades, Dances

By 1913 Estherwood had become the center of Mardi Gras fun and frolic in Acadia Parish. Old and young for 20 miles around came to town to view a parade with music, floats and maskers. The parade went up Main street to Canal, then down on LeBlanc and Second streets. Leading the procession, on horseback and carrying a big flag was the Mardi Gras King, Felix Guillory, and his wife, the Queen. That night for the dance the Roy hall was decorated with bunting and evergreens.[72]

One of the couples who continued the wedding dance tradition at David Roy's hall were Pauline Broussard and Dominic Leleux, who were married at the Estherwood Catholic Church on June 17, 1914.[73]

Newspapers

Two newspapers were published for Estherwood between 1900 and 1905. The first was the *Estherwood Enterprise* and was published by

---

[68] *Ibid*, May 4, 1907
[69] *Daily Signal*, Apr. 4, 1911
[70] *Ibid*, Apr. 10, 1913
[71] *Ibid*, July 8, 1911; July 6, 1912
[72] *Ibid*, Feb. 6, 1913
[73] *Ibid*, June 18, 1914

G. H. Poor.[74] It is not known how long the newspaper remained in existence.

The *Estherwood Call*, edited and published by S. G. Watkins, was first published in early June of 1902. T. C. Tinker edited the paper in 1903 and John P. Hoyt took over some time during 1904.[75] Information on the length of time the newspaper remained in publication is not available.

Vignettes

Many of the Estherwood news items carried in the Crowley newspaper, while of relatively minor importance to an historical work, are nonetheless interesting, and help to fill in the picture of the community's past. Following is a selected few of these vignettes of life in the village between 1900 and 1920:

In the spring of 1900 a large number of Mexican laborers were brought to Estherwood by the Southern Pacific railroad and put to work repairing the tracks. The Mexicans also constructed the siding for the rice mill and built a depot. Several references to the aliens were made in the Estherwood news column during the three months the crew worked there: "The Mexicans are still hammering away at the railroad track . . . there are more than 100 here . . . they make the air fairly resonant at night. These people are the noisest of noisy people, but seem to be good natured with their noise."[76]

The work stint in Estherwood was not altogether happy for the Mexicans. One newspaper report read: "One of the Mexican gang was killed by the train last Saturday night and was buried Sunday by the side of the railroad track where they were stationed at the time."[77]

A well-known area farmer was killed by lightning during the summer of 1900. Adam Istre, riding horseback over a coulee bridge, was knocked off his horse and into the water by the lightning. The accident happened about two and a half miles south of Estherwood. The lightning burned and charred the victim's right side and ripped his clothing into shreds.[78]

A new industry was planned for Estherwood in 1906, but there is no information on the outcome of the plan. A frog farm was started by C. LeBlanc, who had spent $2,000 in eight months constructing and stocking his frog pond. Three acres were fenced off with palings about four feet high, and inside were placed 5,000 frogs which had access to a

[74] *Crowley Signal*, Apr. 13, 1901
[75] *Daily Signal*, June 16, 1902; Mar. 7, July 25, 1904; *Crowley Signal*, Apr. 25, 1903
[76] *Crowley Signal*, Mar. 31, Apr. 14, May 5, 1900
[77] *Ibid*, Apr. 14, 1900
[78] *Ibid*, Aug. 11, 1900

lake 500 feet long and 60 feet wide. LeBlanc planned to divide the enclosure for frogs of various sizes.[79]

A free ferry over Bayou Plaquemine Brulee, established in 1914, gave Estherwood residents access to Prairie Hayes and the oil field. Philoze Myers was the ferryman.[80]

A newsworthy note of 1915 was Ben Barnett's new sugar mill, which had turned out "a fine lot of sorghum syrup." Two years earlier W. M. Hoyt had put up a new process sugar mill to make syrup and brown sugar for himself and his neighbors. The sugar mill was on the Hoyt Ranch, two miles northwest of Estherwood.[81]

An Estherwood inventor achieved a measure of success in 1915 when the cistern he had invented was judged the best in the country. James A. Leighton took the gold medal at the Panama-Pacific Exposition at San Francisco for his patented sanitary cistern. Leighton also was awarded a bronze medal for his patented open-eye sewing needle.[82]

Salt water in the bayou was credited with bringing an unusual type of fish to the Estherwood area in 1902. At the nearby Union relift pumping operation a number of spoonbill catfish (paddlefish) were seen. One of the fish, usually found in the Mississippi and its tributaries, was brought to the *Signal* office; the fish measured four feet from bill to tail.[83]

In 1903 a farmer lost a pocketbook containing a sizable sum of money. The pocketbook, containing $366, was found on the public road by Jesse Miers. Miers turned his find over to Mayor Henry Feitel, who opened the purse and discovered that it belonged to Cyprien Guidry. Guidry was delighted to get his property back.[84]

Not all persons were as honest as Jesse Miers. That same year safe crackers broke into a 3,000 pound safe in the Hoyt company office and made off with $30,000 in cash, crop liens and notes. A previous attempt to open the safe at the Jean Castex store in Mermentau led authorities to believe that expert burglars were operating in the parish.[85]

The Rufus Miers family made the news in 1904. During a severe storm lightning struck the Miers home and severely shocked the inmates.

---

[79] *Daily Signal*, Feb. 8, 1906
[80] *Ibid*, July 11, 1914
[81] *Ibid*, Sept. 13, 1915; Nov. 28, 1913
[82] *Ibid*, June 24, 1915
[83] *Ibid*, July 26, 1902
[84] *Crowley Signal*, Apr. 25, 1903
[85] *Ibid*, July 25, 1903

The Hoyt sawmill, located on Bayou Plaquemine Brulee near Estherwood about 1895. The mill processed the lumber for the Hoyt Brothers lumber business in Estherwood. (Reproduced from Edward T. Hoyt photo)

The bolt came down the stove pipe, passed through the floor knocking the stove leg off and split the foundation block under the house. Mr. and Mrs. Miers, sitting near the stove, were badly shocked. Mrs. Miers was knocked senseless for about 10 minutes.[86]

"Hello, My Creole Belle, Hello," was the title of a new song, published in 1909 by the Wizard Music Co. of Estherwood. The sheet music was for sale at Eckels' Pharmacy in Crowley.[87]

An Estherwood resident set a record for longevity in the parish, perhaps in the state, in 1919. *Grandmere* Alepou Breaux was 107 years old when she died. The former Anderine Clements, she was born May 8, 1812 and died Nov. 12, 1919. The mother of 15, she had more than 100 grandchildren and had been married four times. In substantiation of *Grandmere* Breaux's claim to this great age is the baptismal records of the Catholic church at Grand Coteau (est. 1819) which show an Alexandrine Clement, daughter of Louis Clement and Marianne Stelly, baptized May 26, 1825.[88] (At that time many children were not baptized until they were well up in age because of the distances and difficulties of traveling to a church).

---

[86] *Daily Signal*, Apr. 28, 1904
[87] *Ibid*, June 29, 1909
[88] *Ibid*, Nov. 20, 1919; Hebert, Rev. Donald J., *Southwest Louisiana Records, Vol. 2*, 199.

Midland

Midland first appeared on an Acadia Parish map as Midland Junction. This was when the railroad branch line was constructed from Midland to Eunice, the St. Landry Parish town founded by C. C. Duson in 1894. The place name is derived from the location: Midland is exactly midway between New Orleans and Houston on the Southern Pacific's east-west railway.[1]

Prior to 1900 Midland consisted of three warehouses and one house, all on the north side of the railroad track.[2]

The railroad line was extended from Midland south to Gueydan in 1896, then from Gueydan to Abbeville in 1902.[3] The completion of the line and announced plans by the Southern Pacific to locate a railroad roundhouse* at Midland led to an effort to develop Midland Junction into a town.

Charles H. Cowen was the developer. Had it not been for his untimely death his dream of town building had a strong potential; Midland was linked by railroad to growing communities in St. Landry and Vermil-

---

* A circular building for housing and repairing locomotives

[1] *Daily Signal*, Apr. 17, 1902
[2] "Louisiana Places," Baton Rouge *Morning Advocate*, Apr. 10, 1966
[3] *Crowley Signal*, Feb. 1, 1902; Dec. 24, 1904

The Midland, a three-story hotel built by C. H. Cowen in 1903. The hotel was later dismantled and the lumber used for a residence. (Photo courtesy Vera Cowen Buchanan)

ion Parishes, as well as to points east and west; the place was situated within a vast area of fine rice lands and within a few minutes of the parish seat by train.

Cowen, a native of Rockford, Ill., was born May 2, 1864. He married Helen Nellie Griffiths in 1887 and the following year came south, to Jennings, where he worked as a carpenter and a baker. In 1892 he bought 160 acres of land in Acadia Parish where Midland now stands and shortly thereafter added a 660-acre tract. He became one of the parish's most successful rice farmers. He was the chief incorporator of the Midland Development Company and president of the Midland Rice Milling Company, both chartered in 1902.[4]

An auction sale of town lots on Cowen land south of the railroad track took place April 22, 1902. A total of 156 lots were sold, at prices ranging from $50 to $200 for a total of $13,864.[5]

That summer Midland's first post office was established, a new train station and a section house were built. Other assets were a store, run by a man named Sarkes; a school and a church, the Callahan Lumber Company, a hotel and livery, owned and operated by Cowen.[6]

Cowen built a new three-story hotel, located on the corner of Morse and Ralph streets. The Midland Hotel was opened for business on September 15, 1903. The old hotel building was used as a residence by the Cowen family.

Shortly after the new hotel was opened Cowen lost a leg in a rice threshing accident. He developed septicemia and died October 29, 1903, a little more than a year after he had initiated the several major improvements for Midland. He was 39 years of age. In addition to his farming and business enterprises he was the Midland correspondent for the Crowley newspaper.[7]

Plans for the Midland roundhouse were abandoned; the railroad company found it expedient to locate the facility elsewhere. In 1908, five years after it was built, the Midland Hotel was dismantled and the material used to build a home for Ralph Cowen about a mile south of the town site.[8]

A newspaper, the *Midland Enterprise*, was published at Midland for a year or more. The first issue came out April 27, 1905. Miss Gertrude Callahan, a Washington, La., newspaperwoman, was editor. Later that year the editor married Kirtley Lynch and returned to Washington. The

---

[4] *Ibid*, July 11, Oct. 3, 1903
[5] *Daily Signal*, Apr. 17, 23, 1902
[6] *Crowley Signal*, Feb. 1, 1902; *Daily Signal*, June 21, Aug. 5, 1902; Jan. 19, Mar. 21, 1903
[7] *Crowley Signal*, Oct. 31, 1903
[8] Hilligarde, Nancy, "History of Midland," unpublished history paper; interview, Vera Cowen Buchanan

The Cowen family of Midland, Charles H. and Mrs. Cowen and three of their children, Rosslyn J., Ralph R. and Nellie Katherine. Another daughter, Dorothy, is Mrs. Clyde Heinsz. (Photo courtesy Vera Cowen Buchanan)

Midland newspaper was continued for some time thereafter; there is no information as to when publication was suspended.[9]

First postmaster at Midland was Eugene T. Callahan, appointed June 13, 1902. The post office was located in the Callahan store. Other postmasters were James W. Callahan and Minerva Burke McSherry. Mrs. McSherry was postmistress for 42 years.[10]

The first school at Midland was established in 1903 with May M. Goodell (Goodale) as teacher. Miss Goodell was also the teacher for the 1904-1905 session. By 1907 two teachers, May Holt, principal and June Shultz, conducted classes in a two-room school.[11]

Edmond Etienne had a store in Midland in 1907. The Callahans, whose main interest was lumber, also had a store and a nine room hotel. The Callahan brothers, Herbert, James, Abner and Eugene, owned 874 acres of timber land, cypress and tupelo gum, eight miles from Midland on Bayou Queue de Tortue. Their two sawmills, located on the tract of timberland, could turn out 25,000 feet of lumber a day, most of which was shipped out to other points. The Callahans employed seven men to oper-

[9] *Daily Signal*, Apr. 4, 21, 1905; Apr. 27, 1906; *Crowley Signal*, Nov. 25, Dec. 23, 1905

[10] Register of Postmasters, National Arch. and Rds. Service

[11] Louisiana Places," *Advocate*, Apr. 10, 1966; *Daily Signal*, May 16, 1904; Dec. 14, 1907

The Methodist Church of Midland, built in the early 1900s. The picture was taken by Edward T. Hoyt, whose hobby was photography. (Photo courtesy Lucille Hoyt Hoffpauir)

ate their planing mill and tank factory at Midland, where red cypress tanks, weather boarding, flooring, sash and door were made.[12]

Three farm families which were long associated with Midland area were those of Fremaux Istre, Frank Quebedeaux and Philip Lapleau. Istre and Quebedeaux were established on farms in the Midland vicinity before parish division. The Quebedeaux place, located on Bayou Plaquemine Brulee between Midland and Mermentau, was once noted for its orange orchard and pecan grove. Quebedeaux had 1,300 fine orange trees, and the largest pecan grove in the parish.[13]

Fremaux Istre, born circa 1847, was an influential Acadian who took an active interest in parish affairs. He married Euphemie Broussard; their two children, Emile Istre and Mrs. Adam LeBlanc, were also prominent residents of the Midland-Mermentau section.[14]

Philip Lapleau, naturalized as an American citizen in 1903, operated a rice farm and cattle ranch about two miles west of Midland. He was one of the first Acadia Parish farmers who successfully combined stock raising with rice cultivation. In the fall of 1916, in addition to the more than $50,000 realized from his rice crop, he cleared an extra $1,000 on the sale of steers raised at no extra cost on laid over rice fields.[15]

---

[12] *Daily Signal*, Feb. 15, 1906; Dec. 14, 1907
[13] *Crowley Signal*, Sept. 21, 1907
[14] *Daily Signal*, Jan. 14, 1911
[15] *Ibid*, Sept. 28, 1916

During World War I the O. R. Hopson farm near Midland was used as an emergency landing field for aeroplanes from Gerstner Field, Lake Charles. The landings of the training planes attracted many curious spectators to the scene.[16]

A Methodist church is believed to have been the first religious edifice put up at Midland. The church was built sometime in the early 1900s or before. There is no information on how long the church functioned, or where it was located.

A land transaction of 1914 reveals that there was a Baptist congregation at Midland. The New Morning Star Baptist Church of Midland, represented by Rev. Jarrus J. Wilson, pastor, Ed Lyons and Martin Norman, trustees, bought from Martin Norman Lot 6 in Block 9 for $25.[17]

---

[16] *Ibid*, Jan. 12, 1918
[17] Conveyance Book, S-2, #34638, 407, Acad. Par.

Morse

Morse came into existence because of rice and the railroad. The rice came first and created the need for a railroad—to facilitate the marketing of huge quantities of the grain grown in the southwest corner of Acadia.

The settlement began to build up after 1896, when the Southern Pacific branch line from Midland to Gueydan was completed. A post office, known as Lorna, was established April 30, 1898 with Mrs. M. Belle Gault as postmistress. Mrs Gault served as postmistress for 20 years, until 1918, when Anna K. Sargent was appointed. The first post office was located in "The Post Office Store," a grocery operated by Mrs. Gault's husband, William S. Gault. At the time the village consisted of the post office and grocery, a general store, Louis Jardell blacksmith shop, the railroad depot and a warehouse.[1]

The village was first known as Morse Station. It has been generally accepted that the railroad station was named for S. F. B. Morse, the general passenger agent for Southern Pacific at the time the Morse line was completed. There is, however, another version of how the place got its name. According to the *Crowley Signal* of October 19, 1907, the town was named for Robert Morse of Decatur, Ill., a former resident of the area who owned two farms at Morse and one at Iota; Morse built the second rice mill at Morse and was mill manager for a year. Despite this claim (which may have been made by Robert Morse as a joke) it appears unlikely that the railroad company would have singled out an individual, other than a company executive, for such an honor.

In response to a petition by Lorna post office patrons, the postmaster general agreed to change the name of the post office to Morse, to conform with the name of the railroad station. The change of name became effective July 1, 1900.[2]

Earliest settlers in the Morse community were the Mauboules brothers, Henry A. and Jules S., who homesteaded land in 1892, and became prosperous and well-known farmers. After the railroad came and Morse became a village the Mauboules were leaders in the civic and business affairs of the town.[3]

Available information concerning the beginnings of the village indicate that J. M. Crabtree was the father of the town. In the spring of 1899 Crabtree completed construction on a general merchandise store, known as Crabtree and Gibson store, had ground laid out in town lots and planned a sale of lots.[4]

---

[1] Register of Postmasters, National Archives and Records Service; *Crowley Signal*, Apr. 15, 1899

[2] *Ibid; Ibid*, Apr. 14, 1900

[3] *Crowley Signal*, 50th Anniv. Ed., 57

[4] *Ibid*, Apr. 1, 14, 1899

News briefs in 1900 refer to several other early business places at Morse. These include a reference to "Mr. Caldwell's store," a boarding house run by F. F. Feray, formerly of Estherwood, and the Kollitz warehouse.[5]

According to the *Crowley Signal*'s Golden Anniversary Edition, published in 1949, the first store in Morse was run by J. W. Callahan. The first reference to the Callahan firm found in old files of the *Signal* is in the business directory published Feb. 16, 1901, in which the company advertised lumber and general merchandise.

A two-story business building, 34 by 68 feet, was put up by C. F. Mathews and H. A. Mauboules in 1901. The building, located opposite the depot, housed general merchandise stock valued at $12,000. The firm also built a 50 by 84 foot warehouse.[6]

A news item of 1901 reveals that one of the new businesses in Morse was not welcome in some quarters. The Morse correspondent for the *Signal* wrote: "Sorry to learn that one of the newcomers here will open a saloon—a curse to any place. The building is being erected right in front of our school."[7]

The Mauboules store was re-chartered and expanded in 1902, under the firm name of Mauboules and Guidry. Main incorporators were Martin Guidry Jr., Jules S. and Henry A. Mauboules, dealers in groceries, general merchandise and rice. The company was capitalized at $25,000.[8]

Several other news items about businesses in Morse appeared in the Crowley paper in 1902. One such report read: "Mr. Heath of Crowley has opened a restaurant here, something Morse really needed." The firm of Matthews and Louden was identified as a lumber company.[9]

Morse acquired a hotel in the fall of 1902, built by Harry Wykoff. A little more than two years later Jules Mauboules bought the Wykoff Hotel.[10]

Three rice mills were built in Morse between 1900 and 1920: the White Swan, constructed in 1900; the Morse, 1902; the Liberty, 1918. Additional information on these mills will be found in the chapter on rice.

The growth of the little settlement was severely retarded by fire in the fall of 1902 when two rice warehouses, two lumber yards and two other buildings were destroyed, causing a loss of $15,000, a large amount for the times. Buildings burned were warehouses belonging to Matthews and Mauboules and the Ferre Canal Company; the Callahan lumber yard and the Matthews and Louden lumber yard, a boarding house and store owned by J. H. Callahan.[11]

[5] *Ibid*, Sept. 15, Oct. 13, 1900
[6] *Ibid*, Nov. 16, 1901
[7] *Ibid*, Jan. 19, 1901
[8] *Daily Signal*, June 9, 1902
[9] *Ibid*, Aug. 7, 1902
[10] *Ibid*, Oct. 2, 1902; Mar. 9, 1905
[11] *Ibid*, Oct. 8, 1902

A business directory for the parish, published in the *Crowley Signal* in 1903, listed four advertisements from Morse: the Morse Barber Shop, Adam Albarado; W. S. Gault, general merchandise; Fred Dehm, blacksmith and wood working; Guidry & Mauboules. Another 1903 reference gives the name of Morse's one barroom: the Istre & Leleux Saloon.[12]

Jules Mauboules, Morse's pioneer homesteader, took an early lead in the use of modern improvements. In 1905 he installed an acetylene gas plant for lighting his store and residence.[13]

Business places known to have been operating in Morse in 1907 include the Mauboules store; Mrs. Zamie Kershaw, general merchandise and millinery; Joseph Hanks, general merchandise; Moise Herpin, barber; Alcee Henry, grist mill and feed store.[14]

For some 12 years—from 1907 to 1920—there was only one reference to the business life of Morse in the Crowley paper. This was the publication, in 1919, of the charter of a new and substantial firm, the Morse Hardware and Grocery. Principal stockholders were Alex Brown, J. N. Dubus, Angeles and Marshall Chiasson and I. P. Saal.[15]

There was a dance hall in Morse in 1903. In the fall of that year the *Signal* carried the news of the marriage of Louis Simon and Eliza Miller on September 8, which was "celebrated at a wedding dance at Richard's hall." In 1910 wedding dances were held at Weekly's hall.[16]

Churches, Schools

There was a Catholic church in Morse as early as 1901. The Morse church was a mission of St. Michael's of Crowley, as was the Mermentau church, there being no resident pastor in Mermentau at the time. Father Van Alfen, pastor of the Crowley church, traveled to the two villages by train to celebrate Mass and minister to the spiritual needs of the people.[17]

In 1908 the Diocese of New Orleans, represented by Rev. F. L. Gassler, purchased 10 lots (one-half of Block 3) in the village of Morse. The land was sold to the church by Joseph Francois for $200. The church building was moved two blocks north from its original location onto the newly acquired property and was painted and improved.[18] The Morse church became a mission of Mermentau after Father Fontaine was appointed resident pastor at Mermentau. According to a 1917 map preserved in the records of the Mermentau church, the church at Morse was

[12] *Crowley Signal*, Mar. 21, Dec. 19, 1903
[13] *Ibid*, Dec. 2, 1905
[14] *Ibid*, Dec. 14, 1907
[15] *Daily Signal*, June 19, 1919
[16] *Crowley Signal*, Sept. 12, 1903; Dec. 24, 1910
[17] *Ibid*, July 20, 1901
[18] Conveyance Book 0-2, #31487, 156, Acad. Par.; *Daily Signal*, Mar. 1, 1909

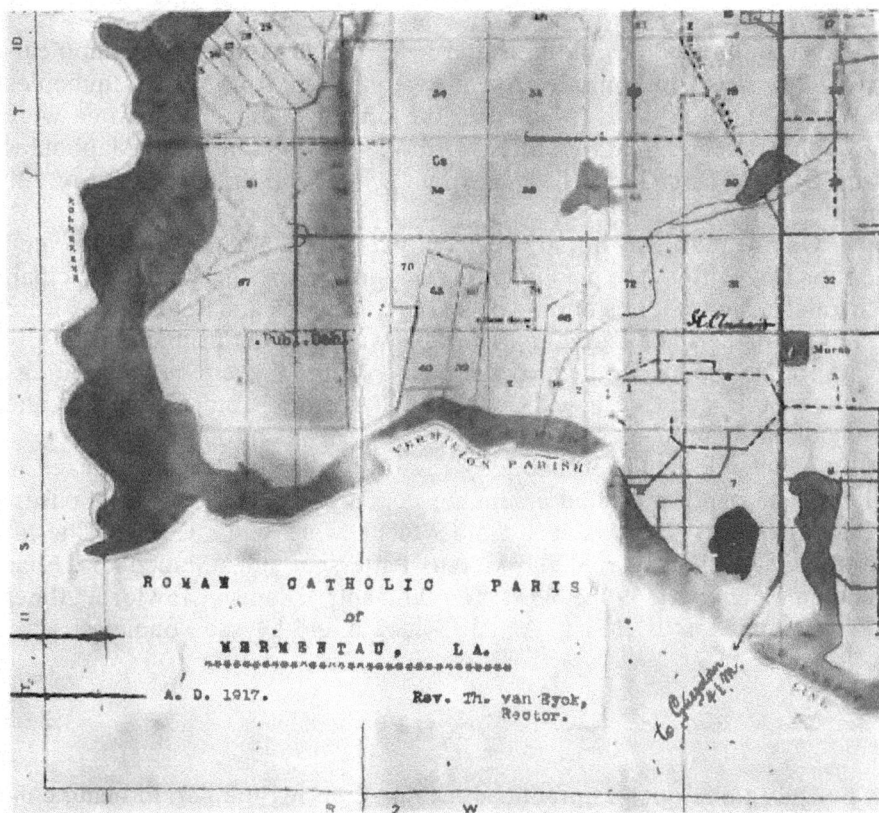

Portion of a 1917 map of the Catholic parish of Mermentau which shows the mission chapel of St. Andrew at Morse. The map also designates the location of two rural schools of the Mermentau-Morse area. (Map courtesy Rev. John Engbers)

named St. Andrew's. The name was later changed to the Church of the Immaculate Conception.

First school teacher for Morse's public school was Mrs. Stella Glass, employed by the Acadia Parish School Board for the 1900-1901 session. She was succeeded by Hattie B. Reilly (1901-1902) and Etta Mulligan (1902-1903).[19]

A new school house was built early in 1902, and the following year the enrollment justified the employment of two teachers, Josie Smith and Clara Jones.[20]

Disaster struck the Morse school a double blow during the 1905-1906 school year. The school building was burned down twice that session. Morse residents rallied to the cause of education: a tax election was called for the Morse school district, to levy a three-mill tax for five years. With the active support of Joseph Francois, school board member; Alcee

---

[19] *Crowley Signal*, Sept. 8, 1900; Sept. 14, 1901; *Daily Signal*, Sept. 3, 1902
[20] *Crowley Signal*, Jan. 11, 1902; Oct. 10, 1903

Henry, the Mauboules brothers and J. M. Crabtree, the tax election carried 32 to 7. Ten lots on Jules Avenue were bought from H. A. Mauboules for the school grounds. Named to the school building committee were Joseph Francois, J. M. Crabtree, Dr. W. T. Patterson, Jules Mauboules and Charles Dommert. The four-room school had an enrollment of 120 pupils in 1907.[21]

On a January day in 1909 the faculty, students and parents celebrated Arbor Day with a tree planting program initiated by the school principal, Samuel Arnette. Rows of oak, china berry, catalpa and poplar trees were planted on the school grounds. The oaks were brought from the woods by Charles Dommert. Mothers of the pupils planted flowers on the grounds. A new style gate, designed to prevent live stock from getting into the school yard and damaging the new plantings, was put up.[22]

A juvenile band, probably a school organization, was organized in 1908. The band presented a summer concert in one of the warehouses. Band members, 14 boys aged from 9 to 13, were Willie Holder, Chester and Harry Dehm, Harold and Marcus Patterson, Jules Mauboules, Elias and Adam Hebert, Willie West, Gerald Gault, Thomas Crawford, Abner Broussard, Marcus Henry, Amedis Richard and Ulysse Sonnier.[23]

Doctors

Only three doctors practiced in Morse during the period being considered. The first was Dr. Walter F. Carstens of New Iberia who located in Morse in 1901.[24]

Dr. Carstens practiced in Morse for almost five years then sold his practice to Dr. W. T. Patterson, who became a leader in the business and civic affairs of the village.[25]

Dr. G. G. Fontenot began a lifetime practice in Morse in 1909. A native of Ville Platte and Tulane graduate he came to Morse to practice in partnership with Dr. Patterson.[26]

The oldest landmark in Morse is the two-story Arthur Crawford home, built about 1900 by Charles Matthews, a Morse lumber man. Rooms on the second floor were rented to school teachers and rice mill employees. Two of the parish's best known rice men, J. J. Cassidy and Wallace Elberson, roomed with the Crawfords.[27]

---

[21] *Daily Signal,* Apr. 28, May 1, 25, June 1, 1906; Dec. 14, 1907
[22] *Ibid,* Jan. 26, 1909
[23] *Crowley Signal,* June 13, 1908
[24] *Ibid,* June 29, 1901
[25] *Daily Signal,* Feb. 21, 1905
[26] *Ibid,* May 27, 1909
[27] Interview, Mrs. Moise Chiasson, 1978

Municipal Officers

Morse achieved the status of a village March 27, 1906 when Governor N. C. Blanchard signed the incorporation proclamation. Appointed as first officials were Alcee Henry, mayor; Dr. W. T. Patterson, Jules Mauboules and J. M. Crabtree, aldermen. Ozeme Hebert was commissioned May 5, 1906 as the first town marshal. He was replaced two months later by Joseph E. Meaux. Dr. Patterson was the first town clerk and Jules Mauboules the first treasurer.[28]

The inauguration of the first municipal administration was properly celebrated in the new village. Judge P. S. Pugh of Crowley administered the oaths of office, Gus Fontenot, clerk of court, made a speech in French. About 100 persons attended the ceremonies and banquet held in the White Swan mill warehouse. The warehouse was decorated with flags and patriotic bunting, and the program included music, speeches and picture-taking.[29]

Initial actions taken by the mayor and council included extending the corporation limits of the village; building a small jail; adopting ordinances which made it unlawful to gamble, be drunk or disorderly, or use vulgar or obscene language. An ordinance also laid out guidelines for the town marshal.[30]

Only three mayors served Morse during the period under study (1900-1920): Alcee Henry, J. M. Crabtree and Arthur Crawford. Crabtree went in as mayor in 1908. Serving with him were J. S. Mauboules, Joseph Hanks and Arthur Crawford, aldermen, and J. E. Meaux, marshal. When Hanks moved away in 1909 Fred Dehm was appointed to replace him on the council. Dr. Patterson resigned as town clerk in 1909 and A. LeBlanc replaced him.[31]

The same officials were returned to office in the 1910 election with the exception of Fred Dehm who was replaced by Charles Dommert.[32]

Arthur Crawford began his first term as mayor in 1912. On the alderman board were Mauboules, Dehm and Dommert. Eraste Hebert was the new marshal.[33]

There is no record of a municipal election being held in Morse in 1914. The names of the same officers appear in the minutes from the time of the 1912 election to the election of 1916.

At a special meeting held June 1, 1914 the council voted to pay the mayor a salary of $5 a month. The town's first board of health, appointed

---

[28] Louisiana Department of State; Morse Town Council Minutes, May 1, 1906
[29] *Daily Signal*, May 16, 1906
[30] Minutes, May 21, 1906
[31] *Ibid*, June 13, 1908; Mar. 4, Sept., 1909; La. Dept. State
[32] Minutes, June 3, 1910; La. Dept. State
[33] Minutes, June 4, 1912; La. Dept. State

at a meeting on January 13, 1915, was composed of Dr. G. G. Fontenot, Alex Brown, J. M. Crabtree and J. M. Chiasson.

Crawford was re-elected mayor in 1916, 1918 and 1920, as was Jules Mauboules, who continued to serve as town treasurer. Newcomers to the council during the 1918-1920 period were Felix Istre and Andrew Henry, Jr., Cleopha Thibodeaux, first elected marshal in 1916, was re-elected in 1918. Joseph Bonvillain was elected marshal in 1920.[34]

Elections in Morse were evidently quiet affairs. As was the case in many small communities, candidates were probably selected by acclamation at Democratic mass meetings and went into office without opposition, thereby making the general election little more than a legal formality. During the first 14 years of Morse's history as a municipality only one election report appeared in the Crowley newspaper. This was the election returns of 1918, when Arthur Crawford won over Alcee Henry 24 to 8, and Cleopha Thibodeaux won re-election by 15 votes over Eric (*sic*) Hebert.[35]

---

[34] Minutes, La. Dept. State
[35] *Daily Signal*, Apr. 18, 1918

Mermentau

Mermentau is the only town on Acadia's only river. The name of the town, derived from the river, is a corruption of Nemento, the name of an Attakapas Indian chief, who with the other Indians of the tribe, lived in a village on the west side of the river about 1776.[1]

Only four of the Spanish land grants situated on the Mermentau River were taken up, according to the official survey plat of Township 10 South Range 3 West. The claimants were Andre Martin, Augustin and Alexandre Nezat, and Joseph Chevalier Piernass, a retired Spanish military officer. Piernass' land grant, located mostly on the west side of the Mermentau, barely extended across the river to take in the confluence of the river and Bayou Queue de Tortue. Martin and the Nezats owned land on both sides of the stream about two and a half miles up river from the Piernass claim.

There is no evidence that any of these people ever lived on their Spanish grant land in Acadia. Martin was one of the first settlers at Vermilionville (Lafayette) and the Nezat brothers came from Pointe Coupee. There are published references to *vacheries* (cattle ranches) being operated by Martin and the Nezats, and it is believed they used their "river bank strips" of land for raising the long horn cattle which once ranged over the southwest Louisiana prairies.[2]

The first person known to have settled on the Acadia Parish side of the river was John Webb, an English sea captain, who in 1827 settled in the cove formed by the river and Bayou Queue de Tortue. The place was known as Tasso Cove, also as Webb's Cove.[3]

Before the Civil War the isolated and sparsely settled river country became a sanctuary for outlaws and slave smugglers. After the war broke out bands of Jayhawkers established camps on the river and from there made forays into the settled areas, robbing and pillaging.[4] Tales and legends of pirates and buried treasure add to the aura of mystery that distinguishes Mermentau's past history.

One merchant established a business on the river before the Civil War. This was Jean Castex, a native of France, who opened a general merchandise store in 1859. Another enterprising Frenchman, Victorin Maignaud of Bordeaux, started out as a peddler in 1866. Maignaud operated the river ferry for 40 years, was postmaster 17 years, owned a store, a hotel, a sawmill and a rice mill.[5]

---

[1] *American State Papers, Public Lands, Vol. III*, 111

[2] Griffin, Harry, *Attakapas Country*, A History of Lafayette Parish, La., 16; Fontenot and Freeland, *Acadia, etc.* 64

[3] *Crowley Signal*, Aug. 25, 1888

[4] *Ibid*; Opelousas *Daily World*, Bicentennial supplement, Vol. III, 36

[5] Fontenot and Freeland, *Acadia*, 166; *Crowley Signal*, Jan. 8, 1910

The Jean Castex store, built by Mermentau's pioneer merchant. The building was located on a corner near the Castex residence on Highway 90. (Photo courtesy A. C. Boudreaux)

The United States government located a post office at Mermentau September 2, 1859. Postmasters (to 1920) were William Cottrell, Helaire Desessarts, John O. Wright, Jules Castel, John A. Rowell, Paul Castel, William Wallis, Jean Castex, Victorin Maignaud, Edward J. Perrault, John W. Cousins, Placide C. Pierce, Guillaume A. Maignaud, Albert S. Johnson, Elia J. Guidry.[6]

When Mermentau was incorporated in 1899 the village claimed 250 inhabitants. The needs of the people were served by 10 business firms: Meehan and Maignaud, general merchandise; Felix Simon, groceries and drugs; Joseph U. Miller, blacksmith and wheelwright; O. Ledeaux, meat market; A. Maignaud, saloon; J. P. Fruge, hotel and livery; Harrison and Case, grocers; the State Lumber Co. (organized in 1900 by Patterson, La., interests); Numa Laviolette, fresh meats, and the general store run by Mermentau's pioneer merchant, Jean Castex. In addition Felix Simon

---

[6] Register of Postmasters, National Archives and Records Service

312

The *Mermentau Messenger* was a six-column eight-page weekly in publication for about three years. The only content of local interest in the issue of Friday, September 12, 1902 was advertising inserted by area business firms. (Copy courtesy Rev. John Engbers)

was agent for New Royal sewing machines, and Joseph U. Miller bought hides.[7]

A transfer line, with "special attention to transferring baggage to and from trains and boats" was operated by J. W. Cousins; Alexandre Gaudet was proprietor of the River Restaurant, and Theodule Duhon was the village barber. William M. Youngblood advertised his services as a "collector of accounts," Adam Wright was a rough rice dealer, Gustave Fruge ran a men's clothing and grocery store.[8]

During this period (1900-1903) Mermentau had a newspaper, the *Mermentau Messenger*, which began publication in the spring of 1900. Publication, not always on a regular basis, was continued until January of 1903.[9]

Three Acadia Parish businessmen invested in a shingle mill at Mermentau in 1905. H. Eugene Lewis, W. E. Lawson of Crowley and John Taylor of Rayne bought the old sawmill on the west side of the river just north of the railroad bridge, and converted it into an up-to-date plant capable of putting out 100,000 shingles per day.[10]

Fires

Disastrous fires were few and far between in Mermentau's early history, or else were not noted in the newspapers. In 1894 Felix Simon's

---

[7] *Crowley Signal*, June 2, 1900; Feb. 16, Dec. 28, 1901
[8] *Ibid*, Mar. 21, July 11, Aug. 8, 1903
[9] *Daily Signal*, July 14, 1902; Jan. 15, 1903
[10] *Ibid*, May 18, 1905

store was destroyed by fire causing a loss of $7,000, a large amount for the times. Simon, a self-made man, had been a clerk for Dupuis and Fremaux store, then went into business for himself on an original investment of $700. Notwithstanding his fire loss was not covered by insurance, he rebuilt his store in 1895 and became one of the parish's leading business men.[11]

Damage amounting to $4,000 was caused by fire in 1915 when A. Romero's dance hall and J. P. Fruge's livery were burned. By that time the village had acquired a chemical engine which enabled the fire company to contain the flames and prevent a conflagration which could have destroyed the entire town.[12]

Municipal Affairs

Mermentau was incorporated as a village in November of 1899. First officials, appointed by the governor on November 14, 1899, were William J. Meehan, mayor; Gustave Fruge, marshal; Felix Simon, John Hoffman and Sidney J. Bouchard, aldermen.[13]

Council meetings were first held in the Southern Pacific depot. Beginning in March, 1903, official business was transacted in a building rented from J. P. Fruge for $21 a year. Council meetings were held in the rented building until 1914, when the contract to build a town hall was awarded to Callahan Lumber Company on a low bid of $346.[14]

Actions taken by the newly appointed village officials included drafting ordinances for the safety, health, morality and general well-being of the residents of Mermentau. These included ordinances prohibiting drunkenness, vulgar language, exposure of person, use of firearms, concealed weapons, fast riding or driving, hogs at large, fighting, cruelty to animals, vagrancy, damage to property, gambling and conducting a disorderly house.[15]

The town marshal was the only salaried official, receiving $20 a month for his services. E. D. Conner was appointed first town clerk and Duplicie Simon the first treasurer. First town attorney was J. G. Medlenka of Crowley.[16]

Mayor Meehan was returned to office by the will of the people at the regular election of 1900. Also elected were Marshal Gustave Fruge, Aldermen Simon and Hoffman. Auguste Maignaud replaced Bouchard on

[11] *Ibid*, Feb. 12, 1903
[12] *Ibid*, Oct. 9, 1915
[13] Louisiana Department of State
[14] Minutes, Mermentau Town Council, Dec. 29, 1899; Mar. 14, 1903; Apr. 21, 1914; *Daily Signal*, Feb. 6, 1900
[15] Minutes, Mermentau Council, Dec. 29, 1899
[16] *Ibid*

Rosalie Castex and Euclide D. Conner on their wedding day in 1898. The bride was one of the twin daughters of Mr. and Mrs. Jean Castex Sr. (Photo courtesy Mrs. John Conner)

the council. Meehan did not complete his two-year term; he resigned in December of 1900.[17]

Thomas C. McCain, a river boat captain, was commissioned mayor to fill the unexpired term. He served for six years, being elected to the office in 1902 and re-elected in 1904 and 1906. Aldermen who served with him were W. H. Cary, Ulysse Duhon, H. M. Ledeaux, N. B. Fruge, A. S. Johnson, Fred Case, D. Maignaud, R. Harrington and P. C. Pierce. Marshals were William Youngblood, N. B. Fruge and A. S. Johnson.[18]

Mayor McCain's term of office took in a critical period in the history of the village and parish—the yellow fever epidemic of 1905, which claimed thousands of victims in New Orleans and other points in Louisiana. The mayor called special meetings of the council three times in 10 days to enact emergency legislation to deal with the crisis.

The council employed N. B. Fruge to assist Marshal Youngblood with guard duty. The marshal served as the day time guard and Fruge as night guard. They were ordered to meet all passenger and freight trains; persons without certificates of good health were not allowed off the train. The village quarantined against New Orleans and against Calcasieu Parish; Calcasieu had set up a detention camp on the west bank of the Mermentau.[19]

A thorough clean-up of the village was ordered. Residents were advised to burn all trash and garbage, to drain mud holes and ditches, to sprinkle lime in privy vaults, and to pour kerosene in all cisterns and water barrels to kill mosquito larvae.[20]

The quarantine was in effect some 60 days, from July 26 to October 3, 1905.[21] The measures taken were evidently effective; there were no reports of the dread disease in Mermentau.

Other actions taken during Mayor McCain's tenure include:

Setting up a village board of health, consisting of Dr. E. J. Perrault, Joseph U. Miller and W. F. Spurgeon.[22]

Ordering sidewalks constructed in the main part of town, from the Meehan and Maignaud store to the A. Maignaud corner, thence east to the Joseph U. Miller shop, the same to be built and kept up by the property owners. The ordinance was adopted at the meeting of May 7, 1901.

Adopting an ordinance prohibiting the storing of offensive or green hides within the corporation limits.[23]

Voting that the town should pay the rent on the school house. Three

---

[17] Louisiana Dept. State
[18] *Ibid*
[19] Minutes, Mermentau Council, July 26, 1905. At that time Calcasieu Parish extended east to the Mermentau River
[20] *Ibid*, Aug. 1, 1905
[21] *Ibid*, Oct. 3, 1905
[22] *Ibid*, Feb. 5, 1901
[23] *Ibid*, June 3, 1902

Jean Castex Sr.
(Photo courtesy Alice Conner Carlin)

years later the council called a tax election setting a five mill tax to run for two years to raise $589.42 to build and maintain a school house. The proposition was approved; 12 ballots and property valued at $8,715 were voted for the measure, and none against.[24]

Issuing a permit to U. Duhon to erect and maintain a race track on Mrs. Duhon's land, the races to be run any day in the week except Sunday. The town agreed to pay a special deputy to keep order at the races. A council ruling made it unlawful for boys under 16 to bet on the races.[25]

Naming a new board of health, with Dr. T. F. Jones chairman, A. S. Johnson and Jean Castex.[26]

A. C. Boudreaux became Mermentau's third mayor in December of 1906, when he was appointed to fill the vacancy created by the resignation of Captain McCain.[27]

Boudreaux, running for the mayor's office in 1908, was opposed by George W. Caldwell, but was victorious by a vote of 19 to 7. In the race for marshal Albert S. Johnson won over H. M. Ledeaux 15 to 11. Four candidates were in the race for the three council seats: J. P. Fruge, R. Harrington, P. C. Pierce and John Broussard. Broussard, with 11 votes, was edged out by the other three candidates.[28]

Marshal Johnson resigned in 1909 and David Fruge was appointed, only to be replaced two weeks later by Honore Sellers.[29]

During Mayor Boudreaux's term of office the town officials authorized the purchase of land for a cemetery. A three-acre tract in the southeast part of town was bought from Dr. Louis Espargelier and his son-in-law, P. Simon, at $40 per acre. A 24-foot square in the cemetery was reserved by the vendors. The move to buy land for a town cemetery was instigated by Dr. Morgan Smith, who was town clerk at the time.[30]

Announced candidates for office in the 1910 election were Captain Henry L. Sweet, another river boat man, and P. C. Pierce, for mayor; J. P. Fruge, R. Harrington, A. C. Boudreaux, John Broussard, Liodice Richard, Manuel Smith, for council; J. D. LeBlanc and Eddie Fruge, for marshal.[31] It is not known if all these candidates qualified and actually ran; state records show that the new slate of officers were Captain Sweet, mayor; Eddie Fruge, marshal; John Fruge, Broussard and Boudreaux, aldermen.

Captain Sweet resigned after six months in office, giving as his reason that he could not do justice to the office on account of being away

---

[24] *Ibid*, Dec. 10, 1902; Nov. 7, Dec. 12, 1905

[25] *Ibid*, Mar. 6, 1906

[26] *Ibid*, May 1, 1906

[27] La. Dept. State

[28] *Crowley Signal*, Apr. 25, 1908; La. Dept. State

[29] La. Dept. State

[30] Minutes, Aug. 3, 1909; Feb. 3, 1910; *Crowley Signal*, Feb. 12, 1910

[31] *Crowley Signal*, Feb. 12, Mar. 19, 1910

on the river so much of the time.[32] One of the ordinances enacted during his short term prohibited the sale of liquor to minors and women. It was also made unlawful for barrooms to serve liquor to white and black customers on the same premises; to have music or entertainment in barrooms, except in open air places, or to display vulgar and obscene pictures.[33]

R. Harrington became mayor by appointment in January of 1911, replacing Captain Sweet. A policy initiated during Mayor Harrington's first year in office was accepted as standard procedure by subsequent administrations. This was financial help provided by the town to keep the school open for a full nine months term.

The first such action came about in April of 1911 in response to a petition asking the council to appropriate $150 to run the school another month. Twenty two citizens signed the petition: A. C. Boudreaux, Mrs. D. Maignaud, Jean Castex Jr., A. L. Papillon, E. Smith, J. D. LeBlanc, A. S. Johnson, E. D. Fruge, J. P. Fruge, R. Harrington, John Broussard, Thomas Inman Jr., R. Wright, D. Richard, Mrs. V. Maignaud, Miss Augustine Maignaud, H. L. Sweet, James Inman, L. Richard, D. J. Fruge, George W. Caldwell and J. Duhon.[34]

Mayor Harrington had no opposition in the 1912 election, but six candidates announced for the council race, and two wanted the marshal's job. Candidates for the council were A. S. Johnson, A. C. Boudreaux, John Broussard, Honore Sellers, J. P. Fruge and Tom Inman Jr.; for marshal, Eddie Fruge, William Myers. Winners were Boudreaux, Broussard and J. P. Fruge for council, and Eddie Fruge, marshal. N. B. Fruge was appointed marshal in 1913, replacing Eddie Fruge.[35]

Interest in office holding picked up even more in the 1914 election. Again Harrington was unopposed for mayor, but five candidates were nominated for council seats, and six for marshal. Running for council were D. Simon, John Broussard, C. P. Guidry, E. D. Fruge and W. F. Stephenson; for marshal, L. Richard, Philosite Gary, Felix Istre, C. E. Istre, J. D. LeBlanc and N. B. Fruge.[36]

The winners were Broussard, Richard and Simon, for council, and C. E. Istre, marshal.[37]

Major actions taken during Mayor Harrington's five years in office included:

Approval of a motion to build an addition to the school house. George W. Caldwell, John Broussard and R. Harrington composed the

[32] *Daily Signal*, Jan. 13, 1911
[33] Minutes, Nov. 29, 1910
[34] *Ibid*, Apr. 4, 1911
[35] *Daily Signal*, Feb. 15, Apr. 23, 1912; La. Dept. State
[36] *Ibid*, Mar. 5, 1914
[37] La. Dept. State

The first steam-powered boat to navigate Bayou Plaquemine Brulee was this tug, which brought what appears to be a barge and a houseboat from Mermentau to Crowley on June 20, 1899. A dredge boat was working on the bayou at this time. (Photo by Edward T. Hoyt)

committee which drew the plan and advertised for bids. J. S. Hellrick's low bid of $485 was accepted.[38]

Construction of the town hall, and purchase of fire fighting equipment in 1914. The town paid $450 for the combination hook and ladder chemical truck. The purchase led to the formation of Mermentau's first fire company, with Mayor Harrington as first fire chief. The roster of Fire Company No. 1 listed 12 members.[39]

State records show that W. F. Stephenson and C. P. Guidry were appointed to the council in 1915, replacing John Broussard and L. Richard, resigned. A few months later John Broussard went back on the council, replacing Stephenson, resigned.

A new mayor, D. Simon, was elected in 1916. Other officials were E. D. Fruge, marshal; Sam Wright, John Broussard and D. LeBlanc, aldermen.[40]

Ranzie Harrington won his fourth term as mayor in 1918. Also elected were Marshal E. D. Fruge, Aldermen C. P. Guidry, O. Meyers and A. C. Boudreaux. Harrington and the incumbent councilmen were returned to office in 1920. Felix Istre was elected marshal.[41]

[38] Minutes, Aug. 6, 13, 1912
[39] *Ibid*, Apr. 21, June 17, 1914; *Daily Signal*, Sept. 4, 1914
[40] La. Dept. State
[41] *Ibid*

A school house for black children was provided by the town during the Harrington administration. The council appropriated $80 to be paid to Joe Thomas for a building for this purpose, to be located on lots belonging to the parish school board.[42]

The town council held regular meetings, with special meetings being called by the mayor as conditions dictated. The minutes of these meetings contain information relating to the business community, also reflect the attitudes of the times. For example:

The first saloon license issued by the council, in conformity with state legislation requiring an official permit to sell intoxicants, was issued to E. F. Myers and E. E. Pridgen in 1910. This apparently was the only saloon in the village, as no other licenses were issued that year. Two years later the Myers license was transferred to Sam Wright. Subsequent permits to operate saloons were granted to D. Maignaud, James Alicotte, Antoine Sarkes and Thomas John, Sam Wright, A. M. Zwan.[43]

A 1907 ordinance provided that only fire-proof flues, of brick or double galvanized iron, could be used in the village.[44]

Noteworthy abstracts from the minute books include the following:

Tax Collector Orthur Ledeaux reported in 1910 that a village resident, T. Moore, refused to pay his tax assessment on two horses, on the grounds that he never owned two horses. Two business firms, those of J. P. Fruge and Smith & LeBlanc, complained of the high price of town licenses, but agreed to pay after the matter was explained.[45]

Dr. T. F. Jones paid for his license to practice medicine, but claimed he carried only the drugs necessary to his practice therefore should not be required to pay for a retail drug license. The following month the marshal reported: "Went to Dr. Jones to collect his drug store license; he asked me to wait another week." Dr. Jones also asked for a six-month license to operate his cold drink stand, but was refused by the council.[46]

A 1915 ordinance prohibited black and white people from patronizing the same pool room, indicating that there was such an entertainment in Mermentau at the time.[47]

The town treasury was enriched as a result of another 1915 ordinance. The ruling prohibited sheep and goats from running loose in the village. As a result Marshal C. E. Istre picked up 43 sheep which were later sold at auction for $1.50 a head, bringing a total of $64.50. After expenses were deducted, $32.25 was turned over to the town.[48]

---

[42] Minutes, Jan. 7, 1919
[43] *Ibid*, Dec. 20, 1910; Apr. 12, 1912; Dec. 16, 1913; Sept. 21, 1916; Apr. 26, 1917; Dec. 23, 1918
[44] *Ibid*, Dec. 3, 1907
[45] *Ibid*, Mar. 1, 1910
[46] *Ibid*, May 3, June 7, 1910
[47] *Ibid*, Feb. 2, 1915
[48] *Ibid*, May 4, 1915

The mayor and council considered the installation of an electric light plant in 1919, but no action was taken on the measure.[49]

American intervention in World War I brought a display of patriotism to Mermentau. The council appropriated $20 for the purchase of an American flag. Writing the minutes of the meeting of May 1, 1917, the town clerk, A. Boyer, noted that the new flag "is now gloriously floating and proudly waving over the town of Mermentau."

Doctors

Dr. Louis Isadore Espargelier was Mermentau's pioneer physician. A native of France, he came to America in 1851 and practiced medicine until within a few years of his death, on April 8, 1917, at age 93.[50]

Dr. Espargelier was known familiarly in Mermentau as "Dr. Louis," demonstrating a long-standing custom of the Acadians, that of dropping the surname of a person (especially when the name was difficult to remember or pronounce) and using only the Christian name, usually with a title, as in the doctor's case. Specific instances of the use of the familiar appellation of Dr. Espargelier appear in the minutes of the Mermentau Town Council of February 3, 1910, when action was taken on the matter of buying land for a cemetery from "Dr. Louis." Also, in the newspaper account of the 1915 cyclone the doctor's name appears as "Dr. Lewis."[51]

Dr. E. J. Perrault came to Mermentau at an undetermined time prior to 1901. He was known to have been there in 1901 and 1903.[52]

Dr. Morgan Smith, a graduate of Vanderbilt University, practiced in the Midland-Morse-Mermentau area for several years, from 1906 to 1909. He served as Mermentau town clerk.[53]

Dr. L. J. Breaux located in Mermentau in November of 1910. He moved to Crowley in 1911.[54]

Churches and Schools

Mermentau's first house of worship, a Catholic church built in 1882, was destroyed by fire in 1886 in the first of a series of calamities which befell the Catholic congregation. A chapel, only large enough to accommodate the women and children, replaced the burned structure in 1891.[55]

---

[49] *Ibid*, July 1, 1919
[50] *Daily Signal*, Apr. 8, 1917
[51] *Ibid*, May 7, 1915
[52] *Crowley Signal*, May 23, 1903; Minutes, Feb. 5, 1901
[53] *Daily Signal*, May 22, 1906; Minutes, Aug. 3, 1909
[54] *Crowley Signal*, Nov. 26, 1910
[55] Booklet, St. John the Evangelist Church, 1977; Baudier, *The Catholic Church in Louisiana*, 452

A larger church building was built sometime before 1900. In August of 1900 a storm blew the church off its foundation, damaging the building beyond use. The statues were moved over to the grocery warehouse belonging to Jean Castex and services were held here until 1908 when the damaged building was raised and repaired. The rebuilt church was like the storm-damaged structure in all respects except one: the real stained glass windows in the first church were not replaced. Some type of colored paper was used on the windows to give the effect of stained glass. Lightning struck the church in the summer of 1914; the wooden building burst into flames and burned down within a short while.[56]

Rev. J. Chasles was the first resident pastor of St. John the Evangelist Church, assigned there in 1882. The first church and rectory were constructed during his pastorate. After the fire of 1886 priests from the Crowley church served Mermentau until 1908, when Rev. Bartholomew Fontaine was assigned resident pastor. Prior to 1920 two other pastors were assigned to Mermentau: Rev. Theo Van Eych (1917-1919) and Rev. A. Verhoeven (1919-1930).[57]

Plans to build a Methodist Episcopal church in Mermentau were announced in 1899. The church building, 28 by 45 feet in dimension, was built on property bought from Euclide D. Conner. The land, Lot 4 of Block 17, was purchased for $40. Rev. J. F. Ross was the pastor in charge. The new church was dedicated November 11, 1900. There is no published information on the length of time the church functioned. The only other reference is a news item of 1902 which reported: "The Methodist Church of Mermentau will give a moonlight excursion on the steamer *Olive* from Mermentau to Lake Arthur."[58]

A congregation of southern Methodists was organized in 1911 by Rev. Martin Hebert of New Iberia. Some 30 members were counted. The following year the board of trustees of the Mermentau Methodist Episcopal Church South, R. Harrington, P. C. Smith, Captain George W. Caldwell, R. A. Smith and A. S. Johnson, announced plans to buy a lot and build a church. The property, Lot 1 in Block 16, was bought from heirs of V. Maignaud for $50. First services were conducted in the new church by Rev. Hebert in March of 1913.[59]

Rev. J. I. Hoffpauir, presiding elder of the Lafayette District, delivered the sermon when the church was dedicated August 9, 1914. The collection netted $160, the amount owed on the church building. After the dedication ceremonies a basket dinner was held under the trees.[60]

---

[56] *Crowley Signal*, Aug. 11, 1900; *Daily Signal*, June 30, 1914; interview, Edna Duhon, 1978

[57] Booklet, St. John the Evangelist, 1977

[58] *Crowley Signal*, Sept. 23, 1899; Nov. 10, 1900; Conveyance Book V, #14993, 623, Acad. Par.; *Daily Signal*, Apr. 15, 1902

[59] *Daily Signal*, May 13, 1911; Nov. 7, 1912; Mar. 6, 1913; Conveyance Book T-2, #37550, 776, Acad. Par.

[60] *Daily Signal*, Aug. 14, 1914

St. John the Evangelist Catholic Church, sketched by Ben Earl Looney from a snapshot of the church made before 1900 by Edward T. Hoyt. The church was damaged in a storm in 1900, struck by lightning and destroyed by fire in 1914.

A Baptist congregation of black people was organized at an undetermined time early in the century. Cora Barker is credited with having been the person who coordinated the efforts of the congregation to build the first church. Two lots were sold to New Hope Baptist Church in 1903 by E. D. Conner. The consideration was $80, and was paid by the church trustees, C. Barker, John Barker, George Caplin, Henry Willard and King Atly.[61]

The church building also served as the first school house for black children. Classes were taught by H. C. Ross of Crowley after the regular three-month session of school was over. At a time prior to 1915 members of the black community got together and gave benefits to raise funds for a one-room school house. This school, located on a hill in the eastern part of town, was destroyed in the 1915 storm.[62]

Other than names of teachers, there is little information available on

[61] Interview, Anita Lapointe Davis, 1978; Conveyance Book B-2, #21821, 737, Acad. Par.

[62] Interviews, Anita L. Davis, Edna Duhon

early public schools of the Mermentau area. Minutes of the Mermentau Town Council show that the town supported measures to improve the educational system, such as providing extra funds to run the school a full nine months.

Teachers at the Mermentau school (1899-1904) included Maud Coffin, Cornelius Scully, Orion Kirkpatrick and Ella M. Cutler. Another early school in the Mermentau area of the Fifth Ward was the John Henry school, where classes were taught (1899-1904) by Mrs. Stella Glass, Lee Hereford and L. P. LeBesque.[63]

St. Mary's, a private school, was in operation in Mermentau for about five years. Philibert Simon, son-in-law of Dr. Louis Espargelier, established the school in 1907. Misses Harriet and Marceline Goudeau were the first teachers. R. C. Trumps took over the school as principal in 1910. Names of some of the 40 students enrolled were given in a 1911 news release published in the *Crowley Signal*: Allia Fruge, Ada LeBlanc, Gladys Smith, Erin Myers, William Beard, Herbert Simpson, Henry Simon, Arthur LeBlanc, Ruth Pridgen, Ava Rice, Vivia Simon and Alphe LeBlanc.[64]

St. Mary's was not a parochial school in the commonly accepted meaning of the term, that is, a school established and maintained by the church parish. The building belonged to Simon, and the teachers were paid by the parents of the pupils. However, there appears to have been a connection between the school and the Catholic church of Mermentau; for instance, the profits from the 1909 school closing program were earmarked for the Catholic rectory building fund.[65]

Addenda

A Woodmen of the World organization was functioning in Mermentau in 1913. The July 4th celebration that year was sponsored by the WOW with a picnic and entertainment on the river near the rice mill. Cold drinks and ice cream were sold, and the games included a greasy pig race, for boys in knee pants, with the pig as the prize. Other competitions were climbing a greased pole with $1 at the top as the prize; a sack race, pocket knife as the prize. In the hen race, the hen was to be turned loose for the ladies to catch and win the hen as a prize. Another ladies' contest was a nail driving contest with a box of candy for the prize. The final game was a three-legged race for boys, with fishing tackle as the prize.[66]

One of the long-time residents of the Mermentau Cove section was

---

[63] *Crowley Signal*, Sept. 16, 1899; Sept. 8, 1900; Sept. 14, 1901; *Daily Signal*, Sept. 3, 1902; May 16, 1904

[64] *Crowley Signal*, Dec. 7, 1907; July 16, 1910; Mar. 25, 1911

[65] *Crowley Signal*, Sept. 10, 1910; *Daily Signal*, June 11, 1909

[66] *Daily Signal*, July 3, 1913

Andrew Henry, who played a leading role in the politics of the area, before and after parish division. A justice of the peace for many years, Henry was known as "Judge Henry." His farm in 1917 was the old John Webb place, where Webb settled in 1827.[67]

The River

The center of interest and activity during Mermentau's entire history has always been the river. Before the trains came and for many years thereafter the river was an important artery for commerce and industry. Until the advent of motorized vehicles and hard surfaced roads the river was the main outlet to market for the bulk of the region's products, such as lumber, rice, oil, cotton, furs and wild game.

Public ferries were operated on the Mermentau for almost a hundred years. More than 50 years before the railroad was built a ferry transported passengers and vehicles from one side of the river to the other, and continued in use for more than 40 years after the railroad bridge spanned the river in 1880. It was 1918 before the police juries of the two parishes involved took definite steps toward building the first highway bridge.[68]

---

[67] *Ibid*, Oct. 18, 1917
[68] *Ibid*, Jan. 3, 1918

Best known of the Mermentau River boats was the *Olive*, the largest of the fleet owned by Captain George W. Caldwell. The *Olive* was a favorite means of transportation for Acadia Parish people to attend the summer camp meetings held each year at Lake Arthur. (Photo reproduced from *Crowley Signal*, Dec. 14, 1907)

So far as is known Hypolite Guidry was the first Mermentau River ferryman. He had ferry rights over the river for almost 20 years, from 1824 to 1841, when he was replaced by James Andrews (Andrus) Sr. Ferry rights were controlled by the police jury; rights to operate a ferry were leased to individuals for a specified length of time, usually five years.[69]

The police jury also set the ferriage rates: so much per person, man on horseback, vehicles and persons in vehicles. Travelers paid ferriage fees to cross the Mermentau until 1909, when the first free ferry was established. The following news item gives the details:

> For the first time in the history of the parish people can cross the river for free. The people of Mermentau, aided by Paul E. Fremaux, Philibert Simon and William F. Spurgeon raised sufficient funds to buy the old ferry, and with the assistance of Calcasieu Parish, to operate a free ferry. The ferry operates from 6 a.m. to 7 p.m.[70]

One of the more interesting facets of life on the river was known as "swamping." Times of high water in the river and swamps was when the swampers went to work, commanding top wages for floating out cypress logs to the sawmills along the river.[71] Weather conditions in the spring of 1903 created perfect conditions for swamping. Writing in the *Crowley Signal* of March 31, 1903, the Mermentau correspondent gave the following graphic description of swamping:

> The river is as high as it has been for 15 years. The swamps are full of water. It is a picturesque sight to stand on the banks and watch the great rafts of logs floating by, to marvel at the hazardous work of the loggers as they bob up and down on unsteady footing while descending the rapid current.

Traffic on the river remained fairly heavy until after World War I. Passenger boats, freight boats and barges plied the waters of the Mermentau to Lake Arthur, Grand Cheniere, points along Lacassine Bayou and even through the Gulf of Mexico to Texas.

The best known passenger-freight boat was the 96-ton steamer the *Olive*, which made round trips every other day from Mermentau to Lake Arthur. Described as "a splendid stern wheel packet," the *Olive* was a popular means of transportation to and from the religious revivals, known as camp meetings. which were held each summer at Lake Arthur. Boat trips were scheduled by train arrival time at the Mermentau depot. Fares on the *Olive* were 50 cents one way, 75 cents round trip.[72]

The *Olive* first belonged to McCain Brothers, then to George W.

[69] Engbers, Rev. John, "Mermentau Memoirs," *Crowley Post-Signal*, Feb. 23, 1978; *Crowley Signal*, Dec. 21, 1901

[70] *Daily Signal*, Aug. 17, 1909

[71] *Ibid*, Feb. 12, 1903

[72] *Ibid*, June 28, 1902

Captain George W. Caldwell was the best known boat captain on the Mermentau. In right photo are Mrs. Caldwell, the former Mary Alzelia Leger, and two of the Caldwell children, William "Bill" and Olive Ruth. (Photo courtesy C. C. Caldwell)

Caldwell who bought out the McCains in 1905. Captain Caldwell started navigating the waters of the Mermentau and its tributaries about 1890. In addition to the *Olive* he owned smaller boats, the *Oscar G.*, the *Josephine*, the *Prima*, the *Goldie*, the *Two Brothers*, the *Gertrude*, the *Lee*, the *Lucy*, the *Clipper*, the *Danton*, and the *Palma*, plus 24 barges. The barges, powered by tug boats, hauled rice, oil, cattle, cotton, wood and general freight to and from points on Bayous Nezpique, Plaquemine Brulee, des Cannes and Lacassine.[73]

Captain Caldwell also operated a commissary on the riverfront. He issued metal tokens that could be redeemed at the commissary in the amounts of 5, 10, 25 and 50 cents and $1. These tokens came to be known as "Mermentau Money."[74]

---

[73] *Ibid*, Dec. 14, 1907; interview, C. C. Caldwell, 1978
[74] Interview, C. C. Caldwell

Some of the captains who piloted boats for the Caldwell Boat Company were F. P. Blackburn, Jack Marion, Henry Sweet, R. F. Edgar and Pullos Legros.[75]

Wild game and furs constituted a large part of the boat freight coming into Mermentau during the winter months. Such cargo was shipped out of Mermentau to market by train.

An amazingly large number of wild ducks was brought in by boat; one day's load in 1903 totaled 1,200 ducks, and the average amount of wild ducks shipped from Grand Cheniere was 10 barrels a day. One fur shipment consisted of 2,500 raccoon and mink skins.[76]

A shipyard was in operation at Mermentau about 1911. One newspaper report stated that pontoons belonging to a dredge boat were undergoing repairs at the "Mermentau shipyards;" a dredge boat was "being built at the shipyards," a gasoline boat, the *Stork*, two houseboats and a small gasoline boat were "at the Mermentau shipyards for repairs," also Captain Caldwell's tug and launch, the *Gertrude* and the *Clipper*. The shipyard was located about a quarter mile up river from the railroad bridge.[77]

An Acadian boat captain was the subject of a laudatory article in a Texas newspaper in 1911. The exploits of the Cajun pilot were reported in a story datelined Port Arthur which appeared in the *Beaumont Enterprise* of October 15, 1911.

The newspaper account told of the schooner *Hebert*, loaded with 40 cords of oak firewood and a number of coops of live chickens which came into Port Arthur from Mermentau. The schooner was convoyed by a gasoline launch *Rosalie*, which was piloted by one Alcide Clement.

The *Rosalie* itself had three cords of the firewood stowed in the cabin, which, according to the newspaper, made "the little vessel . . . top heavy to the danger limit, yet she hit the Gulf between the bars of the Mermentau and Sabine and came into the canal in front of this city (Port Arthur) today."

The newspaper writer appeared quite impressed with the Acadian's navigational skill: "When one finds a frail craft being thrust into danger one naturally looks for a French voyageur on board . . . Alcide Clement . . . is as French as his name would indicate. . . ."

Some interesting facts about boats on the Mermentau are contained in the following abstracts from the Crowley newspaper:

The *Agnes T. Parks* was the mail boat, carrying mail down the river from Mermentau to Lowry every day except Sunday. Captain G. W. Halliburton was a veteran pilot of the *Agnes T. Parks*, starting in 1898, and August Fruge worked on the boat as engineer.[78]

[75] *Crowley Signal*, May 5, 1903; *Daily Signal*, May 25, 1905; Sept. 7, 1911; Jan. 1, 1912
[76] *Daily Signal*, Jan. 15, 22, 29, 1903
[77] *Ibid*, Aug. 5, Sept. 7, 1911; May 5, 1912; interview, Edna Duhon, 1978
[78] *Crowley Signal*, May 30, June 6, 1903

The *Josephine*, one of the boats in the fleet owned by Captain George W. Caldwell. The boat company was in operation on the Mermentau and its tributaries for about 30 years. (Photo courtesy C. C. Caldwell)

In 1903 the steamer *Oscar G.* "made a record-breaking trip to Lacassine country, breaking records of all boats that have run Lacassine Bayou."[79]

In 1906 one of the gasoline launches on the Mermentau was named the *Carrie Nation*.[80]

In February of 1915 the *Tuebor* and the *White Lily*, on their regular runs, brought in 30 barrels of ducks.[81]

As early as 1903 there were pollution problems that affected the river. An oil pipeline which crossed over the stream was accidently broken and the river was covered with oil. At the time it appeared that public concern was more for the loss of the oil than because of the pollution caused by the spill.[82]

The Mermentau boat company magnate, Captain Caldwell, was the first resident of the town to own an automobile. In 1910 the newspaper reporter for Mermentau wrote: "Our little village can now boast of an automobile." Captain Caldwell was the owner of a seven-passenger car, which constitutes a bit of irony since motorized vehicles eventually put the river boats out of business.[83]

[79] *Ibid*, May 23, 1903
[80] *Daily Signal*, July 26, 1906
[81] *Ibid*, Feb. 4, 1915
[82] *Crowley Signal*, Aug. 29, 1903
[83] *Ibid*, Apr. 16, 1910

Legend

The town of Mermentau is not segregated. White families and black families live harmoniously in the same neighborhoods and have done so without problems of any consequence for something like four decades.

How this came about is answered by an old legend. The story, which must be labeled a legend because it cannot be substantiated, is nonetheless credible and could be true:

Until about 1900 white people lived in one area of the town and the blacks in another. One of the black residents was a man named Alfred Barker, a cattle wrangler. Barker would be away from home for several months at a time on the long cattle drives. When the drive was over he always returned home with all the money he had made during the drive.

After one such drive Barker got back to Mermentau with a large amount of money. He went into a saloon where some white men, noticing that he had the money, invited him to get into their card game. Barker accepted and got into a winning streak that seemed to have no end. He won pot after pot until the other card players were broke. For the final round one of the white men put up his property—a lot with a house on it, located in the center of the white section of town. Barker won that also. He and his family moved onto the property he had won, thereby integrating the town.[84]

The Storm

The most disastrous storm in the history of the parish, in terms of human lives lost, hit Mermentau and Egan on the afternoon of May 6, 1915. Seven persons—five from Mermentau and two from Egan—were killed by the storm.

The tornado left a path of destruction some 1,000 feet wide, sweeping into Mermentau from a point about three miles south, thence in a northeasterly direction into the Egan community. The storm came without warning, its approach obscured by the heavy forest south of the village.

The five Mermentau residents killed were Adam Thibodeaux, white, and four members of a black family: Mrs. Belizar "Billy" Premo (Primeaux) and three of her four young children, Andrew, Gertrude and Beulah. Mrs. Premo was seven months pregnant.

The only survivors were Shafter Premo, the eldest child, who was eight years old, and the father, who had gone to Gueydan in search of work earlier in the day. When he returned he found the four bodies lying in the wreckage of his home. One of the children had been disemboweled by flying debris.

---

[84] Interview, Burrell Barker, 1978

Property damage at Mermentau included the home and barn of Ulysse Duhon, the William F. Spurgeon home, the large rice warehouse belonging to Dr. Louis Espargelier—a heavy iron safe in the warehouse was carried 100 feet and dropped on the railroad right-of-way—a sawmill, a school house, large bridge and numerous residences were demolished. All buildings and fences in the storm's path were razed; bodies of many head of cattle and work animals were strewn over the area.[85]

The storm victims were helped by contributions of food, clothing and cash sent by residents of Jennings and Crowley. In Mermentau Mrs. Philibert Simon had charge of distributing the donations, giving to each according to need.[86]

---

[85] *Daily Signal*, May 7, 1915; interviews, Shafter Premo, Edna Duhon, Anita Davis, 1978

[86] *Daily Signal*, May 17, 1915

Acknowledgements

The author wishes to acknowledge, with sincere gratitude, the help given by a number of friends (other than those cited in the bibliography and elsewhere in this book) in the preparation of this second volume of Acadia Parish history. Thanks for invaluable assistance goes to Emerson P. Abshire, Toodie Pierrel Bailey, Elizabeth Lyman Barnett, Minnie Berry, Laurence T. Bliss, Laurent Boudreaux, Phoebe Bone Brown, Erin Dore Canan, Virginia Terrell Christopher, Marie Cook, Ethel Freeland Darden, Annette Leger Dietz, Barbara H. Dietz, Donald W. Doga, Roland Domingue, Bernice Trahan Dugas, Yola Cormier Dugas, Meus Duhon, Helene Lang Embry, Rev. John Engbers, James Forester, Marcus Fowler, Barton Freeland Sr., Barton Freeland Jr., Mary Alice Wynn Freeland, Charles Fruge, Esther Toler Gardiner, Lucille Gautreaux, Dennis Gibson, Lucille F. Gravot, Mary Barker Green, Walter Grotefend, Wilfred Guidry, Paul J. Hardy, Dean Harris, Stella P. Hildreth, Lyle Johnson, Thelma Finley Kleiser, Wilma Knight, Yvonne Reggie LaHood, Beryl Dore Lanier, Judy Leger, Morris Lejeune, Jan Lewis, Burnley Lynch, E. H. Lund Jr., Shirley Peyrefitte Lund, Anna Jane Marks, Rubie Marionneaux, Ann Mire, Milo Nickel, Alfred Norman, Rev. William Ohlenforst, Thelma Pierrel, R. C. Regan, Helen Richard, Lee Riehl, Vincent Riehl, Rev. W. A. Rowell, Jr., George Sabatier, Joyce Sarver, Hilton Smith, H. Leo Spaetgens, Bernice H. Stewart, Millie Doucet Stroderd, Josie Berkens Thevis, Rev. Paul Thibodeaux, Kathleen Toups, Laura Morgan Williams, Adeline Thibodeaux Wimberley, Helen Zaunbrecher.

Bibliography

PRIMARY SOURCES

ACADIA PARISH RECORDS
Abstracts U.S. Land Entries No. 1
Conveyance Books
Donation Books
Official Township Survey Plats
AMERICAN STATE PAPERS, PUBLIC LANDS, VOL. III

LOUISIANA DEPARTMENT OF STATE
Municipal officers of Rayne, Church Point, Iota, Estherwood, Mermentau, Morse

NATIONAL ARCHIVES AND RECORDS SERVICE
Register of Postmasters of Acadia Parish

ST. LANDRY PARISH RECORDS
Conveyance Books
Miscellaneous Suits

CHURCH RECORDS
Archives, Diocese of Lafayette
Archives, Society of Jesus, Grand Coteau
Bethel C.M.E. Church, Crowley, cornerstone inscription
Centenary Methodist Church, Rayne, church history
St. Joseph's Catholic Church, Iota, La.

MUNICIPAL RECORDS
Minute books Crowley, Iota, Mermentau, Morse, Rayne

BOOKS

FONTENOT, Mary Alice, and FREELAND, Rev. Paul B., *Acadia Parish, a History to 1900* (Baton Rouge, 1976)
GRIFFIN, Harry L., *Attakapas Country, a History of Lafayette Parish, La.* (New Orleans, 1959)
GUIDRY, Anita G., *La Pointe de l'Eglise, a History of Church Point, Louisiana, 1800-1973* (Lafayette, La. 1973)
HAIR, Velma Lee, *The History of Crowley, Louisiana*, reprinted from *Louisiana Historical Quarterly, Vol. 27*, 1944 (Master's thesis in History, Louisiana State University, 1941)
HEBERT, Rev. Donald J., *Southwest Louisiana Records, Vol. 2* (Eunice, La., 1975)
KEYES, Frances Parkinson, *Blue Camellia*, New York, 1957
Louisiana Almanac, 1973-1974, James Calhoun, editor, New Orleans
National Cyclopedia of American Biography, New York, 1943
PERRIN, William H., *Southwest Louisiana, Historical and Biographical* (New Orleans, 1891)
Yearbook of Agriculture, official publication United States Department of Agriculture, 1936

BOOKLETS, MAGAZINES

ACADIA PARISH PLANNING BOARD, *Acadia Parish Resources and Facilities*, published in cooperation with Louisiana Department Public Works Planning Division, Sept. 1, 1946
BAUDIER, Roger, *History of Our Lady of the Sacred Heart Catholic Church*, 1954 booklet
Country Gentleman, magazine, July 24, 1920
ROCK ISLAND RAILROAD, *Southwest Trail*, July, 1915
ST. JOSEPH'S SCHOOL, *Golden Jubilee St. Joseph's School, Rayne, 1891-1941*, booklet

ST. JOHN EVANGELIST CHURCH, Mermentau, *History St. John Evangelist Church* (Waco, Tex. 1977)

ST. JOHN LUTHERAN CHURCH, Iota, *75th Anniversary St. John Lutheran*, Oct. 31, 1976

St. Leo's Church and School Directory, 1903-1904; St. Leo's Church

SIGNAL PUBLISHING CO., *The Rice Journal and Gulf Coast Farmer*, magazine, March, 1913

ARTICLES

CRAIG, Myrta Fair, "Three Weil Brothers Bring Rayne Fame as 'Frog Capital of the World,' " *Rayne Acadian-Tribune* supplement, Aug. 30, 1973

CRIPPEN, Charles L., "Surface Canals," *Crowley Signal*, Feb. 16, 1901

ENGBERS, Rev. John, "Mermentau Memoirs," *Crowley Post-Signal*, Feb. 23, 1978

FLEMING, Estelle Bonin, "Rayne Frog Industry Dates Back to 1880s—Donat Pucheu First Shipper," *Rayne Acadian-Tribune* supplement, Aug. 30, 1973

FONTENOT, Mary Alice, "The Schell Canal," Opelousas *Daily World*, Jan. 19, 1969

FONTENOT, Mary Alice, "Le Bon Vieux Temps," *Crowley Post-Signal*, Nov. 13, 1977

GINN, Mildred K., "A History of Rice Production in Louisiana to 1896," *Louisiana Historical Quarterly, Vol. XXIII*

KONDERT, Reinhart, "The Germans of Acadia Parish," *Louisiana Review*, Vol. 6, No. 1

LAVERGNE, Gary, "Homer Barousse, Portrait of an Acadia Parish Politician," *Attakapas Gazette, Vol. XI*, 1976

LEEPER, Clare d'Artois, "Louisiana Places," Sunday *Advocate*

MC NEELY, Dorothy B., "Mermentau Dam Secret for 70 Years Revealed," *Crowley Post-Signal*, Apr. 17, 1977

MC NEELY, Dorothy B., "Acadia College: Educating the Rural Louisianian," *Crowley Post-Signal*, May 15, 1977

PRATHER, Mrs. Ulric, "Baptist Church in Richard Founded in 1899; Pilgrim's Rest Now Boasts 422 Members," *Crowley Daily Signal*, 50th Anniv. Ed., 1949

NEWSPAPERS

Abbeville Meridional, Abbeville, La.

Acadian, Crowley, La.

Acadia Sentinel, Rayne, La.

Beaumont Enterprise, Beaumont, Tex.

Courier, Opelousas, La.

Crowley Daily News, Crowley, La.

Crowley Mirror, Crowley, La.

Crowley Signal and/or *Daily Signal*, Crowley, La.

Crowley Daily Signal, 50th Anniversary Edition supplement, 1899-1949

Crowley Post-Herald, Crowley, La.

Crowley Post-Signal, Crowley, La.

Daily World, Opelousas, La. Bicentennial edition, Vol. III, 36, 1976

Houston Daily Post, Houston, Texas

The Morning Star, Lafayette, La.

New Orleans Item, New Orleans, La.

Rayne Independent supplement, Rayne, La.

Rayne Signal, Rayne, La.

Rayne Tribune, Rayne, La.

Rice Belt News, Crowley, La.

Times-Picayune, New Orleans, La.

UNPUBLISHED

BABINEAUX, Lawson P. Jr., "A History of the Rice Industry in Southwest Louisiana," University of Southwestern Louisiana thesis, 1967

FREELAND, Rev. Paul B., "Mayors of Crowley," "Acadia Parish Officials," Acadia Parish Library

HILLIGARDE, Nancy, "History of Midland," history paper
MC NEELY, Dorothy B., "Crowley City Council Actions;" "Acadia Parish School Board Members," Acadia Parish Library
MEAUX, Ena Broussard, "Graduates of Crowley Schools," Ledoux Library, Louisiana State University at Eunice

INTERVIEWS, ORAL HISTORY

AKOLS, Mrs. Annie, Rayne, La.
ANDRUS, Antonia "DouDouce" Plattsmier, Rayne, La.
ANDRUS, Roy, Rayne, La.
ARCENEAUX, Elton, Crowley, La.
ATTEBERRY, Winston "Skeet," Eunice, La.
BAKER, Sidney, Crowley, La.
BARKER, Burrell, Mermentau, La.
BAROUSSE, Winston, Rayne, La.
BARRAS, Garland D., Lake Charles, La.
BAUR, Lindsey, Crowley, La.
BIEBER, Mrs. Edgar, Branch, La.
BIEBER, Henry, Branch, La.
BOURGAUX, Henry, Rayne, La.
BUCHANAN, Vera Cowen, Crowley, La.
BULLER, George, Opelousas, La.
CALDWELL, C. C., Lake Charles, La.
CARROLL, Bertha Dischler, Lafayette, La.
CASSIDY, J. J., Crowley, La.
CHATELAIN, Wiltz, Rayne, La.
CHIASSON, Mrs. Moise, Morse, La.
CRAIG, Myrta Fair, Rayne, La.
DAVIS, Mrs. Anita LaPointe, Mermentau, La.
DELAHOUSSAYE, B. C., Crowley, La.
DOUCET, Alphonse and Walter, Iota, La.
DUGAS, Mrs. Beatrice, Rayne, La.
DUHON, Mrs. Felix, Mermentau, La.
DUSON, Henry, T., Crowley, La.
EDWARDS, Mathilde, Abbeville, La.
ELEAZAR, Paul, Kaplan, La.
FONTENOT, Roland, Crowley, La.
FOWLER, Helen Lolette, New Orleans, La.
GRAVOT, Marie Bordelais, Iota, La.
GUENO, Leonie Medlenka, Crowley, La.
GUIDRY, Owen, Church Point, La.
HEBERT, Marilyn Morgan, Crowley, La.
HENDERSON, Betty Hebert, Maxie, La.
HENSGENS, Kate and Marie, Eunice, La.
HOFFPAUIR, Lucille Hoyt, Estherwood, La.
JABUSCH, Willa Duhon, Crowley, La.
KAHN, Leo H. and Selma, Lafayette, La.
LEWIS, Jan, Rayne, La.
LOEWER, F. D., Branch, La.
LYONS, Oswald, Crowley, La.
MAY, Jeannette Ross, Crowley, La.
MOSES, Rosebud Young, Jennings, La.
PETE, James Sr., Crowley, La.
PETITJEAN, Irene, Rayne, La.
PHILLIPS, Rev. Thomas, Crowley, La.
PLEASANT, John "Moustique," Rayne, La.
PREMO, Shafter, Mermentau, La.
PRIVAT, Louis, Rayne, La.
RANDEL, Hazel McManus, Eunice, La.

RAYMOND, Jerry McBride, Rayne, La.
REED, Bella Cart, Iota, La.
SCHAFFHAUSEN, Elizabeth and Ann, Eunice, La.
SMITH, Alberdia Clark, Rayne, La.
SONNIER, Vernon, Lafayette, La.
SWEENEY, Etta Stamm, Rayne, La.
TREMIE, Rev. Gene, Lafayette, La.
TRUAX, Steve, Verbie Regan and Grant, Egan, La.
WILSON, Sherman, Crowley, La.
WRIGHT, S. L. Jr., Crowley, La.
ZIEGLER, Magdalen Bossley, Crowley, La.

Index

Dacosta, A., 116
Dacosta, A. F., 100
Daigle, Alexandre, 256
Daigle, Ben, 189, 194, 195, 205
Daigle, Colan, 242
Daigle, Constant, 254
Daigle, Edward, 2, 189, 190, 191, 195, 197, 200, 201, 203
Daigle, Emelie, 200
Daigle, Emelien, 195
Daigle, Emile, 188, 192, 194, 196, 203, 205
Daigle, Ernest, 195, 197
Daigle, Evelina, 201
Daigle, Hermina, 102
Daigle, H. J., 59, 190, 203, 251, 254
Daigle, Homer J., 229
Daigle, J. E., 1, 2, 5, 188, 200, 201, 206
Daigle, J. E., Jr., 195
Daigle, J. E. & Son, 191, 192
Daigle, Joseph E., 186, 197
Daigle school, 8, 241, 242
Daigle, T., 203
Daigle, Theo, 189; firm, 195
Daigle, Theodore, 190, 191, 195, 196, 250
Daigle, Theodule, 186, 200
Daigle, Ursin, 1, 5, 267
Daigle, Valentine, 206
Daily, James, 277
Daily Rice City News, 134
Dalton, Inez, 291
Daniels, M. J., 101, 102
Daniels, S. B., 56
Daniels, S. M., 137
Danum, W. C., 113
D'Aquin, Edmond, 65
D'Aquin, Robert, 56
Darbonne, C., 250
Darbonne, Paul, 224
Dardeau, Edward, 227
Darphin, Ed, 252, 264
d'Augereaux, Gaston, 190
Daughenbaugh, Henry L., 248, 249, 254
David, Arthur, 195
David & Breaux, 191, 194
David, Gilbert, 194
David, Homer, 1, 190
David, Hubert, J., 189, 191, 194, 195, 201, 203, 206
David, J. B., 189
David, John B., 269
David, Jules, 188
David, Mrs. Jules, 191
David, R., 192
David, Ralph, 194, 205
David, Rudolph, 191
Davidson, Neal, 102
Davidson, William, 101
Davis, Andrew J., 244
Davis, Rev. C. L., 145
Davis, Eddie, 65

Davis House, 104
Davis, J. C., 104
Davis, John M., 190, 209, 243
Davis, Louisa, 202
Davis, R. W., 189, 191, 203
DeBellevue, C. B., 2, 5, 253
DeBellevue, L. B., 2, 5
Declouet, Richlobert "Broin," 269
DeGeneres, A. D., 101
Deher, Salem, 102, 117, 118
Dehm, Chester, 308
Dehm, Fred, 209
Dehm, Harry, 308
Dejean, Adolph, 220
Dejean, Felix A., 192
Dejean post office, 220
Dejean school, 7, 220
Delahoussaye, A. B., 5
Delahoussaye, B. C., 65
Delarue, Visca T., 224
Delaune, L. J., 155
Deputy, Elias, 163
Deputy, L. R., 102, 108, 153, 163
Derouen, G., 156
Derouen's Opera House, 153
Desessarts, Hilaire, 312
Deshotels & Dejean store, 220
Deshotels, J. H., 251, 252, 263
Deuran, J. M., 269
Deville, Edmond, 189, 191, 201, 203, 204
Devinne, Rev. Daniel, 209
Deviral, Rev. Charles, 119
Dickerson, Theodore, 50
Dickson, Margaret, 270
Dietz, Edward, 259
Dietz, George, 259
Dietz, John, 259
Dietz, William, 259
Die Deutsche Gesellschaft, 233, 234, 235
diphtheria, 12
Dischler, Charles, 219
Dischler family, 231
"Dix Sous," 156
Dixon, Margaret, 244, 247
Dobbs, David H., 218
Dobson, Henry, 250
Dodson, J. B., 89
Dodson, Dr. W. R., 89
Dollinge & Brown, 58
Dommert, Charles, 308, 309
Dommert family, 232
Donovan brothers, 194
Donovan, Dr. 198
Donzler, Charles, 177
Dore, A. B., 252, 254
Dore, Gordon, 64
Dore, O., 104, 105
Dore family, 64
Dorman, James L., 5
Dorr family, 231

346

Francez drug store, 281
Francez, Louis, 51
Francez, Dr. Z. J., 2, 7, 12, 135, 136, 286, 287, 293
Francis, Mrs. Auzemar, 139
Francois, Joseph, 5, 306, 307, 308
Frank, Abram, 104
Frankel, Jac, 58, 65, 67, 77, 84, 87, 99, 101, 103, 104, 114, 130
Franques, Ben, 195
Franques, Leo, 196, 205, 207, 208
Franques, Leonard, 189
Franques, Lloyd, 131, 189, 190, 191
Fraser, Dr. George, 120
Fraser, Inglis, 275
Freeland brothers, 85, 131
Freeland, C. J., 9, 51, 54, 65, 66, 68, 84, 104, 130, 131, 135, 278
Freeland, Jay, 85, 89, 114
Freeland, Mrs. Jay, 134
Freeland school, 8
Freeland, T. B., 54, 65, 68, 84, 100, 130, 131, 150, 278
Fremaux canal, 77
Fremaux, George, 10
Fremaux, E. W., 58
Fremaux, H. C., 56
Fremaux, Leon, 5, 99
Fremaux, J. O., 51, 56, 63, 64, 295
Fremaux, Paul E., 1, 156, 327
Freeman Bros., 102, 112
Freeman, Rev. F. M., 173
Freeman, Rebekah, 137
Frere, Hugh, 10, 101
Frey family, 228
Frey, John, 228
Frey, John Jr., 236
Frey, Joseph, 228
Frey & Klein, 228
Frey, Louis, 239
Frisbie, Col. S. L., 131
Frisco railroad (see Colorado Southern)
frog farm, 296
frog industry, 159-162
Fruge, Allia, 325
Fruge, Alonzo F., 248
Fruge, August, 329
Fruge, David, 318
Fruge, E. D., 161, 319, 320
Fruge, Eddie, 318, 319
Fruge, Ernest, 252, 254
Fruge, Gustave, 313, 314
Fruge, Homer, 267
Fruge, J. P., 312, 314, 318, 319, 321
Fruge, N. B., 316, 319
Fulton, J. F., 159
Fuselier, Gus, 271
Fuselier, Portalis, 213

Gabelle, James G., 132

Gaidry, Alcee L., 280, 282, 285
Gaidry store, 281
Gamble, William, 268
Gardiner, A. C., 205
Gardiner, J. B., 190, 194
Gardiner, T. L., 102
Gardner, E., 137
Garic, E. G., 58
Garland, B. R., 55
Garrould, Frank E., 270
Garvey, Jake, 56
Garvey, W. G., 63
Gary, Philosite, 319
Gaspard, Telesport, 222
Gassie, Iberia, 123
Gassler, Rev. Francis L., 228, 230, 255, 257, 258, 267, 306
Gates, John W., 87
Gaudet, A. L., 196
Gaudet, Alexandre, 313
Gaudet, E. L., 106
Gaudin, L. P., 100
Gault, Gerald, 308
Gault, Mrs. M. Belle, 304
Gault, William S., 304, 306
Geens, Rev. F. Wenceslaus, 119
Gellert, Rev. H., 120, 266
Genais, Rene, 268
Genais post office, 268
George, Mrs. Mathilda, 105, 117
Gerson, S. R., 101
Gertrude, Sister M., 122
Gibson, Dora E., 122
Gibson, E. M., 59
Gibson, Philip "Pleg," 209
Gielen family, 231
Gilbert, Frank, 50
Gilbert, Rev. M. T., 260
Gil, Jules, 5
Gill, George, 50
Gill, John, 289
Gill, R. E., 75
Gill, J. W., 295
Gillard, Armas, 163
Gilley, G. N., 103
Giozza, Frank, 56, 295
Glass, Stella, 307, 325
Glode, Adam, 137
Glode, Joseph, 137
Gobnait, Sister M., 122
Godchaux, Agnes Putnam, 58
Godchaux, Frank, 31, 55, 58, 65
Godchaux, J. L., 101
Goebel, Carl, 238
Goebel, Elise, 237
Going, S. A., 213, 251
Goldberg, Sam H., 279
"Gold Bugs," 203
Goldstein, Phil A., 111, 124
Goodell, May M., 301

351

John, Tom, 103, 321
Johnson, Albert S., 312, 316, 318, 319, 323
Johnson, Alex, 137
Johnson, A. V., 10, 100, 102
Johnson, Ben, 161
Johnson Bros. Store, 268
Johnson, Catherine, 247
Johnson, Charles J., 216
Johnson & Grehan, 101
Johnson, Jake, 137
Johnson, J. H., 168
Johnson, J. I., 122
Johnson & Lupper, 102
Johnson, Luther V., 100, 102, 106
Johnson, M. G., 239
Johnson, Miguel, 268
Johnson, S. J., 79
Johnson, S. P., 55, 68, 100
Johnson, Dr. Will, 268
Johnson, William F., 173
Johnston, Kathleen, 174
Jolly Boys Brass Band, 202
Jonas Cove School, 244
Jones brothers: 61, 77; farm, 31, 238, 239,
    241; rice mill, 62, 65, 107
Jones, Rev. C. L., 174
Jones, Clara, 307
Jones, Rev. Claude L., 120
Jones, Rev. Eli, 143, 144, 174
Jones, Henry, 77, 145
Jones, Rev. J. D., 174
Jones, J. W., 241
Jones, Mrs. J. W., 267
Jones, N. E. A., 137
Jones' Spur, 241
Jones, Dr. T. F., 318, 321
Jones, Dr. Willie, 256
Jones, Winston, 77, 238
Joplin, F. M., 102
Joseph, Emile, 117, 118
Joseph, John, 117
Joseph, S., 102
Judd, J., 2, 101
Judd, 239
Jumel, Gen. Allen, 128, 158
Jumonville, Alcee, 93, 101
Jumonville, Dora, 123

Kahn, Alfred, 167
Kahn, Herbert, 168
Kahn, Mador, 100
Kahn, Marx B., 131
Kahn, Mervine, 60, 104, 151, 153, 155, 163,
    166, 168, 177, 183
Kahn, Sol, 156
Kahn, Theo store, 95
Kaiser (Wilhelm), 235
Kalid, Mrs. K., 117
Kaplan, Abrom, 31, 51, 52, 53, 56, 65, 74,
    77, 78, 85, 104, 105, 130, 139, 191, 242,
    280, 281, 291

Kaplan & Blum, 101
Kaplan, Henry, 191, 281
Karre, Paul, 105, 117, 118
Karre, S., 117
Kasich, Tony, 104
Keener, Bishop, 173
Keener, Rev. Christian, 173
Keener, Rev. T. S., 173
Keigley, C. C., 59, 61
Keith, Frank, 54
Keller, A. N., 101
Keller, Dennis, 195
Keller, Ellis G., 105
Keller, J. F., 103
Keller, L. A., 153, 163
Kelley, Ora, 155
Kelley, W. B., 101
Kelley, W. C., 131
Kelsey, D. R., 102
Kemmerly, C. E., 4
Kennedy, A. S., 53
Kennedy, Ed, 54
Kennedy, G. A., 104, 105, 153, 156, 177
Kernan, Mrs. Louis, 102
Kerr, E. J., 242
Kerr, Herbert, 242
Kershaw, Mrs. Zamie, 306
Kerysch, Rev. Leo, 119
Key, George, 102, 105
Keyes, Frances Parkinson, 20
Key Stone Ranch, 245
Klein family, 228
Klein, F. J., 1, 7, 228, 229
Klein, Joseph A., 228
Klein, Peter Sr., 230
Klein, Peter, 278
Klein warehouse, 229
Kleinpeter, Dr. E. A., 245
Kleinpeter, Eunice, 244, 258
Kleinschmidt, Rev. W. D., 173
Kleiser, Robert, 50, 103
Khaled, A. J., 117, 118
Khaled, K., 102
Khaled, Joseph, 105, 117
Khaled, Mrs. Mary, 118
Kilbeaux, C., 239
Kilmer, Charles J., 246
Kinder Times, 185
Kingston, P. A., 173
Kinnon, Rev. A., 174
Kirkpatrick, Orion, 211, 325
Kloor family, 232
Kloor, George, 235
Kloor, Louis A., 100, 101, 104, 233, 235
Klondike Saloon, 191
Klumpp family, 232
Klumpp, Joe, 268, 269
Klumpp, John, 269
Kluwe, M., 101
Knapp, Dr. S. A., 21, 42
Knickerbocher, R. W., 103

357

Midland: location, 299; hotel, 299; town lot
sale, 300; newspaper, 300; railroad
roundhouse, 300; post office, 300; school,
301; churches, 303
Midland canal, 75, 76
Midland Development Co., 300
Midland Enterprise, 300
Midland-Eunice railroad branch, 8, 248
Midland rice mill, 63, 65, 67
Midland Rice Milling Co., 300
Mier, Odel, 225
Mier, Ulysse, 225
Miers, James, 225
Miers, Jesse, 63, 297
Miers, Rufus, 297
Miers, Sidonia, 294
Miguez, Nemour, 156
Miles Bros., 102
Miles, G. E., 101, 111, 127
Miles, J. R., 127
Miles, J. W., 100, 116
Miles, Wesley J., 111, 127
Miller, Dautrive, 229
Miller, Dennis, 1, 269, 270
Miller, Eliza, 306
Miller, Ernest, 262
Miller, Eugene, 261, 262
Miller family, 270
Miller, Mrs. G., 254, 255
Miller, Gerasin, 271
Miller, Henry, 253
Miller, Iva E., 229, 239
Miller, H., 102
Miller, James, 263
Miller, Dr. J. F., 136
Miller, Joseph U., 312, 313, 316
Miller, Leopold, 253
Miller, Mrs. Maurice, 239
Miller, Mitchell, 254
Miller-Morris canal, 56, 74, 75, 279
Miller, Olive, 212
Miller, Paul, 253
Miller, Philomen, 251
Miller post office, 270
Miller, Theo, 254
Miller, William, 56, 74
Millerville canal, 77
Millerville post office, 270
Milligan, L. M., 155
Milligan, W. B., 5, 159
Milligan school, 7
Milliken, F. M., 4, 31, 32, 55, 82, 88, 150
Milton, Eula, 122, 275
Milton, Norwood, 102
Milton, William N., 220
Mims, Dr. D. D., 12, 93, 135, 136
minerals springs, 248
Minkin, Joseph, 143
Minkin, Willie, 143
Minton, T. E., 131

Mire, Alexandre, 221
Mitchell, Rev. A. C., 144
Mitchell, Arline, 144
Mitchell, Rev. B. H., 216
Mitchell, Dave, 104
Mitchell, John, 137
Mitchell, Dr. Thomas A., 136
Mitchell, W. B., 214
Moffet, Allen, 54
Monaco, C. F., 102
Montagne Bros., 118
Monteillard, Rev. J. V., 119, 229, 273
Montgomery, Robert, 5
Moore, Alfred T., 241, 243
Moore, Bun, 173
Moore, T., 321
Moore, W. H., 106
Morales, S., 155
Morell, Xavier, 231
Morgan, Joe, 275
Morgan, W. A., 7, 82, 104
Morgan, William, 274
Morning Star Baptist Church, 141, 142, 143,
145
Morris, J. C., 55, 58
Morris, Dr. J. F., 2, 56, 74, 103, 136, 153,
163, 169
Morris, Dr. N. B., 2, 101, 125, 136
Morris, Robert, 62
Morrison, W. E., 239
Morrow, W. K., 62
Morse: origin of name, 304; founder, 304;
rice mills, 305; hotel, 305; fires, 305;
churches, schools, 306, 307, 308; doctors,
308; landmark, 308; municipal officers,
309, 310
Morse, C. A., 95
Morse, C. S., 65, 84
Morse Hardware & Grocery, 306
Morse rice mill, 62
Morse, Robert, 304
Morse, S. F. B., 304
Morton, L. P., 102
Mosley, Henry, 242
Mt. Calvary Baptist Church, 209
Mt. Carmel Convent, 172
Mt. Sinai Baptist Church, 145
Mt. Triumph Baptist Church, 259
Mt. Zion Baptist Church, 145
Mourain, H. C., 295
Mouton, Alexandre, 170
Mouton, Celia B., 141
Mouton, Ernest, 143
Mouton, Dr. G. C., 2, 163, 167, 169, 170
Mouton, Jean, 222
Mouton *vacherie*, 277
Mowata German Baptist Church, 237, 238
Mowata post office, 239
Mowata, origin of name, 238, 239
Mudd, Kate, 50

Parrott, Dr. J. B., 194, 207, 208, 209, 211, 212
Parrott, Olive, 207
Patterson Bros., 153
Patterson, Harold, 308
Patterson, Marcus, 308
Patterson, W. E., 93, 100, 102
Patterson, Dr. W. T., 7, 130, 240, 308, 309
Patin, Rev. James, 144
Patton, J. A., 241, 260
Pavy, P. J., 74
Pearce & Godso, 101
Pearce & Irion, 154
Pefferkorn, A., 101
Pelican rice mill, 56
Pelton, John E., 37, 204, 211
Pemble, Clifton, 262
Pemble, Curtis, 261, 262
Pentacostal Church of Nazarene, 243
People's Bank, 103
People's Cotton Gin, 190
People's Drug Store, 106
People's Independent rice mill, 47, 52, 53, 65
People's Investment Co., 137, 142
People's Lumber Co., 194, 196, 197
Percy, W. R., 5
Perkins, Albert H., 106
Perkins, Linn T., 106
Perkins, Mae, 122
Perkins, W. F., 163
Perrault, Edward J., 312
Perrault, Dr. E. J., 316, 322
Perres, Auguste, 155, 163
Perres, Felix, 168
Perrodin, Charles O., 188
Perrodin, Jules, 60
Perry Point school, 275
Pershing, Gen. John J., 129
Petitjean, Amede, 153, 156
Petitjean, Dermas, 4, 167, 178
Petitjean, Edna, 156
Petitjean, Dr. E. J., 106
Petitjean, Emile, 1
Petitjean, Ernest, 50
Petitjean, Joe, 157
Petitjean, Martin, 4, 8, 156, 167, 183
Petitjean school, 8
Petry, Alice, 131
Petty, James A., 61, 62, 63, 101, 130
Pickett, A. B., 106
Pickett-Crowley rice mill, 50
Pickett, Squire A., 50, 59
Picou, Marie, 134
Pierce, Placide C., 312, 316, 318
Pier, George, 143
Pier, Joe, 143
Pier, Wilfred, 143
Pierrel, A. S., 44
Piernass, Joseph Chevalier, 311

Pietro, John, 11
Pilgrims Rest Baptist Church, 216, 238
Piloff, Jack, 105
Pintard, J. M., 103, 123, 127
Pipes & White, 102
pirate legends, 311
Pitre, Ada, 276
Pitre, Edgar, 224
Pitre, Edna, 276
Pitre, H. M., 276
Pizzalatto, Louis, 118
Pizzalatto, V., 105, 118
Pizzini Hotel, 104
Pizzini, M., 103
Pizzini Restaurant, 105
Philips, Rev. J. C., 145
Phillips school, 7
Phillips, Seward, 273
Phillips, U. S., 77
Philomene, Sister, 171
Plapper, Dr. H. C., 136
Plaquemine Brulee-Branch: post office, 207; school, 7; churches, 209-211; teachers, 211
Platt, J. E., 51, 52, 66, 130
Plattsmier, Anthony, 156
Plattsmier grocery, 156, 184
Pleasance, Emile, 277
Pleasure Pavilion, 158
Pleasant Resort Saloon, 192
Pleasantview, 278
Point Francois, 277
Pointe au Fiere, 278
Pointe-au-Tigre, 278
Pointe-aux-Loups, 248
Poor, G. H., 296
Pond, C. P., 131
Porter, Fannie B., 291
Porter, W. A., 53
Postal Telegraph, 107, 175
Poupeville post office, 185
Poupeville settlement, 151, 170, 174
Poulet, A. C., 154
Poulet, C., 185
Poulet, Mrs. Rosa, 171
Pousson, Arcade, 246
Pousson, Gaudens, 1, 254, 258, 267
Pousson, Hayes, 265
Pousson, James, 254
Pousson, Mathias, 254
Pousson, Matthew Sr., 255
Pousson, M. Jr., 254
Powell, H. H., 295
Powers, Dr. C. L., 5
Powers, J. E., 2
Prados, Louis, 60
Prairie Gregg, 277
Prairie Hayes school, 7
Prairie Mammouth, 265
Prather, C. W., 4

Prather, J., 237
Prather, Mollie, 131
Pratt, Bertha, 290
Pratt, C. H., 259
Pratt, F. M., 86
Preddy, P. A., 156
Premo, Andrew, 331
Premo, Mrs. Belizar, 331
Premo, Beulah, 331
Premo, Gertrude, 331
Premo, Shafter, 331
Price, J. J., 95, 102
Price, W., 103
Pride's Hall, 203
Pridgen, E. E., 321
Pridgen, Ruth, 325
Prien, 265
Primeaux, Valin, 272, 273
Pritchard, Lola, 291
Pritchard, Paul F., 55
Privat, Louis, 156
Prudhomme, Mrs. Annie, 223
Prudhomme post office, 223
Prudhomme, Michel Sr., 223
Prudhomme, Michel Jr., 223
Pucheu, Donat, 153, 159, 170, 175, 251
Pucheu, Mayme, 170
Pugh, Lawrence, 5
Pugh, Philip Sidney, 1, 2, 5, 93, 100, 133, 282, 309
Pulliam, Dr. Seely T., 53, 136
Pulliam, Dr. L. C., 2, 136

Quakers, 266
quarantine, 11
Quebedeaux bridge, 147
Quebedeaux, Frank 147, 302
Quebodeaux, Capt. Atyole, 149, 150
Quereau, F. C., 90
Queue Tortue, 151
Quinn, A. G., 100
Quinn & Villien, 101
Quirk, E. C., 269

race tracks, 126, 127, 182, 205
Raezor, John, 10
Rahm, Philip, 52
Raine, Leonie, 258
Rakestraw, A., 83
Rampmier, Fritz, 259
Rampmier, Karl, 259
Ramsey, M. I., 199, 205
Ramsey, W. H., 220
Randall, Dr. John N., 76
Randle, Rev. T. L., 173
Randolph, Frank, 80, 123, 130, 131
Raney, James, 103
Raney, Dr. R. B., 106, 135, 136
Ransom, C. A., 103
Rasberry, Dave, 250

Rasberry, Zan, 254
Raslan, J., 105
Raslan, Joseph, 117, 118
Raslan, James, 118
rawhide bottom chairs, 230
Raymond, Anthony, 157
Raymond, A. E., 168
Rayne: population, 151, 153; frog industry, 159-162; town hall, 163; municipal officers, 163-168; utilities, 164, 165, 166; medical history, 169-170; churches, 170-174; schools, 174-176; fires, 175, 177, 178; cotton, 178; fire department, 178; first brick building, 177; politicians, 180-182; sports, 182; Bastille Day, 183; post office, 185; newspapers, 185
Rayne Building & Loan Co., 158
Rayne Brick Co., 153
Rayne Cotton Oil Co., 155
Rayne Ginning Co., 154, 178
Rayne Herald, 185
Rayne Ice Co., 153
Rayne News, 185
Rayne Ranger, 185
Rayne rice mill, 60, 65, 153
Rayne Sanitarium, 170
Rayne Signal, 128, 153, 185
Rayne Silver Cornet Band, 183
Rayne State Bank, 153, 155, 159, 168, 169, 177
Rayne Station, 174
Rayne Tribune, 134, 153, 156, 185
Rayon, S., 155
Reams, Rev. I. T., 173
Rearson, Annie, 228
Redlich, Henry B., 7, 268
Redlich, Julia, 268
Redlich post office, 268
Redlich store, 268
Redtop post office, 240
Reed, Adam, 1, 205
Reed, Amos, 254
Reed, Fernest, 5, 269
Reed, James, 254
Reed, Jesse, 235, 253
Reed, Raymond, 268
Regan, Hannah, 247
Regan, J. J., 245, 246, 247
Regan, Johanna, 247
Regan, John, 244, 246
Regan, Katie, 134
Regan, Neal, 247
Regan post office, 244
Regan store, 245
Regan, Tom, 246
Regan warehouse, 247
Reggie, Mrs. Emile, 117
Reiber & W. C. Fleshman, 101
Reilly, Hattie B., 307
Reilly, Ted, 58